AMÉRICA DEL SUR

Mar de las Antillas

Caracas
VENEZUELA
Medellín
Bogotá
COLOMBIA
Río Orinoco
LAS GUAYANAS
(Inglesa)
(Holandesa)
(Francesa)

Océano Atlántico

ECUADOR
Quito
ECUADOR
Guayaquil
Iquitos
Río Negro
Manaus
Amazonas
Río Madeira
Belém
Fortaleza
Río Tocantins

PERÚ

B R A S I L

Callao Lima
Cuzco
Lago de Titicaca
La Paz
Arequipa
Arica
Iquique
BOLIVIA
Sucre
Cuiabá
Río São Francisco
Recife
Salvador
Belo Horizonte

ANDES
LOS
DE
CORDILLERA
ARGENTINA

Río Paraguay
PARAGUAY
Asunción
São Paulo
Santos
Río de Janeiro

Antofagasta
TRÓPICO DE CAPRICORNIO

Océano Pacífico

Tucumán
Córdoba
Rosario
Valparaíso
Santiago
Concepción

Río Paraná
URUGUAY
Porto Alegre
Buenos Aires
Montevideo
Bahía Blanca

Océano Atlántico

ESCALA
900 Millas
1448 Kilómetros

ISLAS FALKLAND

Estrecho de Magallanes
Cabo de Hornos

SPANISH FOR CONVERSATION

Fourth Edition

SPANISH FOR CONVERSATION
A BEGINNING GRAMMAR

JOHN KENNETH LESLIE
Northwestern University

John Wiley & Sons, Inc.
New York London Sydney Toronto

This book was set in Times Roman by
Technical Filmsetters Europe Ltd. It was printed
by Vail Ballou and bound by Vail Ballou. The
designer was Jerry Wilke. Editor and photo
researcher: Hedwig L. Jourdan.

Library of Congress Cataloging in Publication Date:
Leslie, John Kenneth, 1907–
    Spanish for conversation.

    Includes index.
    1.   Spanish language—Grammar—1950–
    I. Title.

PC4112.L46   1976   468′.2′421   75-37774
ISBN 0-471-52810-2

Printed in the United States of America

10 9 8 7 6 5 4 3 2 1

PREFACE

Spanish for Conversation is a basic textbook for the first year of Spanish. It is accompanied by a *Workbook*, a complete laboratory tape program, and an *Instructor's Manual*. The program is based on an oral-aural method that stresses the spoken language.

The textbook includes 2 preliminary lessons, 26 regular lessons, and six reviews. The first 10 lessons contain formal pronunciation sections. The reviews are spaced so that two occur in each quarter or three in each semester. Many schools on the semester system will cover lessons 1–13 in the first semester and lessons 14–26 in the second. Schools on the quarter system might assign lessons 1–9 the first quarter, 10–18 in the second, and 19–26 in the third.

Each regular lesson in the text begins with a Spanish proverb that illustrates one of the lesson's basic points. Some teachers may wish to have their students memorize these proverbs. New verb forms are introduced next, not necessarily so that the students will learn them as paradigms but so that they may *hear* the new forms—*before studying them*—as spoken by the instructor. New vocabulary appears in an *Escuchar y Hablar* section to permit the students to hear and repeat new words and idioms before using them in context. The core of each lesson, a passage in Spanish based on a real-life situation, follows. The students listen to this passage as the instructor reads it or as the accompanying tape is played in the laboratory. The minimum essentials of Spanish grammar are presented in the *Estructura* sections. Certain special constructions and minor points are indicated by superior numbers in the text and explained in the *Notas* which follow most of the "situations."

The Spanish situation in each lesson is not simply a "reading"; it is the basis of the lesson and provides the students with something to talk about in Spanish. The students should learn it as a sequence of ideas, not memorize it word for word. They should learn it well enough to be able to retell the story to themselves, which they should do a number of times as part of their preparation for class. This constant practice leads to fluency and builds up reflexes by which the students can apply the principles of Spanish grammar to their own speaking and writing.

The lessons end with a supplementary *Diálogo* followed by a group of *Preguntas Personales* and cultural notes. The instructor may use the *diálogos* in various ways. For example, the students may be asked to memorize them and take some of the parts in class. The cultural notes, in English, are intended simply to give the students some brief insight into the world of the people whose language they are studying. Readings in Spanish have not been included; many elementary readers are available that provide more reading practice than could be accommodated in this basic book.

Several types of exercise materials are provided. Questions to be answered orally follow each situation. Often these questions may be adapted to a students' personal experience. For instance, a question like "¿Cómo prepara Juan la lección de español?" may logically be followed by "¿Cómo prepara *usted* la lección?" In the verb and *Estructura* sections, exercises under the heading *Práctica* include, among others, subject and item substitutions, tense and structure substitutions, patterned responses, and pattern sentences to be expressed in Spanish. These offer copious and rapid drill and should be done by the students as part of their preparation. In the classroom, with books closed, the students should repeat the models in chorus after the instructor, who then cues the responses as suggested in the exercises. For example, after the model "Es mi traje. Es mío," the instructor gives the cue "Es mi blusa," to which a student responds, "Es mía."

Tareas follow each *Estructura* section. The instruction for the first *tarea* in each lesson reads "Diga en español"; however, many instructors may wish to assign the material as a written exercise. The following *Composición* may, of course, be either oral or written. Further writing exercises appear in the *Workbook*.

This book is for the modern instructor who believes that the class hour should be devoted largely to conversation based on the material studied for the day and enlarged to include related experiences of the student's own. The instructor may wish to retell the story of the day to the class, varying the wording and the order of the details. He or she will find that the situations lend themselves to speedy recapitulation by the student, either orally or in the form of compositions written on the blackboard. The ideas of the situations are so easily retained by the students that frequent impromptu reviews are feasible, with the result that the vocabulary and grammatical principles already studied can be kept fresh in mind and used throughout the course.

For many helpful suggestions for this or earlier editions I thank the following present or former colleagues at Northwestern University: Edwin B. Place, Joseph G. Fucilla, Frederick S. Stimson, Humberto E. Robles, Harvey L. Johnson, José Sánchez, Homero Castillo, Mabel Staudinger, William T. Starr, Robert J. Bininger, Donald G. Castanien, and Gabriel H. Engerrand—and to Eduardo Neale-Silva of the University of Wisconsin. For their careful reading of the manuscript of the fourth edition and their thoughtful suggestions, I thank A. Joe Auseré and Maurice M. Campion of Glendale Community College, Cornelia Field of the College of Alameda, Hershel Frey of the University of Pittsburgh, Samuel Keehn of Los Angeles Pierce College, Carlos M. Morrison of Los Angeles City College, Ormon W. Moulton of Indiana Central College, Lisa Nelson of Stanford University, Stephen H. Richardson of Mercer County College, Cecilia Ross of the University of California at Berkeley, Carlo Vacca of Massachusetts Bay Community College, and Angelo S. Villa of Los Angeles Valley College. A special word of appreciation goes to Hedy Jourdan, who, as editor for Wiley, was of inestimable assistance.

J.K.L.

TO THE STUDENT

Speaking Spanish is fun. Your instructor, aided by the materials in this book, can teach you to speak Spanish—within the range of the vocabulary here presented, of course.

Since the best way to learn a language is to imitate and repeat, imitation and repetition are the core of the method on which this book is built.

Before you study each lesson, listen to the new verb forms as your teacher reads them. Repeat each one as you hear it pronounced. Then listen to the new words used in the lesson, repeating each one after your teacher. Next, either in the laboratory as the tape is played or in the class as your teacher reads, listen to the "situation"—the story or dialogue in the section called *Escuchar y hablar*—around which each lesson is built. Again, repeat after the tape or after your teacher.

The main part of your work in preparing each lesson is to repeat the "situation" to yourself, preferably aloud. Tell yourself the story over and over again, until you can tell it as easily as if you were speaking English, but do not memorize the story word for word. Remember always to imitate the pronunciation and intonation of your teacher.

Study the *Notas* and *Estructura* sections that follow each "situation," for you need to know the basic grammatical structure that is explained in them in order to transfer the words and expressions you are learning to other circumstances—those of your own daily life, for example. Each point of structure is reinforced by practice exercises (*Práctica*) that will help you to remember the basic structure of the language. Do the exercises assigned by your instructor.

Above all, keep speaking Spanish. Get into the habit of repeating to yourself and to your classmates the expressions which you learn. As you learn new words, keep using them to tell your classmates in Spanish what you are doing, what you are going to do, and what you have done recently.

J.K.L.

CONTENTS

SPANISH FOR CONVERSATION

1

The basic sounds of Spanish

VOWELS

Spanish has five vowels: **a**, **e**, **i**, **o**, and **u**. Each Spanish vowel is a single, pure sound. In English many vowel sounds are not single sounds. Instead we tend to drawl them out with a following diphthongal glide. For example, when we say the word *no*, we usually say "no-u." In Spanish the vowel is cut short to one single sound and pronounced "no/." Be careful not to drawl your Spanish vowels. Another difference between English and Spanish pronunciation is the English tendency to reduce unstressed vowels to a neutral sound like "uh," as in *above* or *papa*. This does not occur in Spanish, where each vowel retains its essential sound, even when unstressed.

In the following sections listen carefully as each word is pronounced by your teacher or on the laboratory tape; then repeat.

a is similar to the vowel sound in English *hot*. The tongue lies level in the mouth. The tip of the tongue rests near the lower front teeth.

    Ana   ama   fama

e is similar to *a* in *able* when final in its syllable. It is a closed mid front vowel. The tip of the tongue rests against the lower front teeth. The lips are spread to the sides.

    me   nene   nena

    When followed by a consonant in the same syllable, **e** is similar to the open *e* in *let*.

    papel   el   en

i is similar to *i* in *machine*. It is a high front vowel. The lips are spread to the sides. The tip of the tongue rests against the lower front teeth. Note that the Spanish conjunction **y** (*and*) is pronounced like **i**.

    ni   mina   fina   y

1

o is similar to *o* in *omit* when final in its syllable. It is a mid back vowel. The lips are rounded. The back of the tongue is raised towards the back of the mouth.

no   mono   nona

When followed by a consonant in the same syllable, **o** is similar to *o* in *nor*.

con   compás

u is similar to *oo* in *pool*. It is a high back vowel. The lips are well rounded and trumpet shaped. The back of the tongue is raised towards the back of the mouth, close to the velum.

una   fuma   mula

CONSONANTS

b and **v** are pronounced exactly alike.

1. At the beginning of a word group and after **m** or **n** they are pronounced like English *b*, but less explosively. This sound is a voiced bilabial stop. The lips close, stopping the airstream, then open to release it abruptly. Note that **n** is pronounced **m** before **b** or **v**.

   bola   vaca   ambos   invita

2. In all other positions the sound of **b** and **v** is a voiced bilabial fricative unlike either *b* or *v* in English. The lips do not close, but almost touch, leaving a slit through which the airstream passes continuously. Never allow the upper teeth to touch the lower lip, as in the pronunciation of English *v*.

   Cuba   nave   la bola   la vaca

c followed by **e** or **i** is pronounced like *s* in *send* in Spanish America and in the south of Spain. This is a voiceless alveolar fricative. The tip of the tongue rests against the lower front teeth. The blade of the tongue touches the upper teeth ridges. In northern and central Spain **c** before **e** or **i** is pronounced like the voiceless interdental *th* of English *think*.

centavo   cemento   cima   cine

c followed by all other sounds is like *c* in *cot* (the sound of *k*). This is a voiceless velar stop. The back of the tongue touches the velum, stopping the airstream. There is no aspiration as in English, where a puff of air usually follows the *k* sound.

cama   cola   cuna   clima

d at the beginning of a word group or after **l** or **n** is a voiced dental stop. The tip of the tongue touches the back of the upper front teeth, not the upper teeth ridges as in English.

don   donde   el día   el disco

d in other positions is a voiced dental fricative like English *th* in *neither*. The tip of the tongue touches the edges of the upper front teeth without stopping the airstream. At the end of a word, before a pause, **d** is so weak that it is scarcely heard.

cada   codo   la duda   tomad

f is like English *f*, a voiceless labiodental fricative. The lower lip touches the edges of the upper front teeth, without stopping the airstream.

fama   fina   fuma

g followed by **a**, **o**, **u**, or a consonant has two sounds.

1. At the beginning of a word group or after **n** it is a voiced velar stop, like *g* in *go*. The back of the tongue touches the velum, stopping the airstream.

   gana   gafas   gula   goma

   Notice that **n** before **g** is pronounced like *n* in *single*.

   mango   con ganas

2. In other positions **g** + **a**, **o**, **u**, or a consonant is a voiced velar fricative. The back of the tongue is raised close to the velum without stopping the airstream. The resulting sound is like the weak *g* of English *rugged* when pronounced rapidly.

   hago   mago   vago

   In the combinations **gue** and **gui** the **u** is silent, and the **g** has one of the above sounds, depending on its position.

   1. **guía   un guía**   2. **me guía   pague**

g followed by **e** or **i** is unlike any English sound, but is similar to the *ch* of German *ach* or *Buch*. It is a voiceless velar fricative. The back of the tongue is raised close to the velum, and the airstream passes between tongue and velum without being stopped.

imagen   imagino   gema   gime

h is always silent.

heno   himno   humano

j is like Spanish **g** in the combinations **ge** and **gi**.

majo   baja   jota   jamón

k is a voiceless velar stop, as in English. The back of the tongue is raised against the velum, but there is no following aspiration as in English.

kilo   kilómetro

l is a voiced alveolar lateral articulated with the tip of the tongue against the upper teeth ridges, as in English *leave*.

ala   Lima   luna   él

m is a voiced bilabial nasal, pronounced like English *m*.

malo   ama   mago

n is a voiced alveolar nasal articulated like English *n*, with the tip of the tongue against the upper teeth ridges.

nido   nulo   mina

However, **n** is pronounced **m** before **b**, **v**, **p**, **m**, and **f**.

un bocado   en Vigo   un poco   un mundo   enfada

Before **k**, **g**, and **j** the sound of **n** is velar, as in English *think, single*.

un kilo   un cabo   mango   un joven

p is a voiceless bilabial stop, articulated as in English, except that there is no following aspiration as in *p^hack*.

papá   pico   puma

q occurs only in the combinations **que** and **qui**. It is pronounced like English *k*. The **u** is silent.

que   aquí   aquel

r has two pronunciations.

1. When initial in a word or after **l**, **n**, or **s** it is a voiced alveolar trill. The tip of the tongue strikes the upper teeth ridges several times in quick succession.

   romano   la roca   el robo   un ramo

2. In other positions **r** is a voiced alveolar tap. The tip of the tongue makes a single tap against the upper teeth ridges.

   para   pero   pronto   parte

Note that **s** before **r** is not pronounced; it is assimilated by the **r**. The result is almost as if the **s** were dropped.

las rosas   los ricos

s is a voiceless alveolar fricative, like *s* in *sat*. The tip of the tongue touches the lower front teeth. The blade of the tongue touches the upper teeth ridges.

sano   sino   son

Be careful not to voice an **s** between vowels or at the end of a word, as we often do in English, where we pronounce a *z* in such words as *roses* or *days*.

rosa   cosa   cosas   días

However, Spanish **s** voices to the sound of *z* before a voiced consonant (**b, v, d, g, l, ll, m, n,** and **y**).

los bancos   las vacas   desde   las ganas
los lunes   mismo   asno

t is a voiceless dental stop. The tip of the tongue presses against the back of the upper front teeth—not against the upper teeth ridges as in English. There is no following aspiration as in English *t*.

tan   tuna   mata   lata

w occurs only in foreign words. It is usually pronounced as in English.

Wáshington

x is pronounced variously, depending on its position in a word.

1. Before a consonant it is pronounced like *s* in *seven* or like *ks*.

extremo   explico

2. Between vowels it is pronounced *gs* (with a voiceless *s* like *s* in *seven*) or *ks*.

examen   éxito

y is a voiced palatal fricative. The tip of the tongue presses against the lower front teeth. The middle of the tongue is raised close to the palate. The result of these two tongue positions is a more tense sound, with more audible friction than English *y* in *yes*.

yo   ya   haya   tuyo

z is pronounced like *s* in *sent* in Spanish America and in southern Spain. Like *s*, it voices before a voiced consonant. In central and northern Spain **z** is pronounced like the voiceless *th* of English *think*.

paz   vez   caza   zapato

DIGRAPHS

In addition to the preceding sounds, Spanish has four which are represented by digraphs: **ch, ll, rr** (each of which counts as a single letter), and **ñ**. In dictionaries and vocabularies **ch, ll,** and **ñ** follow **c, l,** and **n,** respectively.

ch is a voiceless palatal affricate, pronounced like English *ch* in *church*.

chico   chocolate   mucho   muchacho

ll is articulated like Spanish **y** in most of Spanish America and parts of Spain. In other parts of Spain it is a voiced palatal lateral, similar to *lli* in English *million*, provided the tip of the tongue presses against the back of the lower teeth.

calle   halla   llama   llave

In the region around Buenos Aires **ll** is pronounced like *s* in *pleasure*.

ñ is a voiced palatal nasal. The tip of the tongue presses the back of the lower teeth. The middle of the tongue makes wide contact with the palate. The sound is similar to *ny* in English *can you*, but with the tip of the tongue against the lower teeth.

año   niño   España   señor

rr (like **r** when initial or after **l**, **n**, or **s**) is a voiced alveolar trill. The tip of the tongue, under tension, strikes the upper teeth ridges several times in rapid succession.

perro   carro   parra   narra

DIPHTHONGS

Spanish vowels are classed as strong (**a**, **e**, **o**) and weak (**i**, or **y**, and **u**). Any combination of a strong and a weak vowel or of two weak vowels forms a diphthong. The vowels of a diphthong are pronounced as they would be if each stood alone, but they are run together into one syllable.

Stress the *strong* vowel in a combination consisting of a strong and a weak vowel.

ai (ay): baile, hay, habláis   **eu:** Europa, europeo
ia: gloria, patria   **ue:** suelo, bueno, vuela
au: aula, causa, jaula   **oi (oy):** boina, hoy
ua: Ecuador, cuaderno, suave   **io:** comió, bebió, idioma
ei (ey): veinte, rey, treinta   **uo:** continuo, inicuo
ie: miel, cielo, cierto

Emphasize the *second* vowel in a combination of two weak vowels.

iu: ciudad, viuda   **ui (uy):** ruido, cuidado, muy

Note that a combination of a strong and a weak vowel whose weak vowel bears a written accent, or a combination of two weak vowels the first of which bears a written accent, is not a diphthong. Neither is a combination of two strong vowels.

   dí-a   rí-o   flú-ido   le-o   ca-e

TRIPHTHONGS

A triphthong is a combination of three vowels: a stressed strong vowel between two weak ones. Pronounce as one syllable.

   iai: estudiáis   **uai, uay:** continuáis, Uruguay
   iei: estudiéis   **uei, uey:** continuéis, buey

A combination of a weak, a strong, and a weak vowel that bears a written accent on the first *weak* vowel breaks down into a vowel plus a diphthong.

   vivirí-ais

Division of words into syllables

1. A Spanish word has as many syllables as it has vowels, diphthongs, and triphthongs.

   bo-ni-ta   fue-ra   es-tu-diáis

   Two strong vowels coming together are separated; so is a combination of vowels prevented by a written accent mark from being either a diphthong or a triphthong.

   te-a-tro   rí-o   flú-i-do   ha-bla-rí-ais

2. A single consonant (including **ch, ll, rr**) between vowels goes with the following vowel.

   pa-se-mos   mu-cha-cha   ha-lla-ron   ca-rro   se-ño-ri-ta

3. Two consonants are usually divided.

   ac-ción   tar-dar   hon-ra   bur-lar   ob-je-to

   However, with one exception, any combination of a consonant plus **l** or **r** which can begin a word in English goes with the following vowel in Spanish.

   ha-bla-ron   sa-cro   so-bre   si-glo

   The exception is **s** plus any consonant; this combination cannot begin a syllable. The **s** therefore goes with the preceding syllable.

   is-la   Es-pa-ña   cons-tan-te   as-cen-sor

4. Three consonants are usually divided after the first one.

   in-glés   im-pre-sión   sal-dré

Stress

Spanish words are usually stressed on the last or the next-to-the-last syllable.

1. Stress the *last* syllable of a word ending in any consonant except **n** or **s**.

   sal-lu-*dar*   na-tu-*ral*   ciu-*dad*   hon-ra-*dez*

2. Stress the next-to-the-last syllable of a word ending in a vowel (or a diphthong) or **n** or **s**.

   her-*mo*-so   bo-*ni*-ta   in-te-re-*san*-te
   glo-ria   es-*tu*-dian   ca-*ba*-llos

3. Any violation of the above two rules is indicated by a written accent on the stressed syllable.

   lá-piz   *ár*-bol   mi-*ró*   bai-*lé*
   na-*ción*   in-*glés*   *jó*-ve-nes   *dí*-ga-me

Note that there is only one written accent in Spanish, and it always means that the syllable which bears it is *stressed*. In addition, it distinguishes two words that would otherwise be spelled alike.

   que   which, that   si if   el the
   ¿qué?   what?   sí yes   él he

Linking of words

Words are normally not pronounced in any language as isolated units but rather as breath groups. Within breath groups in Spanish, individual words will be linked to those following and preceding them according to the following principles:

1. A final vowel and the initial vowel of a following word tend to be pronounced as one syllable.

   lindísima Amapola   mi amigo
   Carlos está aquí   éste es mío
   hablo español   su profesor y usted

2. A final consonant may be linked with an initial vowel of the following word.

   es ella   un alumno   el español

PRÁCTICA

1. Copy the following words. Divide them into syllables and underline the stressed syllable. (EXAMPLE: **aeropuerto—a-e-ro-puer-to.**)

conoce	hablaré	instituir
saben	detrás	veintiséis
sillas	carro	soberbias
tarde	espero	compañía
sueltos	tranquila	Paraguay
trasto	leer	unión
supremo	caen	oiga

2. Explain why the following words have a written accent. (Without the accent the stress would be on a different syllable. Why?)

difícil	jamás	alemán
así	fábrica	baúl
frío	halló	célebre
canción	mártir	quizás

Saludos y despedidas (Greetings and leave-takings)

Now that you have learned how to pronounce Spanish sounds, repeat the following dialogues after your teacher and be prepared to take each one of the parts in class.

SEÑOR LÓPEZ—Buenos días, señora. ¿Cómo está usted?
    (Good morning, señora. How are you?)
SEÑORA GÓMEZ—Muy bien, gracias. ¿Y usted?
    (Very well, thank you. And how are you?)

ANA—Buenas tardes, Inés. ¿Cómo estás?
    (Good afternoon, Inés. How are you?)
INÉS—Bien, gracias. ¿Y tú?
    (Fine, thanks. And you?)

PACO—Buenas noches, Pepe. ¿Cómo estás?
    (Good evening, Pepe. How are you?)
PEPE—Yo, muy bien. ¿Y tú?
    (I'm fine. And you?)

ANA—Adiós. Hasta luego.
    (Good-by. See you later.)
INÉS—¡Hasta pronto! Saludos a la familia.
    (See you soon. Regards to your family.)

Classroom expressions

You will hear your teacher use the following expressions.

1. **Voy a pasar lista.**   I'm going to call the roll. (You answer: **Presente.**)
2. **Repita usted. (Repitan ustedes.)**   Repeat.
3. **Abra usted (Abran ustedes) el libro.**   Open your book(s).
4. **Lea usted (Lean ustedes) en voz alta.**   Read aloud.
5. **Basta.**   That's enough.
6. **Cierre usted (Cierren ustedes) el libro.**   Close your book(s).
7. **Pase usted (Pasen ustedes) a la pizarra.**   Go to the blackboard.
8. **¿No hay tiz ?**   Isn't there any chalk?
9. **Vamos a escribir al dictado.**   We're going to write dictation.
10. **Borren ustedes.**   Erase.
11. **Vaya usted (Vayan ustedes) a su sitio.**   Go back to your seat(s).
12. **Dígame usted.**   Tell me.
13. **Continúe usted. (Continúen ustedes.)**   Continue.
14. **Siga usted. (Sigan ustedes.)**   Continue.
15. **Cierre la puerta, por favor.**   Please close the door.
16. **Abra la ventana, por favor.**   Please open the window.

2

Poco a poco se va lejos.
Little by little one goes far.

Verbs used in this lesson

es is
(yo) hablo I speak
usted habla you speak

son are
(ellos) hablan they speak
los españoles hablan the Spaniards speak

Escuchar y hablar

la* Argentina Argentina
el Brasil Brazil
de of, from
donde *rel. adv.* where
¿dónde? *interrog. adv.* where?
dos two
en in
España *f*. Spain
el español Spaniard, Spanish (*language*)
los Estados Unidos United States
el francés Frenchman, French (*language*)
Francia *f*. France
hermoso beautiful, handsome
Hispanoamérica *f*. Hispanic America
hispanoamericano Hispanic American
Inglaterra *f*. England
el inglés Englishman, English (*language*)

interesante interesting
Italia *f*. Italy
el italiano Italian
la lengua language
México *m*. Mexico
no no; not
el norteamericano American
otro another, other
el país country
el portugués Portuguese
principal principal
que *rel. pron.* that, which
¿qué? *interrog. pron.* what?
¿quién? (*pl.* **¿quiénes?**) *interrog. pron.* who?
también also, too
un, una a (an)
y and

* The definite article shows the gender of the noun it precedes. In most cases where it does not appear, *m.* (*masculine*) or *f.* (*feminine*) follows the noun. The definite article will not be given in the English translation.

11

LAS LENGUAS*

En España los españoles[1] hablan español. En los Estados Unidos los norte-americanos hablan inglés. Un país donde hablan inglés también es Inglaterra. Los ingleses hablan inglés. La lengua que hablan los franceses, en Francia, es el[2] francés. En Italia, los italianos hablan italiano.

En Hispanoamérica hablan dos lenguas principales.[3] Las dos lenguas principales de Hispanoamérica son el español y el portugués. Hablan portugués en el[4] Brasil. En los otros países de Hispanoamérica hablan español. Hablan español en la[4] Argentina. Otro país donde hablan español es México.[5]

Yo hablo inglés. Hablo español también. El inglés es hermoso. El español es también una lengua hermosa. Otra lengua hermosa es el italiano. El portugués es una lengua interesante. Yo no[6] hablo portugués. ¿Qué[7] habla usted?[8]

NOTAS

1. Only proper names and the first word of a sentence are capitalized in Spanish. Adjectives of nationality and names of languages are not capitalized.

   En España los españoles hablan español. In Spain the Spaniards speak Spanish.
   Los ingleses hablan inglés. The English speak English.

2. In general, the definite article is used more often in Spanish than it is in English. It is used, for example, with names of languages—except after **hablar** and after **de** and **en**.

   El francés es interesante. French is interesting.
   Yo hablo francés. I speak French.

   Hablan en español. They're speaking in Spanish.
   la lección de español the Spanish lesson

3. In Spanish a descriptive adjective generally follows its noun.

   dos lenguas principales two principal languages
   una lengua hermosa a beautiful language

4. The definite article is used with names of certain countries.

   el Brasil Brazil   **la Argentina** Argentina

*The superior figures in the above text refer to corresponding explanations in the *Notas* section.

5. The Mexicans spell the name of their country as in English, but with a written accent: **México**. The **x** is here pronounced as Spanish **j**. The Spanish spell the word as it is pronounced: **Méjico**.

6. To make a verb negative in Spanish, place **no** before it.

   Yo hablo español.   I speak Spanish.
   No hablo ruso.   I do not speak Russian.

7. Interrogative words bear a written accent to distinguish them from relatives and conjunctions with which they would otherwise be identical.

   ¿qué? what?   **¿dónde?** where?   **¿quién?** who?

   ¿Qué hablan los españoles?   What do the Spaniards speak?
   ¿Qué lengua hablan en México?   What language do they speak in Mexico?
   ¿Dónde hablan inglés?   Where do they speak English?

8. In questions the subject usually follows the verb, as it does in the English sentence "Have you money enough?" Deviations from this general rule, for the sake of emphasis and euphony, can be learned by observation. An inverted question mark is placed at the beginning of the actual interrogation.

   ¿Qué habla usted?   What do you speak?
   Usted habla español, ¿verdad?   You speak Spanish, don't you?

PREGUNTAS

Conteste (answer) *en español.*

a. 1. ¿Qué hablan los españoles?
   2. ¿Qué hablan los ingleses?
   3. ¿Qué hablan los franceses?
   4. ¿Qué hablan los italianos?

b. 1. ¿Quiénes hablan francés?
   2. ¿Quiénes hablan español?
   3. ¿Quiénes hablan inglés?
   4. ¿Quiénes hablan italiano?

c. 1. ¿Dónde hablan italiano?
   2. ¿Dónde hablan francés?
   3. ¿Dónde hablan español?
   4. ¿Dónde hablan inglés?
   5. ¿Dónde hablan portugués?

d. 1. ¿Qué lengua hablan en España?
   2. ¿Qué lengua hablan en los Estados Unidos?
   3. ¿Qué lengua hablan en la Argentina?
   4. ¿Qué lengua hablan en el Brasil?

e. 1. ¿Es hermoso el español?
   2. ¿Es interesante el portugés?
   3. ¿Es el inglés una lengua hermosa?
   4. ¿Es el italiano una lengua interesante?

f. 1. ¿Habla usted inglés?
   2. ¿Habla usted español?
   3. ¿Habla usted francés?
   4. ¿Habla usted portugués?

Estructura

1. GENDER OF NOUNS

Spanish nouns are always masculine or feminine. Most nouns ending in **-o** are masculine; most nouns ending in **-a** are feminine.

    estado *m.*   state   **lengua** *f.* language

The gender of other nouns must be learned as observed.

    español *m.* Spanish   **país** *m.* country

2. DEFINITE ARTICLE

The definite article has a masculine form **el** and a feminine form **la** to agree with masculine and feminine nouns.

    el inglés   the Englishman   **la lengua**   the language

3. INDEFINITE ARTICLE

The indefinite article has a masculine form **un** and a feminine form **una**.

    un país   a country   **una lengua**   a language

4. PLURAL OF NOUNS

The plural of nouns ending in a vowel is formed by adding **-s** to the singular. The plural of nouns ending in a consonant is formed by adding **-es** to the singular.

    estados   states   **lenguas**   languages
    españoles   Spaniards   **ingleses**   Englishmen

5. PLURAL OF DEFINITE ARTICLE

The definite article has a masculine plural **los** and a feminine plural **las**.

    los países   the countries   **las lenguas**   the languages

PRÁCTICA

Cambie según se indica, siguiendo los modelos. (Change as indicated, following the models.)

a. **El español es la lengua de España.**

    1. el francés   3. el italiano
    2. el inglés   4. el español

b. **Los españoles hablan español.**

1. los ingleses
2. los franceses
3. los italianos
4. los portugueses

c. **México es un país de Hispanoamérica. El español es una lengua de Hispanoamérica.**

1. la Argentina
2. el portugués
3. el Brasil
4. el español

6. ADJECTIVES

Adjectives, like articles, agree in gender and number with the nouns they modify. Adjectives ending in **-o** in the masculine singular change the **o** to **a** for the feminine. Most other adjectives are the same in both masculine and feminine.

otro país   another country
otra lengua   another language
una lengua hermosa   a beautiful language
la lengua interesante   the interesting language

The plural of adjectives is formed the same way as the plural of nouns.

países interesantes   interesting countries
lenguas hermosas   beautiful languages
las lenguas principales   the principal languages

PRÁCTICA

Cambie según se indica, siguiendo los modelos.

a. **México es un país.**
España es otro país.
Inglaterra y Francia son otros países.

1. La Argentina es un país.
   el Brasil
   Italia y México

2. El francés es una lengua.
   el inglés
   el italiano y el español

3. Inglaterra es un país.
   la Argentina
   Francia y el Brasil

4. El portugués es una lengua.
   el italiano
   el inglés y el español

b. **El español es una lengua hermosa.**
El español y el portugués son lenguas hermosas.

1. El italiano es una lengua hermosa.
   el portugués y el español

2. El italiano es una lengua hermosa.
   el francés y el inglés

3. España es un país hermoso.
   España y Francia

4. El Brasil es un país interesante.
   Inglaterra y la Argentina

A newsstand in Lima, Peru, displays daily newspapers and a variety of magazines, including foreign publications.

Intonation

Proper intonation—the rising and falling of voice pitch—is as important as correct pronunciation. Imitate your instructor's intonation as you imitate his or her pronunciation.

The most characteristic feature of Spanish intonation is the fairly uniform level of pitch between the first and last tonic stresses in a short declarative sentence. In a declarative sentence of one word group, the pitch rises until the first stressed syllable is reached, remains at the level of this syllable, and drops on the last stressed syllable.

Us**ted habla español.**

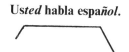

In a declarative sentence of two word groups, the pitch rises higher on the last stressed syllable of the first group; the second group has the pattern illustrated above.

En los *o*tros pa*í*ses/los hispanoameri*c*anos hablan espa*ñ*ol.

In the commonest pattern for questions, the highest pitch is on the first stressed syllable. The pitch then falls, but rises again *after the last stressed* syllable, or on the last syllable, if stressed.

¿No *h*abla usted espa*ñ*ol?

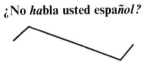

Tarea

Diga a la clase en español.

(Try to say the following sentences in Spanish without hesitation and without referring to the vocabulary.)

1. What do you speak?
2. I speak English and Spanish.
3. I do not speak French.
4. In the United States they speak English.
5. England is another country where they speak English.
6. The Italians speak Italian.
7. The two principal languages of Hispanic America are Spanish and Portuguese.
8. They are beautiful languages, and they are interesting.
9. They speak Portuguese in Brazil.
10. In the other countries of Hispanic America and in Spain they speak Spanish.

PREGUNTAS PERSONALES Y GENERALES

1. ¿Habla usted inglés?
2. ¿Habla usted español también?
3. ¿Habla usted francés, italiano y portugués?
4. ¿Qué lenguas habla usted?
5. ¿Dónde hablan portugués en Hispanoamérica?
6. ¿Dónde hablan francés y dónde hablan italiano?
7. ¿Hablan español en México?
8. ¿En qué otros países hablan español?
9. ¿En qué países hablan inglés?

10. ¿Quiénes hablan inglés?
11. ¿Quiénes hablan español?
12. ¿Es hermoso el español?
13. ¿Son hermosos el inglés y el francés?
14. ¿Es el italiano una lengua hermosa?

Nota cultural

The language you are studying is one of the Romance languages that developed from Latin, the other most important ones in this group being French, Italian, and Portuguese. Spanish grew not from "classic" Latin—but from the language of the common people of Rome. It was brought to the Iberian peninsula by soldiers and colonists at the time of the Roman conquest in the second century B.C. Castilian **(el castellano)**, from which modern standard Spanish evolved, emerged in the ninth century around Burgos, in north central Spain, and spread southward. The first written Spanish that is preserved dates from the tenth century and is found in Latin documents with Spanish words interspersed in the text. The first great literary monument in Spanish, the *Poem of the Cid*, was probably composed about the middle of the twelfth century.

Spanish is spoken by more than 200,000,000 people on four continents. It is the language of eighteen American nations and Spain and is also spoken in North Africa, the Philippines, the Near East, and the United States (which has more than 10,000,000 Spanish speakers).

In Spain itself, Spanish is not the only language. Catalan, another Romance tongue, is spoken in the northeastern region of Catalonia **(Cataluña)**, whose cultural and commercial center is Barcelona. In the northwestern region of Galicia, a dialect of Portuguese, Galician, is spoken. The Basques, straddling the Pyrenees, maintain their own Basque tongue, considered by some to be the survivor of the language of the ancient Iberians.

Donde hay gana hay maña.
Where there's a will there's a way.

Present indicative of regular verbs of the first conjugation

Spanish verbs are grouped into three conjugations according to the ending of the infinitive. The first-conjugation infinitive ends in **-ar,** the second in **-er,** and the third in **-ir.**

hablar   to speak   **aprender**   to learn   **vivir**   to live

The present indicative of verbs of the first conjugation is formed by removing the infinitive ending and adding the following personal endings to the stem:

	SINGULAR	PLURAL
FIRST PERSON	**-o**	**-amos**
SECOND PERSON	**-as**	**(-áis)**
THIRD PERSON	**-a**	**-an**

hablar   to speak

yo hablo   I speak
tú hablas   you speak (*fam.*)
usted habla   you speak
él (ella) habla   he (she) speaks

nosotros (nosotras) hablamos   we speak
[vosotros (vosotras) habláis]   you speak
ustedes hablan   you speak
ellos (ellas) hablan   they speak

Each form of the present tense has two other translations besides the simple translation given above.

Hablo.   I speak.   (I am speaking.   I do speak.)

Hablan.   They speak.   (They are speaking.   They do speak.)

Because the ending of the verb usually identifies the subject in Spanish, subject pronouns (except **usted** and **ustedes**) are commonly omitted. They must be used, however, when the subject of a verb would not otherwise be clear or when they are to be emphasized.

> **Juan y María estudian. *Él* prepara la lección y *ella* contesta a las preguntas.**
> John and Mary are studying. *He* is preparing the lesson and *she* is answering the questions.

> ***Nosotros* estudiamos, pero *ellos* conversan.** *We* are studying, but *they* are talking.

Notice that in Spanish there are two "you" forms. The second person singular **tú** (plural, **vosotros**) is used in familiar situations, such as when speaking to members of one's family, to children, and to close friends.

> **tú hablas** (*a mother would say to her child*)

Usted (plural, **ustedes**) is the polite form; it is used when addressing people with whom one is not on a first-name basis.

> **usted habla** (*a student would say to his instructor*)
> **ustedes hablan** (*a professor would say to his students*)

In Spanish America the **vosotros** form is seldom used.* **Ustedes** is used in both formal and familiar situations. Note that **usted** and **ustedes** are commonly abbreviated to **Ud.** and **Uds.** or **Vd.** and **Vds.,** respectively.

PRÁCTICA

Cambie según el modelo. (Change according to the model.)

> **Yo hablo español. / tú**
> **Tú hablas español.**

1. Yo hablo español.
   tú / usted / ustedes / nosotros / él

2. Ella no conversa mucho.
   yo / nosotros / usted / ellos / tú

3. ¿Estudian ustedes?
   nosotros / tú / yo / ella / usted

* In this text the **vosotros** form will be included in the conjugations. It will not appear in examples or exercises, however.

Present indicative of irregular verb *ser* (to be)

soy I am	**somos** we are
eres you are (*fam.*)	**(sois)** you are (*fam.*)
usted es you are	**ustedes son** you are
es he (she, it) is	**son** they are

PRÁCTICA

Cambie según el modelo.

¿De dónde es usted?
¿De dónde ____ (son) ellos?

1. ¿De dónde ____ tú?
2. ¿De dónde ____ ella?
3. ¿De dónde ____ yo?
4. ¿De dónde ____ usted?
5. ¿De dónde ____ ellas?
6. ¿De dónde ____ nosotros?
7. ¿De dónde ____ ustedes?
8. ¿De dónde ____ él?
9. ¿De dónde ____ Juan y Carlos?
10. ¿De dónde ____ el profesor?

Escuchar y hablar

alto tall
la alumna student *f.*
el alumno student *m.*
bajo short
la casa house
la clase class
como like, as
¿cómo? how?
contestar (a) to answer (to)
conversar to converse
cubano Cuban

delgado thin
escuchar to listen
estudiar to study
explicar to explain
gordo fat
guapo good-looking, handsome *m.*;
  guapa pretty *f.*
hay there is; there are
inteligente intelligent
joven young
la lección lesson

moreno dark-haired
la muchacha girl
el muchacho boy
mucho much; **muchos** many
pequeño small
la pregunta question
preguntar to ask
preparar to prepare
el profesor professor
rubio blond
señor Mr.; sir
simpático nice, congenial
uno, una one
viejo old

IDIOMS

en casa (at) home
en la clase in (the) class

PROPER NAMES

California California
Carlos Charles
Juan John
María Mary
Nueva York New York
Tejas Texas
Virginia Virginia

EN LA CLASE

Hay muchos alumnos en la clase. Hay muchachos y hay muchachas. Hay también un profesor. El profesor es el[1] señor Martínez, don Roberto Martínez.

Uno de los muchachos es Juan. Otro muchacho es Carlos. Una de las muchachas es Virginia. Otra alumna es María.

Juan es de Tejas. Es alto y moreno. Es delgado también.

Carlos no es moreno, como Juan; es rubio. No es alto y delgado; es bajo y gordo. Carlos es de Nueva York.

Virginia es alta y rubia. Es guapa también. Virginia es de California.

La otra muchacha, María, es de Tejas, como Juan. Ella no es rubia, como Virginia; es morena. Y es pequeña. Las dos muchachas son simpáticas.

Los alumnos son jóvenes.[2] El señor Martínez es viejo. Él es inteligente, y los alumnos son inteligentes también.

Yo soy otro alumno de la clase. Soy de Chicago.

No estudiamos en la clase. Preparamos la lección[3] en casa. En la clase el señor Martínez explica la lección. Nosotros escuchamos y contestamos a[4] las preguntas. Conversamos en la clase y hablamos en español.

—[5]¿De dónde es usted?—pregunta el señor Martínez.

—Soy de Chicago, señor—contesto.

—Yo soy de Cuba—contesta el señor Martínez. —Soy cubano.

NOTAS

1. The definite article is used with titles when speaking *about* a person. It is omitted when addressing the person directly.

   El señor Martínez es el profesor.   Mr. Martínez is the professor.
   El profesor Martínez es viejo.   Professor Martínez is old.

   —Sí, señor Martínez.   "Yes, Mr. Martínez."

The definite article is never used with **don** and its feminine **doña**, generally untranslatable titles used only before first names to express respect for an older or distinguished person.

El profesor es don Ramón Martínez.   The professor is Don Ramón Martínez.

2. That syllable of a word which is stressed in the singular is stressed also in the plural. Words like **joven**, therefore, must add an accent in the plural (**jóvenes**), just as words like **inglés** drop their accent in the plural (**ingleses**).

3. Nouns ending in **-ción** are feminine: **la lección.**

4. Certain Spanish verbs are used with prepositions where their English equivalents take no preposition. Your attention will be called to such cases as they occur in the text.

Contestamos *a* las preguntas.   We answer the questions.

5. In Spanish dialogue a dash is used to introduce different speakers. It is not repeated at the end of each speech, unless narrative matter or words introducing the next speech follow in the same paragraph.

PREGUNTAS

1. ¿Hay muchos alumnos en la clase?
2. ¿Quién es el profesor?
3. ¿Quiénes son dos muchachos de la clase?
4. ¿Quiénes son dos muchachas de la clase?
5. ¿De dónde es Juan?
6. ¿Cómo es Juan?
7. ¿Cómo es Carlos?
8. ¿De dónde es Carlos?
9. ¿Cómo es Virginia?
10. ¿De dónde es Virginia?
11. ¿Cómo es María y de dónde es?
12. ¿Son viejos los alumnos?
13. ¿Es joven el señor Martínez?
14. ¿Estudian ustedes en la clase?
15. ¿Dónde preparan ustedes la lección?
16. ¿Quién explica la lección?
17. ¿Habla usted inglés en la clase?
18. ¿De dónde es el profesor?

PRÁCTICA

Cambie según se indica. (Change as indicated.)

1. Yo estudio en casa.
   él / tú / nosotros / ella / ustedes / ellos

2. Ellas contestan a las preguntas.
   yo / usted / nosotros / tú / él

3. Él no explica la lección.
   ustedes / ella / tú / nosotros / yo

4. Tú no escuchas.
   usted / él / ustedes / nosotros / yo / ellas

*Law class at the
University of San
Marcos in Lima. In
South America the
professions with the
greatest prestige are
law, medicine, and
engineering. Many
students use law as an
avenue to a political
career.*

Estructura

USES OF SER

Spanish has two verbs which mean "to be": **ser**, which you have already
learned, and **estar**, which you will learn later.

a. **Ser** is used to express source or origin, that is, to tell where persons or things
   are from.

   Yo soy de Chicago.   I am from Chicago.
   Juan y María son de Tejas.   John and Mary are from Texas.
   El profesor es de Cuba.   The professor is from Cuba.

PRÁCTICA

Haga preguntas (ask questions) *y conteste según el modelo.*

   ¿De dónde es usted? (Nueva York)
   Soy de Nueva York.

   1. ¿Y Virginia? (California)
   2. ¿Y Juan y María? (Tejas)
   3. ¿Y nosotros? (Los Estados Unidos)
   4. ¿Y ustedes? (La Argentina)

5. ¿Y usted? (Los Estados Unidos)
6. ¿Y ella? (México)
7. ¿Y el señor Martínez? (Cuba)
8. ¿Y tú? (España)

b. **Ser** is used with predicate nouns or pronouns. It tells what people or things are.

El señor Martínez es el profesor.　Mr. Martínez is the professor.
Somos norteamericanos.　We are Americans.
Carlos es otro alumno.　Charles is another student.
Es ella.　It is she.

PRÁCTICA

Cambie según el modelo.

¿Qué es usted? ¿Es usted italiano (italiana)?
No, no soy italiano (italiana).

1. ¿Qué es Juan? ¿Es español?
2. ¿Qué es Carlos? ¿Es portugués?
3. ¿Qué es usted? ¿Es usted cubano (cubana)?
4. ¿Qué son Juan y María? ¿Son españoles?
5. ¿Qué es el señor Martínez? ¿Es norteamericano?
6. ¿Qué son ustedes? ¿Son ustedes ingleses?
7. ¿Qué eres tú? ¿Eres francés (francesa)

c. **Ser** is used with an adjective which indicates an essential or inherent characteristic, one that is normally associated with a person or thing. It tells what they are like.

Juan es alto y delgado.　John is tall and thin.
Las muchachas son guapas.　The girls are pretty.
El profesor es viejo.　The professor is old.

PRÁCTICA

Cambie según se indica.

1. Carlos es inteligente.
2. Los alumnos ＿＿.
3. ＿＿ rubios y guapos.
4. La muchacha ＿＿.
5. ＿＿ joven.
6. Los profesores ＿＿.
7. ＿＿ altos y delgados.
8. Las muchachas ＿＿.
9. ＿＿ pequeñas.
10. María ＿＿.
11. ＿＿ inteligente.
12. Nosotros ＿＿.
13. ＿＿ viejos.
14. El señor Martínez ＿＿.

Tareas

Diga a la clase en español.

1. There are many students in the class.
2. Two of the boys are Juan and Carlos.
3. Juan is tall, dark, and handsome.
4. Carlos is short and fat.
5. The two girls are young and pretty.
6. Virginia is from California; Juan and María are from Texas.
7. The professor and the students are intelligent.
8. I study and prepare the lesson at home.
9. Mr. Martínez explains the lessons.
10. The students converse in class and speak in Spanish.

Composición oral o escrita

1. Ask several members of the class where they are from. Then prepare a short talk telling where they are from and what they are like (tall, short, young, pretty, small, good-looking, intelligent). Be prepared to present your talk to the class.

2. Prepare a short talk about the class. Explain who the professor is and what he or she does during the class period (explains the lessons, talks about Hispanic culture). Tell where you prepare the lesson and what kinds of things you do in class (listen, answer questions, converse in Spanish).

Pronunciación

The pronunciation of Spanish **d** depends on its position within a word or phrase. At the beginning of a breath group or after **1** or **n**, Spanish **d** (phonetic symbol [d]) is a voiced dental stop similar to English *d*. However, it is articulated with the tip of the tongue against the upper front teeth, not against the upper teeth ridges as in English. In other positions Spanish **d** is a voiced dental fricative [đ], made by placing the tip of the tongue lightly against the edges of the upper front teeth, without stopping the airstream. The resulting sound is similar to the voiced *th* in *neither*.

Pronounce the following series of words after your instructor.

[d]	[d]	[d]	[đ]	[d] and [đ]
dato	el dato	un dato	cada	dado
día	el día	un día	nada	dedo
diario	el diario	un diario	codo	delgado
daño	el daño	un daño	la dama	despide
Dios	el dios	un dios	la duda	duda
diente	el diente	un diente	la dicha	desdicha

Diálogo

¡OYE, GUAPA! ¿QUÉ ESTUDIAS?

PEPE—¡Oye, guapa![1] ¿Qué estudias?

VIRGINIA—Preparo la lección para[2] la clase de español.[3]

PEPE—¿Es interesante la clase?

VIRGINIA—¡Claro![4] El profesor habla mucho de la cultura hispánica.[5]

PEPE—¿Quién es el profesor?

VIRGINIA—El señor Martínez, don Roberto Martínez y Vanegas.

PEPE—¿Es español?

VIRGINIA—No, es cubano. Es un viejo muy simpático[6] y también muy inteligente. Explica muy bien las lecciones.

PEPE—¿Hablan ustedes en español?

VIRGINIA—Sí, claro. Preparamos la lección en casa y en la clase contestamos a las preguntas y conversamos en español.

[1]¡Oye, guapa! *Hey, beautiful!*
[2]para *for*
[3]la clase de español *Spanish class*
[4]claro *of course, naturally*
[5]cultura hispánica *Hispanic culture*
[6]muy simpático *very nice*

PREGUNTAS PERSONALES

1. ¿Es usted cubano (cubana) o norteamericano (norteamericana)?
2. ¿De dónde es usted?
3. ¿Es usted alto (alta) o bajo (baja)?
4. ¿Es usted joven o viejo (vieja)?
5. ¿Estudia usted en la clase o en casa?
6. ¿Dónde prepara usted la lección?
7. ¿Escucha usted en la clase?
8. ¿A qué contesta usted en la clase?
9. ¿Conversa usted en inglés en la clase?
10. ¿Cómo son las muchachas de la clase?
11. ¿Cómo son los muchachos de la clase?
12. ¿Cómo es el profesor (la profesora)?

Notas culturales

1. In the *Diálogo* Professor Martínez is called **don Roberto Martínez y Vanegas.** You noted that **don** is not translatable, though it is roughly equivalent to *Mr.* and implies respect for a person who is older or distinguished. It is used only before a given name. When only the family name is used, **don Roberto**

Caracas, Venezuela, was the first settlement in South America to achieve independence from Spain. Modern-day Caracas is a systematically planned city with many parks and plazas and wide boulevards. Much of Venezuela's recent development and modernization is due to increased revenues from its oilfields. The country is the world's third largest producer of petroleum.

is addressed as **señor Martínez**. The same is true of the feminine counterpart: **doña Alicia**, but **señora Montalvo**. Notice that **don** and **doña** are not capitalized in Spanish unless they begin a sentence. They are capitalized, however, when abbreviated, as they may be, to **D.** and **Da.**

2. Officially, people in the Spanish-speaking countries have two family names **(apellidos)**, and many of them use both. In the case of Roberto Martínez Vanegas, Martínez was his father's first **apellido**, and Vanegas was his mother's first **apellido**. Often the two family names are joined by **y: Roberto Martínez y Vanegas**. In the telephone book and other lists you look up Don Roberto under Martínez.

Let us say that Don Roberto marries Alicia Montalvo y López. Her name becomes **Alicia Montalvo de Martínez**. She keeps her own name and first **apellido**, adding **de** and her husband's first **apellido**. She thus preserves her identity!

Their children use the father's first **apellido** followed by the first **apellido** of their mother. Their son Roberto is Roberto Martínez Montalvo.

Middle initials are not normally used in the Hispanic countries, but they frequently are in Argentina, where a famous writer and statesman was Domingo F. Sarmiento. The equivalent of *junior* is **hijo** (*son*). The son of Don Roberto Martínez, named after his father, might be referred to as **Roberto Martínez, hijo**.

2

Para aprender nunca es tarde.
It's never too late to learn.

Present indicative of regular verbs of second & third conjugations

The present indicative of regular verbs of the second and third conjugations is formed by removing the infinitive ending (**-er** and **-ir**, respectively) and adding the following personal endings:

	SECOND CONJUGATION		THIRD CONJUGATION	
	Singular	*Plural*	*Singular*	*Plural*
FIRST PERSON	**-o**	**-emos**	**-o**	**-imos**
SECOND PERSON	**-es**	**(-éis)**	**-es**	**(-ís)**
THIRD PERSON	**-e**	**-en**	**-e**	**-en**

Notice that the endings of the second and third conjugations are identical except for the first and second persons plural.

---

aprender   to learn

---

aprendo I learn	**aprendemos** we learn
aprendes you learn (*fam.*)	**(aprendéis)** you learn (*fam.*)
usted aprende you learn	**ustedes aprenden** you learn
aprende he (she) learns	**aprenden** they learn

---

vivir   to live

---

vivo I live	**vivimos** we live
vives you live (*fam.*)	**(vivís)** you live (*fam.*)
usted vive you live	**ustedes viven** you live
vive he (she) lives	**viven** they live

29

PRÁCTICA

Cambie según se indica.

1. Yo* aprendo mucho.
   tú / el alumno / él / ellas / yo / nosotros / usted / ustedes / la muchacha /
   los alumnos

2. Nosotros vivimos en España.
   yo / ella / ellos / la alumna / tú / su padre / ustedes / el señor Martínez /
   el profesor y yo

Present indicative of irregular verb *decir* (to say)

digo I say	**decimos** we say
dices you say(*fam.*)	**(decís)** you say(*fam.*)
usted dice you say	**ustedes dicen** you say
dice he (she) says	**dicen** they say

PRÁCTICA

Cambie según el modelo.

El dice que aprende mucho.
Yo digo que aprendo mucho.

1. el alumno
2. ustedes
3. tú
4. yo
5. las alumnas

6. nosotros
7. la muchacha
8. los alumnos y yo
9. usted
10. el profesor

Escuchar y hablar

el abogado lawyer	**después** *adv.* afterwards;
bueno good	**después de** *prep.* after
la cinta tape	**el día** day
el clima climate	**el ejercicio** exercise
comprender to understand	**entrar (en)** to enter

* As you learned in Lección 1, subject pronouns are commonly omitted in Spanish. They
  are given in the exercises as cues.

escribir   to write
la familia   family
la hermana   sister
el hermano   brother
el ingeniero   engineer
el laboratorio   laboratory
leer   to read
el libro   book
luego   then
la madre   mother
el médico   doctor
muy   very
el padre   father
pero   but

el político   politician
porque   because
que *conj.*   that
un rato   a while
la sala   room
su   his, her

IDIOMS AND OTHER EXPRESSIONS

buenos días   good morning, good day
la sala de clase   classroom
toda la lección   all the lesson, the whole
   lesson

EN LA CLASE Y DESPUÉS DE LA CLASE

El profesor entra en[1] la sala de clase.
—¡[2]Buenos días![3]—dice el profesor.
—¡Buenos días, señor!—dicen los alumnos.
Uno de los alumnos lee un libro. El profesor pregunta: —¿Qué lee usted en el libro? —El alumno contesta: —Leo la lección.
Luego el profesor pregunta: —¿No leen ustedes la lección en casa?—El alumno contesta: —Sí, señor Martínez, leemos la lección en casa, pero yo no comprendo toda la lección.
—¿Cómo preparan ustedes la lección?—dice el señor Martínez.
María contesta: —Escuchamos[4] la cinta en el laboratorio, leemos la lección, contestamos a las preguntas del libro y escribimos los ejercicios. ¡Hay muchos ejercicios y muchas preguntas en el libro!
Después de la clase los alumnos conversan un rato.
Virginia dice que[5] es de California. Explica que su padre es médico y que es muy viejo. Su familia vive en California porque él es viejo y porque el clima[3] de California es bueno.
Carlos dice que es de Nueva York. Dice que su padre es abogado y que es político también.
—Es un político muy bueno—dice Carlos.
Juan explica que María es su hermana. Su familia vive en Tejas. El padre de Juan es ingeniero. No es norteamericano; es español. Pero su madre no es española; es norteamericana.

NOTAS

1. The verb **entrar** requires the preposition **en** when it is followed by an object.

   El profesor entra en la sala.   The professor enters the room.
   Entro en la casa.   I enter the house.

2. An inverted exclamation point precedes an exclamation, just as an inverted question mark precedes a question.

3. The nouns **el día** and **el clima** are masculine although they end in **-a.**

4. **Escuchar** may mean "to listen *to*." It takes no preposition equivalent to English "to."

   Escuchamos la cinta.   We listen *to* the tape.

5. The conjunction **que** (*that*) may not be omitted in Spanish as its English counterpart often is.

   Virginia dice que es de California.   Virginia says (that) she is from California.

PREGUNTAS

1. ¿Quién entra en la sala de clase?
2. ¿Qué dice el profesor?
3. ¿Qué lee uno de los alumnos?
4. ¿Qué no comprende el alumno?
5. ¿Cómo prepara María la lección?
6. ¿Qué hay en el libro?
7. ¿Qué es el padre de Virginia y dónde vive?
8. ¿Qué es el padre de Carlos?
9. ¿Quién es María?
10. ¿Dónde vive la familia de Juan y María?
11. ¿Es norteamericano el padre de Juan y María?
12. ¿Es médico el padre de Juan y María?

PRÁCTICA

Cambie según se indica.

1. Entramos en la sala de clase.
   yo / él / los alumnos / tú / nosotros

2. Usted lee toda la lección.
   los alumnos y yo / yo / ustedes / él / tú

3. Escribo los ejercicios.
   él / ellas / ustedes / tú / nosotros

4. Tú conversas un rato.
   nosotros / usted / ella / ustedes / yo

Puerto Rican festival in Central Park, New York City. The Jones Act of 1917 made Puerto Rico a territory and conferred US citizenship on its people. In 1950 it was elevated to a free commonwealth under the American flag. The greatest influx of Puerto Ricans to this country took place after World War II during a time of economic distress on the island. Many of the newcomers have established roots here —most of them in the New York metropolitan area and the Midwest. Others shuttle back and forth depending on the labor market.

Estructura

1. POSSESSION

The Spanish possessive is expressed by **de** plus the name of the possessor.

> **el padre de Juan** John's father
> **el hermano de María** Mary's brother
> **los libros de los alumnos** the students' books

2. CONTRACTION DEL

The preposition **de** contracts with the masculine definite article **el** to form **del**.

> **las preguntas del profesor** the professor's questions
> **los ejercicios del libro** the exercises of the book

It does not contract with **la, los,** or **las.**

> **la madre de la muchacha** the girl's mother
> **la hermana de los muchachos** the boy's sister

PRÁCTICA

Cambie según los modelos.

a. **¿Quién es? (el padre / Juan)**
   Es el padre de Juan.

   1. ¿Quién es? (la madre / María)
   2. ¿Quién es? (la hermana / el muchacho)
   3. ¿Quién es? (el hermano / la muchacha)
   4. ¿Quién es? (el padre / el profesor)
   5. ¿Quiénes son? (las hermanas / los muchachos)
   6. ¿Quiénes son? (los hermanos / el alumno)
   7. ¿Quiénes son? (las hermanas / el profesor)

b. **¿Qué libro es? (el abogado)**
   Es el libro del abogado.

   1. ¿Qué libro es? (el alumno)
   2. ¿Qué libro es? (la alumna)
   3. ¿Qué libro es? (el ingeniero)
   4. ¿Qué ejercicios son? (los alumnos)
   5. ¿Qué ejercicio es? (Pepe)
   6. ¿Qué clase es? (la profesora)
   7. ¿Qué clases son? (los profesores)
   8. ¿Qué clases son? (el profesor)
   9. ¿Qué médico es? (la madre)
   10. ¿Qué médico es? (el padre)

3. OMISSION OF THE INDEFINITE ARTICLE

The indefinite article is omitted with an *unmodified* predicate noun indicating profession, nationality, religion, or political affiliation.

Su padre es abogado.   His father is a lawyer.
El señor Martínez es español.   Mr. Martínez is a Spaniard.
Soy norteamericano.   I am an American.

But when the predicate noun is *modified*, the indefinite article is used, as in English.

Usted es un político muy bueno.   You are a very good politician.
Es una profesora muy famosa.   She is a very famous professor.

PRÁCTICA

Conteste según los modelos.

a. **¿Qué es usted? ¿Norteamericano (norteamericana)?**
   Sí, soy norteamericano.

   1. ¿Qué es usted? ¿Cubano (cubana)?
   2. ¿Qué es usted? ¿Alumno (alumna)?
   3. ¿Qué es su padre? ¿Médico?
   4. ¿Qué es su padre? ¿Abogado?
   5. ¿Qué es su hermano? ¿Ingeniero?
   6. ¿Qué es don Roberto Martínez? ¿Profesor?

b. **¿Es médico?**
   Sí, es un médico muy bueno.

1. ¿Es abogado?
   Sí, _____ muy inteligente.
2. ¿Es ingeniero?
   Sí, _____ muy bueno.

3. ¿Es político?
   Sí, _____ muy famoso.
4. ¿Es profesora?
   Sí, _____ muy simpática.

---

4. MORE ABOUT THE FEMININE OF ADJECTIVES

Adjectives of nationality ending in a consonant add **-a** to form the feminine.

Su padre es español. His father is Spanish.
Su madre no es española. Her mother is not Spanish.

PRÁCTICA

Cambie según los modelos.

a. **Su padre es norteamericano. ¿Y su madre?**
   Su madre es norteamericana.

1. Su padre es español ¿Y su madre?
2. Su padre es inglés. ¿Y su madre?
3. Su padre es italiano. ¿Y su madre?
4. Su padre es francés. ¿Y su madre?
5. Su padre es portugués. ¿Y su madre?

b. **Los muchachos son italianos. ¿Y las muchachos?**
   Todas son italianas.

1. Los muchachos son franceses. ¿Y las muchachas?
2. Los muchachos son ingleses. ¿Y las muchachas?
3. Los muchachos son norteamericanos. ¿Y las muchachas?
4. Los muchachos son españoles. ¿Y las muchachas?
5. Los muchachos son portugueses. ¿Y las muchachas?

Tareas

Diga a la clase en español.

1. The professor enters the classroom and says, "Good morning."
2. One of the students is reading the lesson.
3. Mr. Martínez asks, "Don't you read the lesson at home?"
4. The student says that he does not understand all the lesson.
5. "How do you prepare the lessons?" asks the professor.
6. The students listen to the tape in the laboratory, they read the lesson, they answer the questions, and they write the exercises.
7. Virginia's father is a doctor.

Students in the school of music at the University of Puerto Rico. Educational opportunities in Puerto Rico have become extensive as a consequence of economic prosperity and increased social mobility.

8. He is old and lives in California, because the climate of California is very good.
9. Charles's father is a lawyer.
10. He is a very good politician, too.
11. John's father is a Spaniard and is an engineer.
12. His mother is not Spanish.

Composición oral o escrita

1. Explain how you prepare the lesson. (You listen to the tape, you read the lesson, you answer the questions, you write the excercises, you speak in Spanish a while, and you learn the whole lesson.)

2. Describe the families of Carlos, Virginia, Juan, and María. (Tell where they live, what their fathers are, and so forth.)

Pronunciación

In Spanish the letters **b** and **v** are pronounced exactly the same. They have two sounds. In an initial position after a pause or after **n** or **m**, they are a voiced bilabial stop similar to English **b** (phonetic symbol [b]). In all other positions they are a voiced bilabial fricative [b̷], made by not quite closing the lips and allowing the airstream to pass through them without being stopped. **N** is pronounced **m** when it appears before **b** or **v**.

Pronounce the following words after your instructor.

[b]	[b]	[ƀ]	[b] and [ƀ]	[ƀ] and [ƀ]
broma	en broma	la broma	barba	la barba
venta	en venta	la venta	boba	la boba
balcón	un balcón	el balcón	verbo	el verbo
vino	un vino	el vino	bravo	el bravo
burro	un burro	los burros	bebo	yo bebo
verso	un verso	los versos	vivo	yo vivo

Diálogo

PEPE ES MUY SIMPÁTICO

MARÍA—Pepe es muy simpático. Es puertorriqueño,[1] ¿no?[2]

VIRGINIA—Sí, su familia es de Puerto Rico, pero viven en Nueva York. Su padre es abogado.

MARÍA—¿Dices que es abogado? ¿No es ingeniero?

VIRGINIA—No, dicen que es un abogado muy famoso. Pero el hermano de su padre es ingeniero.

MARÍA—¿Qué estudia Pepe?

VIRGINIA—Estudia para médico.[3] ¡Y es tan formal![4] Trabaja todo el día y aprende mucho. Pero es muy chistoso[5] también. ¡Las cosas[6] que dice . . . ! ¡Y es tan guapo y baila divinamente![7]

MARIA—Dices que es muy guapo y chistoso y que baila divinamente. ¡La cosa parece seria![8]

[1]puertorriqueño *Puerto Rican*

[2]¿no? *isn't he?*

[3]para médico *to be a doctor*

[4]formal *serious*

[5]chistoso *witty*

[6]cosa *thing, matter*

[7]baila divinamente *he dances divinely*

[8]parece seria *seems (looks) serious*

PREGUNTAS PERSONALES

1. ¿Dónde vive usted?
2. ¿Cómo es el clima donde usted vive?
3. ¿Vivimos en España? ¿Dónde vivimos?
4. ¿Estudia usted mucho y aprende mucho?
5. ¿Escucha usted la cinta?
6. ¿Dónde escucha la cinta?
7. ¿Luego prepara usted toda la lección?
8. ¿Comprende usted toda la lección?
9. ¿Escribe usted todos los ejercicios?
10. ¿Lee usted muchos libros?
11. ¿Aprendemos mucho en la clase?

Notas culturales

Hispanic Education

The educational system of the Hispanic countries differs from ours in various ways. The concept of the college in our sense—an institution beyond the secondary level affording a general education—does not exist. The **colegio** (also called **liceo**, **instituto**, or **escuela secundaria**) is a secondary school plus about the equivalent of two years college work. It corresponds to our high school plus junior college.

Students who complete their studies at the **colegio** receive the **bachillerato**, the bachelor's degree. They then enter the university and immediately pursue a course of specialized study leading to a professional degree. In the universities the intermediate degree is the **licenciatura**, the holder of which is entitled to be called **Licenciado**.

The three professions mentioned in this lesson—law, medicine, and engineering—are the most prestigious. Many of the people you will hear called doctor in Latin America will not be in the field of medicine, but lawyers who hold the degree of Doctor of Laws. Their profession is generally overcrowded. Many law students are not really preparing to practice, but are seeking entrance to government positions.

Universities in Spain and Latin America are usually located in large cities and do not have campuses like our schools—though there are exceptions, as in Mexico City, Bogotá, and Madrid. Hispanic universities are usually crowded and sometimes, especially in Spain, there are not enough places for all those who wish to enter.

3

Cuando en casa estoy, rey soy.
A man is king in his own house.

Present indicative of regular verbs *estar* and *ir*

estar to be	**ir** to go
estoy I am	**voy** I go, am going
estás you are (*fam.*)	**vas** you go, are going (*fam.*)
usted está you are	**usted va** you go, are going
está he (she) is	**va** he (she) goes, is going
estamos we are	**vamos** we go, are going
(estáis) you are (*fam.*)	**(vais)** you go, are going (*fam.*)
ustedes están you are	**ustedes van** you go, are going
están they are	**van** they go, are going

PRÁCTICA

Cambie según se indica.

1. Estamos en casa.
   yo / tú / los alumnos / usted / ustedes / mi hermano y yo

2. Ella no está en la clase.
   nosotros / la profesora / ustedes / tú / yo / el alumno

3. El profesor va a Cuba.
   ustedes / mi padre y yo / usted / tú / yo

4. Ustedes van a casa.
   tú / el alumno / yo / él / Inés y yo / los muchachos

*Knowledge of a foreign
language can lead to
interesting jobs at
home or abroad. Here
a multilingual
Colombian works for
the UN in New York.*

Escuchar y hablar

a   to
¿adónde?   (to) where?
ahora   now
allí   there
la amiga   friend *f.*
el amigo   friend *m.*
la biblioteca   library
bien *adv.*   well
el café   coffee house, café
cansado   tired
con   with
contento   happy
difícil   difficult
enfermo   ill
enojado   angry
fácil   easy
grande   large, big
la historia   history
más   more
perezoso   lazy
poco   little; **un poco**   a little
su, sus   his, her, your, their

todos *pron.*   all
trabajar   to work
tu, tus   your (*fam.*)

IDIOMS AND OTHER EXPRESSIONS

a casa   (to) home
al contrario   on the contrary
al fin   finally
en broma   jokingly
en efecto   in fact
en todas partes   everywhere
por eso   therefore; that's why; for that
   reason
¿qué hacen?   what do they do?
todos los días   every day
tomar un refresco   to have something to
   drink (*literally*, to take a refreshment)
¡vamos!   let's go!
¡vamos a tomar . . . !   let's have . . . !
   (*literally*, let's take . . . !)

ESTAMOS EN LA BIBLIOTECA

Ahora estamos en la biblioteca. La biblioteca es muy grande. Hay muchos libros en todas partes. Muchos alumnos van a la biblioteca todos los días. Allí leen sus libros y estudian sus lecciones.

Juan y María van a la biblioteca con su amigo Carlos y su amiga Virginia. Van a[1] preparar sus lecciones.

Carlos va a estudiar la lección de español.[2] Su lección es muy fácil. Por eso Carlos está muy contento.

María y Virginia van a aprender su lección de francés y Juan va a leer su libro de historia. María y Virginia están contentas, pero Juan, al contrario, está enojado. La lección de ellas es fácil, pero la lección de él es difícil.

Juan no está bien. Está un poco enfermo y por eso no trabaja mucho.

Al fin Juan dice: —No voy a trabajar más. Estoy un poco enfermo. Por eso voy a[3] casa.

—María—dice Carlos en broma—tu hermano no está enfermo. ¡Es perezoso y por eso no va a trabajar más! Yo, al contrario, no soy perezoso, pero estoy cansado. ¡Tú estás cansada también! En efecto, todos estamos cansados. ¡Vamos al café! ¡Vamos a tomar un refresco!

NOTAS

1. The verb **ir** requires the preposition **a** before an infinitive.

    Van a preparar sus lecciones.   They are going to prepare their lessons.
    No voy a trabajar más.   I am not going to work any more.
    ¡Vamos a tomar un refresco!   Let's have something to drink!

2. In English, phrases like "a Spanish lesson" and "an English professor" may have two meanings. The latter may mean either a professor who is English or a professor who teaches English. Sometimes we are forced to phrase the idea in the longer way to make our meaning unmistakable. Spanish always differentiates between the two ideas, but more simply.

    un profesor inglés   an English professor (a professor who is English)
    un profesor de inglés   an English professor (a professor who teaches English)
    un libro español   a Spanish book (a book written in Spanish, published in Spain)
    un libro de español   a Spanish book (a book about Spanish)

3. The preposition **a** means "to." Except in certain idioms, do not use it to translate "at," which is **en**.

    Vamos a casa.   We are going (to) home
    Estamos en casa.   We are at home.

PREGUNTAS

1. ¿Dónde estamos ahora?
2. ¿Cómo es la biblioteca?
3. ¿Qué hay en todas partes?
4. ¿Quiénes van a la biblioteca todos los días?
5. ¿Qué hacen los alumnos en la biblioteca?
6. ¿Qué va a estudiar Carlos?
7. ¿Cómo es su lección de español?
8. ¿Cómo está Carlos?
9. ¿Qué van a hacer María y Virginia?
10. ¿Qué va a leer Juan?
11. ¿Cómo están María y Virginia?
12. ¿Al contrario, ¿cómo está Juan?
13. ¿Cómo es la lección de Juan y cómo es la lección de María?
14. ¿Qué dice Juan?
15. ¿Adónde va?
16. ¿Qué dice Carlos en broma?
17. ¿Cómo están todos los alumnos?
18. ¿Qué más dice Carlos?

PRÁCTICA

a. *Sustituya según se indica.*

1. Yo voy a estudiar.
2. Ella ___ escuchar.
3. Los alumnos ___ leer.
4. Usted ___ hablar.
5. Nosotros ___ escribir.
6. Tú no ___ aprender.
7. Juan no ___ trabajar.
8. Yo no ___ contestar.

b. *Diga en español.*

1. Let's study.
2. Let's ask.
3. Let's learn.
4. Let's read.
5. Let's go in (enter).
6. Let's have something to drink.

c. *Diga en español.*

1. the Spanish lesson
2. the history book
3. the French class
4. the English professor
5. the Spanish lessons
6. the history books
7. the French classes
8. the English professors

Estructura

1. USES OF ESTAR

a. **Estar** is used to express location.

Estamos en la biblioteca.   We are in the library.
Madrid está en España.   Madrid is in Spain.
Las muchachas no están en casa.   The girls are not at home.

b. **Estar** is used with an adjective (sometimes an adverb) which tells the state or condition the subject is in (*tired, angry, well, ill,* and the like). Such states or conditions are often, though not always, temporary.

Juan está enfermo.   John is ill.
Estoy bien.   I'm well.
Las muchachas están enojadas.   The girls are angry.

States or conditions contrast with essential characteristics (like *tall, handsome, old, young*), which are indicated by the use of **ser.**

¿Cómo está Carlos?   How's Charles? (How is he feeling?)
¿Como es Carlos?   What's Charles like?

Juan está malo.   John is sick.
Juan es malo.   John is bad.

PRÁCTICA

a. *Conteste según el modelo.*

¿Dónde está Pepe? (en casa)
Está en casa.

1. ¿Dónde está usted? (en la clase)
2. ¿Dónde está Juan? (en España)
3. ¿Dónde están los alumnos? (en el café)
4. ¿Dónde estás? (en casa)
5. ¿Dónde estamos? (en la biblioteca)

b. *Conteste según el modelo.*

¿ Cómo está el profesor? (muy bien)
Está muy bien.

1. ¿Cómo están los alumnos? (muy contentos)
2. ¿Cómo está su hermana? (muy enferma)
3. ¿Cómo estás tú? (muy enojado, enojada)
4. ¿Cómo están ustedes? (muy bien)
5. ¿Cómo estamos todos? (muy cansados)

The tradition that a chaperon must watch over young women is fading rapidly.

c. *Use **ser** o **estar***.

1. Antonio no ___ en la biblioteca.
2. Nosotros no ___ perezosos.
3. ¿___ todos en la clase?
4. Las muchachas ___ muy cansadas.
5. Las muchachas ___ muy guapas.
6. Tu hermano no ___ enfermo.
7. ¿___ viejo el profesor?
8. Los alumnos ___ jóvenes.
9. Tú no ___ enojado, ¿verdad?
10. Tú ___ cubana, ¿no?
11. Yo no ___ inglés.
12. La lección ___ muy fácil.
13. Ahora nosotros no ___ en casa.
14. Yo no ___ muy alto.
15. Yo ___ en la clase todos los días.

2. POSSESSIVE ADJECTIVES TU AND SU

Possessive adjectives agree in gender and number with the thing possessed.
Tu and **su** have plural forms **tus** and **sus** to agree with plural nouns.

tu lección   your lesson (*fam.*)
tus lecciones   your lessons (*fam.*)
su libro   his (her, your, their) book
sus libros   his (her, your, their) books

Since **su** and **sus** have several meanings each, they might not always be clear.
In such cases a substitute expression is used. The definite article replaces **su** or
sus before the noun and **de** plus a pronoun is added:

el libro
- **de él**   his book
- **de ella**   her book
- **de usted (ustedes)**   your book
- **de ellos (ellas)**   their book

las amigas
- **de él**   his friends
- **de ella**   her friends
- **de usted (ustedes)**   your friends
- **de ellos (ellas)**   their friends

La amiga de él es española pero la amiga de ellos es francesa.   *His* friend
is Spanish, but *their* friend is French.

PRÁCTICA

a. *Diga en español.*

1. Where is his father?
2. Where is their mother?
3. Where is your professor?
4. Where are your brothers?
5. Where are their exercises?
6. Where are her sisters?
7. Where are his doctors?
8. Carlos, where is your book?
9. Mary, where are your friends?
10. John, where are your lawyers?

b. *Diga en español empleando* (using) *dos formas, según el modelo.*

his book: **su libro; el libro de él**

1. his sister
2. her brothers
3. your father
4. your exercises
5. their house
6. their houses
7. her library
8. his lawyers
9. their class
10. your doctors

3. *CONTRACTION* AL

Just as **de** contracts with the masculine definite article **el** to form **del**, the preposition **a** contracts with **el** to form **al**.

> **¡Vamos al café!**   Let's go to the coffee house!
> **al contrario**   on the contrary
> **al fin**   finally

PRÁCTICA

Sustituya según el modelo.

Hablamos al profesor. (la señorita)
Hablamos a la señorita.

1. el médico
2. el abogado
3. la madre
4. la hermana
5. el ingeniero

6. el muchacho
7. los alumnos
8. las muchachas
9. el joven
10. la joven

Tareas

Diga a la clase en español.

1. Many students are in the library every day.
2. The library is large, and there are books everywhere.
3. Carlos is going to study his Spanish lesson.
4. He is happy, because his lesson is easy.
5. María and Virginia are happy, too, because their French lesson is easy.
6. Juan, on the contrary, is angry, because his history book is difficult.
7. Juan is ill, and is not going to work (any) more.
8. Carlos says jokingly that María's brother is lazy, and that's why he's going home.
9. In fact all the students are tired.
10. Let's go to the café and let's have something to drink.

Composición oral o escrita

Tell about going to the library. (You go to the library every day. You read and study there. Describe what the library is like. You are happy, because the Spanish lesson is easy, but other students are angry, because their lessons are difficult.)

Pronunciación

In most positions Spanish **r** is a single tap of the tip of the tongue against the upper teeth ridges (phonetic symbol [r]). **Rr** is strongly trilled, with several rapid taps of the tip of the tongue against the upper teeth ridges (phonetic symbol [r̄]).

Pronounce the following words after your instructor.

[r]	[r̄]
para	parra
pero	perro
caro	carro
coro	corro

When **r** is initial in a word or occurs after **l**, **n**, or **s**, it is strongly trilled, like **rr**.

ramo	rayo	río
el ramo	el rayo	el río
un ramo	un rayo	un río
los ramos	los rayos	los ríos

Diálogo

MARÍA VA A TOMAR UN REFRESCO

CARLOS—Hola,[1] María, ¿adónde vas?

MARÍA—Voy a la biblioteca, como todos los días.

CARLOS—¿Vas a estudiar la lección de español?

MARÍA—¡Sí, claro! Y estoy contenta, porque es muy fácil.

CARLOS—¿Dónde está tu hermano Juan?

MARÍA—Está en casa. Dice que está cansado y que está un poco enfermo. Por eso no va a trabajar en la biblioteca.

CARLOS—Tu hermano es perezoso. Es por eso que no va a estudiar. Pero tú trabajas mucho. ¿No estás un poco cansada? ¡Vamos al café! ¡Vamos a tomar una coca cola!

MARÍA—Bueno.[2] ¡Vamos, pues![3]

[1] hola *hi*

[2] bueno *all right, O.K.*

[3] pues *then*

PREGUNTAS PERSONALES

1. ¿Va usted a la biblioteca todos los días?
2. ¿Qué estudia usted en la biblioteca?

3. ¿Lee usted muchos libros?

4. ¿Son fáciles o difíciles sus lecciones?

5. La lección de español es muy fácil, ¿no?

6. ¿Cómo está usted ahora? (¿cansado? ¿contento? ¿enojado?) ¿Por qué (*Why*)?

7. ¿Está usted bien, o está un poco enfermo?

8. ¿Va usted mucho a los cafés?

9. ¿Qué toma usted en el café?

10. Un amigo dice —¡Vamos al café!— ¿Qué dice usted?

Notas culturales

We have been using *Hispanoamérica* for "Latin America" or "Spanish America." In reality no term in current use, in either Spanish or English, is a satisfactory description of the area. All the names fail to recognize important ethnic, historical, or linguistic elements.

The terms *América Latina* and *Latinoamérica* do not take into account the many non-Latin peoples and languages in the region. *Hispanoamérica* and the similar but less common *Iberoamérica* share the same fault and also fail to recognize the French influence in Haiti. A term that has found much favor among "Latin Americans" is *Indoamérica*, coined by the Peruvian political leader Raúl Haya de la Torre. Yet this name, despite its inventor's protestations to the contrary, slights the Hispanic aspects of the area.

Perhaps the best expression yet found is *Eurindia*, devised by the Argentine scholar Ricardo Rojas. It evokes the coexistence and commingling of European and indigenous ethnic, cultural, and linguistic elements. But it has not caught on, and in all probability never will.

4

Quien puede y no quiere, cuando quiere no puede.
He who can and will not, when he wishes may not.

Present indicative of irregular verbs *querer, tener, poder,* and *ver*

querer to wish, want	**tener** to have
quiero I wish, want **quieres** you wish, want (*fam.*) **usted quiere** you wish, want **quiere** he (she) wishes, wants	**tengo** I have **tienes** you have (*fam.*) **usted tiene** you have **tiene** he (she) has
queremos we wish, want **(queréis)** you wish, want (*fam.*) **ustedes quieren** you wish, want **quieren** they wish, want	**tenemos** we have **(tenéis)** you have (*fam.*) **ustedes tienen** you have **tienen** they have

poder to be able	**ver** to see
puedo I can **puedes** you can (*fam.*) **usted puede** you can **puede** he (she) can	**veo** I see **ves** you see (*fam.*) **usted ve** you see **ve** he (she) sees
podemos we can **(podéis)** you can (*fam.*) **ustedes pueden** you can **pueden** they can	**vemos** we see **(veis)** you see (*fam.*) **ustedes ven** you see **ven** they see

PRÁCTICA

Cambie según se indica.

1. Nosotros queremos trabajar.
   él / tú / ustedes / la muchacha / yo / Paco y yo

2. Yo tengo dos hermanas.
   usted / tú / ellas / el alumno / nosotros / yo

3. Él puede aprender mucho.
   ellos / yo / nosotros / usted / ustedes / él

4. Veo al médico todos los días.
   Juan / tú / ustedes / ella / nosotros / yo

Escuchar y hablar

acompañar to accompany, go with	**las papas fritas** fried potatoes
bastante enough	**para** to, in order to
el bistec steak,	**el plato** plate; **lavar los platos** to wash the dishes
buscar to look for	
el café coffee	**pobre** poor
¡caramba! confound it! gracious!	**¿por qué?** why?
cerca de near	**el reloj** clock; watch
comer to eat	**el tiempo** time
la cuenta bill, check	**tomar** to take; to have (*meals, foods, etc.*)
dejar to leave	
el dinero money	**la universidad** university
exclamar to exclaim	
¡gracias! thank you, thanks; **¡muchas gracias!** thank you very much	IDIOMS AND OTHER EXPRESSIONS
el gusto pleasure	**con mucho gusto** with pleasure
hallar to find	**hasta luego** see you later
invitar to invite	**la hora de comer** dinner time
lavar to wash	**no . . . más que** only
mi, mis my	**tener calor** to be warm
mirar to look at	**tener frío** to be cold
nuestro, nuestra our	**tener hambre** to be hungry
pagar to pay	**tener sed** to be thirsty
	tener que to have to

¡VAMOS AL CAFÉ!

Carlos tiene calor y también tiene mucha sed.
—¡Vamos a tomar un refresco!—dice Carlos.
—Con mucho gusto—dice María.

Carlos quiere invitar a Virginia también, pero no ve a su amiga. No está en la sala de la biblioteca donde estudian Carlos y María.

Carlos busca[1] a Virginia en otra sala y después en otra. Al fin halla a su amiga.

Pero Virginia dice que no puede ir con sus amigos. —No puedo—explica ella—porque no tengo tiempo. Tengo que[2] preparar otras lecciones. Mis otras lecciones son difíciles. No son fáciles como nuestra lección de español.

Por eso Carlos y María dejan a Virginia en la biblioteca. Van a un café muy bueno que está cerca de la universidad.

—¿Qué vas a tomar, María?—pregunta Carlos.

María no tiene sed, como Carlos. Al contrario tiene mucha hambre.

—Quiero un bistec con papas fritas—contesta María.

El[3] pobre Carlos no tiene mucho dinero. Él no toma más que café.

María come todo el bistec y las papas fritas. Después mira[1] el reloj. Luego mira a Carlos y exclama: —¡Caramba! Tengo que ir a casa porque es la hora de comer.[4] ¡Muchas gracias, Carlos! ¡Adiós! ¡Hasta luego!

Y deja a Carlos en el café.

El pobre Carlos no puede acompañar a su amiga. No tiene bastante dinero para[5] pagar la cuenta. Y por eso tiene que lavar los platos en el café.

Cafés and coffee are to Spain and Latin America what bars are to the United States. Often little more than a small room with a few tables, cafés are a favorite meeting place for everyone. An undying Spanish institution is the tertulia—*a group of men who get together to talk and discuss the day's events at their favorite café.*

NOTAS

1. **Buscar**, *to look for,* and **mirar**, *to look at,* do not take prepositions equivalent to the "for" and "at" of their English counterparts.

   Juan busca sus libros.   John is looking for his books.
   María mira el reloj.   Mary looks at the clock.

   But when their direct object denotes a definite person, the "personal **a**" is used as with other verbs. (See *Estructura* section of this lesson.)

   Carlos busca al profesor.   Charles is looking for the professor.
   María mira a Carlos.   Mary looks at Charles.

2. The preposition "to" in *I (you,* etc.) *have to* is translated into Spanish by **que**.

   Tengo que estudiar.   I have to study.
   ¿Tiene usted que pagar?   Do you have to pay?

3. The definite article is used before a proper noun modified by an adjective.

   el pobre Carlos   poor Charles
   la joven María   young Mary

4. Spanish has few true compound nouns. Notice that "dinner time" is **la hora de comer** (*literally,* "time to eat").

5. When "to" with an infinitive in English expresses purpose, it is usually translated into Spanish by **para**.

   Carlos no tiene bastante dinero para pagar la cuenta.   Charles doesn't have enough money to pay the check.
   Estudiamos para aprender.   We study to (in order to) learn.

PREGUNTAS

1. ¿Tiene Carlos mucha hambre?
2. ¿Qué quiere tomar Carlos?
3. ¿A quién busca Carlos?
4. ¿Qué dice Virginia?
5. ¿Cómo son las lecciones de Virginia?
6. ¿Adónde van Carlos y María?
7. ¿Dónde está el café?
8. ¿Qué pregunta Carlos?
9. ¿Tiene María mucha sed?
10. ¿Qué quiere María?
11. ¿Por qué no puede Carlos pagar la cuenta?
12. ¿Qué mira María?

13. ¿Adónde va María?
14. ¿Por qué?
15. ¿Qué tiene que hacer Carlos en el café?

PRÁCTICA

Sustituya según se indica.

1. Yo tengo que estudiar.
2. Tú _____.
3. _____ trabajar.
4. Antonio _____.
5. _____ aprender.
6. Ustedes _____.
7. _____ escribir.
8. Nosotros _____.
9. _____ leer.
10. Yo _____.
11. _____ contestar.
12. Ellas _____.
13. _____ escuchar.
14. Usted _____.

Estructura

1. PERSONAL A

When a noun denoting a definite person is the direct object of a verb, it is preceded by the preposition **a**. This is true of people's names when used as direct objects. This **a** has no equivalent in English and can not be translated. It merely indicates who the object is.

Verb + **a** + direct object person (or name)

Carlos halla a su amiga.   Charles finds his friend.
Ustedes pueden invitar al profesor.   You may invite the professor.
No veo a Virginia.   I don't see Virginia.

The "personal **a**" is also used with **quién** to translate "whom."

¿A quién ve usted?   Whom do you see?
¿A quiénes buscan?   Whom are they looking for?

It is omitted after the verb **tener.**

Tenemos un profesor muy bueno.   We have a very good professor.

PRÁCTICA

a. *Sustituya según el modelo.*

Veo a Juan.
María / Veo a María.

1. Ramón / Veo _____.
2. la muchacha / Veo _____.
3. el profesor / Vemos _____.
4. mis amigos / Invito _____.
5. tu hermano / Invitas _____.

6. mi amiga / Hallo _____.
7. Isabel / Hallamos _____.
8. el médico / Busco _____.
9. tus hermanos / Buscan _____.

b. *Sustituya según el modelo.*

Tengo que buscar al médico.
mi amigo / Tengo que buscar a mi amigo.
el café / Tengo que buscar el café.

1. la profesora
2. el profesor
3. mi reloj
4. mi padre
5. mis amigos

6. el dinero
7. Dolores
8. los platos
9. el libro
10. los médicos

The Chicanos have played a significant part in the cultural development of the United States. Their influence has been strongest in the Southwest where most of their communities are concentrated. In stores such as this one in East Los Angeles, they are able to buy some of their typical products. La Raza Unida and other Chicano political groups have been active in the struggle for better economic, social, and political conditions.

2. POSSESSIVE ADJECTIVES

Like the possessive adjectives **tu** and **su** which you have already learned, **mi** (*my*) has its plural: **mis**. **Nuestro** and **vuestro** have four forms each: masculine and feminine, singular and plural.

SINGULAR	PLURAL	
mi	**mis**	my
tu	**tus**	your (*fam.*)
su	**sus**	his, her, your, its
nuestro, -a	**nuestros, -as**	our
(vuestro, -a)	**(vuestros, -as)**	your (*fam.*)
su	**sus**	their, your

In Spanish America the familiar second person plural (**vuestro, -a, -os, -as**) has been replaced by the formal third person **su**, **sus** (*your*).

Remember that these forms agree with the *thing possessed*, not with the possessor.

mi lección	my lesson	**mis lecciones**	my lessons
tu hermana	your sister	**tus hermanas**	your sisters
nuestra casa	our house	**nuestras casas**	our houses
su libro	his (her, your, their) book	**sus libros**	his (her, your, their) books

You have already learned the substitute construction for **su** and **sus** when the meaning of these words might not be clear.

la casa de ellos y la casa de él   their house and his house
el hermano de usted y el hermano de ella   your brother and her brother

PRÁCTICA

Sustituya según los modelos.

a. **Yo quiero mi dinero. (Juan)**
   Juan quiere su dinero.

   1. Ana
   2. Tú
   3. Nosotros
   4. Ellos
   5. Yo
   6. Ella
   7. Carlos y yo
   8. Ustedes
   9. Usted
   10. El abogado

b. **Teresa ve a sus hermanas. (Yo)**
   Yo veo a mis hermanas.

   1. Usted
   2. Ustedes
   3. Tú
   4. Ellas
   5. Yo
   6. Nosotros
   7. Tomás
   8. Usted y yo

3. *IDIOMS WITH* TENER

Some physical or emotional states in living beings are expressed with **tener** plus a noun.

> **Tengo calor.**   I am warm.
> **Tienen sueño.**   They are sleepy.
> **Carlos tiene miedo.**   Charles is afraid.
> **Tenemos frío.**   We are cold.

Since words such as **calor** and **miedo** are nouns, they must be modified by the adjective **mucho**, not by the adverb **muy**. Two common nouns used in such expressions, **sed** and **hambre**, are feminine. They must therefore be modified by the feminine form **mucha**.

> **Tenemos** *mucha* **sed.**   We are *very* thirsty.
> **¿Tiene usted** *mucha* **hambre?**   Are you *very* hungry?

PRÁCTICA

Diga en español.

1. I am very thirsty.
2. We are very hungry.
3. She is very sleepy.
4. He is not very cold.
5. The boys are not very warm.
6. They are not afraid.

Tareas

Diga a la clase en español.

1. Carlos says that he is very warm and very thirsty.
2. "Let's go to the café and let's have something to drink."
3. "With pleasure," says María.
4. Carlos wants to invite the other girl too.
5. But he does not see Virginia.
6. He looks for his friend in another room.
7. "I can't go to the café," says Virginia, "because I have to study my lessons."
8. "What are you going to have, María?"
9. "I want a steak and fried potatoes, because I am very hungry."
10. Carlos takes only coffee.
11. María looks at the clock and looks at Carlos.
12. Gracious! She has to go home, because it's dinner time.
13. "Thank you very much," she says, and leaves Carlos in the café.
14. Poor Carlos doesn't have enough money to pay the check and has to wash the dishes.

Composición oral o escrita

Tell about an experience you have in a coffee house. (You are thirsty and want to have some coffee. You invite two friends. Tell where the coffee house is. You ask them what they are going to have. They say that they are hungry. They eat a steak and fried potatoes. They look at the clock and say that it is dinner time and that they have to go home. You do not have enough money to pay the check. For that reason you have to wash the dishes.)

Pronunciación

The sound of Spanish **j** is an unvoiced velar fricative. The back of the tongue is raised towards the velum (the soft palate) as if to pronounce English **k**. But the back of the tongue does not touch the velum as in **k**. Instead a small space is left between tongue and velum through which the airstream passes. Spanish **g** before **e** or **i** has a similar sound.

Pronounce the following words after your instructor.

joven	gema	gime
jamón	gente	giro
julio	general	gigante
tajo	genio	gimnasio
lujo	gesto	gitano

Diálogo

MARÍA PUEDE ENGORDAR

CARLOS—¡Hola, Virginia! María y yo tenemos mucha sed. Vamos al café a tomar un refresco. ¿No quieres ir también?

VIRGINIA—Gracias, Carlos, pero no puedo. Tengo que escribir una composición[1] para mi clase de inglés. Además[2] tengo que ver a Pepe en la biblioteca.

(*Carlos y María entran en el café.*)

CARLOS—¿Qué vas a tomar, María, coca cola?

MARÍA—No, tengo hambre. Quiero un bistec con papas fritas.

CARLOS—¿Puedes comer todo eso?[3]

MARÍA—Sí, puedo.

CARLOS—¡Puedes engordar![4]

MARÍA—¡Qué va![5] No tengo miedo[6] de eso.

CARLOS—¡Uf![7] ¡Qué calor![8] No voy a tomar más que coca cola.

[1]composición *composition*

[2]además *besides*

[3]eso *that*

[4]Puedes engordar. *You may get fat (put on weight).*

[5]¡Qué va! *Nonsense!*

[6]tener miedo *to be afraid*

[7]¡Uf! *Phew!*

[8]¡Qué calor! *How hot it is! (What heat!)*

PREGUNTAS PERSONALES

1. ¿Tiene usted hambre?
2. ¿Qué quiere usted comer?
3. ¿Tiene usted mucha sed?
4. ¿Qué quiere usted tomar?
5. ¿Tenemos frío en enero (*January*)?
6. ¿Tenemos calor en julio (*July*)?
7. ¿Tiene usted mucho sueño en la clase?
8. ¿Puede usted comprender todas las preguntas?
9. ¿Puede usted ir al café ahora?
10. ¿Tiene usted que estudiar mucho?

Notas culturales

Food in the Hispanic countries

Typical foods and dishes vary greatly around the Hispanic world. Those with rice as an ingredient are widely used. Nearly everyone has tasted or knows about **arroz con pollo,** which originated in Spain and there contains spicy Spanish **chorizos** (sausages). Variations of this dish are found in Latin American countries, each with its special preparation and flavor. The **paella a la valenciana,** which originated in Valencia, contains seafood like mussels and squid.

Seafood is common in Spain and on seacoasts of Latin America. The Spaniards eat squid in several ways—fried or **en su tinta** (cooked in their own ink). The Peruvians and Chileans have an immense variety of seafood, and in Chile you can get excellent lobsters brought in from the Juan Fernández Islands.

Mexican food is especially attractive to many Americans who like the **picante** (hot, highly seasoned) dishes prepared with chili and other types of hot pepper. **Tamales** are made by wrapping corn husks around a mixture of corn meal and highly seasoned pork or chicken. **Tacos** are tortillas filled with chopped meat, cheese, tomatoes, and lettuce. **Enchiladas** are tacos with a hot sauce and sprinkled with cheese. Peruvians, too, like hot dishes flavored with **ají** (chili pepper) and **ajo** (garlic).

If your palate does not appreciate such highly seasoned foods, you will prefer the **plato típico** of Argentina: beef. In Buenos Aires, order a **bife** or a **baby bife**! Or try the **parrillada,** a mixed grill of several meats from steak to sausages cooked over charcoal.

In the tropical countries you will enjoy the exotic fruits, among them **papayas, chirimoyas** (custard apples), **granadillas** (passion fruit), **mangos,** and **aguacates** (avocados), called **paltas** in Ecuador and Peru, where they may reach a size to dwarf the ones we know.

1

A. *Conteste según el modelo.*

¿Es usted español?
No, no soy español.

1. ¿Habla usted portugues?
2. ¿Va usted a la biblioteca ahora?
3. ¿Tiene usted mucha hambre?
4. ¿Quiere usted comer ahora?
5. ¿Es usted de la Argentina?

B. *Use la forma correcta de **a** + el artículo definido.*

1. Vamos _____ biblioteca.
2. Vamos _____ café.
3. Vamos _____ universidad.
4. Vamos _____ cafés.
5. Vamos _____ clases.

C. *Use la forma correcta de **de** + el artículo definido.*

1. Es el padre _____ muchacho.
2. Es el padre _____ muchacha.
3. Es el padre _____ médico.
4. Es el padre _____ alumnos.
5. Es el padre _____ profesor.

D. *Conteste según el modelo.*

¿De quién es el libro? (Marta)
Es de Marta.

1. ¿De quién es el libro? (el profesor)
2. ¿De quién es el libro? (Ramón)
3. ¿De quién es el libro? (la profesora)
4. ¿De quién es el libro? (los alumnos)
5. ¿De quién es el libro? (las muchachas)

E. *Conteste.*

1. ¿De dónde es usted?
2. ¿De dónde es el señor Martínez?
3. ¿De dónde son Juan y María?
4. ¿De dónde somos nosotros? ¿De Inglaterra?
5. ¿De dónde son los españoles?

F. *Use **ser** o **estar**.*

1. Nosotros _____ jóvenes
2. Nosotros _____ muy enojados.
3. El profesor _____ de Cuba.
4. El profesor _____ muy viejo.
5. El profesor _____ cansado ahora.
6. Pepe no _____ aquí.
7. Los alumnos _____ en la biblioteca.
8. Los alumnos no _____ mexicanos.
9. Usted no _____ del Brasil.

G. *Cambie según el modelo.*

Es una muchacha muy guapa.
Son muchachas muy guapas.

1. Es una lengua muy hermosa.
2. Es una lección muy fácil.
3. Es una clase muy interesante.
4. Es un profesor muy simpático.
5. Es un libro muy difícil.

H. *Conteste según el modelo.*

¿Quieres estudiar?
Sí, vamos a estudiar.

1. ¿Quieres tomar un refresco?
2. ¿Quieres escuchar la cinta?
3. ¿Quieres comer ahora?
4. ¿Quieres ir al café?

I. *Conteste según el modelo.*

¿Puedes ir al café? (estudiar)
No, tengo que estudiar.

1. ¿Puedes ir a casa? (trabajar)
2. ¿Puedes ir a la biblioteca? (ir a casa)
3. ¿Puedes ir a la biblioteca? (ir a mi clase)
4. ¿Puedes ir al café? (preparar la lección)

J. *Use **a**, si es necesario.*

1. Veo _____ el libro.
2. Veo _____ mi amigo Paco.
3. Busco _____ mis libros.
4. Busco _____ mis amigos.
5. Busco _____ Virginia.

K. *Conteste según el modelo.*

¿Qué es el señor Martínez?
Es de Cuba: es cubano.

1. ¿Qué es el señor Pérez? Es de España: _____.
2. ¿Qué es el señor Smith? Es de Inglaterra: _____.
3. ¿Qué es el señor Dupont? Es de Francia: _____.
4. ¿Qué es la señora Gómez? Es de España: _____.
5. ¿Qué es la señora Smith? Es de Inglaterra: _____.
6. ¿Qué es la señora Dupont? Es de Francia: _____.

L. *Conteste según el modelo.*

¿Qué es el señor Martínez? (profesor / simpático)
Es profesor.
Es un profesor muy simpatico.

1. ¿Qué es el señor Blanco? (abogado / famoso)
2. ¿Qué es la señora Martí? (profesora / inteligente)
3. ¿Qué es el señor Pardo? (médico / joven)
4. ¿Qué es el señor Vázquez? (ingeniero / simpático)
5. ¿Qué es el señor Torres? (profesor / viejo)

M. *Cambie según el modelo.*

Yo busco mis libros. (Juan)
Juan busca sus libros.

1. Yo busco mi libro. (Tomás)
2. Yo busco mi libro. (ellas)
3. Yo busco mis libros. (tú)
4. Inés busca sus libros. (nosotros)
5. Inés busca su libro. (ustedes)
6. Inés busca su libro. (nosotros)

N. *Cambie según el modelo.*

Vemos la casa de Carlos.
Vemos la casa de él.

1. Vemos los ejercicios de Ana.
2. Vemos el libro del profesor.
3. Vemos las casas de nuestros amigos.
4. Vemos los ejercicios de los muchachos.
5. Vemos los libros de las alumnas.

O. *Diga en español.*

1. the Spanish lesson
2. the French class
3. the history book
4. the English professor

P. *Diga en español.*

1. I'm very hungry.
2. I'm very thirsty.
3. I'm very warm.
4. I'm very cold.

Q. *Diga a la clase en español.*

1. Tell about the languages of Europe and Latin America and the languages that you speak.
2. Tell about the people in Mr. Martínez's class: who they are; where they are from; what they are like; what you know about their families.
3. Tell where and how we prepare the lessons and what we do in class.
4. Tell about the students in the library: when they go there; what they do there; how they feel about their lessons, and so forth.
5. Tell about Carlos and María in the café.

5

Dios los cría y ellos se juntan.
Birds of a feather flock together.
(God produces them but they get together.)

Present indicative of irregular verbs *saber* and *conocer*

sé	sabemos	conozco	conocemos
sabes	(sabéis)	conoces	(conocéis)
Ud.* sabe	Uds. saben	Ud. conoce	Uds. conocen
sabe	saben	conoce	conocen

Note that these verbs have only one irregular form, the first person singular.

Both **saber** and **conocer** mean *to know*. **Saber** means *to know* in the sense of to have in one's head, to be master of—for instance, to know a fact, a theorem, or a language. It also means *to know how to* when followed by an infinitive.

> **Yo sé la lección.** I know the lesson.
> **El señor Martínez sabe varias lenguas.** Mr. Martínez knows several languages.
> **Sabemos escribir en español.** We know how to write in Spanish.

Conocer means *to know* in the sense of to be acquainted with someone or something.

> **Conozco a Virginia.** I know Virginia.
> **¿No conoce Ud. al profesor?** Don't you know the professor?
> **Conozco esa ciudad.** I am acquainted with that city.

* In Lesson 1 you learned that **usted** and **ustedes** are commonly abbreviated to **Ud.** and **Uds.** or **Vd.** and **Vds.** When abbreviated in this text the forms **Ud.** and **Uds.** will be used.

63

PRÁCTICA

Cambie según se indica.

1. El alumno sabe la lección.
   yo / nosotros / tú / Ud. / los muchachos / él

2. Ellos conocen al señor García.
   tú / Ud. / nosotros / yo / Ud. y yo / Uds.

Commands with *usted* and *ustedes*

Spanish has two forms of direct commands: the "formal" command, used in speaking to persons whom you normally address as **usted**, and the "familiar" command, used in speaking to persons whom you address as **tú**.

The **usted** command of all regular and most irregular verbs is formed on the stem of the first person singular of the present indicative. The **-o** is dropped and replaced by the following endings:

	-ar verbs		**-er** and **-ir** verbs	
	SINGULAR	PLURAL	SINGULAR	PLURAL
	-e	**-en**	**-a**	**-an**

INFINITIVE	FIRST PERSON SINGULAR PRESENT	COMMANDS		
		SINGULAR		PLURAL
hablar	**hablo**	**hable usted**	speak	**hablen ustedes**
aprender	**aprendo**	**aprenda usted**	learn	**aprendan ustedes**
escribir	**escribo**	**escriba usted**	write	**escriban ustedes**

In commands **usted** and **ustedes** follow the verb. They may be omitted. When used, they make the command more polite and less peremptory.

The negative is formed by placing **no** before the command.

No mire usted el reloj.   Don't look at the clock.
No coman ustedes ahora.   Don't eat now.

Familiar commands

In the singular, the familiar command of all regular and most irregular verbs is the same as the third person singular of the present indicative.

habla   speak   **aprende**   learn   **escribe**   write

Guatemalan descendants of the ancient Mayas exhibit their wares at the market center of Chichicastenango. Fine examples of Guatemalan weaving reflect the Indian sense of color and design.

Tú is used only for emphasis. When it is included, it follows the command.

   ¡Habla tú, María!   *You* speak, Mary!

A few verbs have irregular commands. These will be studied later.

In Spanish America, the plural of the familiar command is the same as the plural of the formal command.*

   ¡Hola! Pasen ustedes.   Hi there! Come on in.

The negative singular familiar command of all regular and many irregular verbs is the same as the formal singular, but with **-s** added.

FORMAL COMMAND NEGATIVE SINGULAR	FAMILIAR COMMAND NEGATIVE SINGULAR
No hable usted.	**No hables (tú).**
No aprenda usted.	**No aprendas.**
No escriba usted.	**No escribas.**

The negative plural is the same as the negative plural of the formal command.

   ¡No me digan!   Don't tell me! (You don't say!)

* This is the form that will be used in this book. The form of the familiar plural command that is used in Spain will be studied later.

PRACTICA

Conteste según los modelos.

a. **Quiero hablar.**
   Pues, hable usted.

1. Quiero aprender.
2. Quiero escribir.
3. Quiero escuchar.
4. Quiero leer.
5. Quiero contestar.
6. Quiero comer.
7. Quiero trabajar.
8. Quiero comprender.
9. Quiero estudiar.
10. Quiero preguntar.

b. **Vamos a escribir.**
   No escriban ustedes.

1. Vamos a trabajar.
2. Vamos a comer.
3. Vamos a contestar.
4. Vamos a aprender.
5. Vamos a escribir.
6. Vamos a preguntar.
7. Vamos a escuchar.
8. Vamos a leer.
9. Vamos a estudiar.
10. Vamos a hablar.

c. **¿Puedo escuchar?**
   ¡Sí, claro! ¡Escucha!

1. ¿Puedo hablar?
2. ¿Puedo trabajar?
3. ¿Puedo comer?
4. ¿Puedo preguntar?
5. ¿Puedo contestar?
6. ¿Puedo escribir?
7. ¿Puedo mirar?
8. ¿Puedo leer?
9. ¿Puedo estudiar?
10. ¿Puedo escuchar?

d. **¿Puedo escuchar?**
   ¡No, hombre! ¡No escuches!

1. ¿Puedo hablar?
2. ¿Puedo contestar?
3. ¿Puedo comer?
4. ¿Puedo trabajar?
5. ¿Puedo preguntar?
6. ¿Puedo leer?
7. ¿Puedo estudiar?
8. ¿Puedo mirar?
9. ¿Puedo escribir?
10. ¿Puedo escuchar?

Escuchar y hablar

además besides
aquí here
azul blue
bonito pretty
barato cheap; **más barato** cheaper
los calcetines socks
la camisa shirt
caro expensive
comprar to buy
la corbata necktie, tie
¿cuál? *interr. pron.*
   which (one)? what?

el dólar dollar
examinar to examine
la ganga bargain
hola hello
el hombre man
honrado honest
la lana wool; **de lana** of wool, woolen
la mañana morning; **mañana** tomorrow

necesitar   to need
ochenta   eighty
el precio   price
pues   well! then!
rebajar   to lower
rojo   red
la seda   silk
siempre   always
la tienda   store
el traje   suit
unos, unas   some
ya   already; indeed
el zapato   shoe

IDIOMS AND OTHER EXPRESSIONS

aquí tiene Ud.   here is, here are
ir de compras   to go shopping
mucho gusto de verlos   (I am) very
   pleased to see you
¿qué hace?   what does he do?
¿verdad?   aren't you? don't
   you? isn't it? etc. (**Verdad** is really a
   feminine noun meaning *truth*.)

LOS ALUMNOS VAN DE COMPRAS

Una mañana Carlos dice: —¡Hola, Juan! ¿Quieres ir de compras? Yo quiero comprar un traje, unas camisas y una corbata. Voy a una tienda que conozco. Es la tienda del señor García. Él me conoce y sé que siempre rebaja un poco los precios. ¿No lo conoces tú?

—¡Sí! Lo conozco. Es de Puerto Rico y es un hombre muy honrado.

—Mucho gusto de verlos—dice el señor García. —Uds. estudian el español, ¿verdad?

—Sí, señor,—contesta Juan—lo estudiamos.

—Pues, ¡hablen Uds. en español!

—¡Sí, sí, Carlos, habla en español!—dice Juan.

Carlos dice en español que quiere comprar un traje azul.

—¡Mire Ud.!—dice el señor García. —Aquí tiene Ud. un traje muy bonito. Es de lana.

—¿Cuál es el precio?— pregunta Carlos.

—Ochenta dólares.

—Mira, Carlos, es una ganga—dice Juan. —¡Cómpralo!

—Ya lo sé—dice Carlos. Y lo compra.

Carlos necesita también una corbata. Ve una corbata roja. Es de seda. La examina y la compra, porque es barata.

Carlos examina también unas camisas. Va a comprarlas, pero el señor García dice: —No las compre Ud. Son muy caras. Mañana voy a tener otras más baratas.

Juan ve unos calcetines y unos zapatos que no son muy caros. Los compra.

—¡Adiós, señor García!—dicen Juan y Carlos.

—¡Adiós, señores! Y muchas gracias.

—El señor García—dice Carlos—es un hombre muy honrado. Además nos conoce y por eso siempre rebaja un poco los precios.

PREGUNTAS

1. ¿Qué dice Carlos una mañana?
2. ¿Qué quiere comprar Carlos?
3. ¿Adónde va Carlos?
4. ¿Conoce a Carlos el señor García?
5. ¿Conoce Juan al señor García?
6. ¿Qué pregunta el señor García?
7. ¿Qué contesta Juan?
8. ¿Qué dice luego el señor García?
9. ¿Cuál es el precio del traje de lana?
10. ¿Qué más necesita Carlos?
11. ¿Qué hace Carlos?
12. ¿Por qué no compra Carlos las camisas?
13. ¿Qué compra Juan?
14. ¿Cómo es el señor García?
15. ¿Qué hace siempre el señor García?

Estructura

1. DIRECT OBJECT PRONOUNS

A direct object pronoun takes the place of a noun used as the direct object of a verb. The third person forms (**lo, la, los, las**) agree in gender and number with the nouns they stand for.

me	me	**nos**	us
te	you (*fam.*)	**(os)**	you (*fam.*)

lo	him, you, it (*m.*)	**los**	them, you (*m.*)
la	her, you, it (*f.*)	**las**	them, you (*f.*)

Many Spaniards (not Spanish Americans) use **le** to refer to a masculine person (*him, you*). In Spanish America the familiar plural *os* (*you*) has been replaced by the formal plural (**los, las**).

Lo is also a neuter form (*it*) used to refer to an idea or an action.

> **Lo sé.**   I know it.

Object pronouns are normally placed immediately before the verb. When used with a negative command, they take the normal position—preceding the verb. However, object pronouns follow and are attached to *affirmative* commands and infinitives. They also follow the present participle, which will be discussed later.

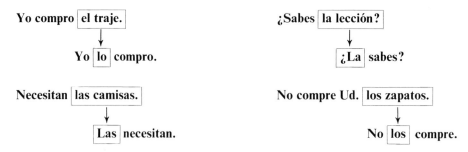

But:

Quiero ver las corbatas.

Quiero verlas.

Compre Ud. los calcetines.

Cómprelos Ud.

In the last example notice that **Cómprelos** has a written accent. An accent is required when an object pronoun is added to a command form of two or more syllables. It is placed over the syllable of the verb which was stressed before the pronoun was added.

PRÁCTICA

Conteste según los modelos.

a. **¿Compra Juan el traje?**
Sí, lo compra.

1. ¿Compra Juan la corbata?
2. ¿Compra Juan los calcetines?
3. ¿Compra Juan las camisas?
4. ¿Compra Juan el libro?
5. ¿Compra Juan las corbatas?
6. ¿Compra Juan los zapatos?
7. ¿Compra Juan la camisa?
8. ¿Compra Juan los trajes?

b. **¿Vas a examinar los zapatos?**
Sí, voy a examinarlos.

1. ¿Vas a examinar el libro?
2. ¿Vas a examinar los libros?
3. ¿Vas a examinar la camisa?
4. ¿Vas a examinar las corbatas?
5. ¿Vas a examinar los calcetines?
6. ¿Vas a examinar el ejercicio?
7. ¿Vas a examinar la lección?
8. ¿Vas a examinar las camisas?

c. **¿Puedo examinar las camisas?**
Sí, Pepe, examínalas.

1. ¿Puedo comprar las corbatas?
2. ¿Puedo leer el libro?
3. ¿Puedo estudiar la lección?
4. ¿Puedo comer el bistec?

5. ¿Puedo lavar los platos?
6. ¿Puedo escribir los ejercicios?
7. ¿Puedo escuchar la cinta?
8. ¿Puedo mirar su reloj?

d. **¿Puedo estudiarlo?**
No, no lo estudie Ud.

1. ¿Puedo mirarlo?
2. ¿Puedo escucharla?
3. ¿Puedo leerlo?
4. ¿Puedo comprarlas?
5. ¿Puedo escribirlos?
6. ¿Puedo aprenderlo?
7. ¿Puedo lavarlos?
8. ¿Puedo examinarlas?

e. **¿Conoce Ud. al señor García?**
Sí, lo conozco.

1. ¿Conoce Ud. a Dolores?
2. ¿Conoce Ud. al profesor?
3. ¿Conoce Ud. a las señoritas?
4. ¿Conoce Ud. a mi hermana?
5. ¿Conoce Ud. a los muchachos?
6. ¿Conoce Ud. al señor López?
7. ¿Conoce Ud. a las alumnas?
8. ¿Conoce Ud. a mis hermanas?

f. *Diga en español.*

1. He knows me.
2. They know us.
3. She knows you, señor.
4. She knows you, señora.

5. Does he know you, Pepe?
6. Does he know you, María?
7. Do they know you, boys?
8. Do they know us?

2. SER *WITH EXPRESSIONS OF MATERIAL*

Ser is used in naming the material of which a thing is made.

El traje es de lana.   The suit is of wool (woolen).
La corbata es de seda.   The tie is (of) silk.

PRÁCTICA

Diga en español.

1. It is a woolen suit.
2. It is a silk tie.
3. I need woolen socks.

4. I need silk ties.
5. Do you have woolen suits?
6. Do you have silk shirts?

Tareas

Diga a la clase en español.

1. "Hello!" says Carlos. "Let's go shopping!"
2. I know a store that is near the university.
3. It is Mr. García's store.
4. He knows me and always lowers the price a little.
5. "I know him, too," says Juan, "and I know that he is from Puerto Rico."
6. Carlos wants a blue suit. "Here it is," says Mr. García.
7. "What is the price of the suit?" asks Carlos.
8. It is a woolen suit, and he buys it because it is a bargain.
9. He needs a red tie, too, and he is going to buy it.
10. Carlos wants some shirts, but Mr. García says, "Don't buy them; they are very expensive."
11. Juan needs shoes and socks, but he does not buy them.
12. Mr. García is an honest man.

Composición oral o escrita

Pretend that you and a fellow classmate are going to a store that is near the university. Tell what you need and what you buy. Tell what your friend needs and what he buys. Tell what he does not buy, and why. Use as many direct object pronouns as you can.

Pronunciación

Spanish vowels must be pronounced clearly and distinctly—never slurred. Failure to pronounce unstressed vowels distinctly may sometimes make the meaning of words unclear.

Pronounce the following pairs of words as your instructor reads them, paying particular attention to the unstressed vowels.

a vs. e		a vs. i	
basar	besar	casa	casi
estudia	estudie	alusión	ilusión
prepara	prepare	amago	imago
señoras	señores	manar	minar
españolas	españoles	pasada	pisada
pasó	pesó	anterior	interior

a vs. o		a vs. u	
vieja	viejo	paré	puré
altas	altos	lanar	lunar
alumnas	alumnos	pañal	puñal
pasar	posar	maleta	muleta
saltar	soltar	maceta	muceta
barbón	Borbón	añoso	uñoso

Diálogo

EL SEÑOR GARCÍA REBAJA LOS PRECIOS

PACO—¡Carlos! ¿Cómo te va?[1]

CARLOS—Perfectamente.[2] Y tú, ¿cómo estás?

PACO—Bien, gracias. ¿Adónde vas?

CARLOS—Voy de compras. Conozco una tienda muy buena que está cerca de la universidad. Es de[3] un puertorriqueño muy simpático. Sé que siempre rebaja un poco los precios, porque me conoce. ¿No quieres acompañarme?

PACO—Pues, sí. Necesito una corbata y unos calcetines, si los hay[4] baratos. ¿Qué vas a comprar tú?

CARLOS—Voy a buscar unas camisas. Las necesito. No tengo ni una buena.[5]

PACO—Quiero también una chaqueta sport.[6] ¿Puedo comprarla en la tienda que conoces?

CARLOS—¡Claro! Cómprala allí. Va a ser muy barata, pero buena.

[1]¿Cómo te va? *How are you (how goes it with you)?*

[2]perfectamente *very well*

[3]es de *it belongs to*

[4]si los hay *if there are any*

[5]ni una buena *(not) even one good one*

[6]chaqueta sport *sport jacket*

PREGUNTAS PERSONALES

1. ¿Va Ud. de compras?
2. ¿Sabe Ud. dónde está una buena tienda?
3. ¿Conoce Ud. la tienda?
4. ¿Qué va Ud. a comprar para su hermano o hermana?
5. ¿Necesita Ud. una chaqueta sport?
6. ¿Va Ud. a comprarla en la tienda del señor García?
7. ¿Tiene Ud. calcetines de lana?
8. ¿Compra Ud. camisas de seda o camisas de lana?
9. ¿Necesita Ud. zapatos? ¿Dónde va a comprarlos?
10. ¿Sabe Ud. el precio del traje que compra Carlos en la tienda del señor García?

Notas culturales

Shopping

1. Most stores in Latin America and Spain are specialized. The **farmacia** (also called **droguería** or **botica**) is just what the name implies; it sells pharmaceutical and medicinal supplies and related items such as soap and toothpaste—but not the wide variety of unrelated articles found in our drugstores. Names of shops usually end in **-ía**. Here is a list of some common ones:

carnicería	butcher shop	**librería**	bookstore
panadería	bakery	**lavandería**	laundry
lechería or	dairy shop	**zapatería**	shoe store
mantequería		**ropería**	clothing store
frutería	fruit store		

Large department stores (**almacenes**) such as El Corte Inglés in Barcelona and Harrod's in Buenos Aires do exist, but are less common than in this country. Another term for department store is **el bazar**.

Markets are a familiar sight along the streets and in the squares of towns all over Latin America and Spain. Some, like those at the Indian fairs in Cuzco and Huancayo, Peru, and Otavalo, in Ecuador, are famous. At the markets one is able to find the attractive local handicrafts at good prices—sarapes, pottery, silver specialties, alpaca rugs. . . .

2. In this lesson we noted that **el señor García rebaja los precios**. Although Carlos did not have to **regatear**, bargaining still goes on in small shops and especially at open-air markets. The vendor, who is often the maker of the handicraft object he or she sells, expects customers to bargain. In stores where the practice is discouraged one may find the sign **precio fijo**.

Most people in the Hispanic countries still shop in small specialized shops. But department stores are gaining in popularity. The El Corte Inglés department store chain has branches such as this one in all major cities of Spain.

Religious paintings and portrait photographs available at the gate to Mexico City's Basilica of Guadalupe.

6

De la mano a la boca se pierde la sopa.
There's many a slip 'twixt the cup and the lip.
('Twixt the hand and the mouth the soup is lost.)

Stem-changing verbs (e > ie and o > ue)

Many Spanish verbs undergo a change of spelling in the stem. Such verbs, called stem-changing verbs, contain either the vowel **e** in the stem (like **pensar**, *to think*) or the vowel **o** (like **volver**, *to return*). In the present indicative verbs of this kind change the **e** to **ie** and the **o** to **ue** whenever the stress falls on these vowels. These changes occur throughout the singular and in the third person plural.

pensar:	**pienso**	I think
sentir:	**sientes**	you regret
volver:	**vuelve**	he returns
dormir:	**duermen**	they sleep

But not every verb with stem vowel **e** or **o** is stem-changing. You learn whether it is or not when you learn the verb. Vocabularies indicate which verbs are stem-changing by giving the change in parentheses after the infinitive, thus: **pensar (ie), sentir (ie), volver (ue), dormir (ue).** You have already seen these changes in the irregular verbs **querer** and **poder.**

Present indicative and command forms of some stem-changing verbs

pensar to think		**sentir** to regret	
*pi*enso	pensamos	*si*ento	sentimos
*pi*ensas	(pensáis)	*si*entes	(sentís)
Ud. *pi*ensa	Uds. *pi*ensan	Ud. *si*ente	Uds. *si*enten
*pi*ensa	*pi*ensan	*si*ente	*si*enten

volver to return		dormir to sleep	
v*ue*lvo	volvemos	d*ue*rmo	dormimos
v*ue*lves	(volvéis)	d*ue*rmes	(dormís)
Ud. v*ue*lve	Uds. v*ue*lven	Ud. d*ue*rme	Uds. d*ue*rmen
v*ue*lve	v*ue*lven	d*ue*rme	d*ue*rmen

The command forms of stem-changing verbs have the same change as the present indicative.

piense Ud.	**piensen Uds.**	**piensa (tú)**
vuelva Ud.	**vuelvan Uds.**	**vuelve (tú)**
duerma Ud.	**duerman Uds.**	**duerme (tú)**

PRÁCTICA

a. *Cambie según se indica.*

1. Yo pienso leerlo.
   Ud. / ellos / nosotros / tú / él

2. Juan no duerme bien.
   yo / nosotros / tú / ella / Uds.

3. Ud. vuelve mañana.
   tú / yo / él / Juan y yo / ellas

4. Yo lo siento mucho.
   María / Uds. / Ud. y yo / ellos / tú

b. *Cambie según el modelo.*

Quiero pensar.
No piense Ud.

1. Vuelvo mañana.
2. Quiero dormir.
3. Lo siento.
4. Pienso mucho.

Present indicative of irregular verb *dar* (to give)

doy	**damos**
das	**(dais)**
Ud. da	**Uds. dan**
da	**dan**

Notice that **dar** has only one irregular form in the present indicative: the first person singular.

PRÁCTICA

Cambie según se indica.

1. Nosotros no damos dinero.
   ellos / tú / él / yo / Ud. y yo

2. Virginia no me da el libro.
   Uds. / nosotros / tú / los alumnos / ella

Escuchar y hablar

blanco   white
la blusa   blouse
bonito   pretty
la compra   purchase
contar (ue)   to count
la chica   girl
el chico   boy
dar   to give
el dependiente   clerk
devolver (ue)   to return, give back
diez   ten
dormir (ue)   to sleep
encontrar (ue)   to find
la falda   skirt
gustar (a)   to be pleasing (to)
hoy   today
las medias   stockings
morir (ue)   to die
mostrar (ue)   to show
mucho   a lot, very much
el novio   sweetheart
pensar (ie)   to think; + *infin.* to intend
preferir (ie)   to prefer
prestar   to lend

sentir (ie)   to regret, be sorry
la señorita   young lady; Miss
si   if, whether
el sombrero   hat
tanto   so much, as much
la vendedora   salesgirl
verde   green
el vestido   dress
volver (ue)   to return, go back

IDIOMS AND OTHER EXPRESSIONS

me gusta   I like it; **me gustan**   I like
   them
me hace falta   I need it; **me hacen falta**
   I need them
me parece   it seems to me
¿Qué le (te) parece . . . ?   How do you
   like . . . ?
por supuesto   of course
¡Qué vestido más bonito!   What a pretty
   dress!
lo siento mucho   I am very sorry

LAS CHICAS VAN DE COMPRAS

—¿Qué piensas hacer hoy, Virginia?—pregunta María.
—Pienso ir de compras. Me hacen falta unas medias y un vestido.
—Pues, yo quiero comprar una falda y una blusa. ¡Vamos de compras!
Las dos chicas van a una tienda muy buena que conoce María. La vendedora
les muestra un vestido muy bonito que les gusta.

—¡Qué vestido más bonito!—exclama Virginia. —Me gusta mucho, pero es de lana y prefiero uno de seda.

—Es una ganga—dice María. —¡Cómpralo!

Pero Virginia no lo compra. Al contrario, examina unas medias. Le gustan y las compra.

María ve una falda de lana que le gusta mucho.

—Qué te parece la falda, Virginia?

—Me parece muy bonita. Es una ganga también.

—Voy a comprarla—dice María.

Ella quiere también una blusa de seda. La vendedora le muestra unas blusas.

—¿No les gustan a Uds. las blusas?—pregunta la vendedora.

—Sí, nos gustan—contestan las chicas. —¡Qué blusas más bonitas!

—Prefiero la blusa blanca[1] a la verde—dice María. —Pero no sé si tengo bastante dinero para comprarla.

—Cuenta tu dinero—le dice Virginia.

María cuenta su dinero, pero no encuentra bastante. —No puedo comprar la blusa—dice. —¡Lo siento mucho!

—Puedo prestarte diez dólares—le dice Virginia. Y le da el dinero.

María compra la blusa, pero dice: —Si no va bien con mi falda roja, voy a devolverla.

—¡Por supuesto! Devuélvala, si quiere—le dice la vendedora.

Luego las dos señoritas vuelven a casa. Están muy contentas, porque les gustan sus compras.

Each year more women in Latin America graduate from the universities and begin careers in government work or the professions. In Maracaibo, Venezuela, this staff handles public relations activities for the governor.

NOTA

1. You have learned several colors: **blanco**, **rojo**, **azul**, **verde**. To these should be added **negro** (*black*), **amarillo** (*yellow*), and **morado** (*purple*). *Light blue* is **azul claro**.

PREGUNTAS

1. ¿Qué pregunta María?
2. ¿Adónde piensa ir Virginia?
3. ¿Qué le hace falta a Virginia?
4. ¿Qué le hace falta a María?
5. ¿Qué les muestra la vendedora?
6. ¿Qué exclama Virginia?
7. ¿De qué es el vestido?
8. ¿Qué prefiere Virginia?
9. ¿Por qué compra Virginia las medias?
10. ¿De qué es la falda que le gusta a María?
11. ¿Qué más les muestra la vendedora?
12. ¿Qué exclaman las chicas?
13. ¿Cuál de las blusas prefiere Maria, la blanca o la verde?
14. ¿Qué hace María con su dinero?
15. ¿Qué le presta Virginia?
16. ¿Va María a devolver la falda?
17. ¿Adónde vuelven las señoritas?
18. ¿Por qué están contentas?

PRÁCTICA

Sustituya según se indica.

1. ¡Qué vestido más bonito!
2. ¡_____ blusas _____!
3. ¡_____ _____ caras!
4. ¡_____ sombrero _____!
5. ¡_____ _____ barato!
6. ¡_____ falda _____!
7. ¡_____ _____ bonita!
8. ¡_____ medias _____!

Estructura

1. INDIRECT OBJECT PRONOUNS

The indirect object pronouns are the same as the direct object pronouns, except in the third person, where there is only one form for the singular (**le**) and one for the plural (**les**).

me	(to) me	**nos**	(to) us
te	(to) you (*fam.*)	**(os)**	(to) you (*fam.*)
le	(to) you, him, her, it	**les**	(to) you, (to) them

In Spanish America the familiar plural **os** has been replaced by the formal plural **les**.

The indirect object pronouns correspond to the English forms *to you, to him,* and so forth, even when the *to* is not expressed. When you have a sentence like "I'll write *him* about it," which means "I'll write *to him* about it," you know you have an indirect object.

Indirect object pronouns follow the same rules for position as the direct object pronouns: they normally precede the verb, but they follow an infinitive and an *affirmative* command.

> **Me muestra el sombrero.**   He shows me the hat. (He shows the hat to me.)
> **¿Qué te parece la blusa?**   How do you like the blouse? (How does the blouse seem to you?)
> **Le doy el dinero.**   I give the money to you (to him, to her).
> **No les preste Ud. el libro.**   Don't lend them the book. (Don't lend the book to them.)

But:

> **Voy a darle el dinero.**   I am going to give you the money.
> **Muéstreme Ud. el sombrero.**   Show me the hat.

PRÁCTICA

Diga en español.

1. They give him the money.
2. They give her the money.
3. They give me the money.
4. They give them the money.
5. They give us the money.
6. They give you the money.
7. He is going to show her the shoes.
8. He is going to show us the shoes.
9. He is going to show them the shoes.
10. He is going to show me the shoes.
11. He is going to show him the shoes.
12. He is going to show you the shoes.

13. Return the hat to him.
14. Return the hat to them.
15. Return the hat to her.
16. Return the hat to us.
17. Return the hat to me.

18. Don't show her the blouse.
19. Don't show us the blouse.
20. Don't show them the blouse.
21. Don't show me the blouse.
22. Don't show him the blouse.

2. CLARIFICATION OF LE AND LES

Since **le** and **les** have several meanings each, a redundant construction may be used to show which meaning is intended. This consists of the preposition **a** plus the appropriate prepositional object pronoun.

Le doy el libro $\left\{ \begin{array}{l} \textbf{a él.} \\ \textbf{a ella.} \\ \textbf{a Ud.} \end{array} \right.$ I give the book $\left\{ \begin{array}{l} \text{to him.} \\ \text{to her.} \\ \text{to you.} \end{array} \right.$

Les doy el libro $\left\{ \begin{array}{l} \textbf{a ellos.} \\ \textbf{a ellas.} \\ \textbf{a Uds.} \end{array} \right.$ I give the book $\left\{ \begin{array}{l} \text{to them.} \\ \text{to them.} \\ \text{to you.} \end{array} \right.$

The redundant construction is often used for emphasis, even when the meaning is otherwise clear. With **usted (ustedes)** it is frequently used merely for politeness.

PRÁCTICA

Cambie según se indica.

Le prestan el libro a él. (a ellas)
Les prestan el libro a ellas.

1. a Ud.
2. a ella
3. a ellos

4. a él
5. a Uds.
6. a ellas

3. REDUNDANT LE AND LES WITH INDIRECT OBJECT NOUNS

A redundant **le** or **les** is normally used in a sentence containing a noun indirect object indicating a person, including people's names.

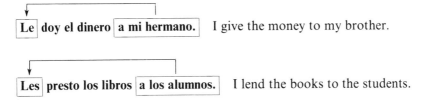

| **Le** | doy el dinero | **a mi hermano.** | I give the money to my brother.

| **Les** | presto los libros | **a los alumnos.** | I lend the books to the students.

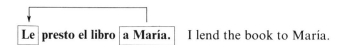 I lend the book to María.

PRÁCTICA

Cambie según se indica.

Le muestro el reloj a mi hermana. (a mis amigos)
Les muestro el reloj a mis amigos.

1. a mi padre
2. a mis profesores
3. a Tomás

4. a la profesora
5. a las chicas
6. al señor Martínez

4. GUSTAR

The Spanish equivalent of *I like the store* makes "store" the subject and says "The store is pleasing to me": **Me gusta la tienda.** Notice that the subject, **tienda**, follows **gustar**.

When the Spanish subject is plural, the verb becomes plural.

Le gustan las tiendas. He likes the stores.

For *I like it* and *I like them*, the Spanish equivalents are "It is pleasing to me" and "They are pleasing to me." But the Spanish speaker omits the subject pronouns "it" and "they" when referring to things and says:

Me gusta. I like it.
Me gustan. I like them.

Since the English subject becomes the Spanish indirect object, the name of the person who likes something, or a noun indicating that person, is always preceded by **a**. The indirect object pronoun is retained, too.

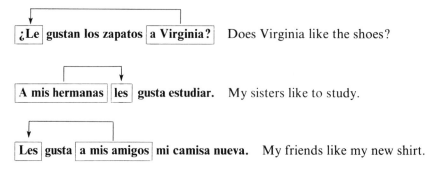

¿Le gustan los zapatos a Virginia? Does Virginia like the shoes?

A mis hermanas les gusta estudiar. My sisters like to study.

Les gusta a mis amigos mi camisa nueva. My friends like my new shirt.

PRÁCTICA

Diga en español.

a. 1. I like the store.
   2. He likes the store.
   3. They like the store.
   4. She likes the store.
   5. You like the store.
   6. You (*plural*) like the store.
   7. We like the store.

b. 1. He likes the socks.
   2. I like the socks.
   3. You like the socks.

4. You (*plural*) like the socks.
5. We like the socks.
6. She likes the socks.
7. They like the socks.

c. 1. María likes the shoes.
   2. Carlos likes the shoes.
   3. Mr. García likes the shoes.
   4. My father likes the shoes.
   5. My brother likes the shoes.
   6. My sister likes the shoes.

5. HACER FALTA *AND* PARECER

Two other expressions similar in construction to **gustar** are **hacer falta** (*to need*) and **parecer** (*to seem, appear*).

> **Me hace falta un traje nuevo.**   I need a new suit.
> **Le hacen falta diez dólares.**   She needs ten dollars.

The question **¿Qué te parece la blusa?** means literally *How does the blouse seem (appear) to you?* It is the equivalent of *How do you like the blouse?* or *What do you think of the blouse?*

> **¿Qué les parece la universidad?**   How do you like the university?
> **¿Qué le parecen las clases?**   What do you think of the classes?

Answers to such questions may be:

> **Me parece buena.**   It seems good to me.
> **Me parecen muy buenas.**   They seem very good to me.
> **Me gusta.**   I like it.   **Me gustan.**   I like them.

PRÁCTICA

a. *Conteste según el modelo.*

> **¿Qué le hace falta a Ud.?**
> **(zapatos nuevos)**
> **Me hacen falta zapatos nuevos.**

1. unas camisas blancas
2. una blusa verde
3. unos calcetines de lana
4. unas corbatas de seda
5. una chaqueta sport
6. diez dólares

b. *Cambie y conteste según el modelo.*

¿Qué le parece a Ud. la universidad?
(las clases)
¿Qué le parecen a Ud. las clases?
Me parecen muy buenas. Me gustan.

1. las tiendas   4. el café
2. la biblioteca   5. las lecciones
3. los profesores   6. el libro

c. *Diga en español.*

1. How do you like the ties, señor?
2. How do you like the ties, señores?
3. How do you like the tie, señora?
4. How do you like the tie, señoras?
5. How do you like the tie, Juan?
6. How do you like the ties, María?

Tareas

Diga a la clase en español.

1. María and Virginia intend to go shopping.
2. They need dresses, shoes, and blouses.
3. The salesgirls show them some hats.
4. Virginia sees some stockings that she likes, and she buys them.
5. How do you like the woolen skirt?
6. She prefers one of silk.
7. The salesgirl shows her some blouses.
8. Maria is going to buy them.
9. But she does not know whether she has enough money to buy them.
10. Virginia lends her ten dollars.
11. She returns the purchases if her sweetheart doesn't like them.
12. The young ladies return home.

Composición oral o escrita

Pretend that you and a girl friend go shopping. Tell where you go, what the sales person shows her, what she likes, what you like, what she buys, what she does not buy, and why.

Pronunciación

Pronounce the following words as your instructor reads them, paying particular attention to the pairs of unstressed vowels.

e vs. **i**		e vs. **o**		e vs. **u**	
pelar	pilar	escuche	escucho	melar	mular
pesó	pisó	puede	puedo	regido	rugido
bebió	vivió	quiere	quiero	se pone	supone
legué	ligué	pedido	podido	se frió	sufrió
relegó	religó	prescrito	proscrito	se vio	subió
case	casi	atentar	atontar	se marcha	su marcha

Diálogo

UN REGALO PARA MAMÁ[1]

Isabel encuentra a Teresa en una tienda en México.

ISABEL—¡Chica! ¡No me digas![2] ¡Tú en el centro![3]

TERESA—¿Te sorprende?[4] ¿No sabes que me gusta ir de compras?

ISABEL—¿Qué buscas?

TERESA—Me hace falta un regalo para mamá. Mañana es su cumpleaños.[5]

ISABEL—¿Qué piensas regalarle?[6]

TERESA—No sé. ¿Qué le doy? Piénsalo[7] tú.

ISABEL—¿Una blusa?

TERESA—No le gustan las blusas. Prefiere vestidos.

ISABEL—¿Por qué no le das unos artículos[8] de plata nacional?[9] No son caros. ¿Unos pequeños ceniceros?[10]

TERESA—No le gustan los ceniceros de plata.

ISABEL—¡Mira! Aquí hay unos aretes.[11] ¿Qué te parecen?

TERESA—Muy bonitos. Me gustan. (*A la vendedora.*) ¿Cuánto valen[12] los aretes?

LA VENDEDORA—Treinta[13] pesos.

TERESA—Bueno, me llevo éstos.[14] Favor de envolvérmelos.[15]

LA VENDEDORA—¡Cómo no![16]

TERESA—Gracias.

LA VENDEDORA—De nada.[17]

[1]un regalo para mamá *a gift for mother*

[2]¡No me digas! *Don't tell me!*

[3]en el centro *downtown*

[4]sorprender *to surprise*

[5]el cumpleaños *birthday*

[6]regalar *to give (as a gift)*

[7]Piénsalo. *Think about it.*

[8]el artículo *article*

[9]la plata nacional *national (Mexican) silver*

[10]el cenicero *ashtray*

[11]los aretes *earrings*

[12]¿Cuánto valen? *How much are they worth?*

[13]treinta *thirty*

[14]me llevo éstos *I'll take these*

[15]Favor de envolvérmelos. *Please wrap them for me.*

[16]¡Cómo no! *Of course!*

[17]De nada. *You're welcome.*

PREGUNTAS PERSONALES

1. ¿Le gusta a Ud. ir al centro?
2. ¿Piensa Ud. ir de compras hoy?
3. ¿Qué le hace falta?
4. ¿Encuentra Ud. en la tienda las cosas que le hacen falta?
5. ¿Prefiere Ud. camisas azules o camisas blancas?
6. ¿Prefiere Ud. corbatas rojas o corbatas verdes?

A saddle shop in Santo Domingo de los Colorados, Ecuador, caters to the region's cowhands.

7. En una tienda, cuando Ud. encuentra una chaqueta barata, ¿qué exclama?
8. Cuando le paga a la vendedora, ¿cuenta Ud. su dinero?
9. ¿Qué le parecen los precios por aquí?
10. ¿Les muestra Ud. sus compras a sus amigas?
11. ¿Devuelve Ud. a la tienda muchas de sus compras?

Notas culturales

In the *Diálogo*, Teresa pays in **pesos**, since she is in Mexico. The **peso**, however, is not the universal monetary unit in the Hispanic world. Some countries have currencies named after famous men: the **colón** (Columbus) in Costa Rica and El Salvador, the **sucre** in Ecuador, the **bolívar** in Venezuela, the **balboa** in Panamá. Guatemala has the **quetzal**, named after the colorful national bird; Honduras, the **lempira**; Nicaragua, the **córdoba**; Perú, the **sol**; Chile, the **escudo**; and Paraguay, the **guaraní**, named after the Indians of the region. Brazil, it might be added, has the **cruzeiro**. Spain uses the **peseta**.

The **peso** or other monetary unit is usually divided into 100 **centavos**. But not everywhere: Spain, Venezuela, and Paraguay have the **céntimo**; Chile and Uruguay have **centésimos**.

7

El que primero se levanta, primero se calza.
The early bird catches the worm.
(He who gets up first gets his shoes on first.)

Reflexive verbs

Reflexive means "bending back." A reflexive verb is one whose action "*reflects back*," directly or indirectly, upon its subject.

me lavo I wash myself (I wash)
me digo I tell myself (I say to myself)

The object is a reflexive pronoun, which has the same person and number as the subject; it also has the same form, whether it is a direct object or an indirect object. In vocabularies and dictionaries reflexive verbs appear with the pronoun **se** attached to the infinitive.

lavarse to wash		**vestirse** to dress	
me lavo	**nos lavamos**	**me visto**	**nos vestimos**
te lavas	**(os laváis)**	**te vistes**	**(os vestís)**
Ud. se lava	**Uds. se lavan**	**Ud. se viste**	**Uds. se visten**
se lava	**se lavan**	**se viste**	**se visten**

Note that the first two persons, singular and plural, of the reflexive pronouns are the same as the direct and indirect object pronouns for these persons. Only the third person differs: **se** (*himself, herself, itself, yourself, themselves, yourselves*).

Many Spanish reflexives may be translated by English reflexives.

Carlos se lava.   Charles washes himself.

But many others are not likely to be, or cannot be, translated by English reflexives.

> **Me acuesto.** I go to bed.
> **Ud. se viste.** You get dressed.
> **María se sienta.** Mary sits down.
> **Ellos se despiertan.** They wake up.
> **Ella se va.** She goes away.
> **¿Cómo se llama Ud.?** What is your name? (How do you call yourself?)

PRÁCTICA

Cambie según se indica.

1. Los muchachos se acuestan tarde.
   yo / Ud. / nosotros / tú / ellas

2. Nosotros nos vestimos.
   Uds. / yo / tú / ella / ellos / Ud. y yo

3. Ramón no se despierta.
   ellos / tú / ella / nosotros / yo / Uds.

4. El viejo se sienta.
   tú / Ud. y yo / yo / Uds. / Ud. / nosotros

More stem-changing verbs

Other stem-changing verbs have a final stem vowel **e** which changes to **i** whenever it is in the stressed syllable—that is, throughout the singular and in the third person plural of the present indicative and in the command forms. All verbs that change **e** to **i** are third-conjugation verbs.

pedir to ask for		**despedirse (de)** to take leave of	
p*i*do	pedimos	me desp*i*do	nos despedimos
p*i*des	(pedís)	te desp*i*des	(os despedís)
Ud. p*i*de	Uds. p*i*den	Ud. se desp*i*de	Uds. se desp*i*den
p*i*de	p*i*den	se desp*i*de	se desp*i*den

Commands:

p*i*da Ud.	p*i*dan Uds.	p*i*de (tú)
desp*í*dase Ud.	desp*í*danse Uds.	desp*í*dete (tú)

Chapultepec Park was the first point in the Valley of Mexico taken and fortified by the invading Aztecs. Montezuma built a summer palace here and in 1793 Chapultepec Castle was begun on the same site. Today the park is a way of life for Mexicans. Crowds of people spend Sunday afternoons picnicking on the grass, rowing on the lake, and strolling through the castle.

PRÁCTICA

Cambie según se indica.

1. Ellos piden un refresco.
   Ud. / Ud. y yo / Antonio / las alumnas / tú / yo

2. Yo pido café.
   Ud. / ellas / nosotros / tú / Héctor / tú y yo

3. Tomás se despide de ellos.
   yo / tú / Ud. / María y yo / las chicas

Some easy irregular verbs

Three common irregular verbs are easy to learn because they have only one irregular form in the present indicative: the first singular, which ends in **-go**. All the other forms are regular.

hacer to do, make		**poner** to put, place		**salir** to leave, go out	
hago	hacemos	pongo	ponemos	salgo	salimos
haces	(hacéis)	pones	(ponéis)	sales	(salís)
hace	hacen	pone	ponen	sale	salen

Venir (*to come*) is like the preceding verbs in the first singular. In the other forms it is like the **e > ie** stem-changing verbs.

vengo	venimos
vienes	(venís)
viene	vienen

PRÁCTICA

a. *Cambie según se indica.*

1. Todos los días hacemos mucho aquí.
   Alberto / yo / tú / tú y yo / mis amigos

2. ¿Sale Ud. a la calle ahora?
   Uds. / Anita / nosotros / yo / tú

3. ¿Dónde ponemos el regalo?
   yo / tú / nosotros / Uds. / Ud.

4. Pepe viene siempre a este restorán.
   Ud. / Uds. / yo / nosotros / tú

b. *Conteste afirmativamente.*

1. ¿Haces mucho en la universidad ahora?
2. ¿Hacen Uds. mucho en la universidad ahora?
3. ¿Hacen mucho sus amigos en la universidad ahora?
4. ¿Sales de casa temprano?
5. ¿Salen Uds. temprano?
6. ¿Salen de casa temprano los alumnos?
7. ¿Vienes temprano a la clase?
8. ¿Vienen Uds. temprano a la clase?
9. ¿Viene temprano el profesor?
10. ¿Pones el libro aquí?
11. ¿Ponen Uds. el libro aquí?
12. ¿Pone el profesor el libro aquí?

Escuchar y hablar

acostarse (ue) to go to bed
bañarse to take a bath
la cara face
el cuarto quarter (hour)
el desayuno breakfast

despedirse (i) (de) to take leave of, say good-by to
los dientes teeth
doce twelve
la fruta fruit

el huevo egg; **huevos fritos** fried eggs
irse to go away, go off
el jugo juice
levantarse to get up
limpiar to clean
llamarse to be called, be named;
  me llamo my name is
la mano hand
medio *adj.* half
menos less
la mesa table
mientras while
la naranja orange
nueve nine
o or
ocho eight
el pan tostado toast
el panecillo roll
pedir (i) to ask for; to order (*in a restaurant, etc.*)
peinarse to comb one's hair

poner to put; **ponerse** to put on
el restorán restaurant
sentarse (ie) to sit down
servir (i) to serve; **servirse (i)** to serve oneself
siete seven
tarde late
la tarde afternoon, evening
temprano early
vestirse (i) to dress, get dressed

IDIOMS AND OTHER EXPRESSIONS

a las siete y media de la mañana at seven-thirty in the morning
son las nueve menos cuarto it's a quarter to nine
por la mañana in the morning
por la noche at night
¿a qué hora? at what time?
¿Qué hora es? What time is it?

POR LA MAÑANA

Yo no soy perezoso. Me levanto temprano por la mañana. Puedo levantarme temprano porque me acuesto temprano por la noche y, además, duermo bien. Juan y Carlos son perezosos. No se levantan temprano, porque se acuestan tarde. Yo me levanto a las siete de la mañana. Ellos se levantan a las ocho o a las ocho y media. Yo me acuesto a las diez o a las diez y media de la noche. Ellos se acuestan a las doce o a las doce y media.

Me levanto a las siete de la mañana. Me lavo las manos¹ y la cara.² Me limpio los dientes. Luego me baño. Después me visto y me peino.

Me pongo la chaqueta y voy a un restorán para tomar el desayuno. Pido fruta, pan tostado y café.

Hoy, mientras tomo el desayuno, Juan y Carlos vienen al restorán con un amigo. Su amigo se llama Arturo.

—¡Siéntense Uds.!—les digo.

Ellos se sientan a mi mesa. Juan pide jugo de naranja y huevos fritos. Carlos pide café y un panecillo. Yo me sirvo más café.

—¿Qué hora es?—pregunta Juan.

—Son las nueve menos cuarto—contesta Carlos.

—Me parece—dice Juan—que nosotros nos levantamos más tarde todos los días.

—¡Sí, es tarde!—exclamo y me levanto de la mesa. Me despido de mis amigos y me voy a la clase.

NOTAS

1. Notice that **la mano** is feminine.

2. Instead of possessive adjectives (**mi**, **su**, etc.) the definite article is normally used with parts of the body and articles of clothing. In Spanish it is obvious who the speaker is.

    Levanto *la* mano.   I raise *my* hand.
    Ricardo se pone *la* chaqueta.   Ricardo puts on *his* jacket.

    The possessor may be indicated by a reflexive or indirect object pronoun.

    ***Me* lavo la cara.**   I wash *my* face.
    Ella *le* lava la cara.   She washes *his* face.

PREGUNTAS

1. ¿Se levanta Ud. tarde o temprano?
2. ¿Por qué puede Ud. levantarse temprano?
3. ¿Se levantan temprano Juan y Carlos?
4. ¿A qué hora se levanta Ud.?
5. ¿A qué hora se acuesta Ud.?
6. ¿A qué hora se acuestan Juan y Carlos?
7. ¿Qué hace Ud. por la mañana cuando se levanta?
8. Después, ¿qué se pone Ud. y adónde va?
9. ¿Qué pide Ud. en el restorán?
10. ¿Quiénes vienen al restorán?
11. ¿Cómo se llama el amigo de Juan y Carlos?
12. ¿Qué les dice Ud.?
13. ¿Qué hacen sus amigos?
14. ¿Qué piden?
15. ¿Qué se sirve Ud.?
16. ¿Qué hora es?
17. Por eso, ¿qué hace Ud.?

Estructura

1. REFLEXIVE PRONOUNS

Reflexive pronouns follow the same rules for position as the other object pronouns. That is, they normally precede the verb. When they are the object of an infinitive or an affirmative command, however, they follow.

Me levanto a las siete.   I get up at seven o'clock.
Se sientan a mi mesa.   They sit down at my table.

But:

Voy a levantarme.   I am going to get up.
¡Siéntense Uds.!   Sit down!

PRÁCTICA

a. *Conteste.*

1. Al entrar en la clase, ¿se sientan Uds.?
2. Al salir de la clase, ¿se despide Ud. del profesor?
3. Después de tomar el desayuno, ¿se sirve siempre más café?
4. ¿Se baña Ud. por la mañana o por la noche?
5. ¿Se levantan Uds. tarde?
6. ¿Se acuesta tarde o temprano su amigo?
7. ¿Se peina Ud. todos los días?
8. ¿Se pone Ud. los zapatos todos los días?
9. ¿Se viste Ud. antes de tomar el desayuno?
10. ¿Cómo se llama su hermana?

b. *Cambie según se indica.*

1. Él quiere ponerse el sombrero.
   yo / ellos / Ud. y yo / tú / Uds.

2. Uds. tienen que vestirse ahora.
   él / yo / nosotros / tú / ellas

c. *Sustituya según se indica.*

1. ¡Levántese Ud.!
   vestirse / sentarse / acostarse / despertarse

2. ¡No se acuesten Uds.!
   despedirse / sentarse / levantarse / bañarse

3. ¡Lávate!
   bañarse / despedirse / peinarse / vestirse

2. CARDINAL NUMBERS 1–12

Notice that **uno** (*one*) has the feminine form **una**, while the other cardinal numbers given below are invariable. **Uno** becomes **un** before a masculine noun:
Yo tengo un hermano.

un(o), una	one	**siete**	seven
dos	two	**ocho**	eight
tres	three	**nueve**	nine
cuatro	four	**diez**	ten
cinco	five	**once**	eleven
seis	six	**doce**	twelve

PRÁCTICA

a. *Diga en español.*

1 más (*plus*) 1 son 2   6 + 2 = 8

2 + 1 = 3   7 + 2 = 9

3 + 1 = 4   8 + 2 = 10

4 + 1 = 5   9 + 2 = 11

5 + 1 = 6   10 + 2 = 12

6 + 1 = 7   11 + 1 = 12

b. *Cuente en español de 1 a 12.*

3. TELLING TIME

¿Qué hora es?   What time is it?

Es la una.
It's one o'clock.

Es la una y media.
It's one-thirty.

Es la una y cuarto.
It's a quarter after one.

Son las dos.
It's two o'clock.

Son las tres y cinco.
It's five after three.

Son las nueve.
It's nine o'clock.

Notice the use of **la** and **las** in the time expressions. **La** stands for **la hora** and **las** stands for **las horas**; but the word **hora (horas)** itself is not expressed.

The singular verb **es** is used with one o'clock. From two o'clock on **son** is used. Time between the hour and the half-hour is expressed by adding **y** and the minutes. Time between the half-hour and the next hour is expressed by giving the next hour less (**menos**) the minutes:

Son las seis menos diez.
It's ten minutes to six.

Son las siete menos cuarto.
It's quarter to seven. (6:45)

When the hour is specified, **de** is the equivalent of *in* or *at* in the phrases **de la mañana** (*in the morning*), **de la tarde** (*in the afternoon, evening*), **de la noche** (*at night*). When no definite hour is specified, **por** is used for *in* or *at*: **por la mañana** (*in the morning*), **por la noche** (*at night*).

Me levanto a las seis de la mañana.   I get up at six in the morning.
Siempre estudio por la noche.   I always study at night.

PRÁCTICA

Conteste según se indica.

a. **¿Qué hora es?**

1.

2.

3.

4.

5.

6.

Picking cotton in the Rio Bravo district in northwest Mexico. Traditionally, textiles and food processing have been Mexico's leading industries. Pueblo and Mexico City are centers for the manufacturing of cotton yarn and textiles. Since World War II the growth of other industries has been encouraged with protective tariffs, special tax exemptions, and subsidies. The most important new industry is steel.

b. **¿Qué hora es? 2:15**
   Son las dos y cuarto.

1. 2:30	7. 8:10
2. 1:00	8. 11:15
3. 1:30	9. 11:45
4. 3:15	10. 6:50
5. 5:30	11. 8:55
6. 6:05	12. 3:45

c. **¿Se baña Ud. por la mañana?**
   Sí, me baño por la mañana.

1. ¿Se viste Ud. por la mañana?
2. ¿Trabaja Ud. por la tarde?
3. ¿Estudia Ud. por la noche?
4. ¿Se despierta Ud. temprano por la mañana?
5. ¿Lee Ud. por la tarde?
6. ¿Se acuesta Ud. tarde por la noche?

d. **¿A qué hora se despierta Ud.? 6 a.m.**
   A las seis de la mañana.

1. ¿A qué hora se levanta Ud.? 6:30 a.m.
2. ¿A qué hora se viste Ud.? 6:45 a.m.

3. ¿A qué hora va Ud. a la clase? 8:50 a.m.
4. ¿A qué hora come Ud.? 1:00 p.m.
5. ¿A qué hora va Ud. a la biblioteca? 3:30 p.m.
6. ¿A qué hora va Ud. al café? 5:00 p.m.
7. ¿A qué hora estudia Ud. la lección? 9:00 p.m.
8. ¿A qué hora escribe Ud. los ejercicios? 11:00 p.m.
9. ¿A qué hora se acuesta Ud.? 11:45 p.m.

Tareas

Diga a la clase en español.

1. We get up early in the morning, because we go to bed early at night.
2. We get up at seven in the morning, but they get up at eight-thirty.
3. She washes her hands and face and goes out.
4. They clean their teeth and bathe.
5. He gets dressed and combs his hair.
6. I put on my jacket and go off to the restaurant.
7. He orders fried eggs and orange juice every day.
8. My friends come to the restaurant and I say to them, "Sit down at my table."
9. They sit down and order coffee and toast.
10. It is a quarter to ten and I take leave of my friends.

Composición oral o escrita

Tell what you do when you get up in the morning, where you have breakfast, what you like for breakfast, and what you do afterwards.

Pronunciación

Pronounce the following pairs of words after your instructor, paying particular attention to the pairs of unstressed vowels.

i vs. **o**		**i** vs. **u**		**o** vs. **u**	
casi	caso	piñal	puñal	osar	usar
cursi	curso	pintura	puntura	moral	mural
trinar	tronar	pinchar	punchar	tornar	turnar
millar	mollar	avisar	abusar	borlar	burlar
mijar	mojar	vigía	bujía	moleta	muleta
tinillo	tonillo	tirón	turón	topé	tupé

Diálogo

¡OYE, PEPE! ¡LEVÁNTATE!

Miguel y Pepe son compañeros de cuarto.[1] Viven en una residencia de estudiantes.[2]

MIGUEL—¡Oye, Pepe! ¡Levántate! Son las siete y cuarto.

PEPE—¡Ay![3] ¡Déjame dormir![4]

MIGUEL—¡No, hombre![5] Es tarde. Son las siete y cuarto y tienes una clase a las ocho.

PEPE—No puedo levantarme. Tengo sueño.

MIGUEL—Es porque siempre te acuestas tarde. Siempre te acuestas a la una o a las dos. Debes[6] acostarte más temprano.[7]

PEPE—¿Cómo puedo acostarme más temprano cuando tengo que preparar tantas lecciones?

MIGUEL—¡Anda![8] Levántate. No debes faltar a la clase.[9]

PEPE—Bueno. Me levanto. Pero no me da la gana.[10]

[1]compañeros de cuarto *roommates*	[6]debes *you ought to*
[2]residencia de estudiantes *dormitory*	[7]más temprano *earlier*
[3]¡Ay! *Oh!*	[8]¡Anda! *Come on!*
[4]déjame dormir *let me sleep*	[9]faltar a la clase *to miss class*
[5]hombre *man*	[10]no me da la gana *I don't feel like it*

PREGUNTAS PERSONALES

1. ¿Cómo se llama Ud.?
2. ¿Cómo se llama el rector (presidente) de la universidad?
3. ¿Cuántos hermanos tiene Ud.?
4. ¿A qué hora toma Ud. el desayuno?
5. Cuando Ud. toma el desayuno en un restorán, ¿qué pide?
6. ¿Le gusta a Ud. la fruta?
7. ¿Le gustan a Ud. los huevos fritos?
8. ¿Cuántas clases tiene Ud.?
9. ¿Tiene Ud. clases por la mañana? ¿A qué hora?
10. ¿Tiene Ud. clases por la tarde? ¿A qué hora?
11. ¿A qué hora tenemos nuestra clase de español?
12. ¿Tiene Ud. una clase a las seis de la mañana?
13. ¿Tiene Ud. una clase a las cuatro de la tarde?
14. ¿Prepara Ud. les lecciones por la mañana?
15. ¿Cuándo estudia Ud., por la mañana o por la noche?
16. ¿A qué hora se acuesta Ud.?
17. ¿Duerme Ud. bien?

Notas culturales

Time in Hispanic countries

1. In addition to the way of telling time that was presented in this lesson, the use of the European twenty-four hour system is widespread—especially in the case of train schedules and the like. At two o'clock in the afternoon you may find a sign on the door of a shop in Seville reading **Cerrado de 14 a 16,30**.

2. In the Hispanic countries it is the general practice for stores and offices to close for two or even three hours in the afternoon while everybody goes home for lunch. There have been attempts to discourage this practice— during World War II, for example, to save gas and ease the transportation problem—but they have not succeeded. In Lima the typical store hours are from nine-thirty to twelve-thirty and from four to seven or eight. In Buenos Aires, however, the big stores remain open from nine until seven.

3. The Hispanic daily schedule being different from ours, you may find that you have to make adjustments in the matter of meal hours, which tend to be late. Lunch is commonly around two or three o'clock, and dinner around nine or ten at night. But if you are hungry you can always find a place to eat, as in many **cafeterías** in Madrid—not cafeterias in our sense, but lunch rooms, usually with counter service. The names of two snacking times may take you by surprise. In Chile and Venezuela you may be served **onces** (*elevens*), not at eleven o'clock, but late in the afternoon. In a café in Bogotá you may note that the menu offers **medias nueves**, a mid-morning snack that you won't get at nine-thirty, but around eleven. In the late afternoon the **confiterías** (*tearooms*) in Buenos Aires, a product of English influence in Argentina, do a thriving business.

"El Silbo" (The Whistler), a resident of the Canary Islands.

LECCIÓN

8

Salió del lodo y cayó en el arroyo.
Out of the frying pan into the fire.
(He got out of the mud and fell into the stream.)

Preterit of regular verbs

Spanish has two simple past tenses: the imperfect, which you learn later, and the preterit. The preterit is formed by adding the following endings to the infinitive stem. Notice that the endings for the second and third conjugations are the same.

FIRST CONJUGATION		SECOND AND THIRD CONJUGATIONS	
-é	-amos	-í	-imos
-aste	(-asteis)	-iste	(-isteis)
-ó	-aron	-ió	-ieron

hablar	aprender
hablé I spoke	**aprendí** I learned
hablaste you spoke	**aprendiste** you learned
Ud. habló you spoke	**Ud. aprendió** you learned
habló he (she) spoke	**aprendió** he (she) learned
hablamos we spoke	**aprendimos** we learned
(hablasteis) you spoke	**(aprendisteis)** you learned
Uds. hablaron you spoke	**Uds. aprendieron** you learned
hablaron they spoke	**aprendieron** they learned

Note the written accent on the first and third persons singular.

Large areas of Ecuador are covered with mountains, flood plains, forests, and tropical jungles. Only about eleven per cent of the country is cultivated, and much of this land is devoted to exportable crops. Ecuador is the largest exporter in the world of bananas—with Europe now being the principal customer.

PRÁCTICA

Cambie según se indica.

1. Ud. preparó la lección.
   yo / Ud. y yo / ellos / tú / nosotros / Tomás

2. Yo escribí el ejercicio.
   nosotros / ella / ellas / tú / yo

3. Nosotros comimos bien.
   Uds. / tú / Uds. y yo / yo / Pepe

Preterit of stem–changing verbs

Stem-changing verbs that end in **-ar** or **-er** have no change in the preterit. Those that end in **-ir** have a change in the third person, singular and plural, of the preterit: final stem vowel **e** becomes **i**; final stem vowel **o** becomes **u**:

s*i*ntió	d*u*rmió	p*i*dió
s*i*ntieron	d*u*rmieron	p*i*dieron

PRÁCTICA

Cambie según se indica.

1. Tú dormiste bien.
   Carmen / nosotros / ellas / yo / Uds. / él

2. Yo lo sentí mucho.
   Ud. y yo / él / Uds. / yo / ella / tú / Ud.

3. Nosotros pedimos café.
   yo / Ud. / tú / él / ellos / tú y yo / Uds.

Escuchar y hablar

agradable agreeable
antes before, earlier
argentino Argentine
asistir (a) to attend
ayer yesterday
bastante rather, quite
la canción song
cantar to sing
clásico classic
la comida meal; dinner
la composición composition
la cordillera mountain range
la cosa thing
describir to describe
despertarse (ie) to wake up, awaken
divertirse (ie) to have a good time
la geografía geography
el guitarrista guitarist
hasta until
el lado side; **al lado de** next to, beside

la leche milk
la música music
ocurrir to occur, happen
la orquesta orchestra
la pampa pampa(s)
para for
pasar to pass, spend (*time*); to happen
popular popular
el programa program
quince fifteen
la selva forest
sobre on
Sudamérica South America
la televisión television
típico typical
tocar to play (*an instrument, song, etc.*)
tropical tropical
veinte twenty
la vida life

AYER

Ayer pasé un día típico.

Me desperté bastante temprano. Me levanté a las siete y media. Me bañé, me lavé la cara, me limpié los dientes y me peiné. Luego me vestí.

A las ocho y cuarto tomé un buen[1] desayuno con jugo de naranja, huevos fritos, café y pan tostado.

Estudié un rato y después asistí a[2] la clase del señor Martínez.

El señor Martínez habló de cosas muy interesantes. Habló de la vida hispanoamericana. Describió la geografía de los países de Sudamérica. Describió la cordillera de los Andes, la pampa argentina y la selva tropical.

Por la tarde trabajé tres horas. Estudié la lección de español y la aprendí. Luego escribí una composición para mi clase de inglés.

A las seis y media comí con Juan y Carlos en un buen restorán. Pedimos bistec con papas fritas, leche y café. Me gustó mucho la comida.

Después, en la librería al lado del restorán, Juan compró un libro muy interesante sobre Sudamérica y me lo regaló. Pero ocurrió también una cosa que no me gustó. Carlos me pidió quince dólares y se los presté. Dice que va a devolvérmelos mañana.

Luego Juan, Carlos y yo volvimos[3] a mi casa para ver unos programas[4] de televisión. Vimos unos programas muy interesantes. Dos chicas muy guapas cantaron canciones cubanas. Cantaron media hora. Una orquesta mexicana tocó música clásica mexicana. Nos gustó mucho la música.

Mis amigos se despidieron a las once. Se acostaron y durmieron bien. Pero yo no me acosté. Miré otro programa hasta las doce menos veinte. En el otro programa un guitarrista[5] español tocó canciones populares españolas que me gustaron mucho. A las doce me acosté y dormí bien.

Ayer pasé un día muy agradable. Trabajé mucho pero me divertí también.

NOTAS

1. **Bueno** becomes **buen** before a masculine singular noun.
2. **Asistir** requires the preposition **a** before a following object.

   Asistí al teatro.   I attended the theater.
   Asistieron a la clase.   They attended the class.

3. Recall that when a plural subject includes the first person singular pronoun **yo**, the verb must be in the first person plural.

   Juan, Carlos y yo volvimos a mi casa.   John, Charles, and I returned to my house.
   Mis dos amigos y yo vimos el programa.   My two friends and I watched the program.

4. Note that **el programa** is masculine. Many Spanish nouns ending in **-ma** are masculine.

   el drama   the drama
   el poema   the poem
   el telegrama   the telegram

5. Note that **el guitarrista** is masculine. Nouns denoting living beings retain the biological gender, regardless of the ending **-o** or **-a**.

   el poeta   the poet   **la modelo**   the model   **el novelista**   the novelist

PREGUNTAS

1. Ud. se despertó tarde, ¿verdad?
2. ¿A qué hora se levantó Ud.?
3. ¿A qué hora se vistió Ud.?
4. ¿A qué hora tomó Ud. el desayuno?
5. ¿Qué tomó Ud.?
6. ¿A qué clase asistió Ud.?
7. ¿De qué habló el señor Martínez?
8. ¿Qué describió?
9. ¿Cuánto tiempo trabajó Ud. por la tarde?
10. ¿Qué escribió Ud.?
11. ¿A qué hora comió Ud.?
12. ¿Con quiénes comió?
13. ¿Qué pidieron Uds.?
14. ¿Qué compró Juan?
15. Carlos le pidió dinero, ¿verdad?
16. ¿Se lo prestó Ud.?
17. ¿Qué miraron Uds. después de comer?
18. ¿Qué cantaron las dos chicas?
19. ¿Qué tocó la orquesta?
20. ¿A qué hora se despidieron Juan y Carlos?
21. ¿Cómo durmieron Juan y Carlos?
22. ¿Miró Ud. otro programa hasta las doce?
23. ¿Quién tocó canciones españolas?
24. ¿A qué hora se acostó Ud.?
25. ¿Durmió Ud. bien?

Estructura

1. USE OF THE PRETERIT

The preterit states an act that was completed in past time. It tells us that the act came to an end. It may be graphed thus:

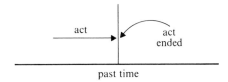

To identify such acts it is helpful to remember that the preterit is used in the following cases:

a. When the time of the act was instantaneous or nearly so.

Me desperté temprano.   I woke up early.
¿Entró Ud. en la tienda?   Did you go into the store?
Se sentaron a la mesa.   They sat down at the table.

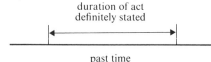

b. When the *duration* of the time is definitely stated.

Cantaron media hora.   They sang half an hour.
Por la tarde trabajé tres horas.   In the afternoon I worked three hours.
Mi padre vivió en España veinte años.   My father lived in Spain twenty years.

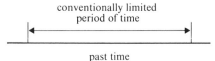

c. When the time was the conventional period of time for the act that took place.

Asistí a la clase del señor Martínez.   I attended Mr. Martínez's class.
Vimos un programa de televisión.   We watched a television program.
¿Comiste en un restorán?   Did you have dinner in a restaurant?

conventionally limited
period of time

past time

Mexico City has some of the most exciting museums in the world, including the Museum of Anthropology, opened in 1964. It was designed by Pedro Ramírez Vásques, who followed the ancient Indian tradition of combining buildings with open spaces. The museum houses interesting relics from Mexico's past, including the statue of the Aztec goddess Coatlicue and the Aztec Calendar. It also displays panoramas showing how Mexicans live today in different regions of the country.

PRÁCTICA

Cambie según los modelos.

a. **¿Va Ud. a estudiar ahora?**
No, estudié antes.

  1. ¿Va Ud. a trabajar ahora?
  2. ¿Va Ud. a comer ahora?
  3. ¿Va Ud. a cantar ahora?
  4. ¿Va Ud. a divertirse ahora?
  5. ¿Va Ud. a bañarse ahora?
  6. ¿Va Ud. a volver ahora?

b. **¿Estudia José ahora?**
No, estudió ayer.

  1. ¿Trabaja José ahora?
  2. ¿Estudia José ahora?
  3. ¿Canta José ahora?
  4. ¿Se divierte José ahora?
  5. ¿Se baña José ahora?
  6. ¿Vuelve José ahora?

c. **¿Preparan la lección?**
No, la prepararon ayer.

  1. ¿Escriben los ejercicios?
  2. ¿Escuchan la cinta?
  3. ¿Aprenden la lección?

  4. ¿Piden bistec?
  5. ¿Tocan la guitarra?
  6. ¿Estudian las lecciones?

d. **¿Preparan Uds. la lección?**
No, la preparamos ayer.

  1. ¿Escriben Uds. los ejercicios?
  2. ¿Escuchan Uds. la cinta?
  3. ¿Aprenden Uds. la lección?
  4. ¿Piden Uds. bistec?
  5. ¿Estudian Uds. las lecciones?

e. **¿Canté bien?**
Sí, cantaste bien.

  1. ¿Hablé bien?
  2. ¿Aprendí bien?
  3. ¿Trabajé bien?
  4. ¿Escribí bien?
  5. ¿Contesté bien?
  6. ¿Comí bien?

2. TWO OBJECT PRONOUNS

When both indirect and direct object pronouns are used in the same sentence, the indirect precedes the direct. Both normally precede the verb, but they follow an infinitive and an affirmative command.

  Te lo presto. I lend it to you.
  ¿Quieres dármelo? Will you give it to me?
  Préstemelos Ud. Lend them to me.

When both pronouns are in the third person, the indirect object pronouns **le** and **les** change to **se**.

  Se lo mostré. I showed it to him (to her, to you, to them).
  Voy a prestárselos. I am going to lend them to him (to her, to you, to them).

When the meaning of **se** might not be clear from the context, we use the same redundant construction that we learned in Lesson 6 to clarify **le** and **les**.

Se los presté a ella.   I lent them to her.

Se lo mostraron a Ud.   They showed it to you.

The redundant construction may also be used for emphasis.

No se lo prestaron a él; se lo prestaron a ella.   They didn't lend it to him; they lent it to her.

The following are the various possible combinations of indirect and direct object pronouns:

me lo	**nos lo**
me la	**nos la**
me los	**nos los**
me las	**nos las**
te lo	**os lo**
te la	**os la**
te los	**os los**
te las	**os las**

se lo
se la
se los
se las

PRÁCTICA

Sustituya según los modelos.

a. **Me pidieron el dinero.**
   Me lo pidieron.

1. Me prestaron el libro.
2. Te mostraron la casa.
3. Nos pidieron las corbatas.
4. Nos prestaron el coche.
5. Me pidieron los zapatos.
6. Te mostraron la biblioteca.

b. **¿Van a darme la blusa?**
   ¿Van a dármela?

1. ¿Van a darme los libros?
2. ¿Van a darte el sombrero?
3. ¿Van a darme los calcetines?
4. ¿Van a darnos las camisas?
5. ¿Van a darme el dinero?
6. ¿Van a darte las corbatas?

c. **Préstele el libro a ella.**
   Présteselo.

   1. Préstele el dinero a él.
   2. Présteles las camisas a ellos.
   3. Préstele los zapatos a Juan.
   4. Préstele la falda a ella.
   5. Présteles las blusas a ellas.
   6. Préstele el traje a él.

d. **No le muestre el reloj a él.**
   No se lo muestre.

   1. No les muestre la casa a ellos.
   2. No le muestre los ejercicios a él.
   3. No les muestre el traje a ellos.
   4. No les muestre las medias a ellas.
   5. No le muestre la camisa a él.
   6. No les muestre los calcetines a ellos.

---

3. CARDINAL NUMBERS 13–20

trece	thirteen	**diecisiete**	seventeen
catorce	fourteen	**dieciocho**	eighteen
quince	fifteen	**diecinueve**	nineteen
dieciséis	sixteen	**veinte**	twenty

PRÁCTICA

a. *Diga en español.*

$12 + 1 = 13$ $16 + 1 = 17$

$13 + 1 = 14$ $17 + 1 = 18$

$14 + 1 = 15$ $18 + 1 = 19$

$15 + 1 = 16$ $19 + 1 = 20$

b. *Cuente en español de uno a veinte.*

Tareas

Diga a la clase en español.

1. Carlos woke up at eight-thirty yesterday.
2. He got up, washed his face, bathed, dressed, and combed his hair.
3. At nine o'clock he had a good breakfast and then attended Spanish class.
4. Mr. Martínez talked about the geography of South America.
5. In the afternoon Carlos worked four hours and wrote a composition.
6. At quarter after six we had dinner in a good restaurant.
7. He asked me for ten dollars, and I lent them to him.
8. They went back to his house and watched some television programs.
9. Two girls sang Cuban songs, and an orchestra played Mexican classical music.

10. Carlos went to bed at ten minutes to twelve and slept well.
11. He worked a lot yesterday, but he had a good time, too.

Composición oral o escrita

1. Tell what you did when you got up this morning.
2. Tell what your friends bought yesterday and how they liked what they bought.

Pronunciación

Between vowels Spanish **s** is an unvoiced sound like the *s* in *sat*. Pronounce the following words after your instructor.

casa	blusa	hermoso
mesa	uso	famoso
rosa	cosa	gracioso

Before voiced consonants (**b**, **d**, **g**, **l**, **m**, and **n**) Spanish **s** is voiced like English *z*. Pronounce the following words after your instructor.

los besos	los gastos	los meses
las voces	las gangas	las mesas
los días	es lunes	es nuestro
las doce	es linda	es nuevo

Diálogo

¡DIOS MÍO! ¡QUÉ DÍA PASÉ!

EDUARDO—¡Hombre! No te vi ayer en la clase.

ROBERTO—¡Dios mío![1] ¡Qué día pasé!

EDUARDO—¿Malo,[2] eh? ¿Qué pasó?[3]

ROBERTO—En primer lugar,[4] me desperté tarde y falté a la clase.[5] Luego salí mal[6] en un examen en la clase de matemáticas.

EDUARDO—¿Te preocupas por[7] eso?

ROBERTO—No. En verdad no me preocupo mucho. Luego Pepe me pidió diez dólares y le presté el dinero. Probablemente[8] no va a devolvérmelo.

EDUARDO—¡Siempre te digo que no debes prestar dinero!

ROBERTO—Tienes razón. No debo hacerlo. Pero además le presté mi coche[9] para ir al centro. Y, ¿sabes lo que[10] pasó? ¡Lo destrozó![11]

---

[1] ¡Dios mío!   *Good heavens!*
[2] malo   *bad*
[3] ¿Qué pasó?   *What happened?*
[4] en primer lugar   *in the first place*
[5] faltar a la clase   *to miss class*
[6] salir mal   *to fail*

[7] preocuparse por   *to worry about*
[8] probablemente   *probably*
[9] el coche   *car*
[10] lo que   *what*
[11] Lo destrozó.   *He wrecked it.*

PREGUNTAS PERSONALES

1. ¿Vio Ud. ayer un programa de televisión?
2. Tocó un guitarrista español, ¿verdad? ¿Le gustó la música?
3. ¿Asistió Ud. ayer a todas sus clases?
4. ¿Aprendió Ud. cosas interesantes?
5. ¿Durmió Ud. en las clases?
6. ¿Cuántas horas trabajó Ud. ayer?
7. ¿Compró su amigo un traje nuevo?
8. ¿Le mostró a Ud. el traje?
9. ¿Qué le pareció el traje?
10. ¿Habló Ud. ayer con sus amigas mexicanas?
11. ¿A qué hora se despidió Ud. de ellas?
12. ¿Halló Ud. su libro de español?
13. ¿Dónde lo encontró—en la biblioteca?
14. ¿Le prestó Ud. dinero a un amigo?
15. ¿Le devolvió a Ud. el dinero?
16. ¿Dónde comió Ud. ayer—en casa o en un restorán?
17. ¿Se lavó Ud. las manos antes de comer?
18. ¿A qué hora volvió Ud. a casa?
19. ¿Se divirtió Ud. ayer?
20. ¿Nos divertimos en la clase ayer?

Notas culturales

1. In the *Diálogo* Roberto says "**Dios mío**," which is about equivalent to our "Good heavens!" The Spanish speaker frequently uses sacred names in exclamations like this. When a person sneezes, someone may say "**¡Jesús!**" He means no blasphemy. Such phrases go back to the Middle Ages and originated as a cry for help in time of trouble. There used to be a sign on the city wall of Ávila, beside the entrance, which said "Within these walls begging and blasphemy are prohibited."

2. Instead of **automóvil** (*auto*), Roberto uses the word **coche**, equivalent to our everyday term *car*. A Mexican would say **carro**. Such common terms vary from country to country. The commonest term for *bus* is **autobús**. In some South American countries it is abbreviated, as in English, to **bus**. In Colombia and Panama you may hear it called **chiva**, which means *goat*. It is said that the first busses in Panama were made by Chevrolet. Hearing "Chevvy," it was natural to think of **chiva**. You can imagine them jumping the ruts like so many goats. In Cuba and Puerto Rico a bus is a **guagua**. But when you are in Chile, don't say you are going to take the **guagua**. They may think you are a kidnapper. There **la guagua** means *the baby*!

In Valencia, Spain, elaborate fallas *(statues) are erected during the festival of San José.*

9

El que tuvo y retuvo guardó para la vejez.
Waste not, want not.
(He who had and kept saved for his old age.)

Some irregular preterits

ser to be, **ir** to go		**dar** to give		**hacer** to do, make	
fui	fuimos	di	dimos	hice	hicimos
fuiste	(fuisteis)	diste	(disteis)	hiciste	(hicisteis)
Ud. fue	Uds. fueron	Ud. dio	Uds. dieron	Ud. hizo	Uds. hicieron
fue	fueron	dio	dieron	hizo	hicieron

estar to be		**tener** to have	
estuve	estuvimos	tuve	tuvimos
estuviste	(estuvisteis)	tuviste	(tuvisteis)
Ud. estuvo	Uds. estuvieron	Ud. tuvo	Uds. tuvieron
estuvo	estuvieron	tuvo	tuvieron

PRÁCTICA

Cambie según se indica.

1. El alumno fue a la biblioteca.
   yo / nosotros / ellos / Ud. / tú / ella

2. Ellos le dieron el dinero.
   Ud. / tú / nosotros / yo / Ud. y yo / sus amigos

3. Yo no lo hice.
   ellas / tú / Ud. / yo / nosotros / Ana

4. Tú estuviste en el café.
   Juan / nosotros / yo / ellos / él

5. Ud. tuvo que hacerlo.
   yo / tú / nosotros / ellos / Uds. / el médico

Some preterits with orthographic changes

Some types of Spanish verbs have orthographic (spelling) changes. Such changes are made in order to preserve the sound of the final consonant of the stem where the addition of a personal ending would otherwise alter its sound.

In the first person singular of the preterit, verbs ending in

> **-car** change **c** to **qu**
> **-gar** change **g** to **gu**
> **-zar** change **z** to **c**

buscar (*to look for*):	**busqué**	**explicar** (*to explain*):	**expliqué**
pagar (*to pay*):	**pagué**	**llegar** (*to arrive*):	**llegué**
empezar (*to begin*):	**empecé**	**comenzar** (*to begin*):	**comencé**

In the preterit of verbs like **leer** (*to read*) whose infinitive stem ends in a strong vowel, the **i** of the ending changes to **y** in the third person singular and plural. In all other persons the **i** of the ending bears a written accent.

le**í**	le**í**mos
le**í**ste	le**í**steis
le**y**ó	le**y**eron

PRÁCTICA

a. *Cambie según se indica.*

1. Ud. buscó a los alumnos.
   tú / yo / Ud. y yo / ellos / ella

2. Mis amigos llegaron a las dos.
   Ud. / nosotros / tú / él / yo

3. Tú comenzaste a trabajar.
   nosotros / yo / Uds. / tú y yo / él

4. Nosotros leímos la lección.
   yo / tú / Ud. / ella / Uds.

b. *Cambie según el modelo.*

¿Compró Ud. el coche?
  Sí, lo compré ayer.

1. ¿Buscó Ud. a su amiga?
2. ¿Pagó Ud. la cuenta?
3. ¿Empezó Ud. los ejercicios?
4. ¿Explicó Ud. las lecciones?
5. ¿Comenzó Ud. el libro?
6. ¿Leyó Ud. la lección?

Escuchar y hablar

aceptar to accept
el actor actor
la actriz actress
anoche last night
al año year
casi nearly, almost
el cine movies
comenzar (ie) to begin
conocido well-known
¿cuánto? how much? **¿cuántos?** how many?
dar to give; to show (*a movie*)
diciembre *m.* December
divertido amusing
empezar (ie) to begin
entretanto meanwhile
entretener to entertain
el examen examination
la flor flower
la gardenia gardenia
la invitación invitation
el joven young man

los jóvenes young people
lindo pretty
llegar (a) to arrive, reach
el mes month
mono cute
la película film, movie
pronto soon
se (to) him, her, you, them
sólo only
tan *adv.* so, as
tanto *adv.* so much
el teatro theater
la vez time

IDIOMS AND OTHER EXPRESSIONS

no importa it doesn't matter
por fin finally
sobre todo especially
tener (veinte) años to be (twenty) years old
a veces at times, sometimes

EL CINE

A veces[1,2] el señor Martínez entra en la sala de clase y dice:—¡Buenos días, jóvenes!

Pero no somos tan jóvenes. María tiene diecisiete años. Carlos y Virginia tienen dieciocho años. Juan tiene diecinueve años y yo tengo veinte años.

Nos gusta mucho el cine. El señor Martínez dice que nos gusta porque somos jóvenes.

Anoche fui al cine. Busqué a mis amigos para invitarlos. Empecé a[3] buscarlos en el café, pero no los encontré allí. Fui luego a la biblioteca, donde por fin los encontré.

En la biblioteca Virginia me preguntó: —¿Quieres prestarme tu libro de español? Lo necesito. Préstamelo.

Tuve que prestárselo. —Te lo presto con gusto—le expliqué—porque voy al cine. ¿No quieren Uds. acompañarme?

Pero sólo María aceptó mi invitación. Los otros prefirieron estudiar, porque pronto empiezan los exámenes—en diciembre. Estuvieron tres horas en la biblioteca, donde leyeron y estudiaron mucho. Carlos leyó casi todo su libro de historia.

Entretanto María y yo fuimos al cine. Llegué al[4] teatro con ella a las ocho y media. En una tienda al lado del teatro vi unas gardenias muy lindas. Compré una y se la di a María. Pagué un dólar, pero no importa . . . ¡a ella le gustan tanto las flores!

En el teatro dieron una película de Cantiflas, el conocido actor mexicano. Cantinflas hizo cosas muy divertidas que nos entretuvieron mucho. Me gustó la película—¡sobre todo las actrices mexicanas muy lindas y muy monas!

NOTAS

1. Nouns ending in **-z** in the singular change the **z** to **c** before adding the plural ending **-es**.

la vez	**las veces**
la actriz	**las actrices**

2. **La vez** means *time* in the sense of *instance*.

   la primera vez   the first time
   Siempre leo la lección tres veces.   I always read the lesson three times.

   Time in the general or abstract sense is **el tiempo**.

   No puedo hacerlo; no tengo tiempo.   I can't do it; I haven't time.
   El tiempo vuela.   Time flies.

   Time in the sense of *hour, the time of day,* is **la hora**.

   ¿Qué hora es?   What time is it?

3. Verbs of beginning require the preposition **a** before an infinitive.

   Empecé a buscarlos.   I began to look for them.
   Comenzaron a cantar.   They began to sing.

4. **Llegar** requires the proposition **a** before a following noun.

   Llegué al teatro.   I reached the theater.
   Ayer llegó a España.   He arrived in Spain yesterday.

PREGUNTAS

1. ¿Adónde fue Ud. anoche?
2. ¿A quiénes buscó Ud.?
3. ¿Dónde comenzó a buscarlos?
4. ¿Dónde los encontró?
5. Virginia le pidió su libro, ¿verdad? ¿Tuvo Ud. que prestárselo?
6. ¿Qué le explicó?

7. ¿Qué les preguntó Ud. a sus amigos?
8. ¿Quién aceptó su invitación?
9. ¿Qué prefirieron hacer los otros?
10. ¿Por qué?
11. ¿Cuánto tiempo estuvieron sus amigos en la biblioteca?
12. ¿Qué hicieron?
13. ¿Qué hizo Carlos?
14. ¿A qué hora llegó Ud. al teatro?
15. ¿Qué compró Ud.?
16. ¿A quién se la dio?
17. ¿Qué dieron anoche en el teatro?
18. ¿Qué hizo Cantiflas?

Estructura

1. CARDINAL NUMBERS: THE TWENTIES

The twenties may be written as one word or three—the form in one word being more common.

21 **veintiuno, veintiún, veintiuna**
   (veinte y uno, veinte y un, veinte y una)
22 **veintidós (veinte y dos)**
23 **veintitrés (veinte y tres)**
24 **veinticuatro (veinte y cuatro)**
25 **veinticinco (veinte y cinco)**
26 **veintiséis (veinte y seis)**
27 **veintisiete (veinte y siete)**
28 **veintiocho (veinte y ocho)**
29 **veintinueve (veinte y nueve)**

The final **-o** of **veintiuno (veinte y uno)** drops before a masculine noun.

veintiún libros   But: **veintiuna veces**

PRÁCTICA

a. *Cuente de 20 a 29.*

b. *Diga en español.*

1. 21 + 1 = 22
2. 21 jóvenes + 2 = 23
3. 21 blusas + 3 = 24
4. 24 casas + 1 = 25
5. 25 + 1 = 26
6. 26 + 1 = 27
7. 27 + 1 = 28
8. 28 + 1 = 29

2. CARDINAL NUMBERS 30–100

30	**treinta**	70	**setenta**
40	**cuarenta**	80	**ochenta**
50	**cincuenta**	90	**noventa**
60	**sesenta**	100	**cien**

From the thirties through the nineties units are expressed by simply adding **y** and the numbers **uno** to **nueve**. Numbers ending in **uno** drop the **-o** before a masculine noun.

treinta y uno	**setenta y siete actrices**
treinta y un libros	**noventa y nueve años**
cuarenta y una veces	**cien personas**

PRÁCTICA

a. *Lea en español.*

1. Hay 31 actores.
2. Hay 41 actrices.
3. Hay 51 flores.
4. Hay 61 profesores.
5. Hay 71 jóvenes.
6. Hay 81 muchachas.
7. Hay 91 hombres.
8. Hay 100 casas.

b. *Diga en español.*

1. 31 más 5 son 36
2. 34 más 3 son 37
3. 42 más 7 son 49
4. 43 más 5 son 48
5. 56 más 1 son 57
6. 55 más 4 son 59
7. 60 más 6 son 66
8. 62 más 2 son 64
9. 71 más 6 son 77
10. 72 más 4 son 76
11. 86 más 1 son 87
12. 84 más 4 son 88
13. 91 más 8 son 99
14. 94 más 6 son 100

3. EXPRESSIONS OF AGE

Age is expressed with **tener** followed by the number of years.

Mi hermana tiene trece años.   My sister is thirteen years old.
Yo tengo veinte años.   I am twenty years old.
¿Cuántos años tiene Ud.?   How old are you?

Sometimes the word **edad** (*age*) is used as follows:

¿Qué edad tiene Juan?   How old is John?
Tiene diecinueve años de edad.   He is nineteen.

Like other large European cities, Madrid has undergone rapid change during recent years. Cabs and subways have replaced trolleys, acres of new apartments have been built on the outskirts, and modern neon lighting has been installed. The heart of the city's shopping area is the Gran Vía, *the Avenue of José Antonio.*

PRÁCTICA

Conteste según el modelo.

¿Cuántos años tiene su hermano? 20
Tiene veinte años.

1. ¿Cuántos años tiene su hermana? 18
2. ¿Cuántos años tiene el muchacho? 13
3. ¿Cuántos años tiene Ud.? 19
4. ¿Cuántos años tienen sus amigos? 16
5. ¿Cuántos años tienen las alumnas? 14
6. ¿Cuántos años tienen las muchachas? 17
7. ¿Cuántos años tiene Isabel? 21
8. ¿Cuántos años tiene Roberto? 15
9. ¿Cuántos años tiene Berta? 31
10. ¿Cuántos años tiene la profesora? 44
11. ¿Cuántos años tiene el profesor? 57
12. ¿Cuántos años tiene la señora? 66
13. ¿Cuántos años tiene el médico? 77
14. ¿Cuántos años tiene el abogado? 89
15. ¿Cuántos años tiene el viejo? 91

4. THE MONTHS OF THE YEAR

enero	January	**julio**	July
febrero	February	**agosto**	August
marzo	March	**septiembre**	September
abril	April	**octubre**	October
mayo	May	**noviembre**	November
junio	June	**diciembre**	December

Note that the names of the months are spelled with small letters.

PRÁCTICA

a. *Conteste según el modelo.*

¿En qué mes es su cumpleaños?
Mi cumpleaños es en el mes de enero.

1. ¿En qué mes es el cumpleaños de su hermano?
2. ¿En qué mes es el cumpleaños de su hermana?
3. ¿En qué mes es el cumpleaños de su mamá?
4. ¿En qué mes es el cumpleaños de su papá?
5. ¿En qué mes es el cumpleaños de su novio (novia)?

b. *Conteste.*

1. ¿Cuántos días hay en abril y junio?
2. ¿Cuántos días hay en mayo y julio?
3. ¿Cuántos días hay en febrero?
4. ¿Cuántos días hay en septiembre y noviembre?
5. ¿Cuántos días hay en enero y agosto?
6. ¿Le gusta más el mes de diciembre o el mes de junio?
7. ¿Prefiere Ud. el mes de octubre o el mes de marzo?

5. DATES

Except for **el primero** (*the first*), cardinal numbers are used in expressing dates in Spanish.

el primero de diciembre   the first of December
el dos de noviembre   the second of November (November second)
el treinta y uno de julio   July thirty-first

Following are questions and answers used in expressing dates:

¿Cuál es la fecha?   What is the date?
¿Qué fecha es hoy?   What's the date today?
¿A cuántos (del mes) estamos?   What day of the month is it?
Hoy es el siete de septiembre.   Today is September seventh.
Estamos a dieciséis (de junio).   It's the sixteenth (of June).

No equivalent of English *on* is used with dates.

¿Cuándo fue Ud. a Puebla? El tres de julio.   When did you go to Puebla? On the third of July.

PRÁCTICA

a. *Conteste según el modelo.*

¿Cuándo fueron a Guadalajara?   (On the nineteenth of March.)
El diecinueve de marzo.

1. ¿Cuándo fueron a Veracruz?   (On the first of August.)
2. ¿Cuándo fueron a Monterrey?   (On the sixteenth of September.)
3. ¿Cuándo fue Ud. a Morelia?   (On the twenty-fourth of October.)
4. ¿Cuándo fue Ud. a Oaxaca?   (On the twenty-seventh of November.)
5. ¿Cuándo fuiste a Mazatlán?   (On the thirtieth of December.)
6. ¿Cuándo fuiste a Chihuahua?   (On the thirty-first of January.)

b. *Conteste.*

1. ¿Qué fecha es hoy?
2. ¿Cuál es la fecha?
3. ¿A cuántos estamos?
4. ¿Cuál es la fecha de su cumpleaños?
5. ¿Cuál es la fecha del cumpleaños de su novio (novia)?

Tareas

Diga a la clase en español.

1. I looked for María and Virginia last night in order to invite them to go to the movies.
2. I began to look for them in the coffee house, and I found them in the library.
3. Virginia asked me for my Spanish book, and I had to lend it to her.
4. She preferred to study, because the exams begin soon—on December sixth.
5. She and Carlos were in the library three hours.

6. Maria accepted my invitation, and we went to the movies.
7. We reached the theater at eight-thirty.
8. I bought a gardenia and gave it to her.
9. They showed a Mexican picture.
10. The well-known Mexican actor, Cantinflas, did many amusing things.

Composición oral o escrita

We went to the movies last night. Tell who went with us, what time we reached the theater, how long we were in the theater, what picture they showed, who the actors and actresses were, whether you liked the picture, and what you did afterwards.

Pronunciación

The sound of **g** followed by **a**, **o**, or **u** is similar to **g** in *go* when initial after a pause or after **n** (phonetic symbol: [g]). Pronounce the following words after your instructor.

ganga	tengo	un gato
gato	vengo	un gusto
gota	rango	un guapo
gusto	mango	un guante

In other positions **g** followed by **a**, **o**, or **u** is a fricative sound produced by raising the back of the tongue towards the soft palate, but without making contact (phonetic symbol: [ǥ]). Pronounce the following words after your instructor.

la ganga	una gota	mi gusto
su gato	la gorra	sus gastos

In the combinations **gue** and **gui** the **u** is silent, and the **g** has one of the above pronunciations, depending on its position. Pronounce the following series of words after your instructor.

[g]	[g]	[ǥ]
guerra	en guerra	la guerra
guerrero	un guerrero	otro guerrero
guía	con guía	mi guía
guitarrista	un guitarrista	otro guitarrista

Diálogo

ANTONIO ES MUY GENEROSO[1]

RICARDO—¿Adónde fuiste anoche? Te busqué en tu cuarto pero no estuviste.

ANTONIO—Ayer fue mi cumpleaños, el cuatro de mayo. Fui al cine con Beatriz.

RICARDO—¿Qué película viste?

ANTONIO—Una de Buñuel, el director español. No recuerdo[2] el título.[3]

RICARDO—¿Te gustó?

ANTONIO—Sí. Me gustó mucho. Le gustó a Beatriz también. Sólo que[4] tuve que pagar demasiado[5] por los boletos.[6] Los teatros son muy caros ahora. Pero no importa. Nos divertimos.

RICARDO—A propósito,[7] me hace falta mi libro de español que te presté.

ANTONIO—No puedo devolvértelo ahora. No lo tengo.

RICARDO—¿No lo tienes? ¿Qué hiciste con mi libro?

ANTONIO—Se lo presté a Beatriz. ¡Lo siento mucho! Ella me lo pidió y . . . tuve que prestárselo. Así soy yo.[8] ¡Soy muy generoso!

[1]generoso *generous*
[2]recordar (ue) *to recall*
[3]el título *title*
[4]sólo que *only*
[5]demasiado *too much*
[6]el boleto *ticket*
[7]a propósito *by the way*
[8]Así soy yo. *That's the way I am.*

PREGUNTAS PERSONALES

1. ¿Hizo Ud. mucho ayer?
2. ¿Fue Ud. al centro?
3. ¿Fue de compras?
4. ¿Qué buscó Ud. en las tiendas?
5. Ud. compró una chaqueta, ¿verdad? ¿Pagó Ud. mucho?
6. Su amigo compró una chaqueta también, ¿verdad? ¿Qué le pareció a Ud.?
7. Su amiga compró una falda que no le gustó a Ud., ¿verdad? ¿Qué le explicó Ud. a su amiga?
8. ¿A qué hora llegó Ud. a la clase hoy?
9. ¿Leyó Ud. un libro ayer?
10. ¿Empezó Ud. anoche a escribir una composición?
11. ¿A qué hora empezó la película que Ud. vio anoche?
12. ¿Le dio Ud. un regalo a su novio (novia)?
13. ¿Qué le regaló Ud.?
14. ¿Cuánto tiempo estuvo Ud. en la biblioteca ayer?
15. Su amigo le pidió a Ud. veinte dólares, ¿verdad? ¿Se los prestó Ud.?
16. ¿Tuvo Ud. que trabajar mucho ayer?

Festivities honoring the Virgin Mary in Salamanca, Spain. The elaborate charro costume is typical of the province. In addition to the world-famous ferias of Seville and other major cities, Spain has hundreds of small-town festivals which draw people from surrounding villages. Most of the festivals celebrate religious events.

17. ¿Cuántas horas trabajó Ud.?
18. ¿Pagó Ud. veinticinco o treinta dólares por la chaqueta que compró ayer?
19. ¿Cuánto pagó Ud. por sus zapatos nuevos?
20. ¿Se divirtió Ud. ayer?

Notas culturales

1. National Holidays

In Latin America, most of the holidays celebrating independence come in May, July, August and September. Following are some of the national holidays of the Hispanic world. Read them in Spanish.

May 25	Argentina
July 5	Venezuela
July 18	Spain
July 20	Colombia
July 28	Peru
August 10	Ecuador
August 25	Uruguay
September 7	Brazil

September 15	Costa Rica, El Salvador, Guatemala, Honduras, Nicaragua
September 15–16	Mexico
September 18	Chile

2. *Other Holidays*

The Hispanic world observes many saints' days, celebrating the patron saint of a town or village, and has many **fiestas, ferias** (fairs), and **romerías** (a combination of picnic and pilgrimage to the local shrine). Such activities range from the delightful tradition of the blessing of the animals on the day of San Antonio Abad, January 17, to the elaborate processions of Holy Week (**Semana Santa**) in Seville.

The festivities of **Navidad** (Christmas) mainly take place on **Nochebuena** (Christmas Eve) with the **misa del gallo** (midnight mass) and Christmas dinner. One of the most attractive customs of the season is the Mexican and Guatemalan **posada**, commemorating the journey to Bethlehem of Mary and Joseph and their search for shelter at an inn. The **posadas** ("inns"), which begin on December 16 and continue to **Nochebuena**, are processions of children bearing a litter with statues of Mary and Joseph. They are not admitted to the houses at which they stop, for "there is no room at the inn." On Christmas Eve they are finally admitted, and a party takes place. The Christmas greeting is **"Felices Pascuas."**

El día de Año Nuevo calls for New Year's gifts, **aguinaldos. Nochevieja** (New Year's Eve) is celebrated with noisemaking and merrymaking. The New Year's greeting is **"Feliz Año Nuevo."**

Children in the Hispanic countries receive their "Christmas" presents on January 6, **el día de los Reyes**. This commemorates the bearing of gifts to the infant Jesus by the Three Magi.

Easter is **la Pascua de Resurrección** or **la Pascua Florida**, and Easter Sunday is **Domingo de Resurrección**. The processions of bejewelled statues of the **Virgen María** accompanied by **penitentes** (penitents) are an impressive and colorful sight in the cities of Spain.

In the Spanish countries one celebrates not only his birthday, but his saint's day, the **día de su santo**, after whom he was named.

2

A. *Use **saber** o **conocer**.*

1. Yo no _____ al señor Baena.
2. ¿_____ tú la lección?
3. Nosotros no _____ dónde están.
4. Francisco _____ a las chicas.

B. *Conteste según el modelo.*

¿Puedo comprar los calcetines?
Sí, cómo no, cómprelos Ud.

1. ¿Puedo mirar el reloj?
2. ¿Puedo examinar los zapatos?
3. ¿Puedo leer el libro?
4. ¿Puedo escuchar la cinta?
5. ¿Puedo comer las papas fritas?

C. *Conteste según el modelo.*

¿Puedo comprar los calcetines?
Claro, Pepito, cómpralos.

1. ¿Puedo mirar el reloj?
2. ¿Puedo examinar los zapatos?
3. ¿Puedo leer el libro?
4. ¿Puedo escuchar la cinta?
5. ¿Puedo comer las papas fritas?

D. *Conteste según el modelo.*

¿Escuchamos la cinta ahora?
No, no la escuchen Uds.

1. ¿Miramos la televisión ahora?
2. ¿Escribimos los ejercicios ahora?
3. ¿Leemos el libro ahora?
4. ¿Compramos las corbatas ahora?
5. ¿Comemos el bistec ahora?

E. *Conteste en forma negativa.*

1. ¿Piensas ir de compras hoy?
2. ¿Vuelves tarde?
3. ¿Duermes bien?
4. ¿Siempre pides café?
5. ¿Te despides de nosotros ahora?

F. *Conteste afirmativamente.*

1. ¿Haces mucho hoy?
2. ¿Sales ahora?
3. ¿Vienes mañana?
4. ¿Te pones la corbata?

G. *Conteste con frases completas.*

1. ¿Te levantas tarde?
2. ¿Te acuestas temprano?
3. ¿Te vistes ahora?
4. ¿Se lava Tomás la manos?
5. ¿Se bañan ahora?
6. ¿Nos vestimos ahora?

H. *Exclame Ud. según el modelo.*

Mire el vestido. (bonito)
¡Qué vestido más bonito!

1. Mire el libro. (interesante)
2. Mire el reloj. (caro)
3. Mire las corbatas. (bonitas)
4. Mire la casa. (pequeña)

I. *¿Qué hora es?*

1. 1:30	4. 7:06
2. 1:45	5. 8:09
3. 3:20	6. 11:40

J. *Conteste según se indica.*

1. ¿Cuántos años tiene tu hermano?
   (26 años)
2. ¿Cuántos años tiene tu hermana?
   (15 años)
3. ¿Cuántos años tiene el médico?
   (37 años)
4. ¿Cuántos años tiene el profesor?
   (39 años)

K. *Lea las fechas.*

1. el 1.° de enero
2. el 13 de julio
3. el 16 de septiembre
4. el 24 de noviembre
5. el 31 de diciembre

L. *Conteste según el modelo.*

¿Vas a estudiar la lección ahora?
No, la estudié ayer.

1. ¿Vas a aprender la lección?
2. ¿Vas a escuchar la cinta?
3. ¿Vas a comprar zapatos?
4. ¿Va Juan a mirar el programa?
5. ¿Va Juan a leer el libro?
6. ¿Va Juan a escribir los ejercicios?
7. ¿Va Ud. a buscar a sus amigos?
8. ¿Va Ud. a empezarlo ahora?
9. ¿Va Ud. a pagar la cuenta?
10. ¿Van a pedir café?
11. ¿Van a servir bistec?
12. ¿Van a devolver el regalo?

M. *Conteste con frases completas.*

1. ¿Adónde fue Ud. anoche?
2. ¿Hizo Ud. cosas interesantes hoy?
3. ¿Estuvo Ud. en la clase ayer?
4. ¿Tuvo Ud. que trabajar ayer?

N. *Conteste con frases completas.*

1. ¿Le gusta a Ud. el jugo de naranja?
2. ¿Le gustan a Ud. los huevos fritos?
3. ¿Les gusta a Uds. el cine?
4. ¿Les gustó a Uds. la película?
5. ¿Le gustaron a Ricardo las camisas que compré?
6. ¿Le hace falta a Ud. un sombrero nuevo?
7. ¿Le hacen falta calcetines?
8. ¿Qué le parece el clima por aquí?

O. *Conteste según el modelo.*

¿Me dio Ud. el dinero?
Sí, se lo di.

1. ¿Me dio Ud. el reloj?
2. ¿Me prestó Ud. el coche?
3. ¿Me mostró Ud. la chaqueta?
4. ¿Le dieron a Ud. los libros?
5. ¿Le prestaron a Ud. las blusas?
6. ¿Les mostraron a Uds. la biblioteca?
7. ¿Les dio a Uds. el regalo?
8. ¿Nos prestó Ud. el dinero?
9. ¿Nos devolvió Ud. los libros?

P. *Diga a la clase en español.*

1. Tell what time you got up yesterday and what you did when you got up.
2. The rest of your day was a typical one. Tell what you did in the morning and in the afternoon.
3. You went shopping with a friend. Tell in detail what you looked for, how you liked what you saw, and what you bought.
4. Tell how you spent last evening (dinner, the movies, watching television, and so forth).

10

Hoy por ti mañana por mí.
One good turn deserves another.
(Today for you, tomorrow for me.)

Imperfect indicative of regular verbs

The imperfect is formed by adding the following endings to the infinitive stem:

FIRST CONJUGATION		SECOND AND THIRD CONJUGATIONS	
-aba	-ábamos	-ía	-íamos
-abas	(-abais)	-ías	(-íais)
-aba	-aban	-ía	-ían

Note the written accent over the first person plural of the first conjugation and throughout the second and third conjugations.

hablar		aprender		vivir	
hablaba	hablábamos	aprendía	aprendíamos	vivía	vivíamos
I was speaking		I was learning		I was living	
I used to speak		I used to learn		I used to live	
I spoke		I learned		I lived	
hablabas	(hablabais)	aprendías	(aprendíais)	vivías	(vivíais)
Ud. hablaba	Uds. hablaban	Ud. aprendía	Uds. aprendían	Ud. vivía	Uds. vivían
hablaba	hablaban	aprendía	aprendían	vivía	vivían

Only three Spanish verbs are irregular in the imperfect:

ir to go		ser to be		ver to see	
iba I was going, etc.	íbamos	era I was, etc.	éramos	veía I saw, etc.	veíamos
ibas	(ibais)	eras	(erais)	veías	(veíais)
Ud. iba	Uds. iban	Ud. era	Uds. eran	Ud. veía	Uds. veían
iba	iban	era	eran	veía	veían

PRÁCTICA

Cambie según se indica.

1. Yo me levantaba tarde todos los días.
   Ud. / tú / nosotros / ellos / Ud. y yo

2. Nosotros no comíamos mucho.
   yo / ella / tú / ellas / Ud. / tú y yo

3. Tú siempre escribías todos los ejercicios.
   ella / Uds. / Ramón / yo / nosotros

4. Ellos siempre iban temprano a la clase.
   tú / tú y yo / Uds. / nosotros / Teresa

5. Yo veía muchas películas.
   Ud. y yo / ellas / mi padre / tú / él

6. Ud. no era perezoso.
   tú / yo / Uds. / nosotros / los muchachos

Escuchar y hablar

el abuelo grandfather
los abuelos grandparents
una barbaridad (de) a huge amount (number) (of)
el caballo horse
el campo country
la ciudad city
conmigo with me
desgraciadamente unfortunately
enorme enormous
la fiesta celebration
la finca farm
el ganado cattle
había there was, there were
el habitante inhabitant
manso gentle
mejor better, best
mí (*obj. of prep.*) me
el niño child (*m.*), **la niña** child (*f.*)
nadar to swim
pescar to fish

la piscina swimming pool
quinientos five hundred
el rancho ranch
el río river
el rodeo roundup
el trabajo work
triste sad
la vaca cow
el vaquero cowboy
vender to sell
el verano summer
visitar to visit

IDIOMS AND OTHER EXPRESSIONS

¡claro que sí! of course (I did, we were, etc.)!
con frecuencia frequently
montar a caballo to ride horseback
tal vez perhaps, maybe
de vez en cuando from time to time

LA FINCA Y EL RANCHO

—¿Dónde vivías cuando eras niña, Virginia?—preguntó Carlos. —¿En California?

—No, vivía en Colorado. Fuimos a California cuando tenía nueve años. Y tú, ¿dónde vivías?

—En Nueva York, donde vivimos ahora.

—¿En la ciudad o en el campo?

—En la ciudad como ahora. Pero cuando era niño iba con frecuencia al campo. Visitaba la finca de mi abuelo. Iba con frecuencia porque me gustaba visitar a mis abuelos.[1] Pasaba con ellos un mes of dos meses del verano.

—¿Era grande la finca?

—No, no era grande, pero había veinticinco vacas y tres caballos hermosos. Había un río cerca de la finca. Los muchachos de las otras fincas pescaban conmigo en el río casi todos los días. Y cuando teníamos calor, nadábamos en el río. Para mí los meses que pasaba en el campo eran los mejores del año. Siempre estaba muy triste cuando tenía que volver a la ciudad.

—María y yo—explicó Juan—íbamos también a visitar a nuestros abuelos cuando éramos niños. Nuestro abuelo tenía un rancho enorme en Tejas. Había una piscina donde nadábamos. Mi abuelo tenía una barbaridad de ganado—quinientas o tal vez mil vacas. Y había muchos caballos en el rancho.

—¿Montaban Uds. a caballo?

—¡Claro que sí! Montábamos con frecuencia porque siempre había caballos mansos para nosotros. Todos los días veíamos cosas muy interesantes. Había rodeos y de vez en cuando fiestas de los vaqueros que trabajaban en el rancho. Pero desgraciadamente no podemos volver al rancho. Mi abuelo lo vendió el 31 de diciembre de 1975.

NOTA

1. Spanish uses the masculine plural to designate groups of people containing individuals of both sexes.

   mis abuelos y mis padres   my grandparents and my parents
   sus hermanos   his brother and sister (brothers and sisters)

PREGUNTAS

1. ¿Dónde vivía Virginia cuando era niña?
2. ¿Cuándo fue su familia a California?
3. ¿Dónde vivía Carlos?
4. ¿Adónde iba Carlos con frecuencia?
5. ¿A quiénes visitaba?
6. ¿Cuánto tiempo pasaba Carlos con ellos en el verano?

7. ¿Cuántas vacas había en la finca de su abuelo?
8. ¿Qué había cerca de la finca?
9. ¿Quiénes pescaban en el río?
10. ¿Cuándo nadaba Carlos?
11. ¿Cómo estaba Carlos cuando tenía que volver a la ciudad?
12. ¿Adónde iban Juan y María cuando eran niños?
13. ¿Qué tenía su abuelo?
14. ¿Cómo era el rancho?
15. ¿Qué había en el rancho?
16. ¿Qué hacía Juan con frecuencia?
17. ¿Qué veían Juan y María todos los días?
18. ¿Quiénes trabajaban en el rancho?
19. ¿Qué había de vez en cuando en el rancho?
20. ¿Cuándo vendió el rancho el abuelo de Juan y María?

Estructura

1. USE OF THE IMPERFECT INDICATIVE

The imperfect expresses an act that was not completed in past time. It tells what *used to happen* or what *was happening*. The beginning and ending of the action are ignored. Fundamentally it expresses:

a. Customary or repeated past action (equivalent to English *used to, would*).

Visitaba a mis abuelos.   I used to visit my grandparents.
Nadábamos en el río.   We would (used to) swim in the river.

b. An action which covered a relatively long period of time, but the duration of which is never stated or delimited.

Cuando éramos niños, nuestro abuelo tenía una finca.   When we were children, our grandfather had a farm.
Había muchos caballos en el rancho.   There were many horses on the ranch.

c. An action that was going on when another act happened.

Yo leía cuando él entró.   I was reading when he entered.
Mientras estudiaban, ella fue al cine.   While they were studying, she went to the movies.

2. PRETERIT VERSUS IMPERFECT

The *preterit* expresses a completed act. It tells what happened, what incident occurred. It is a narrative tense.
The *imperfect*, not delimited in time, tells (1) what used to happen or (2) what was happening or what state of affairs existed, often as the attendant circumstances of some other act. It is a descriptive tense.

Railroads, highways, and air traffic paths meet in Mexico City, connecting the capital with major population centers. Within the city the first of three subway lines was completed in 1969. Designed to accommodate four million persons a day, it has helped Mexico City cope with transportation problems resulting from its rapid growth.

Observe the uses of these two tenses in the following sentences:

Abrí la puerta. I opened the door. (*Completed act—instantaneous.*)

Sonó el teléfono. The telephone rang. (*Completed act—instantaneous.*)

Mientras yo *abría* la puerta, *sonó* el teléfono. While I was opening the door, the telephone rang. (*What was happening, time not delimited, when something else happened.*)

***Pasé* las vacaciones en el campo, donde *vivió* mi abuelo cuarenta años.** I spent my vacation in the country where my grandfather lived forty years. (**Pasé** = *conventionally limited period of time;* **vivió** = *duration of time definitely stated.*)

***Pasaba* las vacaciones en el campo, donde *vivía* mi abuelo.** I used to spend my vacations in the country where my grandfather lived. (**Pasaba** = *what used to happen, time not delimited;* **vivía** = *what state of affairs existed, time not delimited.*)

PRÁCTICA

Diga en español.

1. They used to live in Spain.
   They lived there twenty years.

2. I was not looking for them.
   I looked for them last night.

3. He would always go to the movies in the evening.
   He went to the movies last night.

4. You were very thirsty.
   You had (took) something to drink.

5. They always ate in a restaurant.
   Yesterday they ate in a restaurant.

6. She was very tired.
   She was in class three hours.

7. We always saw interesting things.
   Yesterday we saw some interesting things.

8. I was beginning to look for them.
   I began to look for them.

9. When he was young, he worked a lot.
   Yesterday he worked nine hours.

10. She would always listen to me.
    She didn't listen to me last night.

---

3. PREPOSITIONAL FORMS OF THE PERSONAL PRONOUN

Except for **mí** and **ti**, the personal pronouns used as the object of a preposition are the same as the subject pronouns. You have been using the third person forms in the redundant construction to clarify **le**, **les**, and **se**.

mí me	**nosotros (-as)** us
ti you (*fam.*)	**(vosotros) (-as)** you (*fam.*)

usted you	**ustedes** you
él him, it	**ellos** them
ella her, it	**ellas** them

El libro es para mí.   The book is for me.
Siempre había caballos para nosotros.   There were always horses for us.
Pasaba mucho tiempo con ellos.   I used to spend a lot of time with them.

With the preposition **con** there are special forms for the first and second persons singular: **conmigo, contigo.**

Vivían conmigo.   They lived with me.
¿Fue al cine contigo?   Did he go to the movies with you?

PRÁCTICA

Conteste según el modelo.

> **¿Para quién es el traje?** (him)
> **El traje es para él.**

1. ¿Para quién es el traje? (you)
2. ¿Para quién es la falda? (her)
3. ¿Para quién es el sombrero? (me)
4. ¿Para quién es la corbata? (him)
5. ¿Para quién son las flores? (her)
6. ¿Para quién son las camisas? (us)
7. ¿Para quién son las gardenias? (you, *plural*)
8. ¿Para quién son los zapatos? (them)
9. ¿Con quién trabajaban? (her)
10. ¿Con quién comían? (him)
11. ¿Con quién estudiaban? (me)
12. ¿Con quiénes vivían? (us)
13. ¿Con quiénes conversaban? (you, *plural*)
14. ¿Con quién hablaban? (with you, Juan)

4. CARDINAL NUMBERS ABOVE 100

101	ciento uno, -a	1000	mil
102	ciento dos	1008	mil ocho
199	ciento noventa y nueve	1200	mil doscientos, -as
200	doscientos, -as	1980	mil novecientos ochenta
207	doscientos siete	2000	dos mil
300	trescientos, -as	2010	dos mil diez
400	cuatrocientos, -as	3593	tres mil quinientos noventa y tres
500	quinientos, -as	5701	cinco mil setecientos uno
600	seiscientos, -as	100.000*	cien mil
700	setecientos, -as	500.000	quinientos mil
800	ochocientos, -as	1.000.000	un millón
900	novecientos, -as		

Starting with **doscientos**, the hundreds have a feminine form.

> **doscientas mujeres**   **trescientas cinco alumnas**

*Note that Spanish uses a period to punctuate thousands. A comma is used as a decimal point.

There is no equivalent of *a* or *one* before **cien** or **mil**, but there is before **millón**. **Millón** is followed by **de** before a noun. Like any other noun, it has a plural: **millones**.

> **ciento uno** one hundred (and) one
> **mil casas** a (one) thousand houses
> **un millón de libros** a (one) million books
> **dos millones de habitantes** two million inhabitants

Y is used only between tens and units.

> **sesenta y seis**   But: **ciento dos**
> **setenta y siete**   **doscientos cuatro**
> **noventa y nueve**   **doce mil siete**

Spanish speakers do not count or express dates by hundreds after 1000 (*eleven hundred, nineteen seventy nine*, etc.). Instead they express such numbers in terms of a thousand.

> **1492 mil cuatrocientos noventa y dos**
> **1979 mil novecientos setenta y nueve**

PRÁCTICA

Lea en español.

a.
1. 100 + 70 = 170
2. 100 + 85 = 185
3. 200 + 100 = 300
4. 300 + 100 = 400
5. 400 + 100 = 500
6. 500 + 100 = 600
7. 600 + 100 = 700
8. 700 + 100 = 800
9. 800 + 100 = 900
10. 900 + 100 = 1000

b.
1. 1500
2. 1669
3. 1970
4. 3400
5. 4700
6. 1000 alumnos
7. 1400 casas
8. 100.000 hombres
9. 600.000 libros
10. 1.000.000 de habitantes

5. DATES

De is normally used before the year in expressing dates.

> **el 4 de julio de 1776**
> **el 2 de mayo de 1808**

Since the 1960s a large investment has been made to develop the agriculture of Paraguay, one of the most underdeveloped countries of Latin America. Livestock production accounts for more than one third of its agricultural output. Here a cowboy rounds up heifers on an estancia, *or large ranch.*

Lea estas fechas importantes.

1. el 4 de julio de 1776 (independencia de los Estados Unidos)
2. el 16 de septiembre de 1810 (independencia de México)
3. el 14 de julio de 1789 (día nacional de Francia)
4. el 12 de octubre de 1492 (descubrimiento de América)
5. el 2 de mayo de 1808 (independencia de España)
6. el 19 de diciembre de 1824 (independencia del Perú)
7. el 11 de noviembre de 1918 (Día del Armisticio)

Tareas

Diga a la clase en español.

1. When I was a child, I lived in a city of nearly two million inhabitants.
2. But I went to the country frequently to visit my grandparents.
3. They had horses and twenty-five cows on their farm.
4. The boys on the other farms used to fish with me.
5. When we were warm, we would swim in the river.
6. Juan's grandfather had an enormous ranch in Texas.
7. There were five hundred or maybe a thousand cows on the ranch.
8. We would ride horseback nearly every day.
9. María would go with us, too.

10. We would see many interesting things.
11. When it was warm, we used to swim in the pool.
12. But we can't go back: our grandfather sold the ranch on December 31, 1975.

Composición oral o escrita

Imagine that your grandparents had a farm when you were a child. Tell what you used to see there and what you used to do.

Pronunciación

In Spanish **n** is pronounced like **m** before **b**, **v**, **p**, **f**, and **m**. Pronounce the following words after your instructor.

en Vigo	un país	enfermo	un millón
en Barcelona	un padre	en febrero	un mexicano
un burro	en parte	en francés	en marzo
un vaso	en portugués	en Francia	en mayo

Before **g**, **j**, **qu**, **k**, and **c** (when pronounced as **k**), Spanish **n** is like *n* in *think*. Pronounce the following words after your instructor.

un gasto	un joven	un queso
un gusto	un jueves	con quien
un guitarrista	con Juan	un kilo
un guisante	en julio	en casa
un guante	un gimnasio	un caballo
un guapo	un general	un café

Diálogo

¡TAMAÑO DE UN SELLO POSTAL!

CARLOS—Tú decías, Juan, que tenías abuelos en Tejas. Pero tú padre es español, ¿verdad? ¿Cómo es que tus abuelos vivían en Tejas?

JUAN—Eran los padres de mi mamá. Tenía otros abuelos en España—los padres de papá.

CARLOS—¿Ibas a visitarlos con frecuencia?

JUAN—Con frecuencia, no. Pero los visité varias[1] veces. Papá nos llevó[2] a verlos.

CARLOS—¿Tenían ellos también un rancho?

JUAN—No; no hay «ranchos» en España. Hay grandes haciendas[3] en el sur.[4] Pero mis abuelos españoles no eran del sur.

CARLOS—¿En qué parte de España vivían, pues?

JUAN—En el norte,[5] la parte que llaman la España verde. Tenían varias pequeñas fincas cerca del pueblo[6] donde vivían. Eran muy pequeñas—del tamaño de un sello postal[7]—y no producían[8] más que fruta y unas legumbres.[9]

[1]varios *several*

[2]llevar *to take*

[3]la hacienda *landed estate, ranch*

[4]el sur *south*

[5]el norte *north*

[6]el pueblo *town*

[7]del tamaño de un sello postal *the size of a postage stamp*

[8]producir *to produce*

[9]la legumbre *vegetable*

PREGUNTAS PERSONALES

1. Cuando Ud. era niño (niña), ¿iba con frecuencia al cine?
2. ¿Fue Ud. al cine anoche?
3. Cuando era niño (niña), ¿visitaba Ud. con frecuencia a sus abuelos?
4. ¿Visitó Ud. a sus abuelos ayer?
5. Cuando era niño (niña), ¿leía Ud. muchos libros?
6. ¿Leyó Ud. un libro ayer?
7. Cuando era niño (niña), ¿tomaba Ud. café o leche?
8. ¿Tomó Ud. café o leche anoche?
9. Cuando era niño (niña), ¿veía Ud. muchos programas de televisión?
10. ¿Vio Ud. anoche un programa de televisión?
11. Cuando era niño (niña), ¿estudiaba Ud. mucho?
12. ¿Estudió Ud. mucho anoche?
13. Cuando era niño (niña), ¿tocaba Ud. la guitarra?
14. ¿Tocó Ud. la guitarra anoche?
15. Cuándo era niño (niña), ¿le gustaba a Ud. la leche?
16. ¿Le gustó a Ud. el café en el restorán?

Notas culturales

1. Cattle raising is very important in many Latin American nations, and terms relating to this activity vary from country to country. Juan's grandfather had a **rancho**. We borrowed the word *ranch* from the Mexicans. **Rancho** means *ranch* in various places, but in Mexico it generally denotes a small farm. A large country estate or ranch is an **hacienda** in Mexico, an **estancia** in Argentina and Uruguay, an **hato** in Venezuela, Ecuador, Cuba, and Puerto Rico, and a **fundo** in Chile. The colorful, picturesque horsemen of the Americas are **vaqueros** in Mexico, **gauchos** on the vast pampas of Argentina, **llaneros** (*plainsmen*) on the great plains of Venezuela and Colombia, and **huasos** in Chile. The Mexican **charro** is a skilled horseman whom you

will see showing off the magnificent silver trappings of his horse in Chapulte-pec Park on Sundays. The horsemen of the Americas, especially the **gauchos** and the **llaneros**, have given rise to much colorful literature.

2. In the cattle country of the western United States the influence of Mexico is seen everywhere. When American farm boys first went to the Southwest and became cowboys, they had to learn their trade from the Mexicans. With the newly acquired skills came a whole new vocabulary: lasso, from **lazo** (*loop, knot*); lariat, from **la reata** (*rope*); chaps **(chaparrejos)**; rodeo (*roundup*); mustang; pinto, and a host of others. Our western style of riding, "neck-reining," was also learned from the Mexicans.

11

Aquéllos son ricos que tienen amigos.
Those are rich who have friends.

More irregular preterits

decir to say, tell		venir to come		querer to wish, want	
dije	dijimos	vine	vinimos	quise	quisimos
dijiste	(dijisteis)	viniste	(vinisteis)	quisiste	(quisisteis)
Ud. dijo	Uds. dijeron	Ud. vino	Uds. vinieron	Ud. quiso	Uds. quisieron
dijo	dijeron	vino	vinieron	quiso	quisieron

Note that there is no **i** in the personal ending of **dijeron**.

PRÁCTICA

Cambie según se indica.

1. Ud. no dijo eso.
   tú / ellos / yo / Uds. / nosotros / Ramona

2. Ellas vinieron ayer.
   él / tú / Ud. / yo / Ud. y yo / ellas

3. Él no quiso decírselo.
   nosotros / Uds. / yo / Ud. / tú / Inés

Escuchar y hablar

el abrigo overcoat, coat
allá there (*after verbs of motion*); back there
aquel, aquella that; **aquellos, aquellas** those; **aquél** the former
aunque although

el béisbol baseball
caminar to walk
demasiado too; too much
el deporte sport
durante during
ese, esa, eso that; **esos, esas** those

esquiar to ski
la estación season
este, esta this; **estos, estas** these
¡estupendo! great!
la excursión outing
favorito favorite
el hockey hockey
importante important
el invierno winter
jugar (ue) to play
menos less, least; fewer, fewest
la montaña mountain
nevar (ie) to snow
la nieve snow

patinar to skate
pintoresco picturesque
el tenis tennis
vasto vast

IDIOMS AND OTHER EXPRESSIONS

el año pasado last year
hace buen tiempo the weather is good
hace calor it's warm (hot)
hace (mucho) frío it's (very) cold
hacer una excursión go on an outing
¿qué tiempo hace? how's the weather?
vale la pena de it's worth while
el verano que viene next summer

EL VERANO Y EL INVIERNO

MARÍA—El verano es mi estación favorita.

CARLOS—¿Sí, eh? A mí me gusta más el invierno. Por eso vine a esta universidad, porque aquí hace bastante frío en el invierno.

MARÍA—No, hombre, el verano es la mejor estación del año. Hay menos deportes en el invierno. Durante los meses de junio, julio y agosto hace calor y casi siempre hace buen tiempo. Juan y yo siempre pasamos el verano en Tejas. Allí pasamos casi todo el día a caballo. Hacemos muchas excursiones a caballo. Siete u[1] ocho amigos nos acompañan y nos divertimos mucho. Me gusta nadar también. Y también juego[2] al tenis. A Juan le gusta jugar al béisbol.

CARLOS—Pues, yo prefiero el invierno, aunque hace mucho frío. En el verano hace demasiado calor. Y a esos deportes del verano prefiero los deportes de diciembre, enero y febrero. Me gusta mucho patinar y jugar al hockey. A veces me pongo el abrigo y salgo para caminar en la nieve. Como nieva mucho aquí, aprendí a[3] esquiar.

JUAN—¿Pero no sabes que puedes esquiar en el verano?

CARLOS—¿Qué quieres decir con eso?

JUAN—Cuando hace calor aquí, hace frío en la Argentina y en Chile. En aquellos dos países hay montañas muy altas donde puedes esquiar. Debes ir allá el verano que viene. Además vale la pena de ver aquellos países. La Argentina y Chile son países importantes e[1] interesantes. Son muy pintorescos también, éste con sus montañas cerca del Pacífico y aquélla con su vasta pampa.

CARLOS—Bueno. ¿Por qué no vamos allá? ¿Quieres acompañarme? ¿Qué dices?

JUAN—¡Estupendo! Sólo que el año pasado le pedí a papá el dinero para ir a Chile y no quiso[4] dármelo.

NOTAS

1. **O** (*or*) becomes **u** before a word beginning with **o** or **ho**.

   siete u ocho   seven or eight
   este coche u otro   this car or another one

   Y becomes **e** before a word beginning with **i** or **hi**.

   Es interesante e importante.   It's interesting and important.
   padre e hijo   father and son

2. **Jugar** (*to play*) is like stem-changing verbs with stem vowel **o** $>$ **ue**. It takes the preposition **a** before the name of a sport.

   Estas chicas juegan al tenis.   These girls play tennis.
   Nosotros jugamos al béisbol.   We play baseball.

3. **Aprender,** like verbs of motion (**ir,** *to go*) and verbs of beginning (**empezar** and **comenzar**), requires the preposition **a** before a following infinitive.

   Aprendieron a esquiar.   They learned to ski.

4. **Querer** has special meanings in the preterit.

   Affirmative: **Quisieron hacerlo.**   They *tried* to do it.
   Negative: **No quisieron pagarme.**   They *would not* (*refused to*) pay me.

PREGUNTAS

1. ¿Cuál es la estación favorita de María?
2. ¿Cuál es la estación favorita de Carlos?
3. ¿Por qué vino Carlos a esta universidad?
4. ¿Qué dice María del verano?
5. ¿Cuáles son los meses del verano?
6. ¿Qué tiempo hace en el verano?
7. ¿Dónde pasan el verano Juan y María?
8. ¿Qué hacen cuando están en Tejas?
9. ¿Cuántos amigos los acompañan?
10. ¿Qué dice Carlos del verano?
11. ¿Cuáles son los meses del invierno?
12. ¿Qué le gusta a Carlos?
13. ¿Qué aprendió Carlos?
14. ¿Dónde puede Carlos esquiar en el verano?
15. ¿Qué tiempo hace en la Argentina y en Chile en el verano?
16. ¿Qué hizo Juan el año pasado?
17. Cuando Juan pidió dinero, ¿se lo dio su papá?

Estructura

1. USE OF HACER TO EXPRESS WEATHER

Some states of the weather are expressed with **hace** and a noun. The commonest ones are the following:

Hace calor.	It's warm (hot).	**Hace viento.**	It's windy.
Hace frío.	It's cold.	**Hace buen tiempo.**	The weather's good.
Hace fresco.	It's cool.	**Hace mal tiempo.**	The weather's bad.
Hace sol.	It's sunny.	**¿Qué tiempo hace?**	How's the weather?

Since words such as **calor** and **frío** are nouns, the Spanish adjective **mucho** takes the place of the English adverb *very* (as in "*very* warm").

Hace mucho frío. It's *very* cold.

PRÁCTICA

a. *Conteste en español.*

1. ¿Qué le parece el clima aquí?
2. ¿Hace mucho frío en el invierno?
3. ¿Hace mucho calor en el verano?
4. ¿Generalmente hace fresco por la noche?
5. ¿Generalmente hace buen tiempo en junio?
6. ¿Hace viento con frecuencia?
7. ¿Hace mucho sol hoy?
8. ¿Generalmente hace mal tiempo en febrero?
9. ¿Qué tiempo hace en enero?
10. ¿Qué tiempo hace hoy?
11. ¿Le gusta a Ud. el clima aquí?

b. *Diga en español.*

1. How's the weather today?
2. It's very cold.
3. It's very cool.
4. It's very windy.
5. It's very sunny.
6. It's very warm.
7. The weather's good.
8. The weather's bad today.

This residential street in the Lima suburb of San Isidro is a fine example of modern colonial-style architecture in Peru.

2. DEMONSTRATIVE ADJECTIVES

Spanish has three demonstrative adjectives: **este**, *this*; **ese**, *that*; **aquel**, *that*. Each has four forms: masculine singular, feminine singular, masculine plural, and feminine plural.

SINGULAR		PLURAL	
Masculine	*Feminine*	*Masculine*	*Feminine*
este	esta	estos	estas
ese	esa	esos	esas
aquel	aquella	aquellos	aquellas

Ese means *that*, referring to something or someone near or associated with the person spoken to. **Aquel** also means *that*, but refers to something or someone at a distance from both the person speaking and the person spoken to.

    este libro y ese libro de Ud.   this book and that book of yours
    esta casa y aquella casa   this house and that house (over there)

PRÁCTICA

a. *Conteste según el modelo.*

¿Prefieres esta corbata?
No, prefiero esa corbata.

1. ¿Prefieres este reloj?
2. ¿Prefieres estos zapatos?
3. ¿Prefieres estas blusas?
4. ¿Prefieres esta falda?
5. ¿Prefieres estos calcetines?

b. *Conteste según el modelo.*

¿Quiere Ud. ese sombrero?
No, quiero este sombrero.

1. ¿Quiere Ud. esos libros?
2. ¿Quiere Ud. esa chaqueta?
3. ¿Quiere Ud. ese traje?
4. ¿Quiere Ud. esos regalos?
5. ¿Quiere Ud. esas medias?

c. *Conteste según el modelo.*

¿Compró Ud. esta casa?
No, compré aquella casa.

1. ¿Compró Ud. estos calcetines?
2. ¿Compró Ud. estas blusas?
3. ¿Compró Ud. este libro?
4. ¿Compró Ud. esta falda?
5. ¿Compró Ud. este reloj?

3. DEMONSTRATIVE PRONOUNS

The demonstrative pronouns are the same in form as the demonstrative adjectives, except that they bear a written accent to distinguish them from the adjectives.

aquellos muchachos y *éste*   those boys and this one
esta blusa y *ésa*   this blouse and that one
esta casa y *aquélla*   this house and that one
este coche y *aquéllos*   this car and those

Each demonstrative pronoun has a neuter form which refers to an action, statement, or idea or to an object that has not been identified—rather than to a specific thing of determined gender. The neuter forms do not have a written accent.

esto   this   **eso**   that   **aquello**   that

¿Qué es esto?   What is this?
Por eso . . .   That's why . . . for that reason . . .
Me gusta aquello.   I like that.

Note that these neuter pronouns have no written accent, since there is no corresponding adjective from which they must be distinguished.

PRÁCTICA

a. *Conteste según el modelo.*

¿Prefiere Ud. este sombrero?
No, prefiero ése.

1. ¿Prefiere Ud. esta camisa?
2. ¿Prefiere Ud. estas flores?
3. ¿Prefiere Ud. estos zapatos?
4. ¿Prefiere Ud. este regalo?

b. *Conteste según el modelo.*

¿Quieres esa corbata?
No, quiero ésta.

1. ¿Quieres esos calcetines?
2. ¿Quieres esa falda?
3. ¿Quieres esas medias?
4. ¿Quieres ese vestido?

c. *Conteste según el modelo.*

¿Le gusta este café?
Sí, pero me gusta más aquél.

1. ¿Le gusta esta casa?
2. ¿Le gustan estos trajes?
3. ¿Le gustan estas flores?
4. ¿Le gusta este teatro?

d. *Diga en español.*

1. What is this?
2. What is that?
3. I don't like this.
4. I don't like that.
5. Who said this?
6. Who said that?
7. Who did this?
8. Who did that?

e. *Conteste según los modelos.*

¿Qué es eso? (mi chaqueta sport)
Esto es mi chaqueta sport.

¿Qué es aquello? (el Teatro Nacional)
Aquello es el Teatro Nacional.

1. ¿Qué es eso? (mi traje nuevo)
2. ¿Qué es eso? (mi vestido nuevo)
3. ¿Que es eso? (el dinero que te devuelvo)
4. ¿Qué es aquello? (la Biblioteca Nacional)
5. ¿Qué es aquello? (el Palacio Nacional)
6. ¿Qué es aquello? (la Catedral)

Tareas

Diga a la clase en español.

1. María said that summer is her favorite season, but Carlos said that he prefers the winter.
2. It is quite cold here in winter.
3. It is hot in June, July and August, but it's always good weather.
4. Juan and María always spend the summer in Texas.
5. They go on many outings on horseback.
6. Seven or eight friends go with them.
7. They play baseball and tennis and have a good time.
8. Carlos doesn't like summer, because it's too hot.
9. The months that he likes best are December, January, and February.

Stretching 4,000 miles from the shores of the Caribbean to Tierra del Fuego in southern Argentina, the Andes are the most extensive high mountain system in the world. In Bolivia they attain their greatest width of 400 miles.

10. He likes to skate and ski.
11. In August he can ski in Chile and Argentina where it is cold.
12. In those countries there are very high mountains.
13. In this country we can't ski in July and August.

Composición oral o escrita

Explain why you like summer and why you like winter. Tell what you do in each of these seasons, what sports you take part in, and where you go.

Diálogo

¡UF! ¡QUÉ CALOR!

ANITA—¡Uf! ¡Qué calor! ¡Esto parece un horno!¹

JULIÁN—¿Por qué no damos un paseo² en mi coche para refrescarnos?³

ANITA—¿Qué dijiste? ¿Tienes coche?

JULIÁN—¡Claro! Ya tengo mi coche. Lo compré ayer.

ANITA—¿Dónde está tu coche?

JULIÁN—Ahí mismo.⁴ Al otro lado de la calle.⁵ ¿Qué te parece?

ANITA—¡Estupendo! Me gusta ese color naranja.⁶ ¿Y tiene aire acondicionado?⁷

JULIÁN—Sí. Con el calor que hace aquí en el verano, hace falta. Y tiene calentador⁸ también.

ANITA—Con el frío que hace aquí en el invierno, es indispensable.

JULIÁN—Te gusta mi coche, ¿eh? Fue una ganga. No tiene más que[9] ciento veinte mil kilómetros. Pero necesito gasolina. Lo primero[10] que tenemos que hacer es pasar por[11] la estación de servicio.[12]

(*En la estación de servicio.*)

EL GARAJISTA[13]—¿Lleno el tanque?[14]

JULIÁN—Ponga treinta litros,[15] por favor. Necesito aceite[16] también. Mañana vuelvo para que lo engrasen.[17]

ANITA—¡Mira el precio de la gasolina! ¡Está por las nubes![18]

[1]el horno   *furnace*

[2]dar un paseo   *to take a ride*

[3]refrescarse   *to cool off*

[4]ahí mismo   *right over there*

[5]la calle   *street*

[6]naranja   *orange*

[7]aire acondicionado   *air conditioning*

[8]el calentador   *heater*

[9]no . . . más que   *only*

[10]lo primero   *the first thing*

[11]pasar por   *to stop by*

[12]la estación de servicio   *service station*

[13]el garajista   *garage attendant*

[14]¿Lleno el tanque?   *Shall I fill the tank?*

[15]el litro   *liter*

[16]el aceite   *oil*

[17]para que lo engrasen   *to have it greased*

[18]por las nubes   *sky high*

PREGUNTAS PERSONALES

1. ¿Tiene Ud. hermanas? ¿Cuántos años tienen?
2. ¿Cuántos años tiene su hermano?
3. ¿Cuál es su estación favorita?
4. ¿Cuáles son sus deportes favoritos?
5. ¿Le gusta nadar?
6. ¿Sabe Ud. esquiar?
7. ¿Le gusta a Ud. más el verano que el invierno? ¿Por qué?
8. ¿Qué le parece el clima de aquí?
9. Ud. tiene coche, ¿verdad? ¿De qué color es? ¿Color naranja?
10. ¿Tiene su coche aire acondicionado?
11. ¿Por qué hace falta el aire acondicionado?
12. ¿Tiene calentador?
13. ¿Por qué es indispensable un calentador?
14. ¿Qué le parece el precio de la gasolina por aquí?

Notas culturales

Measurements

1. The Hispanic countries use the metric system. In the *Diálogo* Julián's car has gone 120,000 **kilómetros**, so an odometer registering miles would show about 75,000. You buy gasoline by the **litro**, candy by the **gramo**, and are allowed so many **kilos** of baggage on the airplane.

    Some equivalents between the metric system and English measurements:

1 **metro**	3.28 feet	1 foot	0.30 **metro**
	1.09 yard	1 yard	0.91 **metro**
1 **kilómetro**	0.62 mile	1 mile	1.60 **kilómetro**
1 **litro**	1.05 quart	1 quart	0.94 **litro**
	0.26 gallon	1 gallon	3.78 **litros**
1 **gramo**	0.03 ounce	1 ounce	28.35 **gramos**
1 **kilo**	2.20 pounds	1 pound	0.45 **kilos**

2. Temperature is measured in degrees centigrade. If you want to know how warm you are in one of the tropical countries of South America or how cool it is in Madrid on a brisk winter morning, you multiply the centigrade reading by $\frac{9}{5}$ and add 32.

Climate

Anyone who travels to Latin America should be prepared for a variety of climates and temperatures. The climate in Argentina and Chile—the southern-most countries of South America—varies depending on one's distance south of the equator. Argentina extends from the tropical northern region of the Chaco, through the pleasant temperate zone of the central pampa, to the Antarctic territory of southern Patagonia. Chile, with a coastline of 2,600 miles, ranges from the northern nitrate desert, through the temperate central valley around Santiago and the land of lakes and forests beyond, to the extreme southern tip with its fjords and glaciers. In the temperate regions the seasons are the reverse of ours: when it is winter in Chicago, it is summer in Santiago. In the brisk winters of Buenos Aires and Santiago temperatures may go as low as thirty-five degrees Fahrenheit; summers can be hot, with the thermometer going over one hundred degrees.

Elsewhere in Latin America temperatures vary with elevation. Some of the most important cities are at high altitudes: Mexico City, 7,300 feet; Bogotá, 8,500 feet; Quito, 9,200 feet; Cuzco, 11,250 feet; La Paz, 11,900 feet. The climate of Quito, which is practically on the equator, is spring-like with little variation from month to month. The high temperature is rarely over seventy degrees, and the low is usually in the mid-forties. At higher altitudes mean temperatures are lower.

Close to the equator the seasons are divided into wet and dry. In Colombia the rainy seasons are April to July and September to December; the other months are considered summer.

Visitors to the high mountainous regions of Bolivia and Peru often feel symptoms of mountain sickness (**soroche**). By the same token, the Indians of these regions are so thoroughly adapted to their habitat that they suffer altitude sickness when they descend to sea level.

12

Mejor pan duro que ninguno.
Half a loaf is better than none.
(Stale bread is better than none.)

More irregular preterits

poder to be able		**poner** to put, to place		**saber** to know	
pude	pudimos	puse	pusimos	supe	supimos
pudiste	(pudisteis)	pusiste	(pusisteis)	supiste	(supisteis)
Ud. pudo	Uds. pudieron	Ud. puso	Uds. pusieron	Ud. supo	Uds. supieron
pudo	pudieron	puso	pusieron	supo	supieron

PRÁCTICA

Cambie según se indica.

1. Ud. no pudo hacerlo.
   Uds. / yo / tú / nosotros / ella

2. Nosotros nos pusimos el sombrero.
   ella / Uds. / tú / yo / Ud. y yo

3. Él lo supo ayer.
   yo / tú / nosotros / Ud. / ellas

Escuchar y hablar

la asignatura   course
bien   very
caliente   hot
colorado   red
enamorado   in love

el enamorado   sweetheart
entonces   then
francamente   frankly
jamás   never, not . . . ever
llover (ue)   to rain

153

las matemáticas mathematics
nada nothing, not . . . anything
nadie nobody, no one
naturalmente naturally
ni . . . ni neither . . . nor
ninguno none, not . . . any
nunca never, not . . . ever
observar to observe
el otoño autumn
peor worse, worst
perdidamente hopelessly
ponerse to become, turn (*pale, red, etc.*)
la primavera spring
replicar to answer, retort
resistir to stand; to resist
sentirse (ie) to feel
señalar to indicate; point at
tampoco neither, not . . . either

la taza cup
el tenis tennis
tranquilamente calmly

IDIOMS AND OTHER EXPRESSIONS

al entrar on entering
después de sentarnos after sitting down
eso de that matter of
a mí no not me; not I (*with gustar, etc.*)
por estar enamorada on account of
  being in love
prestar atención to pay attention
salir aprobado to pass (*a course*)
salir mal to fail, flunk
tomar el sol to take (sit in) the sun
me da vergüenza it makes me ashamed

EL OTOÑO Y LA PRIMAVERA

Ayer fuimos al café a tomar un refresco. Al entrar[1] no vimos a ninguno de nuestros amigos. Pero después de sentarnos vimos al señor Martínez. Lo invitamos a tomar café con nosotros.

—Gracias—nos dijo al sentarse con nosotros. —Voy a tomar una taza de café bien caliente. Hace mucho frío esta mañana.

—Éste—dijo María (y señaló a Carlos)—dice que le gusta el invierno.

—A mí no—replicó el profesor Martínez. —Tampoco me gusta el verano. No puedo resistir ni el frío del invierno ni el calor del verano. Para mí . . . el otoño. Como saben Uds., escribo mucho. En septiembre, octubre y noviembre, cuando hace fresco, puedo trabajar tranquilamente. Entonces escribo más que nunca.[2]

—Pronto viene la primavera—observó Virginia. —¡Ésa es la estación que a mí me gusta!

—La primavera—dijo el señor Martínez—es para los jóvenes y para los enamorados. Y no siempre hace buen tiempo. En marzo hace viento y en abril llueve mucho.

—¡Pero el mes de mayo es el mejor del año!—exclamó Virginia.

—Es el peor para los profesores. Se lo digo francamente: los alumnos se sienten muy perezosos y no prestan atención. En la universidad nadie quiere hacer nada. Se toma el sol; se juega al tenis o al béisbol; pero no se trabaja. En la primavera no se estudia jamás.

—Eso de no estudiar—dijo María—me da vergüenza. La primavera pasada no pude[3] trabajar. Quise estudiar para salir aprobada en la asignatura de matemáticas. Pero no pude. Al fin supe[3] que salí mal.

—¡Naturalmente!—exclamó el señor Martínez.—Ud. no pudo estudiar por estar perdidamente enamorada, ¿verdad?

María se puso colorada, pero no dijo nada.

NOTAS

1. **Al** plus an infinitive means *on* or *upon* plus the English present participle. It often takes the place of an adverbial clause of time.

   al entrar upon entering (when we entered)
   al sentarse on sitting down (when he sat down)

2. After comparisons in Spanish, negative pronouns, adjectives, and adverbs nadie, nunca, etc.) are used, whereas English uses their affirmative counterparts (*anybody*, *ever*, etc.).

   Escribo más que nunca. I write more than ever.
   Trabaja más que nadie. He works more than anybody.

Aficionados *at the Malaga bullring look on as the matador passes the bull with his* muleta. *Although almost every city in Spain has a bullring, in Latin America soccer, not bull-fighting, is the king of sports.*

3. **Poder** and **saber** are other verbs that have special meanings in the preterit. **No pude** means *I could not* in the sense "I tried to but couldn't." **Supe** means *I learned, I found out.*

No pude estudiar.   I couldn't study.
Lo supe ayer.   I learned it (found out about it) yesterday.

These special meanings (**quise, pude, supe**) grow out of the basic use of the preterit to express a completed, instantaneous act.

PREGUNTAS

1. ¿Adónde fuimos ayer?
2. ¿Vimos a alguno de nuestros amigos al entrar en el café?
3. Después de sentarnos, ¿a quién vimos?
4. ¿Qué nos dijo el señor Martínez?
5. ¿Le gusta el invierno al señor Martínez?
6. ¿Le gusta el verano?
7. ¿Por qué no le gusta ni el verano ni el invierno?
8. ¿Cuál es la estación favorita del profesor Martínez?
9. ¿Por qué?
10. ¿Cuáles son los meses del otoño?
11. ¿Qué dijo el señor Martínez de la primavera?
12. ¿Qué tiempo hace en marzo?
13. ¿En abril?
14. ¿Qué dijo Virginia del mes de mayo?
15. ¿Qué dijo el señor Martínez del mes de mayo?
16. ¿Cómo se sienten los alumnos en la primavera?
17. ¿Qué se hace en la primavera?
18. ¿Pudo María estudiar la primavera pasada?
19. ¿Salió María aprobada en la asignatura de matemáticas?
20. ¿Qué dijo el señor Martínez y cómo respondió María?

Estructura

1. INDEFINITE PRONOUN SE

The indefinite pronoun **se** is often used to express the English indefinite pronoun *one* (or indefinite *we, you, they, people*).

Se puede trabajar.   One can work.
Se juega al tenis.   People play tennis.
Pero no se trabaja.   But they don't work.
No se estudia jamás.   You never study. (One never studies.)

PRÁCTICA

Diga en español.

1. One doesn't know.
2. One doesn't listen.
3. One doesn't read.
4. One doesn't learn.
5. One doesn't explain.
6. One doesn't understand.

2. FORMATION OF ADVERBS

Many adverbs are formed by adding the termination **-mente** to the feminine form of the adjective. If the adjective bears a written accent, the adverb retains it.

completo	complete	**completamente**	completely
constante	constant	**constantemente**	constantly
feliz	happy	**felizmente**	happily
fácil	easy	**fácilmente**	easily

PRÁCTICA

Cambie según el modelo.

fácil: fácilmente

1. difícil
2. típico
3. reciente
4. lento
5. sencillo
6. principal
7. nuevo
8. franco

3. AFFIRMATIVE WORDS AND THEIR NEGATIVE COUNTERPARTS

AFFIRMATIVES		NEGATIVES	
alguien	someone, somebody	**nadie**	no one, nobody, not . . . anyone
algo	something	**nada**	nothing, not . . . anything
alguno, -a **algún**	some, any	**ninguno, -a** **ningún**	no, none, not . . . any
siempre	always	**nunca** **jamás**	never, not . . . ever
también	also, too	**tampoco**	neither, not . . . either
o . . . o	either . . . or	**ni . . . ni**	neither . . . nor

Spanish and English differ in the use of negative words in that Spanish frequently uses a double negative. Negative words may precede or follow the verb. When they follow, **no** must precede the verb.

Alguien estuvo aquí.   Somebody was here.
Nadie estuvo aquí.   Nobody was here.
Aquí no estuvo nadie.   Nobody was here.

¿Quieres algo?   Do you want something?
No quiero nada.   I don't want anything.
Nada quiero.   I want nothing.

¿Siempre preparas la lección?   Do you always prepare the lesson?
No la preparo nunca (jamás).   I never prepare it.
Nunca (jamás) preparo la lección.   I never prepare the lesson.

Yo trabajo y ella trabaja también.   I work, and she works too.
Yo no trabajo y ella no trabaja tampoco.   I don't work, and she doesn't work either.
Yo no trabajo. Tampoco trabaja ella.   I don't work. She doesn't work either.

O le gusta la música o no le gusta.   Either you like music or you don't.
¿No te gusta ni el piano ni el violín?   Don't you like either the piano or the violin?
Ni el uno ni el otro.   Neither one. (Neither the one nor the other.)

Alguno and **ninguno** drop the final **-o** before a masculine singular noun.

Algún político dijo eso.   Some politician said that.
Ningún político lo dijo.   No politician said it.
No lo dijo ningún político.   No politician said so.

When used as the direct object of a verb, **alguien** and **nadie** and **alguno** and **ninguno** (when referring to persons) must be preceded by the personal **a**.

¿Llamaste a alguien?   Did you call anybody?
No, no llamé a nadie.   No, I didn't call anybody.

¿Conoces a alguna cubana?   Do you know any Cuban girl?
No, no conozco a ninguna cubana.   No, I don't know any Cuban girl.

Algo and **nada** may be used as adverbs.

Este coche fue algo caro.   This car was rather (somewhat) expensive.
Esta lección no es nada difícil.   This lesson isn't at all (isn't a bit) difficult.

PRÁCTICA

1. *Conteste según los modelos.*

a. **¿A quién vio Ud.?**
   No vi a nadie.

   1. ¿A quién buscó Ud.?
   2. ¿A quién llamó Ud.?
   3. ¿A quién encontró Ud.?
   4. ¿A quién visitó Ud.?

b. **¿Qué hiciste Ud. esta mañana?**
   No hice nada.

   1. ¿Qué viste esta mañana?
   2. ¿Qué dijiste esta mañana?
   3. ¿Qué encontraste esta mañana?
   4. ¿Qué leíste esta mañana?

2. *Conteste según los modelos.*

a. **¿Qué libro quiere Tomás?**
   Ninguno; no quiere ningún libro.

   1. ¿Qué sombrero quiere Tomás?
   2. ¿Qué corbata quiere Tomás?
   3. ¿Qué traje quiere Tomás?
   4. ¿Qué chaqueta quiere Tomás?

b. **¿A cuál de estas muchachas conocen Uds.?**
   No conocemos a ninguna.

   1. ¿A cuál de estos jóvenes conocen Uds.?
   2. ¿A cuál de estas chicas conocen Uds.?
   3. ¿A cuál de estos médicos conocen Uds.?
   4. ¿A cuál de estas profesoras conocen Uds.?

c. **¿Hay cafés por aquí?**
   Hay algunos, pero no me gusta ninguno.

   1. ¿Hay tiendas por aquí?
   2. ¿Hay restoranes por aquí?
   3. ¿Hay teatros cerca de aquí?
   4. ¿Hay universidades en esta ciudad?

3. *Conteste según los modelos.*

a. **¿Estudia Ud. mucho?**
   No, no estudio nunca.
   No estudio jamás.

   1. ¿Trabaja Ud. mucho?
   2. ¿Baila Ud. mucho?
   3. ¿Se divierte Ud. mucho?
   4. ¿Juega Ud. mucho al tenis?

b. **Ud. no estudia nunca ¿Y ella?**
   Ella no estudia tampoco.

   1. Ud. no trabaja nunca. ¿Y ella?
   2. Ud. no baila nunca. ¿Y ella?
   3. Ud. no se divierte nunca. ¿Y ella?
   4. Ud. no juega nunca. ¿Y ella?

c. **¿Cuál prefieres? ¿Este reloj o ése?**
   No me gusta ni el uno ni el otro.

   1. ¿Cuál prefieres? ¿Esta raqueta o ésa?
   2. ¿Cuál prefieres? ¿Este sombrero o ése?
   3. ¿Cuál prefieres? ¿Esta mesa o ésa?
   4. ¿Cuál prefieres? ¿Este regalo o ése?

4. *Conteste según los modelos.*

a. **¿Es fácil la lección?**
   Sí, es algo fácil.

   1. ¿Es guapa esa chica?
   2. ¿Es cara la gasolina?
   3. ¿Son ricos esos jóvenes?
   4. ¿Son generosos esos viejos?

b. **¿Es inteligente ese chico?**
   No, no es nada inteligente.

   1. ¿Es simpática esa muchacha?
   2. ¿Es bueno el clima?
   3. ¿Son interesantes esos libros?
   4. ¿Son razonables los precios?

5. *Diga en español.*

1. Is there anybody in the house? No, nobody.
2. Do you see anybody?
3. Have you something for me? No, nothing.
4. Are there stores nearby? Yes, some.
5. Some day they're going to return.
6. Someone said that.
7. Some boys play tennis.
8. I need something more.
9. Either you like it or you don't.
10. That book is rather difficult, and it's not at all interesting.

Tareas

Diga a la clase en español.

1. The students went to the café yesterday.
2. On entering, they didn't see any of their friends.
3. After sitting down, they saw Mr. Martínez.
4. "It's cold this morning," said Mr. Martínez.
5. "I need a cup of hot coffee."
6. Professor Martínez doesn't like either winter or summer.
7. He prefers the autumn, when it's cool and he can work calmly.
8. It's always cool in September, October, and November.
9. It's windy in March, and it rains a lot in April.
10. But in May the weather's good.
11. "One doesn't study in spring," said the professor.
12. Nobody wants to do anything.

Composición oral o escrita

Tell what the weather is like in the spring and autumn months, what you do then, and what sports you enjoy.

Diálogo

INESITA NO QUIERE HACER NADA

FELIPE—¡Inesita! ¿Tú por aquí a estas horas?
INÉS—¡Evidentemente![1]
FELIPE—¿Quieres hacer algo esta noche?
INÉS—¿Cómo qué, por ejemplo?[2]
FELIPE—Hay un buen concierto[3] de Beethoven.
INÉS—No me gusta nada[4] la música clásica.
FELIPE—Probablemente hay algunas buenas películas en los teatros.
INÉS—No quiero ver ninguna de ellas. Me dicen que todas son horribles.

Since the seasons south of the equator are the reverse of the seasons north of it, Argentina and Chile have become popular vacation spots for Europeans and North Americans seeking relief from the heat of summer. Modern lifts in Bariloche, Argentina, transport hikers and skiers to the slopes.

FELIPE—¿No hay ni siquiera[5] una buena?

INÉS—Así dicen.

FELIPE—¿Vamos a la discoteca[6] a escuchar los discos[7] nuevos?

INÉS—¡Eso tampoco!

FELIPE—¡Quieres ir a bailar?

INÉS—Tampoco. Hace mucho[8] calor para eso.

FELIPE—¿Quieres tomar algo?

INÉS—¡Ni hablar![9]

FELIPE—¿Ni siquiera un café?

INÉS—Me quita el sueño.[10]

FELIPE—¿Qué quieres hacer, pues?

INÉS—Nada. No quiero hacer nada.

FELIPE—¿Estás segura?[11]

INÉS—No tengo ganas de hacer nada.

FELIPE—¡Nunca quieres hacer nada! Bueno, te acompaño a casa.

INÉS—¡Eso no! Más que nada, tengo ganas de estar sola.

[1]evidentemente *obviously*
[2]por ejemplo *for example*
[3]el concierto *concert*
[4]nada *(not) at all*
[5]ni siquiera *(not) even*
[6]la discoteca *record shop*

[7]el disco *record*
[8]mucho = demasiado
[9]¡Ni hablar! *Not on your life!*
[10]Me quita el sueño. *It keeps me awake.*
[11]seguro *sure*

PREGUNTAS PERSONALES

Conteste con respuesta negativa, como en el modelo.

¿A quién buscó Ud. ayer?
No busqué a nadie.

1. ¿A quién vio Ud. anoche?
2. ¿Conoce Ud. a alguna de esas chicas?
3. ¿Vio Ud. algo?
4. ¿Estuvo Ud. alguna vez en Cuba?
5. ¿Llamó Ud. a alguien?
6. ¿Le gusta a Ud. alguna de estas corbatas?
7. ¿Le dijeron algo nuevo?
8. ¿Es Ud. siempre perezoso (perezosa)?
9. ¿Hay alquien en esa sala?
11. ¿Hay algo de interés en ese libro?
11. ¿Invitó Ud. a alguno de estos chicos?
12. ¿Va Ud. siempre a España a pasar las vacaciones?
13. ¿Leyó Ud. todos estos libros?
14. ¿Le gustan todas las estaciones del año?
15. ¿Tiene Ud. ganas de hacer algo?

Notas culturales

1. **Béisbol** is not the favorite sport of the Hispanic world. But it is popular in the countries nearest to the United States—Mexico and Cuba. Far more popular is **fútbol**—not our type of the game, but soccer. Enormous stadiums, like those in Madrid and Barcelona, have been built. Many people follow the progress of the teams with tremendous enthusiasm. Interest often reaches fever pitch, and discussions of the opposing teams can lead to heated arguments and even riots in the stadiums.

2. **Jai alai** is a game of Basque origin. It is similar to handball, except that the ball is caught and returned in a basket (**cesta**) strapped to the player's arm. Played with a hard ball, it is a fast and even dangerous game. Professional matches are played in a **frontón** (court) with high walls on three sides. The spectators are protected by a wire screen on the fourth side. Much betting takes place at the matches.

3. The bullfight (**corrida de toros**) is not a sport, but a spectacle and a ritualized art. It opens with a parade into the arena of the bullfighters and their retinues in their showy silk and velvet costumes. When the bull is loosed, he is played with capes to test his qualities. He is then lured to attack the **picador**, who is mounted on a blindfolded horse protected by padding. The

picador holds off the bull by plunging a lance into the neck muscle to weaken it. **Banderilleros** then place darts with bright-colored streamers in the bull's neck to weaken him further. The final act consists of **faenas** by the **matador de toros**, who plays the bull by waving in front of him the **muleta**, the small red cloth, finally dispatching the animal by plunging his sword between the shoulder blades. Usually six bulls are fought by three alternating **matadores**.

Bullfighting is not universal in the Hispanic countries. It is identified especially with Spain, Portugal (where the bull is not killed), Mexico, and Peru. Only occasionally are there **corridas** in Colombia, Venezuela, and Guatemala.

Mother Earth, *a painting by the Mexican muralist Diego Rivera.*

13

Lo mío, mío, y lo tuyo de entrambos.
What's mine is mine, and what's yours belongs to both of us.

Past participle of the regular verb

The past participle is formed by removing the infinitive ending and adding to the stem the following endings: **-ado** for the first conjugation and **-ido** for the second and third conjugations.

hablar:	**hablado**	spoken
aprender:	**aprendido**	learned
vivir:	**vivido**	lived

When the verb stem ends in **-a**, **-e**, or **-o**, the ending **-ido** bears a written accent: **caer, caído** (*fallen*); **leer, leído** (*read*).

Present perfect indicative

The present perfect tense (*I have spoken, he has studied,* etc.) is formed in Spanish by combining the present tense of the auxiliary verb **haber** (*to have*) with the past participle. It is normally used where we use the present perfect in English.

SINGULAR		PLURAL	
he	hablado	hemos	hablado
has	aprendido	(habéis)	aprendido
ha	vivido	han	vivido

In compound tenses the past participle never changes to the feminine or the plural. Nothing can stand between **haber** and the past participle. Therefore, object pronouns precede the forms of **haber**. In questions, subjects follow the past participle.

Los he comprado.   I have bought them.
Se han divertido.   They have had a good time.
¿Lo ha aprendido Ud.?   Have you learned it?

165

A family in Colombia. In Hispanic countries the family tends to be a large and tightly knit group with a deep sense of solidarity. Often several generations live together. The father is the apparent head of the family who wields authority and disciplines the children. In spite of this, the Hispanic family has traditionally been a matriarchy. The mother knows how to pull strings behind the scenes and work her will. Much love and affection are lavished on the children; yet, respect for the parents is instilled early and children are seldom disrespectful.

PRÁCTICA

Cambia según se indica.

1. Hemos contestado bien.
   yo / Ud. / ellas / tú / tú y yo / los alumnos

2. No han vivido en España.
   tú / Ud. / yo / nosotros / mis padres

3. ¿Ha aprendido Ud. mucho?
   Uds. / tú / nosotros / yo / él / ellas

Irregular past participles

Some past participles are irregular. Among the verbs you have learned so far, the following have irregular past participles:

decir:	**dicho**	said
escribir:	**escrito**	written
hacer:	**hecho**	done, made
morir:	**muerto**	died (dead)
poner:	**puesto**	put, placed
ver:	**visto**	seen
volver:	**vuelto**	returned, gone back
devolver:	**devuelto**	returned, given back

PRÁCTICA

Conteste según el modelo.

¿Va Ud. a estudiar la lección?
Ya he estudiado la lección.

1. ¿Va Ud. a ver al profesor?
2. ¿Va Ud. a devolver el traje?
3. ¿Va Ud. a escribir la composición?
4. ¿Va Ud. a ponerse la chaqueta?
5. ¿Va Ud. a hacer el trabajo?
6. ¿Va Ud. a decir la verdad?
7. ¿Va Ud. a volver?
8. ¿Va a morir el viejo?

Past perfect indicative

The past perfect, or pluperfect, tense (*I had spoken, they had been,* etc.) is formed in Spanish by combining the imperfect tense of **haber** with a past participle. It is used in Spanish as we use the same tense in English.

SINGULAR		PLURAL	
había	hablado	habíamos	hablado
habías	aprendido	(habíais)	aprendido
había	vivido	habían	vivido

PRÁCTICA

a. *Cambie según se indica.*

1. Ella había salido antes.
   yo / ellos / tú y yo / él / tú / Ud.

2. Uds. habían vuelto más temprano.
   tú / él / yo / nosotros / ellas / Ud.

b. *Conteste según el modelo.*

¿Quién compró el coche? (Julián)
Dijeron que Julián lo había comprado.

1. ¿Quién vio la película? (Beatriz)
2. ¿Quién leyó el libro? (Anita)
3. ¿Quién pagó la cuenta? (tú)
4. ¿Quién perdió el dinero? (tú)
5. ¿Quién dijo eso? (nosotros)
6. ¿Quiénes ganaron el campeonato? (nosotros)
7. ¿Quién encontró el reloj? (Uds.)
8. ¿Quién prestó el dinero? (Ud.)

Escuchar y hablar

antes   before; earlier
brillante   brilliant
caído *past. part. of* **caer**   fallen
el campeonato   championship
la cita   date
contra   against; to (*in scores*)
el domingo   (on) Sunday
el equipo   team
la excursión de estudio   field trip
el fútbol   football
ganar   to win
la geología   geology
el guante   glove
el jueves   (on) Thursday
la jugada   play (*in a game*)
el lunes   (on) Monday
el martes   (on) Tuesday
el miércoles   (on) Wednesday
el mío   mine

el nuestro   ours
el partido   game (match)
perder (ie)   to lose
preocuparse   to worry
recordar (ue)   to remember
el sábado   (on) Saturday
el suelo   ground
el suyo   theirs (his, hers, yours)
el tanto   point (*in a game*)
el viernes   (on) Friday

IDIOMS AND OTHER EXPRESSIONS

la clase del miércoles   the Wednesday
   class
eran las doce   it was twelve o'clock
no hay que   there's no need to
pasado mañana   the day after tomorrow
¡qué (jugada)!   what a (play)!

EL PARTIDO DE FÚTBOL

CARLOS—¿Qué hiciste ayer? No te vi.

JUAN—¿Ayer? Vamos a ver ... ayer fue lunes ... Ah, sí, fui al campo. El domingo unos amigos que estudian geología me habían invitado a hacer una excursión de estudio con ellos. La hicimos ayer.

CARLOS—¿Se divirtieron Uds.? ¿Fue interesante la excursión?

JUAN—Mucho.[1]

CARLOS—¿Quieres ir al cine conmigo?

JUAN—Hoy no puedo. Los martes siempre tengo que escribir una composición para la clase del miércoles. Empecé a escribirla anoche, pero había vuelto tarde de la excursión. Eran las doce, y no pude terminarla.

CARLOS—¿Pasado mañana, entonces?

JUAN—Tampoco. El jueves voy a salir con Virginia. Y tengo una cita con ella el viernes. Tiene que ser la semana que viene.

CARLOS—¿La semana que viene? Pues, ¿qué haces el sábado?

JUAN—¿No recuerdas? El sábado vamos al partido de fútbol. El partido va a ser muy importante y quiero verlo.

(*El sábado*)

JUAN—¡Qué jugada! ¿Has visto, Virginia? ¡Otros siete tantos!

VIRGINIA—¿Quiénes van a ganar?

JUAN—Nosotros, por supuesto. Los dos equipos son buenos. El de ellos ha jugado muy bien, pero el nuestro ha jugado mejor. El suyo no puede ganar. ¿Te ha gustado el partido?

VIRGINIA—Sí, claro! Me he divertido mucho.

JUAN—¡Mira, Virginia! Hemos ganado. ¡Cuarenta y nueve tantos contra treinta y seis! Los nuestros han ganado el campeonato.

VIRGINIA—Las jugadas han sido brillantes, ¿verdad?

JUAN—Brillantes y ... ¡caramba! He perdido mis guantes. ¿Los has visto tú? Tal vez han caído al suelo. No quiero perderlos.

VIRGINIA—No importa. No hay que preocuparte. ¡Te doy los míos!

NOTA

1. Where English uses the word *very* standing alone, Spanish uses **mucho**.

PREGUNTAS

1. ¿Qué habían hecho los amigos de Juan?
2. ¿Adónde habían ido?
3. ¿Le había gustado a Juan la excursión?
4. ¿Adónde quiere ir Carlos?

5. ¿Qué día es hoy?
6. ¿Por qué no puede Juan acompañar a Carlos?
7. ¿Qué hace Juan los martes?
8. ¿Por qué no puede ir Juan el jueves?
9. ¿Qué van a hacer Juan y Carlos el sábado?
10. ¿Cómo son los dos equipos?
11. ¿Cuál ha jugado mejor?
12. ¿Quiénes han ganado?
13. ¿Con cuántos tantos ganaron?
14. ¿Qué han ganado además del partido?
15. ¿Qué ha perdido Juan?
16. ¿Qué le dice Virginia?

Estructura

1. POSSESSIVE PRONOUNS

The possessive pronouns in Spanish are as follows:

el mío	**la mía**	**los míos**	**las mías**	mine
el tuyo	**la tuya**	**los tuyos**	**las tuyas**	yours
el nuestro	**la nuestra**	**los nuestros**	**las nuestras**	ours
(el vuestro)	**(la vuestra)**	**(los vuestros)**	**(las vuestras)**	yours
el suyo	**la suya**	**los suyos**	**las suyas**	yours, his, hers, its, theirs

The possessive pronoun agrees in gender and number with the thing possessed, not with the possessor.

mi corbata   my necktie: *la mía*   mine
nuestra casa   our house: *la nuestra*   ours
sus padres   your (his, her, their) parents: *los suyos*   yours (*his, hers, theirs*)

The definite article is part of the pronoun and must always be used.

las mías   mine   **el nuestro**   ours   **los suyos**   yours

Since **el suyo (la suya, los suyos, las suyas)** may be ambiguous, the ambiguity is avoided by substituting as follows:

el de él his		**el de ellos** theirs *m.*
el de ella hers		**el de ellas** theirs *f.*
el de usted yours		**el de ustedes** yours

El de él is changed to **la de él, los de él, las de él,** and so forth depending on the gender of the thing possessed.

> **los guantes de Ud. y los de ella**   your gloves and hers
> **mi casa y la de ellos**   my house and theirs
> **nuestros libros y los de él**   our books and his

These longer forms are also used for emphasis.

PRÁCTICA

Sustituya según los modelos.

a. **Tengo mi corbata.**
   Tengo la mía.

1. Ud. tiene su corbata.
2. Ud. tiene sus camisas.
3. Él tiene sus zapatos.
4. Él tiene su casa.
5. Tenemos nuestra finca.
6. Tenemos nuestro caballo.
7. Tenemos nuestros guantes.
8. Tú tienes tus ejercicios.
9. Tú tienes tu invitación.
10. Tienen su orquesta.
11. Tienen sus calcetines.
12. Tienen su libro.
13. Ella tiene sus blusas.
14. Tengo mis sombreros.
15. Tengo mis ideas.

b. **¿Has visto el rancho de su abuelo?**
   ¿Has visto el de él?

1. ¿Has visto la casa de María?
2. ¿Has visto el sombrero de Tomás?
3. ¿Has visto la finca de su padre?
4. ¿Has visto el programa de las niñas?
5. ¿Has visto los trajes de mi hermano?
6. ¿Has visto las vacas del vaquero?

2. DAYS OF THE WEEK

el lunes (on) Monday		**el viernes** (on) Friday	
el martes (on) Tuesday		**el sábado** (on) Saturday	
el miércoles (on) Wednesday		**el domingo** (on) Sunday	
el jueves (on) Thursday			

> **El jueves voy al cine.**   On Thursday I am going to the movies.
> **Ayer fue lunes.**   Yesterday was Monday.
> **Los sábados no trabajo.**   On Saturdays I don't work.
> **Los martes tienen dos clases.**   On Tuesdays they have two classes.

The names of the days of the week are masculine. They are not capitalized. Except after **ser**, they are used with the definite article. The English preposition *on* is not translated literally. **Sábado** and **domingo** form their plurals regularly. The names of the other days have the same form for both singular and plural.

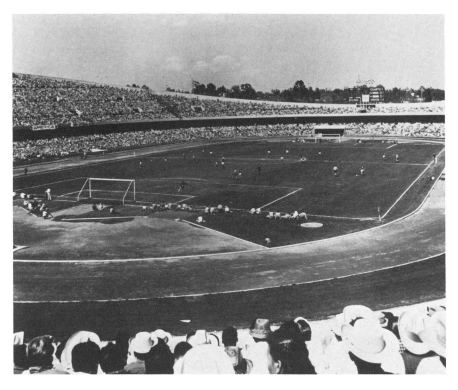

Mexicans are aficionados of many sports. Besides the world's largest bullring, Mexico City has two enormous soccer stadiums which are almost always filled to capacity—the National Stadium and the Olympic Stadium at University City, shown here.

PRÁCTICA

Conteste en español.

a. 1. ¿Cuántas clases tiene Ud. el lunes?
   2. ¿Qué hace Ud. el martes?
   3. ¿Siempre escribe Ud. una composición el miércoles?
   4. ¿Qué va Ud. a hacer el jueves?
   5. ¿Va Ud. al cine el viernes?
   6. ¿Tiene Ud. una cita el sábado?
   7. ¿Tiene Ud. clases los domingos?

b. 1. Si hoy es lunes, ¿qué día fue ayer?
   2. Si hoy es martes, ¿qué día va a ser mañana?
   3. Si hoy es jueves, ¿qué día va a ser pasado mañana?
   4. Si hoy es domingo, ¿qué día va a ser mañana?
   5. Si hoy es sábado, ¿qué día fue ayer?

3. *IMPERFECT TENSE OF* SER *IN TIME EXPRESSIONS*

The imperfect of **ser** is used in telling time in the past. As in expressions of time in the present, the plural is used from *two o'clock* on.

Era la una y media de la tarde.   It was one-thirty in the afternoon.
Eran las diez de la mañana.   It was ten o'clock in the morning.

PRÁCTICA

Diga en español.

1. It was nine o'clock.
2. It was twelve-thirty.
3. It was a quarter after one.
4. It was seven o'clock in the morning.
5. It was four o'clock in the afternoon.
6. It was eleven o'clock at night.

Tareas

Diga a la clase en español.

1. Yesterday was Friday.
2. On Monday Juan had gone on (made) a field trip with some students of geology.
3. "Was the trip interesting?" "Very."
4. Carlos invites him to go to the movies on Tuesday, but he can't go because he has to write a composition for his Wednesday class.
5. On Thursday he is going out with Virginia.
6. On Friday he has a date too.
7. The football game has been very interesting; we have seen some brilliant plays.
8. The two teams have played well, but ours has been better.
9. Theirs is not going to win.
10. Ours has won—with forty-nine points!
11. And they have won the championship, too.
12. Virginia has had a very good time.
13. Juan has lost his gloves.
14. Virginia says that she is going to give him hers!

Composición oral o escrita

We have been attending a football game. Tell who has accompanied us, how the two teams have been, which has played better, which has won, whether we have won the championship, and whether we have had a good time.

Diálogo

LOS CUBANOS EN LOS ESTADOS UNIDOS

MARÍA—El señor Martínez ha sido muy amable[1] para conmigo.[2] Me ha ayudado[3] mucho. Me ha explicado las lecciones cuando no las he comprendido bien.

VIRGINIA—Es muy buena persona. Papá me ha dicho que ha habido[4] muchos cubanos como él que han tenido que dejar su país para venir al nuestro.

MARÍA—Y aquí han hecho un papel[5] muy importante. Ha venido mucha gente[6] profesional.

VIRGINIA—Sí. Papá dice que muchos de los cubanos han sido profesores que han venido con su doctorado[7] de la Universidad de la Habana o de otras universidades cubanas.

MARÍA—Entre ellos ha habido también muchos médicos que han hecho un papel muy importante en nuestros hospitales. Nos hacían falta los médicos cubanos, como nos hacían falta los profesores cubanos.

VIRGINIA—¿Has estado alguna vez[8] en Cuba?

MARÍA—No. Ha sido imposible ir a Cuba. Pero algún día[9] quiero ver la bella isla tropical del Caribe.[10]

[1]amable *kind*	[7]el doctorado *doctorate*
[2]para conmigo *to (towards) me*	[8]alguna vez *ever*
[3]ayudar *to help*	[9]algún día *sometime*
[4]ha habido *there have been*	[10]la bella isla tropical del Caribe *the*
[5]hacer un papel *to play a role*	*beautiful tropical island of the*
[6]la gente *people*	*Caribbean*

PREGUNTAS PERSONALES

1. ¿Ha estado Ud. en Cuba?
2. ¿Han estado sus padres en España?
3. ¿Ha vivido Ud. en México?
4. ¿Ha hecho Ud. mucho hoy?
5. ¿Ha visto Ud. una película de Buñuel?
6. ¿Han escrito sus amigos los ejercicios?
7. ¿Se ha puesto Ud. los guantes en la clase?
8. ¿Ha habido muchos alumnos en la clase?
9. ¿Le ha prestado Ud. dinero a su amigo?
10. ¿Le ha devuelto su amigo el dinero que Ud. le prestó?
11. ¿Ha dicho Ud. siempre la verdad?
12. ¿Ha muerto el viejo profesor?
13. ¿Han comido Uds. en un restorán?

14. ¿Le ha gustado la comida?
15. ¿Han vuelto sus amigos del centro?
16. ¿Ha visto Ud. el partido de fútbol?
17. ¿Quiénes han ganado el partido—nuestro equipo o el de ellos?
18. ¿Hemos ganado el campeonato?
19. ¿Tiene Ud. sus guantes o los de Virginia?
20. ¿Tiene Ud. su libro o el de Pablo?
21. ¿Conoció Ud. a esa chica ayer, o la había conocido antes?
22. ¿Vio Ud. esa película anoche, o la había visto antes?
23. ¿Preparó Ud. la lección esta mañana, o la había preparado antes?
24. ¿Escribió Ud. los ejercicios esta mañana, o los había escrito antes?
25. ¿Leyó Ud. esta lección hoy, o la había leído antes?

Notas culturales

1. Just as the Cubans in the United States are making important contributions, so is another group of Hispanic descent, the Chicanos. The Chicanos are Spanish-speaking citizens or residents of the United States of Mexican heritage. The term first came into prominence in the 1930s and seems to be an ingenious combination of two words: the first syllable of the name of the Mexican state, Chihuahua, and the last syllable of *mexicano*. It is not a disparaging word, but a much needed term expressive of the Mexican-American's identity, self-awareness, and self-respect. Many Chicanos have distinguished themselves as writers, artists, scholars, and as business and professional leaders.
2. To the Mexicans, the Yankee is a *gringo*. It has been said that when numbers of Americans were migrating to Texas, then a part of Mexico, they could be heard singing, as they crossed the plains, a Scottish ballad, "Green Grow the Rashes, Oh." The Mexicans applied to them the first two words of the song, corrupted to *gringo*. But this is apocryphal. Others than Americans have been called *gringos*. In Argentina the term was applied to the many Italian immigrants who settled there. The word really seems to be a corruption of **griego**, meaning Greek, and to have been applied to any foreigner.

The Plaza de España in Madrid. Statues of Don Quijote and Sancho Panza in front of the monument to Cervantes.

3

A. *Conteste en el imperfecto, como en el modelo.*

¿Trabajas mucho ahora?
No, pero antes trabajaba mucho.

1. ¿Vas al cine con frecuencia? No, pero antes _____ todas las noches.
2. ¿Aprendes mucho ahora? Ahora no, pero antes _____ mucho.
3. ¿Se levanta Ud. temprano? No, pero antes _____ temprano todos los días.
4. ¿Ves a Rosita con frecuencia? No, pero antes la_____ todos los días.
5. ¿Eres algo perezoso, ¿verdad? No, pero antes _____ muy perezoso.
6. ¿Hay muchos estudiantes en la clase de latín? Ahora no, pero antes _____ muchos.

B. *Conteste con un pronombre, como en el modelo.*

¿Son para Ud. estos regalos?
No, no son para mí.

1. ¿Son para María? / ¿Son para Juan? / ¿Son para mí?
2. ¿Son para Uds.? / ¿Son para mis amigos? / ¿Son para Ud.?

C. *Lea en español.*

1. 101 vacas
2. 303 personas
3. 1400 alumnos
4. 2500 pesos
5. 3500 pesetas
6. 1756
7. 1812
8. 1978
9. 500.000 habitantes
10. 3.000.000 de libros

D. *Cambie al pretérito, según el modelo.*

Paco estudia mucho.
Paco estudió mucho.

1. Tomás puede hacerlo.
2. Ana no quiere salir.
3. Pepe me lo dice.
4. Isabel se pone los zapatos.
5. Ud. viene tarde.
6. Las chicas no lo saben.
7. Mis amigos no pueden hacerlo.
8. Los alumnos lo dicen.
9. Los chicos no quieren pagar.
10. Uds. se ponen los guantes.

177

E. *Conteste según el modelo.*

¿Estuviste en el café?
No, no estuve en el café.

1. ¿Dijiste eso?
2. ¿Pudiste hacerlo?
3. ¿Lo supiste ayer?
4. ¿Te pusiste los guantes?
5. ¿Viniste temprano?

6. ¿Lo supieron Uds. ayer?
7. ¿Quisieron Uds. venderlo?
8. ¿Dijeron Uds. eso?
9. ¿Se pusieron Uds. los guantes?
10. ¿Vinieron Uds. tarde?

F. *Conteste con frases completas.*

1. ¿Hace mucho calor hoy?
2. ¿Hace mucho frío hoy?
3. ¿Hace fresco hoy?
4. ¿Hace viento hoy?
5. ¿Hace mucho sol?
6. ¿Qué tiempo hace hoy?

7. ¿En qué meses hace calor?
8. ¿En qué meses hace frío?
9. ¿Cuáles son los meses de la primavera?
10. ¿Cuáles son los meses del otoño?

G. *Sustituya según se indica.*

Me gusta esta película.

café / biblioteca / deportes / flores / cafés / casas

H. *Sustituya según se indica.*

¿Quieres prestarme ese libro?

corbata / abrigo / guantes / taza / tazas / zapatos

I. *Sustituya según se indica.*

este abrigo y aquél

universidad / universidades / caballo / caballos

J. *Haga preguntas y conteste, como en el modelo.*

¿Te gusta este coche?
No me gusta éste; prefiero ése.

blusa / abrigo / libros / camisas / sombreros

K. *Diga en español.*

1. This is easy.
2. That is interesting.
3. What is this?
4. I don't like that.

L. *Conteste según el modelo.*

¿Estudian Uds. mucho?
No, aquí no se estudia.

¿Trabajan Uds.? / ¿Leen Uds.? / ¿Bailan Uds.? / ¿Aprenden Uds.?

M. *Conteste usando **nada**, **nadie**, **ninguno**, **ninguna** o **tampoco**.*

1. ¿Qué tiene Ud.? No tengo _____.
2. ¿Qué haces? No hago _____.
3. ¿Quién está en la otra sala? _____ está en la otra sala.
4. ¿A quién vio Ud. anoche? Anoche no vi _____.
5. ¿Tiene Ud. algún amigo en México? No tengo _____ amigo en México.
6. ¿Tienes alguna amiga en Bolivia? No tengo _____ amiga en Bolivia.
7. No conozco a Margarita. Yo no la conozco _____.

N. *Conteste según el modelo.*

¿Cuándo va Ud. a vender el coche?
Lo he vendido ya.

1. ¿Cuándo va Ud. a hacer el trabajo?
2. ¿Cuándo vas a escribir los ejercicios?
3. ¿Cuándo van Uds. a ver la película?
4. ¿Cuándo van Uds. a decir la verdad?
5. ¿Cuándo van tus amigos a devolver el dinero?
6. ¿Cuándo va el niño a ponerse el abrigo?

O. *Conteste según el modelo.*

¿Leyó Ud. ese libro anoche?
No, lo había leído antes.

1. ¿Compró Ud. esos regalos el miércoles?
2. ¿Hizo Juan todo ese trabajo esta mañana?
3. ¿Perdió Ana sus guantes esta noche?
4. Tus amigos escucharon la cinta ayer, ¿verdad?
5. Uds. vieron a Rosita el viernes, ¿no?

P. *Cambie según el modelo.*

La casa de Tomás es grande.
La suya es grande.

1. El padre de Jacinta es ingeniero.
2. Los amigos de María son simpáticos.
3. La abuela de los chicas es muy vieja.
4. Mis hermanas son muy jóvenes.
5. Mi novia es muy guapa.
6. Nuestra casa es bastante pequeña.
7. Tus regalos son muy caros.

Q. *Diga en español.*

1. Explain what Carlos used to do on his grandfather's farm and what Juan and María used to do on their grandfather's ranch.
2. Tell why you like summer and why you like winter. Tell what you like to do in both seasons.
3. Tell why Professor Martínez prefers the autumn and why he does not like spring.
4. Describe the last football game: who played, how the teams were, who won, what the score was, and whether we won the championship.

LECCIÓN

14

No te acostarás sin saber cosa más.
We learn something every day.
(You won't go to bed without learning something more.)

Future indicative of regular verbs

The future tense is formed by adding the following endings to the whole infinitive. The endings are the same for all three conjugations.

-é	-emos
-ás	(-éis)
-á	-án

hablar

hablaré	I shall speak	hablaremos	we shall speak
hablarás	you will speak	(hablaréis)	you will speak
hablará	he (she) will speak	hablarán	they will speak

aprender		vivir	
aprenderé	aprenderemos	viviré	viviremos
aprenderás	(aprenderéis)	vivirás	(viviréis)
aprenderá	aprenderán	vivirá	vivirán

Note the written accent over each of the endings except the first person plural.

PRÁCTICA

Cambie según se indica.

1. Estaré aquí mañana.
   tú / Roberto / Roberto y yo / Ud. / Uds. / yo

2. Leerán todo el libro.
   Ud. / yo / ellos / nosotros / él / tú

3. No escribirás una composición todos los días.
   los alumnos / Paco / nosotros / yo / Ud. / tú

Future indicative of irregular verbs

The future of many irregular verbs is regular: **seré**, *I shall be*; **estaré**, *I shall be*; **iré**, *I shall go*; etc. The future of some others is not; but the irregularity always occurs in the infinitive stem, never in the endings.

Some irregular futures:

hacer		decir		salir		tener	
haré	haremos	diré	diremos	saldré	saldremos	tendré	tendremos
harás	(haréis)	dirás	(diréis)	saldrás	(saldréis)	tendrás	(tendréis)
hará	harán	dirá	dirán	saldrá	saldrán	tendrá	tendrán

PRÁCTICA

a. *Cambie según se indica.*

1. Tú no harás nada.
   yo / Ud. / Ud. y yo / ellas / tú / las chicas

2. Se lo diré mañana.
   nosotros / tú / Uds. / Pepe / ellos / yo

3. Saldremos temprano por la mañana.
   ellas / yo / Inés y yo / Uds. / él / tú

4. Tendrán que pagar mucho.
   Anita / tú / yo / Clara y yo / él / tus amigos

b. *Cambie al singular, según el modelo.*

Ellos me contestarán.
Él me contestará.

1. Iremos a México.
2. Trabajaremos mucho.
3. Seremos buenos.
4. Lo veremos.
5. Lo haremos.

6. Uds. lo leerán.
7. Uds. saldrán temprano.
8. Uds tendrán frío.
9. Ellas lo harán.
10. Ellos lo dirán.

c. *Continúe según el modelo.*

Tú quieres estudiar y _____.
Tú quieres estudiar y estudiarás.

1. Yo quiero hacerlo y lo _____.
2. Ellos quieron decirlo y lo _____.
3. Tú quieres salir y _____.
4. Ellas quieren tenerlo y lo _____.
5. Queremos bailar y _____.

6. Tú quieres hablar y _____.
7. Tú quieres volver y _____.
8. Ellos quieren sentarse y _____.
9. Juan quiere acostarse y _____.
10. Quieren ir y mañana _____.

The city of Chichén Itzá in Yucatan was originally built by the Mayas in A.D. 530. Under its Toltec-Aztec conquerors, it rose to prominence again around 1200. By using the corbelled arch, Mayan builders were able to make greater use of stone and produce massive structures that have withstood the rigors of time. This temple, built on a pyramid and reached by steep stairways, is characteristic of Mayan architectural style.

Escuchar y hablar

bailar to dance
bajar to go down
el comedor dining room
la cubierta deck
descansar to rest
habrá *3d pers. sing., fut. of* **haber** there will be
la medianoche midnight
el mediodía noon
la merienda light lunch, picnic lunch
mío my, of mine
muchísimo very much
nuestro of ours
el paisaje landscape
pasearse to stroll
por for; around
primero first

¡qué (linda)! how (pretty)!
segundo second
sobre on
subir to go up
suyo of his (hers, yours, theirs)
tanto so; so much
tercero third
el vapor steamer, boat
varios several

IDIOMS AND OTHER EXPRESSIONS

a bordo on board
a la luz (light) **de la luna** (moon) by moonlight
otra vez again
río arriba up the river
si las hay if there are any

UNA EXCURSIÓN EN VAPOR

Carlos ha dicho que un amigo suyo ha hecho una excursión río arriba en vapor. Fue muy agradable, y mañana nosotros también haremos la excursión.

Será mi primera excursión en vapor, pero para varios amigos míos será la segunda o la tercera.

Tendremos que salir de casa a las siete de la mañana. Virginia, Juan y su hermana María irán con nosotros. También irán otros amigos nuestros. Irán muchos alumnos de la universidad. Habrá tal vez noventa o cien personas a bordo.

Saldrá el vapor a las ocho y cuarto. Pasaremos la mañana paseándonos por la cubierta y mirando el paisaje. Al mediodía comeremos una merienda. Luego descansaremos un rato y como nos gusta tanto hablar español, lo hablaremos. Nos gustan las canciones españolas y las cantaremos.

Pasaremos la tarde divirtiéndonos en la cubierta, cantando y hablando.

A la hora de comer bajaremos al comedor. Después de comer subiremos otra vez a la cubierta. Habrá una buena orquesta a bordo y bailaremos a la luz de la luna.

Yo me pasearé con una amiga mía y bailaré con ella.

—¡Dios mío!—le diré—¡qué linda eres y qué bien bailas!

Compraré unas flores, si las hay a bordo, y se las daré.

¡Qué agradable será la excursión!

Estaremos a bordo hasta medianoche o hasta la una divirtiéndonos muchísimo.

PREGUNTAS

1. ¿Qué ha dicho Carlos?	11. ¿Qué cantaremos?
2. ¿Cómo fue la excursión?	12. ¿Cómo pasaremos la tarde?
3. ¿Qué haremos nosotros?	13. A la hora de comer, ¿adónde iremos?
4. ¿Quiénes irán con nosotros?	14. ¿Qué haremos después de comer?
5. ¿Cuántas personas habrá a bordo?	15. ¿Qué haremos por la noche?
6. ¿A qué hora saldrá el vapor?	16. ¿Qué habrá a bordo?
7. ¿Cómo pasaremos la mañana?	17. ¿Con quién se paseará Ud.?
8. ¿Qué haremos al mediodía?	18. ¿Qué le dirá Ud.?
9. ¿Qué haremos después?	19. ¿Qué comprará Ud., si las hay?
10. ¿Qué lengua hablaremos?	20. ¿Hasta qué hora estaremos a bordo?

Estructura

1. POSSESSIVE ADJECTIVES—STRESSED FORMS

mío, mía, míos, mías	my, mine, of mine
tuyo, tuya, tuyos, tuyas	yours, of yours
nuestro, nuestra, nuestros, nuestras	our, ours, of ours
(vuestro, vuestra, vuestros, vuestras)	yours, of yours
suyo, suya, suyos, suyas	yours (his, hers, theirs), of yours (his, hers, theirs)

The stressed forms of the possessive adjective follow the noun. Their forms are the same as those of the possessive pronouns (Lesson 13), but they are used without the accompanying definite article. Like the other possessives, they agree in gender and number with the thing possessed.

a. Their commonest meaning is *of mine, of yours,* etc.

   un amigo suyo   a friend of his (hers, yours, theirs)
   unas amigas mías   some friends of mine

b. They are used as predicate adjectives with the verb **ser**.

   ¿De quién es la corbata? Es *mía*.   Whose tie is it? It is *mine*.
   ¿De quién es el sombrero? Es *suyo*.   Whose hat is it? It is *yours* (*his, hers, theirs*).

c. **Suyo**, like **su** and **el suyo**, may be ambiguous. When it is, the phrases **de él, de ella, de usted, de ellos, de ellas,** or **de ustedes** are substituted for it.

   un libro de usted   a book of yours
   un tío de ellos   an uncle of theirs
   ¿Son de ustedes los libros?   Are the books yours?

d. **Mío** (*my*) and **nuestro** (*our*) are used in direct address and exclamations.

Hijo mío, ¿qué haces? Son (my son), what are you doing?
Padre nuestro que estás en los cielos . . . Our Father which art in Heaven . . .
¡Dios mío! My goodness!

PRÁCTICA

a. *Sustituya según el modelo.*

Son mis zapatos.
Son unos zapatos míos.

1. Es mi vestido.
2. Es su hermana.
3. Son tus amigos.
4. Son tus libros.
5. Es su profesor.
6. Es nuestra amiga.
7. Son nuestras chaquetas.
8. Son mis corbatas.

b. *Sustituya según el modelo.*

Es mi traje.
Es mío.

1. Es mi blusa.
2. Son mis calcetines.
3. Es su tienda.
4. Son sus guantes.
5. Son tus ejercicios.
6. Es nuestra finca.
7. Son nuestros libros.
8. Es tu casa.

c. *Diga en español, empleando dos formas, según el modelo.*

an uncle of his
un tío suyo
un tío de él

1. a tie of his
2. books of theirs
3. flowers of hers
4. a suit of yours
5. a farm of theirs
6. friends of his
7. a house of theirs
8. a brother of hers
9. a sister of yours
10. sisters of his

2. PRESENT PARTICIPLE

The present participle (English *speaking, learning,* etc.) is formed by adding
-ando to the infinitive stem of all regular and irregular verbs ending in **-ar** and
-iendo to the infinitive stem of all regular and most irregular verbs ending in
-er or **-ir**.

hablar:	**habl***ando*	speaking	**estar:**	**est***ando*	being
aprender:	**aprend***iendo*	learning	**ser:**	**s***iendo*	being
vivir:	**viv***iendo*	living	**ver:**	**v***iendo*	seeing

Stem-changing verbs ending in **-ir** change **e** to **i** and **o** to **u** in the present participle.

sentir:	**sint***iendo*	regretting
morir:	**mur***iendo*	dying
pedir:	**pid***iendo*	asking

Verbs like **leer** (whose stem ends in a strong vowel) change the **i** of the ending to **y: leyendo** (*reading*).

The following irregular verbs have irregular present participles.

decir:	**diciendo**	saying
ir:	**yendo**	going
poder:	**pudiendo**	being able

Object pronouns, including reflexives, follow and are attached to the present participle. A present participle with a pronoun attached requires a written accent.

Puesto que me gusta estudiar el español, pasé la tarde *estudiándolo*.   Since I like to study Spanish, I spent the afternoon *studying it.*

Pasaremos la mañana *paseándonos* por la cubierta.   We shall spend the morning *strolling* around the deck.

Estarán a bordo hasta la una *divirtiéndose muchísimo*.   They will be on board until one o'clock *having a very good time.*

PRÁCTICA

Conteste según el modelo.

¿Cómo pasarás la tarde? ¿Vas a estudiar?
Pasaré la tarde estudiando.

1. ¿Vas a aprender?
2. ¿Vas a escribir?
3. ¿Vas a leer?
4. ¿Vas a pasearte?
5. ¿Vas a divertirte?

6. ¿Vas a dormir?
7. ¿Vas a vestirte?
8. ¿Vas a cantar?
9. ¿Vas a comer?
10. ¿Vas a bailar?

3. ORDINAL NUMBERS

primer(o)	first		**sexto**	sixth
segundo	second		**séptimo**	seventh
tercer(o)	third		**octavo**	eighth
cuarto	fourth		**noveno**	ninth
quinto	fifth		**décimo**	tenth

The ordinal numbers agree in gender and number with the nouns they modify. Beyond **décimo** they are normally replaced by the cardinal numbers.

Ordinal numbers may precede or follow their nouns. They follow when they denote a member of a recognized series. **Primero** and **tercero** drop the **-o** when they precede a masculine singular noun. The definite article is not used in titles as in English (*Charles the Fifth*, etc.).

el primer libro   the first book
libro primero   Book One
las primeras flores de mayo   the first flowers of May
la cuarta lección   the fourth lesson
lección cuarta   Lesson Four
Carlos Quinto   Charles the Fifth
Alfonso Trece   Alfonso the Thirteenth

PRÁCTICA

Diga en español.

1. the first day
2. the first class
3. the second lesson
4. Lesson Two
5. the third man
6. the third person
7. Charles the Fourth
8. the fifth week
9. the sixth house
10. the seventh month
11. Fernando the Seventh
12. the eighth time
13. the ninth day
14. Alfonso the Tenth
15. Alfonso the Thirteenth

Tareas

Diga en español.

1. Tomorrow I'll go on a boat trip up the river.
2. Some friends of mine and some friends of yours will go with me.
3. It will be my first trip by boat.
4. I'll leave at nine-thirty.
5. I'll spend the morning strolling around the deck and looking at the landscape.
6. At noon I'll eat a picnic lunch.
7. In the afternoon we'll sing Cuban songs.
8. After dinner we'll go up on deck again.
9. There will be a good orchestra on board which will play in the evening.
10. Our sweethearts will be with us, and we'll dance by moonlight.
11. We'll be on board until midnight having a very good time.
12. My goodness! How interesting it will be!

Composición oral o escrita.

Tell about a boat trip that you (*singular*) will take next week.

Diálogo

¡TÚ EN MÉXICO!

Carlos se encuentra con Rafael y su amigo Arturo en el Zócalo de México.

RAFAEL—¡Hombre! ¡Tú en México! ¡Cuánto me alegro[1] de verte! ¿Cómo te va?[2]

CARLOS—Perfectamente. Y tú, ¿cómo estás?

RAFAEL—Muy bien. Pero, ¿cuándo llegaste? Yo no sabía que venías a México.

CARLOS—Llegué anoche. Tenía la intención[3] de llamarte por teléfono.[4]

RAFAEL—Éste es mi amigo Arturo.

CARLOS—Tanto gusto.[5]

ARTURO—El gusto es mío.

RAFAEL—¿Cuánto tiempo estarás aquí?

CARLOS—Pienso quedarme quince días.[6]

RAFAEL—¡Qué bueno![7] Oye. Mañana vamos a Xochimilco. ¿No quieres acompañarnos? Irá toda mi familia. Tendrás la oportunidad[8] de conocerlos.

CARLOS—Muchas gracias. Será un gran placer.[9]

RAFAEL—Lo encontrarás muy interesante. Verás las islas flotantes.[10] Verás los hermosos jardines.[11] Nos pasearemos[13] por los famosos canales. Y comeremos platos típicos mexicanos.

[1] ¡Cuánto me alegro! *How happy I am!*
[2] ¿Cómo te va? *How are you? How goes it with you?*
[3] tener la intención *to intend*
[4] llamar por teléfono *to phone, call (on the telephone)*
[5] Tanto gusto. *Pleased to meet you.*
[6] quince días *two weeks*
[7] ¡Qué bueno! *How nice!*
[8] la oportunidad *opportunity*
[9] el placer *pleasure*
[10] isla flotante *floating island*
[11] el jardín *garden*
[12] nos pasearemos *we'll ride*

PREGUNTAS PERSONALES

1. ¿Irá Ud. a México algún día?
2. ¿Irá Ud. en coche?
3. ¿Quiénes irán con Ud.?
4. ¿Estudiará Ud. en una universidad mexicana?
5. ¿Trabajará Ud. en México?
6. ¿Comprará Ud. regalos para sus padres?
7. ¿Visitará Ud. Xochimilco?
8. ¿Qué verá Ud. allí?
9. ¿Qué comerá Ud. allí?

One result of Mexico's Revolution of 1910 was a great flourishing of mural art. Murals depicting Mexican history by Diego Rivera, a leader in the new movement, adorn the walls of the National Palace.

10. ¿Le gustarán los platos típicos mexicanos?
11. ¿Le gustará la música mexicana?
12. ¿Vivirá Ud. mucho tiempo en México?
13. ¿Cuánto tiempo pasará Ud. en México?
14. Ud. se divertirá mucho en México, ¿verdad?
15. ¿Volverá Ud. en coche?

Notas culturales

We have seen how two proposed terms for Latin America—*Indoamérica* and *Eurindia*—were designed to emphasize the ethnic and cultural inheritance of the indigenous races of the area. In pre-Columbian times the three most important peoples of the New World were the Incas in Peru and the Mayas and Aztecs in Middle America. (The Aztecs and Incas will be discussed in following chapters.)

The Mayas

At about the beginning of the Christian Era the Mayas evolved a civilization in Middle America. Their civilization flourished between A.D. 300 and 900 in what is now Guatemala, Honduras, El Salvador, and southern Mexico. Thereafter they declined in prosperity, abandoned their cities, and emigrated to Yucatán, where their civilization had a second flowering from about 1000 to 1400. During that time they were conquered by the Toltecs, who preceded the Aztecs in Mexico and whose culture fused with the Mayan.

The Mayas were creative people whose cities contained pyramids and magnificent temples and palaces decorated with colorful frescoes and brilliantly painted sculptures. They were also skilled engineers who built good bridges and roads that were surfaced with cement and sloped to the sides, allowing water to run off. The Mayas possessed a hieroglyphic written language recorded on deerskin or paper of maguey fiber and often cut into stone. Highly advanced in mathematics, they used a vigesimal numerical system and discovered the concept of zero. Their astronomical knowledge enabled them to develop a calendar more accurate than any other invented before the sixteenth-century Gregorian.

Present-day descendants of the Mayas number about two million, and most of them occupy the same territory as did their ancestors. They have retained their language, but their culture is now a mixture of pre-Columbian Indian and European.

Santiago Tlatelolco in Mexico City, showing ruins of an Aztec market, a Spanish colonial church, and modern apartment buildings.

15

Más vale poco que nada.
A little is better than nothing.

Conditional of regular verbs

The conditional tense, like the future (Lesson 14), is formed by adding certain endings to the whole infinitive. The conditional endings are

-ía	-íamos
-ías	(-íais)
-ía	-ían

hablar

hablaría	I would speak	hablaríamos	we would speak
hablarías	you would speak	(hablaríais)	you would speak
hablaría	he (she) would speak	hablarían	they would speak

aprender		vivir	
aprendería	aprenderíamos	viviría	viviríamos
aprenderías	(aprenderíais)	vivirías	(viviríais)
aprendería	aprenderían	viviría	vivirían

Note the written accent on the first **i** of the ending throughout.

193

PRÁCTICA

Cambie según se indica, siguiendo el modelo.

Sabían que él cantaría. (Uds.)
Sabían que Uds. cantarían.

1. Sabían que *él* cantaría.
   yo / tú / nosotros / Ud. / Ud. y yo / ellos

2. Parecía que *Ud.* volvería.
   nosotros / Uds. / yo / tú / ellos / ella

3. Expliqué que *nosotros* escribiríamos.
   yo / tú y yo / ellos / tú / Ud. / él

Irregular conditionals

Whenever the stem of the future is irregular, the same irregularity is found in the conditional. Here are the conditionals of each of the four irregular verbs whose futures you learned in Lesson 14. (Only the first person singular of each is given.)

INFINITIVE	FUTURE	CONDITIONAL
hacer	**haré**	**haría** I would do, make
decir	**diré**	**diría** I would say
salir	**saldré**	**saldría** I would leave
tener	**tendré**	**tendría** I would have

PRÁCTICA

Cambie según se indica.

1. Explicaron que *yo* lo haría.
   tú / Ud. / nosotros / él / ellas

2. Sabían que *tú* lo dirías.
   yo / ellos / Ud. / Ud. y yo / Uds.

3. Parecía que *Ud.* no saldría.
   Uds. / tú / nosotros / yo / tú y yo / él

4. Dijo que *él* lo tendría.
   tú / yo / nosotros / Uds. / ellos

More irregular futures and conditionals

INFINITIVE	FUTURE	CONDITIONAL	
querer	querré	querría	I would wish
saber	sabré	sabría	I would know
poder	podré	podría	I would be able
haber	habré	habría	I would have (gone, etc.)
poner	pondré	pondría	I would put, place
venir	vendré	vendría	I would come
valer	valdré	valdría	I would be worth

PRÁCTICA

a. *Cambie el singular por el plural, según el modelo.*

Yo querré hablar.
Nosotros querremos hablar.

1. Yo sabré estudiar.
2. Tú podrás hacerlo.
3. Él se pondrá la chaqueta.
4. Yo vendré pronto.
5. La casa valdrá mucho.
6. Tú querrás salir.

7. Yo sabría estudiar.
8. Tú podrías hacerlo.
9. Él se pondría la chaqueta.
10. Yo vendría pronto.
11. La casa valdría mucho.
12. Tú querrías salir.

b. *Cambie el plural por el singular, según el modelo.*

Uds. podrán volver pronto.
Ud. podrá volver pronto.

1. Ellos sabrán estudiar.
2. Ellas podrán hacerlo.
3. Nosotros nos pondremos el abrigo.
4. Nosotros vendremos pronto.
5. Los libros valdrán mucho.
6. Nosotros querremos salir.

7. Ellos sabrían estudiar.
8. Nosotros podríamos hacerlo.
9. Nosotros nos pondríamos el sombrero.
10. Ellas vendrían pronto.
11. Los libros valdrían mucho.
12. Nosotros querríamos salir.

Escuchar y hablar

la cancha (tennis) court
el chico boy, fellow
desocupado unoccupied, free
esperar to wait
el gasto expense
generoso generous
el gimnasio gymnasium
ligero light
más . . . que more than
mayor older, oldest
el minuto minute
pesar to weigh
prometer to promise
quedarse to remain, stay
la raqueta racket
responder to answer

solo alone
el tío uncle

IDIOMS AND OTHER EXPRESSIONS

¿Dónde estará Juan? Where can John be?
a estas horas at this time
de al lado next
me gusta más I like (it) better
pasar por aquí to come by here
(las tres) en punto (three o'clock) sharp
querer decir to mean
sabrás you must know, you probably know
más tiempo longer
vale la pena it's worth while

UN PARTIDO DE TENIS

VIRGINIA—¿Dónde estará tu hermano mayor?

MARÍA—¿Juan? Estará jugando al tenis o estará en el gimnasio. Tú sabrás que le gustan los deportes. Todos los días a estas horas va al gimnasio o juega al tenis o al béisbol.

VIRGINIA—Eso querrá decir que no vendrá a buscarme. Son las tres y media ya. Anoche prometió que vendría por mí a las tres y que jugaríamos un partido de tenis. Me prometió que pasaría por aquí a las tres en punto. Ahora tendré que quedarme en casa. ¡No podría ir sola!

MARÍA—No valdría la pena esperar más tiempo. Pero no tendrás que quedarte en casa. Yo me pondré los zapatos de tenis, buscaré mi raqueta, e iré contigo.

(*Quince minutos después—en las canchas de tenis.*)

VIRGINIA—Esa raqueta tuya me gusta más que la mía. Parece más ligera que ésta.

MARÍA—Esta raqueta es un regalo de un tío mío. Me la regaló cuando volví a la universidad esta semana. Me dio también cien dólares para los gastos de la universidad.

VIRGINIA—Ese tío tuyo es más generoso que mi padre. ¡Él no me dio tanto!

MARÍA—¡Mira! Hay dos canchas desocupadas. ¿Prefieres ésta o aquélla? Ésta más cerca es más interesante que aquélla. ¡Porque en la cancha de al lado están jugando aquellos dos chicos tan guapos!

VIRGINIA—¡Sí, claro! ¡Vamos a tomar ésta! Es la más interesante.

PREGUNTAS

1. ¿Qué pregunta Virginia?
2. ¿Qué responde María?
3. ¿Qué le gusta a Juan?
4. ¿Adónde va Juan todos los días a estas horas?
5. ¿A qué juega?
6. ¿Qué hora es?
7. ¿Qué prometió Juan anoche?
8. ¿Qué tendría que hacer Virginia?
9. ¿Qué no podría hacer Virginia?
10. ¿Qué le dice María?
11. ¿Qué se pondrá María?
12. ¿Qué buscará?
13. ¿Cuál de las raquetas le gusta más a Virginia?
14. ¿Por qué?
15. ¿Quién le regaló la raqueta a María?
16. ¿Cómo es el tío de María?
17. ¿Cuál de las canchas prefieren las señoritas?
18. ¿Por qué?

Estructura

1. SPECIAL USES OF THE FUTURE AND CONDITIONAL

In Spanish the future tense is also used to express conjecture or probability in present time. The English equivalent is in the present tense and uses expressions such as *probably, must, I wonder, do you suppose,* and *can.*

¿Dónde estará Juan?   Where can John be? I wonder where John is. Where do you suppose John is?

Estará en el gimnasio.   He is probably in the gymnasium. He must be in the gymnasium.

Tú lo sabrás.   You must know it. You probably know it.

The conditional tense expresses the same ideas in past time.

¿Dónde estaría Juan ayer?   Where could John have been yesterday? I wonder where John was yesterday. Where do you suppose John was yesterday?

Estaría en el gimnasio.   He probably was in the gymnasium. He must have been in the gymnasium.

Tú lo sabrías.   You must have known it. You probably knew it.

PRÁCTICA

a. *Diga en español.*

1. María is probably at home.
2. She is probably studying.
3. She probably works a lot.
4. She must like to play tennis.
5. She must like horses.

b. *Diga en español.*

1. Where do you suppose Juan and Carlos were?
2. What do you suppose they were doing?
3. Where do you suppose they went?
4. They probably were in the gymnasium.
5. They probably played tennis, too.
6. They probably didn't study.

2. THE PROGRESSIVE CONSTRUCTION: ESTAR *PLUS THE PRESENT PARTICIPLE*

Estar plus the present participle forms the progressive tense. This tense is used to express an action *in progress at the moment*. It stresses the fact that the action is actually in progress.

    Están jugando al tenis ahora.   They're playing tennis now.
    María está leyendo ahora.   Mary is reading now.

Otherwise the simple present tense expresses English *to be* plus the present participle.

    Estudiamos matemáticas este año.   We're studying math this year.
    Aprende mucho en la universidad.   He is learning a lot at the university.

Note that the present participle of **ir (yendo)** is not used in the progressive construction.

    Vamos a comer ahora.   We're going to eat now.
    Va a jugar al béisbol.   He's going to play baseball.

Object pronouns following a present participle are attached to the participle. When pronouns are added, the participle takes a written accent over the **-ándo** or **-iéndo.**

    Estoy estudiándolo.   I am studying it.
    Están vistiéndose.   They are getting dressed.

But in progressive tenses object pronouns may come before **estar**.

> **Lo estoy estudiando.**
> **Se están vistiendo.**

Other tenses of **estar** may be used to form the progressive.

> **Estaba tocando el piano cuando entré.**   She was playing the piano when I came in.
> **Estará jugando al tenis.**   He is probably playing tennis.

PRÁCTICA

Cambie según los modelos.

a. **Leo mucho.**
   Pero no estoy leyendo ahora.

   1. Trabajo mucho.
   2. Como mucho.
   3. Estudio mucho.
   4. Escribo mucho.
   5. Juego mucho.

b. **Hablan mucho, ¿verdad?**
   Sí, pero no están hablando ahora.

   1. Aprenden mucho, ¿verdad?
   2. Cantan mucho, ¿verdad?
   3. Juegan mucho, ¿verdad?
   4. Bailan mucho, ¿verdad?
   5. Comen mucho, ¿verdad?

c. **¿Se divierten mucho?**
   Sí, están divirtiéndose ahora.
   Se están divirtiendo ahora.

   1. ¿Se pasean mucho?
   2. ¿Se bañan mucho?
   3. ¿Se visten temprano?
   4. ¿Se levantan temprano?
   5. ¿Se acuestan temprano?

3. COMPARISON OF ADJECTIVES AND ADVERBS

The comparative of adjectives and adverbs is formed with **más** (*more*) or **menos** (*less*). The superlative is the same in form, but its meaning is made clear by the context. With both the comparative and the superlative of adjectives, the definite article is used or omitted depending on the meaning, just as in English.

POSITIVE	COMPARATIVE AND SUPERLATIVE
alto tall	**(el) más alto** (the) taller, tallest
caro expensive	**(el) menos caro** (the) less (least) expensive
cerca near	**más cerca** nearer, nearest

María es inteligente, Juan es más inteligente, pero Carlos es el más inteligente.
Mary is intelligent, Juan is more intelligent, but Charles is the most intelligent.
Paca es la más bonita de las dos.   Paca is the prettier of the two.
Es la más bonita de todas.   She's the prettiest of all.
Éstos son mis zapatos más nuevos.   These are my newest shoes.

In comparisons, **que** is used for English *than*. However, **de** is used before numerals.

Esa raqueta es más ligera que ésta.   That racket is lighter than this one.
Esta cancha está más cerca que aquélla.   This court is nearer than that one.
Tengo más de cien pesos.   I have more than a hundred pesos.

After a superlative, **de** is used for English *in*.

Carlos es el alumno más inteligente de la clase.   Charles is the most intelligent student in the class.
Ésa es la ciudad más pintoresca de Guatemala.   That's the most picturesque city in Guatemala.

PRÁCTICA

Cambie según los modelos.

a. **Juan es muy alto. (Carlos)**
   Es más alto que Carlos.

1. María es muy pequeña. (Virginia)
2. Esta lección es muy fácil. (la otra)
3. Estos calcetines son muy caros. (ésos)
4. Ellos son muy inteligentes. (yo)
5. Esa raqueta es muy ligera. (la mía)
6. Su padre es muy rico. (el mío)

b. **Ése es muy inteligente.**
   Sí, es el más inteligente de todos.

1. Ése es muy viejo.
2. Ésa es muy rica.
3. Ésos son muy interesantes.
4. Ésas son muy hermosas.
5. Ése es muy pobre.
6. Ésos son muy baratos.
7. Ése es muy joven.
8. Ésas son muy pequeñas.

c. **Ése es el hombre más rico. (la ciudad)**
   Ése es el hombre más rico de la ciudad.

1. Ésa es la casa más vieja. (la ciudad)
2. Ésa es la chica más guapa. (el mundo)
3. Ése es el chico más perezoso. (la clase)
4. Ése es el restorán más caro. (el país)

d. **¿Es caro el traje?**
   Es menos caro que el otro.

1. ¿Es interesante el libro?
2. ¿Es difícil la lección?
3. ¿Es inteligente el chico?
4. ¿Es divertida la película?

e. **¿Tienes veinte pesos?**
   Tengo más de veinte pesos.

1. ¿Tienes dos camisas?
2. ¿Tienes diecisiete años?
3. ¿Tienes seis hermanos?
4. ¿Tienes cuatro boletos?

Markets are a way of life in South America. This one in Guadalajara, Mexico, is open every day of the week and features everything from fresh produce to local handicrafts.

4. IRREGULAR COMPARISONS OF ADJECTIVES

The following four adjectives have irregular comparisons:

POSITIVE	COMPARATIVE AND SUPERLATIVE
bueno good	**(el) mejor** (the) better, best
malo bad	**(el) peor** (the) worse, worst
grande large	**(el) mayor** (the) older, oldest
	(the) larger, largest
pequeño small	**(el) menor** (the) younger, youngest
	(the) smaller, smallest

Grande and **pequeño** also have regular forms **(más grande, más pequeño)** which refer strictly to size (*larger, smaller*). **Mayor** and **menor** usually, though not always, refer to age (*older, younger*), in which case they follow the noun. **Mejor** and **peor** regularly precede the noun.

> **Juan es el hermano mayor de María.**   John is Mary's older brother.
> **María es la hija menor.**   Mary is the youngest daughter.
> **Lima es la ciudad más grande del Perú.**   Lima is the largest city in Peru.
> **Pepe es el mejor alumno de la clase.**   Pepe is the best student in the class.

PRÁCTICA

Conteste según el modelo.

¿Es ésta la mejor película?
No, es la peor.

1. ¿Es éste el peor mes del año?
2. ¿Es ésta la mejor camisa?
3. ¿Son éstos los mejores zapatos?
4. ¿Son éstas las peores medias?
5. ¿Es ésta la hermana menor?
6. ¿Es éste el hermano mayor?
7. ¿Es ésta la ciudad más grande del país?
8. ¿Es éste el país más pequeño de
   Hispanoamérica?

5. IRREGULAR COMPARISONS OF ADVERBS

Four adverbs have irregular comparisons:

POSITIVE	COMPARATIVE AND SUPERLATIVE
mucho much	**más** more, most
poco little	**menos** less, least
bien well	**mejor** better, best
mal badly	**peor** worse, worst

Yo trabajo mucho, pero él trabaja más.
Yo como poco, pero ella come menos.
Él canta bien, pero ella canta mejor.
Ella escribe mal, pero yo escribo peor.

PRÁCTICA

Conteste según el modelo.

¿Trabaja Ud. más que Juan?
No, trabajo menos que Juan.

1. ¿Estudia Ud. más que Pepe?
2. ¿Hace Ud. menos que Lola?
3. ¿Aprende Ud. más que Ernesto?
4. ¿Habla Ud. menos que José?
5. ¿Canta Ud. mejor que Ana?
6. ¿Escribe Ud. peor que Dolores?
7. ¿Juega Ud. mejor que Roberto?
8. ¿Baila Ud. peor que su amigo?

Tareas

Diga en español.

1. "Where can Juan be?" Virginia asked María.
2. He must be playing tennis.
3. You probably know that he goes to the gymnasium at this time every day.
4. Then he won't come for me.
5. He promised her that he would come for her at three o'clock sharp and that they would play a game of tennis.
6. It wouldn't be worth while to wait for him, but you won't have to stay home.
7. I'll put on my tennis shoes and go with you.
8. I like that racket of yours better than mine.
9. It is lighter than mine.
10. It is a gift of a very generous uncle of hers.
11. That uncle of yours is more generous than my father.
12. Which tennis court do you prefer: that one or this one?
13. That court is more interesting than this one, because those two good-looking fellows are playing in the next court.
14. Let's take the more interesting court!

Despite the rigors of climate at high altitudes, sixty percent of Bolivia's population lives in the Altiplano, the Andean plateau, at elevations up to 14000 feet above sea level. Nowhere else in the world do industrialized cities, towns, railroads, and highways exist at such elevations. These Indian children attend school in the mining town of Llallagua.

Composición oral o escrita.

Suppose you could go on a boat trip up the river today. Tell what time you would leave, what friends would go with you, how you would spend the day (you would stroll around the deck, you would sing Spanish songs, you would have a picnic lunch, etc.), and what time you would return home.

Diálogo

ERNESTO TIENE UN PROBLEMA

ERNESTO—Tengo un problema. ¿Quieres ayudarme?

PEPITO—¡Cómo no! ¿Cuál es tu problema?

ERNESTO—¿Conoces a Lola?

PEPITO—¿Esa rubia? ¡Ya lo creo![1] Es la más linda[2] de todas estas chicas.

ERNESTO—Pues, estoy chiflado por[3] ella y ni siquiera quiere mirarme.[4] Tú que yo,[5] ¿qué harías?

PEPITO—La llamaría por teléfono y le pediría una cita.

ERNESTO—Cuando llamo, siempre dicen que no está en casa.

PEPITO—Entonces le enviaría[6] flores.

ERNESTO—No le gustan las flores. Tiene una alergia.[7]

PEPITO—Pues, entonces le escribiría invitándola al baile[8] de la semana que viene.[9]

ERNESTO—No contestaría.

PEPITO—En ese caso,[10] no haría nada. No pensaría más en ella.[11]

ERNESTO—Eso sería imposible. Pero tú podrías ayudarme.

PEPITO—¿Cómo?

ERNESTO—Podrías hablar con ella.

PEPITO—¿Para qué?

ERNESTO—Para decirle que estoy loco por ella.

PEPITO—No, no podría hacer eso.

ERNESTO—¿Por qué no?

PEPITO—Porque yo también estoy chiflado por esa rubia.

[1]¡Ya lo creo! *I should say so!*

[2]linda *pretty*

[3]estar chiflado (loco) por *to be crazy about*

[4]ni siquiera quiere mirarme *she won't even look at me*

[5]tú que yo *if you were I*

[6]enviar *to send*

[7]la alergia *allergy*

[8]el baile *dance*

[9]de la semana que viene *next week's*

[10]en ese caso *in that case*

[11]No pensaría más en ella. *I'd forget her.*

PREGUNTAS PERSONALES

1. ¿Querría Ud. ser rico (rica)?
2. En ese caso, ¿sería Ud. feliz?
3. En ese caso, ¿tendría Ud. que trabajar mucho?
4. En ese caso, no trabajaría tanto, ¿verdad?
5. En ese caso, ¿estudiaría Ud. tanto?
6. En ese caso, ¿comería todos los días en un buen restorán?
7. En ese caso, ¿pagaría Ud. siempre la cuenta en el restorán?
8. En ese caso, ¿preferiría Ud. estudiar en una universidad española?
9. En ese caso, ¿visitaría a sus amigos en España?
10. En ese caso, ¿me llevaría Ud. a Europa?
11. En ese caso, ¿iría Ud. a México?
12. En ese caso, ¿le gustaría ir a Chile?
13. En ese caso, ¿pasaría Ud. siempre las vacaciones en Hispanoamérica?
14. En ese caso, ¿les daría Ud. muchos regalos a sus amigos?
15. En ese caso, ¿compraría Ud. un coche nuevo?
16. En ese caso, ¿me daría Ud. noventa dólares?
17. En ese caso, ¿me prestaría cien dólares?
18. En ese caso, ¿me pagaría lo que me debe?

Notas culturales

The Aztecs

Less creative than the Mayas, the Aztecs were a warrior nation that occupied central Mexico from coast to coast in the fifteenth and early sixteenth centuries. Their impressive capital, Tenochtitlán (where Mexico City now stands), lay on islands in a lake and was joined to the mainland by causeways. Rather than cultural innovators, the Aztecs were borrowers who assimilated much from the Mayas and Toltecs—the peoples they conquered. With them they shared the pyramidal style of temple architecture. They built impressive roads and aqueducts. A feature of Aztec agriculture was the "floating gardens," patches of reclaimed swampland used for raising crops. They developed a form of picture writing on skins and cloth. Their practical knowledge of astronomy, botany, and medicine was considerable. Aztec craftsmen were fine jewelers, working in gold, silver, jade, and turquoise, and were excellent potters and weavers. They were skillful in featherwork and created cloaks and ceremonial garments that were brilliant mosaics of feathers.

The Aztecs had a complex social and political organization. But under a system more democratic than that of the Incas each family was allotted sufficient land for its maintenance. Religion was a central element of Aztec life and they had many gods. The rites of the temple required human sacrifice, and as the power of the Aztecs grew, the number of sacrifices increased.

Diplomacy was not the Aztecs' strong point—they did not know how to gain the friendship of the peoples they conquered. Consequently, when the Spaniards came to the New World, they were able to convince other Indian tribes to help them conquer the Aztecs.

The language of the Aztecs was Nahua, which is of the same linguistic family as one of the tongues spoken by the Indians in the United States. Today over one million people in Mexico still speak Nahua.

16

No dejes para mañana lo que puedas hacer hoy.
Don't put off till tomorrow what you can do today.

Present subjunctive of regular verbs

The present subjunctive of all regular and of most irregular verbs is formed by adding the following endings to the stem of the first person singular of the present indicative:

FIRST CONJUGATION		SECOND AND THIRD CONJUGATIONS	
-e	-emos	-a	-amos
-es	(-éis)	-as	(-áis)
-e	-en	-a	-an

hablar		aprender		vivir	
hable	hablemos	aprenda	aprendamos	viva	vivamos
hables	(habléis)	aprendas	(aprendáis)	vivas	(viváis)
hable	hablen	aprenda	aprendan	viva	vivan

The subjunctive has various meanings, which will be explained to you as you study its uses. It is most frequently used in clauses introduced by **que** (*that*) or some other conjunction.

Ojalá que aprendan mucho.   I hope (that) they learn a lot.

207

PRÁCTICA

Cambie según los modelos.

a. **Ojalá que Uds. compren el coche. (él)**
   Ojalá que él compre el coche.

   1. Ojalá que compren la casa.
      ella / tú / nosotros / Uds. / Pepe / mis padres

   2. Ojalá que Uds. aprendan mucho.
      yo / tú / ellas / él / nosotros / Ud.

b. **Ojalá que cantes bien. (bailar)**
   Ojalá que bailes bien.

   1. Ojalá que cantes bien.
      escuchar / escribir / contestar / leer

   2. Ojalá que él escriba pronto.
      bajar / aprender / cantar / subir

   3. Ojalá que aprendamos mucho.
      leer / comprar / comer / bailar

   4. Ojalá que no esperen mucho tiempo.
      cantar / leer / hablar / escribir

Escuchar y hablar

el apartamento apartment
el ascensor elevator
así so, thus
el avión plane, airplane
bajar (de) to go down; to get out of, off (*a vehicle*)
el coche car
el convidado guest
cortés polite
la costumbre custom
la criada maid, servant
delante de in front of
encantado delighted (to meet you)
enseñar to show

estacionar to park
funcionar to work, run
grande, gran great
la impresión impression
Jaime James
el piso floor; **el piso bajo** ground floor; **el piso principal** main floor
presentar to introduce
la realidad reality
Santo, San Saint
la sicología psychology
simplemente simply
último last
el viaje trip

IDIOMS AND OTHER EXPRESSIONS

en avión   by plane
hacer un viaje   to take (make) a trip
hay que + *infin.*   one must, it is
   necessary to
de modo que   so (that)

pase Ud.   come in
Tengo mucho gusto en conocerlo.   I am
   pleased to meet you. How do you do?
tomar el pelo   to kid, to pull someone's
   leg

ENTREMOS EN LA CASA DE JAIME

Hemos hecho un viaje a España. Es nuestro primer viaje, pero no será el
último. Hicimos el viaje en avión. En Madrid hemos conocido[1] a un joven
español muy simpático que se llama Jaime Montero. Nos hemos visto casi
todos los días y él nos ha enseñado casi toda la gran ciudad. Esta tarde nos ha
invitado a ir a su casa para conocer a su familia. Jaime ha estacionado el coche
en la calle de San Ildefonso delante de una gran casa de apartamentos.

JAIME—Ésta es su casa. Entremos para conocer a mi familia.
CARLOS—¿Nuestra casa?
JAIME—Naturalmente quiero decir que es mía. Pero a nosotros no nos parece
   muy cortés decir simplemente que es nuestra. De modo que al enseñársela
   por primera vez a un amigo, le decimos que es su casa. Es la costumbre
   española. Vivimos en el primer piso. Tomemos el ascensor, pues.
CARLOS—¡Jaime! ¡No nos tomes el pelo! ¡Que tomen los otros el ascensor!
   Si Uds. viven en el primer piso, yo me quedo aquí. No hay que subir.
MARÍA—¡Que se quede aquí este chico! Yo comprendo que hay que subir.
   Aquí estamos en el piso bajo. Luego viene el piso principal y luego el primer
   piso. En realidad Uds. viven en el tercer piso, pero los españoles lo llaman
   primer piso, ¿no es verdad?
JAIME—Así es. Y es muy buena sicología cuando no funciona el ascensor.
   ¡Bueno, pues, subamos!

Toda la familia Montero está en casa. Jaime nos presenta a su mamá, doña
Matilde, a su padre, don Ricardo, y a sus dos hermanos menores y a su hermana
mayor.

DOÑA MATILDE—Tengo mucho gusto en conocerlos. Encantada. Pasen
   Uds. Siéntense.
DON RICARDO—Sí, sentémonos y hablemos de sus primeras impresiones de
   España.
DOÑA MATILDE—Beatriz, hija, llama a la criada. Que prepare café para
   nuestros convidados.

NOTA

1. **Conocer** often means *to meet*, especially in past tenses.

   Los conocí ayer.   I met them yesterday.
   Hemos conocido a un joven español.   We have met a young Spaniard.

PREGUNTAS

1. ¿Qué hemos hecho?
2. ¿Cómo hemos venido a Madrid?
3. ¿A quién hemos conocido en Madrid?
4. ¿Cómo se llama el joven español?
5. ¿Qué nos ha enseñado Jaime?
6. ¿A dónde nos ha invitado?
7. ¿Dónde ha estacionado el coche?
8. ¿Qué nos dice al estacionar el coche?
9. ¿En qué piso vive su familia?
10. ¿Qué exclama Carlos?
11. ¿Por qué hay que tomar el ascensor?
12. ¿Qué explica María?
13. ¿Quiénes están en la casa de Jaime?
14. ¿Qué nos dice doña Matilde al conocernos?
15. ¿Qué nos dice después?
16. ¿Qué nos dice don Ricardo?
17. ¿Qué le dice doña Matilde a su hija mayor?

Estructura

1. THE SUBJUNCTIVE IN COMMANDS

Since Lesson 5 you have been using the third person singular and plural of the subjunctive with Ud. and Uds. to express formal commands.

   Aprenda Ud.   Learn.   **Siéntense Uds.**   Sit down.

The first person plural of the subjunctive also expresses commands (*Let's . . .*).

   Entremos en la casa.   Let's go in the house.
   Tomemos el ascensor.   Let's take the elevator.
   Subamos.   Let's go up.

Object pronouns, including the reflexive pronoun **nos**, follow this form in the affirmative and are attached to it. Note that a written accent is then required. Note also that reflexive verbs drop the final **-s** before adding **nos**.

    Tomémos*lo*. Let's take *it*.   **Sentémo*nos*.** Let's sit down.

But:

    No *lo* tomemos. Let's not take *it*.
    No *nos* sentemos aquí. Let's not sit down here.

PRÁCTICA

Conteste según los modelos.

a. **Preferimos entrar.**
   Entremos.

   1. Preferimos bajar.
   2. Preferimos escribir.
   3. Preferimos trabajar.
   4. Preferimos vivir.

b. **Queremos tomarlo.**
   Tomémoslo.

   1. Queremos comerlo.
   2. Queremos escribirlo.
   3. Queremos aprenderla.
   4. Queremos leerlas.

c. **Preferimos sentarnos.**
   Sentémonos.

   1. Preferimos bañarnos.
   2. Preferimos levantarnos.
   3. Preferimos lavarnos.
   4. Preferimos acostarnos.

d. **No queremos tomarlo.**
   No lo tomemos.

   1. No queremos comerlo.
   2. No queremos escribirlo.
   3. No queremos aprenderla.
   4. No queremos leerlas.

2. INDIRECT COMMANDS

An indirect command is expressed with the third person singular or plural of the present subjunctive. This is the equivalent of English *let* or *have* plus a verb. **Que** usually introduces the indirect command. Object pronouns precede the verb. Notice that in the examples the subject follows the verb, but subject pronouns are used only for emphasis.

    Que prepare café. Let her (Have her) prepare coffee.
    Que lo prepare. Let her (Have her) prepare it.
    Que lo prepare *ella*. Let *her* prepare it.
    Que se queden aquí. Let them stay here.
    Que lo escriba Inés. Let Inés write it.

Sometimes—usually in set phrases—this construction is equivalent to English *may*, expressed or unexpressed, plus a verb. Here **que** is often omitted.

    ¡Viva el Presidente! Long live the President!
    ¡No lo quiera Dios! (May) God forbid (it).
    Que duerma bien. (May you) sleep well.

Senior citizens in Madrid. In the Hispanic world family loyalty remains strong; the elderly are better provided for than in many other countries.

PRÁCTICA

a. *Conteste según el modelo.*

Juan quiere trabajar.
Que trabaje, pues.

1. Dolores quiere cantar.
2. Ellos quieren leer.
3. Ramón quiere descansar.
4. Ellas quieren comer.
5. Don Ricardo quiere escuchar.
6. Ellos quieren aprender.

b. *Conteste según el modelo.*

¿Lo compro yo o lo compra él?
Que lo compre él.

1. ¿Lo escribo yo o lo escribe ella?
2. ¿Lo pago yo o lo paga él?
3. ¿Lo estaciono yo o lo estaciona él?
4. ¿Lo leo yo o lo lee ella?
5. ¿Lo pregunto yo o lo pregunta él?

3. FAMILIAR COMMANDS

You learned in Lesson 5 that the singular of the familiar imperative has the same form, for most verbs, as the third person singular of the present indicative.

habla (tú) speak   **aprende (tú)** learn   **escribe (tú)** write

You also learned that in reflexive verbs the reflexive pronoun **te** follows and is attached to this affirmative form.

siéntate (tú) sit down   **duérmete (tú)** go to sleep

PRÁCTICA

Conteste según el modelo.

Quiero levantarme.
Pues, levántate.

1. Quiero sentarme.
2. Quiero bañarme.
3. Quiero vestirme.
4. Quiero despedirme.
5. Quiero acostarme.
6. Quiero lavarme.

For the plural of the familiar imperative we have been following Spanish-American usage in using the third person plural command with **ustedes**.

    siéntense Uds. sit down   **escriban Uds.** write

In Spain, however, the plural of the familiar imperative has a special form. For all verbs it is formed by dropping the **-r** of the infinitive and substituting **-d**. The subject, which may be used for emphasis, is **vosotros**.

    hablad (vosotros) speak
    aprended learn
    escribid write

Reflexive verbs add the second person plural reflexive pronoun **os**, after dropping the final **-d**. Note the accented **í** in the third conjugation.

    sentaos sit down   **vestíos** get dressed

But in the plural of the verb **irse** (*to go away*) the **-d** is not dropped: **idos**.

PRÁCTICA

Cambie según el modelo.

Queremos hablar.
Pues, hablad.

1. Queremos comer.
2. Queremos salir.
3. Queremos escuchar.
4. Queremos venir.
5. Queremos sentarnos.
6. Queremos vestirnos.
7. Queremos despedirnos.
8. Queremos irnos.

The singular imperative of a few common verbs is irregular, but the plural is always regular.

decir:	di	decid	salir:	sal	salid
hacer:	haz	haced	ser:	sé	sed
ir:	ve	id	tener:	ten	tened
poner:	pon	poned	venir:	ven	venid

PRÁCTICA

Cambie según el modelo.

Quiero salir.
Bueno, pues, sal.

1. Quiero venir.
2. Quiero ir.
3. Quiero decirlo.
4. Quiero hacerlo.

5. Quiero tenerlo.
6. Quiero serlo.
7. Quiero ponérmelo.

The familiar imperative is used only in the affirmative. To express a familiar command in the negative, the second persons singular and plural of the present subjunctive are used. The subject pronouns **tú** and **vosotros** may be expressed for emphasis. Remember that in Spanish America the third person plural with **Uds.** replaces the second person plural.

no hables	**no habléis**	don't speak
no aprendas	**no aprendáis**	don't learn
no escribas	**no escribáis**	don't write
no te levantes	**no os levantéis**	don't get up
no te laves	**no os lavéis**	don't wash

PRÁCTICA

a. *Conteste según el modelo.*

¿Puedo hablar?
No, no hables.

1. ¿Puedo bailar?
2. ¿Puedo escribir?
3. ¿Puedo cantar?
4. ¿Puedo entrar?

5. ¿Puedo escuchar?
6. ¿Puedo leer?
7. ¿Puedo contestar?

b. *Conteste según el modelo, empleando dos formas: la española y la hispano-americana.*

¿Se puede bailar?
No, no bailéis.
No, no bailen Uds.

1. ¿Se puede hablar?
2. ¿Se puede escribir?
3. ¿Se puede cantar?
4. ¿Se puede entrar?

5. ¿Se puede escuchar?
6. ¿Se puede leer?
7. ¿Se puede contestar?

4. SHORTENING (APOCOPE) OF ADJECTIVES

a. In addition to **uno**, **alguno**, and **ninguno**, the following common adjectives drop the final **-o** before a masculine singular noun:

bueno   good   **primero**   first
malo   bad   **tercero**   third

Hace buen tiempo.   It's good weather.
Hace mal tiempo.   The weather's bad.
el primer piso   the first floor
el tercer día   the third day

But:

la primera lección   the first lesson
buenos amigos   good friends

b. **Grande** drops the final syllable before any singular noun, masculine or feminine. **Ciento**, as we have seen, drops its final syllable before any noun.

una gran ciudad   a great city
cien personas   a hundred people

But:

grandes ciudades   great cities

c. **Santo** (*Saint*) drops the final syllable before a masculine saint's name, except those beginning with **Do-** and **To-**.

San Juan   **San Carlos**

But:

Santo Domingo   **Santa Ana**

PRÁCTICA

Diga en español.

1. no student
2. no farm
3. some day
4. some library
5. bad weather
6. a good book
7. the first day
8. the first lesson
9. the third man
10. a great country
11. a hundred days
12. a hundred girls
13. a hundred boys
14. Saint Mary
15. Saint Dominick
16. Saint John

5. MORE ABOUT THE REFLEXIVE PRONOUN

The plural reflexive pronouns may express reciprocal relationship (*each other, one another*).

Nos hemos visto.   We have seen each other (one another).
Se verán mañana.   They will see each other tomorrow.
Se escribían con frecuencia.   They wrote to each other frequently.

PRÁCTICA

Diga en español.

1. They see each other.
2. They know each other.
3. They write to each other.
4. We see each other.
5. We know each other.
6. We write to each other.

Tareas

Diga en español.

1. The students have taken a trip to Spain.
2. They made the trip by plane.
3. It is their first trip, but it won't be the last.
4. They have met a very nice young Spaniard whose name is Jaime Montero.
5. They have seen each other every day.
6. Jaime invites them to go to his house to meet his family.
7. He parks the car and says, "Let's go in. This is your house."
8. They live on the third floor, but they call it (the) first floor.
9. "Let the others take the elevator," says Carlos. "I'm staying here."
10. He does not know that it is necessary to take the elevator.
11. "Let him stay here," says María. "This is only the ground floor."
12. Jaime introduces them to his family.
13. "Come in," they say. "We are pleased to meet you."
14. "Where is the maid?" asks doña Matilde. "Have her prepare coffee."

Composición oral o escrita

One of your friends tells you that her younger brother is not learning enough Spanish in high school (**la escuela superior**). Give some advice about what he should do: Let him (have him) study more. Have him prepare the lesson every day, learn all the new words, listen to the tapes, answer the questions, write the exercises, speak Spanish every day, etc. Use as many *regular* verbs as you can in such indirect commands.

Diálogo

¿PEPITO? ¡QUE ESTUDIE SOLO!

MANOLO—Alicia, dime, ¿quieres ir a mi casa para conocer a mi familia?

ALICIA—Hoy no puedo. Tengo que ir a la biblioteca.

MANOLO—¿Mañana, entonces?[1]

ALICIA—¡Conforme![2] Tengo vivo deseo de[3] conocer a tus papás[4] y a tus hermanos.[5] ¿Cuántos hermanos tienes?

MANOLO—Tengo siete, un hermano mayor y seis hermanas menores. También vive con nosotros mi abuela.

ALICIA—¿Es viuda[6] tu abuela?

MANOLO—Sí. Mi abuelo murió hace unos años.[7] Te voy a presentar también a mis tíos[8] y a mis cinco primos.[9] Viven en la casa de al lado. Con ellos vive mi bisabuela,[10] una viejecita[11] vivaracha[12] de noventa años.

ALICIA—Bueno, te dejo ahora para ir a la biblioteca.

MANOLO—¿Por qué tanta prisa?[13] Quédate[14] aquí un rato. Tomemos un refresco.

ALICIA—¡Imposible! Le prometí a Pepito que estudiaría con él.

MANOLO—¡Que se lo lleve el diablo![15] ¡Que estudie solo!

[1]entonces *then*

[2]¡Conforme! *Agreed!*

[3]tengo vivo deseo de *I'm eager to*

[4]papás *parents*

[5]hermanos *brothers and sisters*

[6]la viuda *widow*

[7]hace unos años *some years ago*

[8]tíos *aunt and uncle*

[9]primos *cousins*

[10]bisabuela *great-grandmother*

[11]la viejecita *little old lady*

[12]vivaracho *sprightly*

[13]¿Por qué tanta prisa? *What's your hurry?*

[14]quédate *stay*

[15]¡Que se lo lleve el diablo! (*Let the*) *Devil take him!*

PREGUNTAS PERSONALES

1. ¿Es numerosa tu familia?
2. ¿Cuántos hermanos tienes?
3. ¿Quién es el hermano mayor?
4. ¿Cuántos años tiene?
5. ¿Tienes hermanas menores?
6. ¿Cuántos años tienen ellas?
7. ¿Vive tu abuela con tus papás?
8. ¿Vive todavía tu bisabuela?
9. ¿Cuántos primos tienes?
10. ¿Viven cerca de tu casa?

The fortress of Machu Picchu in Peru is thought to have been a last Inca stronghold against the Spanish conquerors. Abandoned after the death of Atahualpa in 1572, it was rediscovered by Hiram Bingham of Yale in 1911. The architectural style of the Incas involving use of huge rectangular stones is much in evidence here.

Notas culturales

The Incas

The great Inca civilization of South America arose on the foundations of earlier cultures that developed in Peru after the introduction of agriculture, perhaps ten centuries before the Christian Era. A strong pre-Inca state evolved in the highlands around Tiahuanaco south of Lake Titicaca. The Tiahuanacans were builders of stone temples and palaces and of strong forts with which they defended their empire as they extended it to the coastal regions between A.D. 700 and 1000. As the power of the Tiahuanaco people declined around 1100, the Incas came to the fore, centering a new empire at Cuzco north of Lake Titicaca. During the next three hundred years they spread to adjacent highland regions. Then with a burst of imperialism after 1400 they extended their territory to the coast. They moved northward to part of what is now Ecuador and southward to present-day Bolivia, the northern half of Chile, and northwest Argentina.

The Incas were great builders and engineers. They constructed forts, temples, and palaces of huge stone blocks so carefully cut and fitted together without mortar that the blade of a knife could not be inserted between them. An impressive network of paved roads and suspension bridges linked the empire and, with a system of post runners, ensured rapid communication. Aqueducts and canals transported water for irrigation, and hillsides were terraced to prevent erosion. As potters, jewelers, and metal workers, Inca craftsmen were highly skilled. They fashioned ornaments of gold and silver and utensils and implements of copper and tin. Talented weavers produced excellent cloth from cotton yarn and from the hair of the vicuña and alpaca.

The Incas cultivated a wide variety of crops, chief among them being maize, potatoes, beans, tomatoes, and squash. They domesticated the llama, which was their beast of burden and also provided meat; the alpaca, whose hair was made into woolen cloth; and the guinea pig, whose flesh was a delicacy. In the realm of science they had considerable knowledge of mathematics, astronomy, and medicine. Their surgeons were particularly adept at the operation of trepanning. Curiously, they had no written language, but they evolved a system of **quipus**, knotted strings by which accounts were kept and information recorded.

The Incan political and social system was a rigid form of socialism. At the head of the state was the ruler, the Inca, and below him were the nobles, the priests, and the workers. Every worker between the ages of twenty-five and fifty was assigned tasks according to his ability and became either a farmer or a craftsman. The workers supported the entire population.

Land was not privately owned; every parcel was allocated by the state to one of three uses: to support the Inca, to support the priests, or to support the local community. Craftsmen were supplied with food and other necessities in return for the articles they produced, which became the property of the state. Forced labor in the mines, on roads, or in other public construction was required of all the able-bodied from time to time. There was security for all, but freedom was unknown.

Library of the Monastery of El Escorial near Madrid.

17

No pidas peras al olmo.
Don't expect the impossible.
(Don't ask pears of the elm tree.)

Present subjunctive of stem–changing verbs

Stem-changing verbs in **-ar** and **-er** have the same changes in the present sub-junctive as in the present indicative. Final stem vowel **e** becomes **ie** and final stem vowel **o** becomes **ue** whenever the stress falls on the **e** or **o**, that is, throughout the singular and in the third person plural.

	pensar		volver
p*i*ense p*i*enses	pensemos (penséis)	v*u*elva v*u*elvas	volvamos (volváis)
p*i*ense	p*i*ensen	v*u*elva	v*u*elvan

Verbs ending in **-ir** also have the same changes in the present subjunctive as in the present indicative. But they have an additional change in the sub-junctive: in the first and second persons plural, **e** becomes **i** and **o** becomes **u**.

	sentir		dormir		pedir
s*i*enta s*i*entas	s*i*ntamos (s*i*ntáis)	d*u*erma d*u*ermas	d*u*rmamos (d*u*rmáis)	p*i*da p*i*das	p*i*damos (p*i*dáis)
s*i*enta	s*i*entan	d*u*erma	d*u*erman	p*i*da	p*i*dan

PRÁCTICA

Cambie según se indica.

1. Quieren que *yo* lo cuente.
   tú / él / Ud. y yo / Ud. / ellas

2. Quieren que *Ud.* se vista pronto.
   ellos / tú / yo / nosotros / ella

3. Quieren que *nosotros* nos sentemos aquí.
   yo / Uds. / tú y yo / él / tú / Ud.

4. No quieren que *él* muera.
   yo / ellos / Ud. / tú / nosotros

5. No quieren que *yo* lo pierda.
   Ud. / Uds. / tú / tú y yo / ellas

Escuchar y hablar

acá   here
el arte   art
célebre   famous, celebrated
cerrar (ie)   to close
la colección   collection
contener   to contain
el cuadro   picture, painting
dormirse (ue)   to go to sleep
especialmente   especially
famoso   famous
fastidiado   annoyed
el fastidio   boredom
el hotel   hotel
impaciente   impatient
impresionante   impressive
insistir   to insist
lentamente   slowly
listo   ready
llevar   to take
magnífico   magnificent, superb
morirse (ue)   to die; to be dying

el museo   museum
la obra   work (*of art*)
el pintor   painter
precisamente   just at this moment
el punto de interés   point of interest
sonar (ue)   to sound, ring
la técnica   technique
el timbre   bell

IDIOMS AND OTHER EXPRESSIONS

¡Cuánto gusto de verte!   How glad (I am)
   to see you!
dar con   to meet, run into
dormir la siesta   to take a siesta
se hace tarde   it is becoming late
largo rato   a long while
de pronto   suddenly
pierde cuidado   don't worry
volver a + *infin.*   to (do something)
   again

The Prado Museum in Madrid was one of the first art gallerys in the world; it now houses the foremost collection of paintings of the Spanish school, including works by Goya, Velázquez, and El Greco.

EN EL MUSEO DEL PRADO

Esta tarde quiero visitar un museo muy famoso. Es el famoso Musco del Prado. Este museo contiene colecciones impresionantes de cuadros españoles. Hay una colección especialmente impresionante de las obras de un gran pintor español, el célebre Velázquez.

Quiero que Juan me acompañe, porque a él le gusta el arte. Pero francamente, deseo que Carlos se quede en el hotel o que visite otro punto de interés. A él no le gusta el arte, y no quiero que se duerma en el museo ni que se muera de fastidio mirando los hermosos cuadros de los pintores españoles.

Hemos dormido la siesta. Se hace tarde, y quiero que Juan se vista pronto para no perder tiempo. Pero él se viste lentamente y yo me pongo impaciente. Al fin está listo y vamos al museo. Llegamos bastante tarde.

En el museo damos con Jaime Montero. Están con él Virginia y María.

—¡Cuánto gusto de verte!—le digo. —Sé que sabes mucho del arte español y deseo que me muestres la Sala de Velázquez.

—Precisamente íbamos allá—contesta Jaime.

Nos lleva a esa sala, donde vemos cosas magníficas. Jaime me explica la técnica del gran pintor español.

Virginia y María quieren que pasemos a otra sala para ver las obras de Murillo, de Zurbarán y de otros pintores. Así lo hacemos. Pero pronto dicen que están cansadas y quieren sentarse para descansar.

—Aunque las pobres muchachas están cansadas, no quiero que se sienten— le digo a Jaime, fastidiado. —Si se sientan, vamos a perder tiempo, y hay mucho que[1] ver. Se quedarán aquí largo rato y no volveremos a[2] ver los cuadros de Velázquez.

Pero las muchachas insisten y se sientan.

—Dejémoslas aquí con Juan—le digo a Jaime. —Quiero que vuelvas conmigo a la sala de Velázquez para volver a examinar esos magníficos cuadros.

De pronto suena un timbre.

—No hay tiempo—dice Jaime. —Van a cerrar.

—Pero no quiero que cierren el museo. Quiero ver más.

—Pierde cuidado—dice Jaime. —Mañana será otro día y volveremos acá.[3]

NOTAS

1. After negative and indefinite expressions and those containing a numeral, English *to* is translated with Spanish **que**.

   No hay nada que hacer.   There's nothing to do.
   Hay mucho que ver.   There's much to see.
   ¿Tiene algo que comer?   Does he have anything to eat?
   Tengo tres cartas que escribir.   I have three letters to write.

2. **Volver** requires the preposition **a** before a following infinitive. In this construction **volver a** means *again*.

   Volveremos a ver los cuadros.   We'll see the paintings *again*.
   Volvió a leer ese libro.   He read that book *again*.

3. **Acá**, like **allá**, is frequently, though not always, used after verbs of motion.

   Volvermos acá.   We'll come back here.
   Vamos allá.   Let's go over there.

PREGUNTAS

1. ¿Qué quiere Ud. visitar esta tarde?
2. ¿Cuál es el museo que quiere visitar?
3. ¿Qué contiene?
4. ¿Cuál es una colección especialmente impresionante que contiene?
5. ¿Por qué desea Ud. que Juan le acompañe?

6. ¿Quiere Ud. que Carlos visite el museo?
7. ¿Por qué quiere Ud. que Juan se vista pronto?
8. ¿A quiénes encuentran Uds. en el museo?
9. ¿Qué sabe Jaime?
10. ¿Qué quiere Ud. que le muestre Jaime?
11. ¿Qué le explica Jaime?
12. ¿Qué quieren Virginia y María?
13. ¿Qué quieren hacer ellas poco después?
14. ¿Adónde quiere Ud. que vuelva Jaime?
15. ¿Qué suena de pronto?
16. ¿Qué quiere decir eso?

PRÁCTICA

a. *Conteste según el modelo.*

¿Hay algo que ver?
No, no hay nada que ver.

1. ¿Hay algo que hacer?
2. ¿Hay mucho que estudiar?
3. ¿Hay algo que leer?
4. ¿Hay cartas que escribir?
5. ¿Hay lecciones que estudiar?

b. *Conteste según el modelo.*

¿Visitó Ud. el museo?
Sí, y volveré a visitarlo.

1. ¿Vio Ud. a Paquita?
2. ¿Ud. dijo eso?
3. ¿Leyeron Uds. la carta?
4. ¿Estudiaron Uds. la lección?
5. ¿Escucharon ellos la cinta?
6. ¿Hicieron eso?

Estructura

1. NOUN CLAUSE VERSUS INFINITIVE

We have seen that an infinitive may be the object of a verb.

Quiero estudiar.   I want to study.
No puedo volver.   I can't go back.

A noun clause may also be the object of a verb. This is a clause which is used as a noun. It always begins with **que** (*that*).

MAIN VERB		NOUN CLAUSE	
Sé	que	**rebaja los precios.**	I know (that) he lowers the prices.
Dice	que	**lo hará mañana.**	He says he'll do it tomorrow.

In English, in expressions like "I want to study" and "I want you to study," we use an infinitive, whether the subject of the infinitive is the same as that of the main verb, or whether it represents a different person. But in Spanish, when a second subject is introduced into the sentence, we replace the infinitive with a noun clause. We are really saying "I want that you study."

Quiero que tú estudies.   I want *you* to study.

2. SUBJUNCTIVE MOOD IN THE NOUN CLAUSE

Some main verbs require the subjunctive in a dependent noun clause. Verbs of *wishing* and *desiring* require the subjunctive in such clauses.

MAIN VERB	NOUN CLAUSE	
Quiero	**que Juan me acompañe.**	I want Juan to go with me.
Desean	**que Carlos se quede.**	They wish Carlos to stay.
No queremos	**que cierren el museo.**	We don't want them to close the museum.

PRÁCTICA

a. *Sustituya siguiendo el modelo.*

Quieren que Ud. visite el museo. (yo)
Quieren que yo visite el museo.

1. Quieren que Ud. visite el museo.
   yo / tú / nosotros / él / ellos

2. Quieren que Juan los acompañe.
   tú / nosotros / yo / Ud. y yo / Uds.

3. Quieren que Uds. vuelvan.
   él / tú / nosotros / yo / ellas

4. Quieren que pasemos a otra sala.
   Ud. / tú / yo / él / ellas / tú y yo

5. Quieren que nos vistamos inmediatamente.
   yo / Ud. / tú / nosotros / él / ellos

6. No desean que Ud. les muestre los cuadros.
   tú / yo / Ud. y yo / ellas / él

7. No desean que Paco se quede en el hotel.
   Uds. / tú / él / yo / tú y yo / Ud.

8. No desean que yo me duerma.
   ella / tú / nosotros / Ana / ellos

"The Working Class," by José Clemente Orozco. Orozco was renowned as a painter of canvases as well as some of the greatest murals produced in the twentieth century. He focused his powerful style on the fundamental problems of man and his social institutions.

b. *Cambie según se indica.*

Quiero volver. (él)
Quiero que él vuelva.

1. Quiero leer. (ella)
2. Quiero hablar. (ellos)
3. Quiero volver. (tú)
4. Quiero contar. (Uds.)
5. Quiero bailar. (ella)

6. Ud. quiere comer. (ellos)
7. Ud. quiere comprender. (él)
8. Ud. quiere sentarse. (nosotros)
9. Ud. quiere quedarse aquí. (yo)
10. Ud. quiere vestirse. (ellas)

3. POSITION OF ADJECTIVES

There are two kinds of adjectives: limiting adjectives (sucn as numerals, demonstratives, possessives, interrogatives, indefinites, negatives) and descriptive adjectives.

a. Limiting adjectives regularly precede the noun.

treinta muchachos	**sus camisas**
el primer viaje	**¿qué lección?**
este museo	**ningún pintor**

b. Descriptive adjectives usually follow the noun. They regularly follow when they differentiate the noun from others of its class.

un pintor español   a Spanish painter (not a French or an English painter)
una colección impresionante   an impressive collection (not an ordinary collection)
un museo famoso   a famous museum (not just any museum)

But when the descriptive adjective denotes an inherent or logical characteristic of the person or thing named by the noun, it precedes. An inherent characteristic is one which is normally associated with the person or thing. A logical characteristic is one which, in the light of our previous knowledge, is associated with the person or thing.

la blanca nieve   the white snow (Snow is inherently white; normally, whiteness is a characteristic of snow.)
la hermosa naturaleza   beautiful nature (Nature is inherently beautiful.)
el gran Simón Bolívar   the great Simón Bolívar (In the light of what we know about Bolívar, greatness is a logical characteristic of his.)
el famoso Cervantes   the famous Cervantes (In the light of our knowledge of Cervantes, fame is a logical characteristic of his.)

To illustrate further these two uses of the descriptive adjective:

We say **un museo famoso,** *a famous museum,* to distinguish a museum which is famous from just any museum. If we talk about *the famous Prado Museum,* we say **el famoso Museo del Prado,** since the Prado, being one of the great museums of the world, is logically famous.

Notice that differentiating adjectives are words that we stress. They follow the noun because this is the stressed position. Adjectives that normally precede their noun will follow the noun when stressed.

Es un buen libro.   It's a good book.
Es un libro muy bueno.   It's a very good book.
Este es nuestro primer viaje.   This is our first trip.
Viven en la Avenida Primera.   They live on First Avenue (not Fifth Avenue, etc.).

Some adjectives vary in meaning, depending upon whether they follow or precede the noun. When they follow the noun, they are differentiating adjectives and usually carry their basic meaning.

el muchacho pobre   the poor (not rich) boy
el pobre muchacho   the poor (pitiful) boy
un hombre grande   a big man
un gran hombre   a great man
un traje nuevo   a new suit
un nuevo traje   another suit

PRÁCTICA

Diga en español.

1. It's a famous museum.
   It's the famous Prado Museum.

2. It's an interesting city.
   It's the interesting city of Madrid.

3. It's a large university.
   It's the great University of Salamanca.

4. He's a Mexican actor.
   He's the well-known actor Cantinflas.

5. Murillo is a good painter.
   Goya is a very good painter.

6. Mr. González is a poor man.
   Poor Mr. González is very ill.

Tareas

Diga en español.

1. Today you want to visit a very famous museum, the famous Prado Museum.
2. It has some very impressive collections of Spanish paintings.
3. You want Juan to go with you, but you wish Carlos to stay in the hotel.
4. You don't want him to go to sleep or to die of boredom.
5. It's getting late and you want Juan to dress quickly.
6. In the museum you run into Jaime and the two girls.
7. You want Jaime to show you the Velázquez Room.
8. He takes you there and explains to you the great Spanish painter's technique.
9. Virginia and María want you to go into another room.
10. They are tired and want to sit down.
11. You want Jaime to return with you to the Velázquez Room to see those paintings again.
12. Suddenly a bell rings.
13. You don't want them to close the museum.
14. "Don't worry," says Jaime. "We can come back here tomorrow."

Composición oral o escrita

You visit a famous museum near where you live. You want a friend to go with you, because he or she knows a lot about art. Tell whom you want to go with you, what collections the museum contains, what paintings you want your friend to show you, whom you run into in the museum, and what they want you to see.

Diálogo

EN EL PARQUE ZOOLÓGICO[1]

JAIME—Dime, María. ¿No estás cansada de todos estos museos?

MARÍA—Hasta cierto punto,[2] te lo confieso.[3]

JAIME—¿Quieres que te lleve al parque zoológico? Aquí hay un magnífico parque nuevo.

MARÍA—¡Ésa sí que es una idea genial![4] Me fascinan[5] los animales.

(*Más tarde, en el parque zoológico.*)

JAIME—¡Ven acá, María! ¡Ve el león![6]

MARÍA—Mis, mis, mis.[7]

JAIME—¡Ten cuidado![8] No te acerques[9] demasiado.

MARÍA—Este león no es más que un gato[10] grande. Los leones no son tan feroces[11] como los lobos.[12] Aquí están los lobos en la jaula[13] de al lado.

JAIME—Tus, tus, tus.[14]

MARÍA—¿Crees que éste es un perro?[15]

JAIME—El lobo no es tan feroz como lo pintan.[16] Tiene buen carácter, como el perro. Y a propósito del[17] perro, tú sabes que es el amigo más leal[18] del hombre. Y ¿sabes otra cosa? Yo soy tu amigo más leal.

(*María no dice nada.*)

JAIME—¿No dices nada? ¡No dices tus ni mus![19] Bueno, hace calor. ¿Quieres que te compre un helado?[20]

[1]el parque zoológico *zoo*	[10]el gato *cat*
[2]hasta cierto punto *up to a certain point*	[11]feroz *ferocious*
	[12]el lobo *wolf*
[3]confesar *to confess, admit*	[13]la jaula *cage*
[4]¡Ésa sí que es una idea genial! *That certainly is a marvellous idea!*	[14]Tus, tus, tus *Here, boy (calling dog)*
	[15]el perro *dog*
[5]fascinar *to fascinate*	[16]pintar *to paint*
[6]el león *lion*	[17]a propósito de *speaking of*
[7]Mis, mis, mis *Here, kitty*	[18]leal *loyal, faithful*
[8]tener cuidado *to be careful*	[19]no decir tus ni mus *to say nothing*
[9]acercarse *to get close to*	[20]el helado *ice cream*

PREGUNTAS PERSONALES

1. ¿Te gustan los animales?
2. ¿Tienes animales en casa—un perro, un gato?
3. ¿Qué nombre le has puesto a tu perro?
4. ¿Qué nombre le has puesto a tu gato?

5. Cuando llamas al gato, ¿qué dices?
6. Cuando llamas al perro, ¿qué dices?
7. ¿Tienes tu caballo propio?
8. ¿Hay un buen parque zoológico en la ciudad donde vives?
9. ¿Vas allá de vez en cuando?
10. ¿Qué animales te gustan más en el parque zoológico—los elefantes, los leones, los tigres, los monos (*monkeys*)?
11. ¿Quieres que te muestre el parque zoológico de esta ciudad?

Notas culturales

Don't overlook the museums if you travel to the Hispanic countries. You will find many fascinating treasures of every imaginable sort. The finest is the Museo del Prado in Madrid, where under near-perfect lighting conditions you can appreciate the paintings of the great masters of Spain's Golden Age—Velázquez, El Greco, Murillo, Ribera, Zurbarán, and those of the more modern Goya. In Barcelona you will want to see the new Picasso collection.

In Mexico City your interest in archeology will be aroused by a visit to the magnificent new Museo Nacional de Antropología with its superb collections that bring to life the cultures of the Aztecs, Mayans, and other pre-Columbian peoples. In Mexico, too, you will want to see the impressive works of the great twentieth-century muralists, like Rivera's enormous fresco at the Teatro Insurgentes in the capital and those of the Palacio de Cortés in Cuernavaca. In Lima, the Museo de Antropología y Arqueología will open your eyes to the fascinating culture of the Incas.

If you are interested in the Middle Ages, and even if you aren't, don't miss the Armería Real, in Madrid, with its impressive collection of armor. Look around for smaller, less well known museums, like the private Peruvian Gold Museum at Monterrico, near Lima, and the little exhibit at the Agricultural Experiment Station in Lima, where you can appreciate the absolute realism of the Incas in their exact pottery reproductions of fruits and vegetables.

Regional dancers from the Canary Islands.

18

No digas que llueve hasta que truene.
Don't count your chickens before they're hatched.
(Don't say it's raining till you hear the thunder.)

Regular present subjunctive of some irregular verbs

Among the irregular verbs which form their present subjunctive regularly—that is, on the stem of the first person singular of the present indicative, after dropping the **-o**—are the following:

INFINITIVE	FIRST PERSON SINGULAR PRESENT INDICATIVE	FIRST PERSON SINGULAR PRESENT SUBJUNCTIVE
decir	**digo**	**diga**
conocer	**conozco**	**conozca**
hacer	**hago**	**haga**
poder	**puedo**	**pueda**
poner	**pongo**	**ponga**
querer	**quiero**	**quiera**
salir	**salgo**	**salga**
tener	**tengo**	**tenga**
valer	**valgo**	**valga**
venir	**vengo**	**venga**
ver	**veo**	**vea**

PRÁCTICA

Cambie según se indica.

1. Quieren que *yo* se lo diga.
   Ud. / tú / nosotros / ellas / él

2. Quieren que *Ud.* lo haga pronto.
   tú / ella / yo / nosotros / Uds.

3. Quieren que *tú* lo pongas aquí.
   Ud. / yo / Ud. y yo / él / ellos

4. Quieren que *él* lo tenga para mañana.
   yo / nosotros / ellas / tú / Ud.

5. Desean que *Uds.* salgan ahora.
   nosotros / tú / ellas / él / yo

6. Desean que *nosotros* también vengamos.
   Ud. / Uds. / yo / tú y yo / él / tú

7. Desean que *conozcas* a Rosita.
   yo / Ud. / ellas / tú y yo / tú

8. Desean que *veamos* la ciudad.
   Pepe / yo / Ud. y yo / ellas / tú

Present subjunctive of *dar*, *estar*, and *ir*

dar		estar		ir	
dé	demos	esté	estemos	vaya	vayamos
des	(deis)	estés	(estéis)	vayas	(vayáis)
dé	den	esté	estén	vaya	vayan

PRÁCTICA

Cambie según se indica.

1. Quieren que *yo* se lo dé mañana.
   Ud. / él / ellos / Ud. y yo / tú

2. Quieren que *ella* vaya allá.
   yo / tú / él / nosotros / ellas

3. Desean que *Uds.* estén aquí.
   tú / yo / él / tú y yo / ellas

Spain is divided into twelve historic regions, each with its own special character and customs. The whitewashed houses and cobbled streets of Mijas are typical for Andalusia.

Escuchar y hablar

acabar to finish
aconsejar to advise
Andalucía Andalusia (*region in southern Spain*)
andaluz, andaluza Andalusian
antes de before
el asunto matter
avisar to inform, let know
el consejo (piece of) advice
el contacto contact
Córdoba Cordova
decidirse a to decide to
desde from
El Excorial (*monastery near Madrid*)
esperar to hope
la estación station
Horacio Horace

inmediatamente immediately
insistir (en) to insist (on)
maravilloso marvellous
el negocio business
la oportunidad opportunity
el par pair, couple
partir to start, leave
permitir to permit, allow
Sevilla Seville
sugerir (ie) to suggest
el sur south
el taxi taxi
el teléfono telephone
terminar to finish
el tren train
urgente urgent
urgir to be urgent

IDIOMS AND OTHER EXPRESSIONS

acabar de (+ *infin.*)   to have just
   + *past part.*

cuanto antes   as soon as possible

dígame   hello (*answering the telephone*)

estar de vuelta   to be back

Habla Jaime.   Jaime speaking.
   (This is Jaime.)

hacer el favor de (+ *infin.*)   please

¡mira!   look!

oiga   hello (*calling on the telephone*)

¿qué hacer?   what to do? what shall I
   do?

en seguida   at once

a tiempo   in time

¡vaya un viaje!   what a trip!

HAGAMOS UN VIAJE A ANDALUCÍA

Eran las nueve y media de la mañana cuando sonó el teléfono.

—¡Dígame!

—¡Oiga! Habla Jaime Montero. ¿Con quién hablo?

—Con Horacio Jones.

—Mira. Mi padre acaba de decirme que vaya a Córdoba en nuestro coche. Es un asunto de negocios y es muy urgente. Sugiere que te lleve a ti y también a tus amigos. Queremos que todos tengan la oportunidad de conocer el sur de España. ¿Podríais estar listos a las tres de la tarde?

—Muchas gracias. ¡Vaya un viaje! Nos gustaría mucho acompañarte. Pero mira, mis amigos están hoy en El Escorial. Tomaron el tren de las ocho[1] y no volverán hasta las siete. ¿Qué hacer?

—¿Me permites que te dé un consejo?

—¡Cómo no! ¿Qué me aconsejas?

—Que tomes el tren de las diez y que vayas a buscarlos. Te aconsejo que salgas inmediatamente a la calle y que tomes un taxi. Llegarás a tiempo a la estación y será posible hallarlos en El Escorial. Pueden estar de vuelta antes de las tres. Espero que vengan, porque será un viaje muy agradable. Al terminar nuestros negocios en Córdoba, iremos a Sevilla, esa maravillosa ciudad andaluza. Pasaremos un par de días allí y luego iremos a Granada para ver la Alhambra. Mira, al volver a Madrid haz el favor de llamarme por teléfono desde la estación para avisarme.

—Bueno, voy en seguida.

—Muy bien. Pero papá insiste en que estemos listos a las tres. Urge el negocio y debemos partir cuanto antes. Espero que encuentres a tus amigos y que se decidan a hacer el viaje.

Eran las diez menos veinte cuando salí del hotel. Pero llegué a tiempo a la estación, tomé el tren de las diez y encontré fácilmente a mis amigos en El Escorial. Eso nos permitió estar de vuelta a tiempo.

NOTA

1. Expressions like "the eight o'clock train" and "the twelve o'clock bus" are in Spanish **el tren de las ocho** and **el autobús de las doce**.

PREGUNTAS

1. ¿A qué hora suena el teléfono?
2. ¿Quién llama?
3. ¿Qué dice?
4. ¿Qué le acaba de decir su padre?
5. ¿Qué sugiere su padre?
6. ¿Por qué quieren que Uds. acompañen a Jaime?
7. ¿Adónde han ido los amigos de Ud.?
8. ¿Qué tren tomaron?
9. ¿A qué hora volverán?
10. ¿Qué le aconseja Jaime?
11. ¿A qué hora podrían Uds. estar de vuelta?
12. ¿Qué ciudades visitarán Uds.?
13. ¿Qué quiere Jaime que haga Ud. al llegar a la estación?
14. ¿A qué hora desea Jaime que Uds. estén listos?
15. ¿Qué hora era cuando Ud. salió del hotel?
16. ¿Llegó Ud. tarde a la estación?

Estructura

1. SUBJUNCTIVE MOOD IN THE NOUN CLAUSE—CONTINUED

a. Verbs of *commanding* and *requesting* require the subjunctive in a dependent noun clause.

Mi padre me dice que vaya.   My father tells me to go. (My father tells me that I go.)

Les ruego que estén listos a las tres.   I beg you to be ready at three o'clock. (I beg you that you be ready . . .)

Le pido a Carlos que me acompañe.   I ask Charles to go with me. (I ask Charles that he go with me.)

Note that, unlike **querer** and **desear,** these verbs of commanding and requesting may take an indirect object in the main clause.

| Me | dice que vaya. | He tells | me | to go. |

| Les | ruegan | a Uds. | que vengan. | They ask | you | to come. |

| Le | pide | a Carlos | que vuelva. | He asks | Charles | to return. |

Some common verbs of commanding and requesting are

pedir (i)   to ask, request   **mandar**   to command
rogar (ue)   to beg, request   **decir**   to tell

Do not confuse the two meanings of **decir. Decir** means (1) *to tell* in the sense of "to inform" and (2) *to tell* in the sense of "to order." The second meaning takes the subjunctive in a dependent noun clause, as you have just seen. The first you have been using since early in the book, with the indicative:

Haga Ud. el favor de *decir*le *que ha llamado* el señor Núñez. Please *tell* him *that* Mr. Núñez *has called.*

Many verbs of causation similar in idea to verbs of commanding and requesting also require the subjunctive in a dependent noun clause.

preferir (ie)   to prefer   **dejar**   to let, allow
sugerir (ie)   to suggest   **impedir (i)**   to prevent
aconsejar   to advise   **proponer**   to propose, suggest
permitir   to permit   **insistir en**   to insist on

Me aconseja que tome el tren.   He advises me to take the train.
Les propongo que salgamos temprano.   I suggest to them that we leave
   early.

PRÁCTICA

a. *Cambie según se indica, siguiendo el modelo.*

Tomo un taxi. (Sugieren que . . .)
Sugieren que tome un taxi.

1. Voy a la estación en seguida.
   aconsejan que / insisten en que / prefieren que

2. Me avisan a tiempo.
   les ruego que / les digo que / les propongo que

3. Se lo damos mañana.
   Ud. sugiere que / Ud. permite que / Ud. aconseja que

4. Ella sale hoy.
   no impiden que / insisten en que / prefieren que

5. Lo ponen aquí.
   les sugiero que / les propongo que / les permito que

Dominating the city of Granada is the Alhambra, the fabulous palace of the Moors who ruled the province for nearly eight centuries. Moslem art reaches heights of splendor in the numerous courtyards and the palace rooms with walls of molded and carved plaster inscribed in Arabic. The Alhambra was once known as the "red house," probably because the plateau on which it is located is fortified with walls and towers of reddish sun-dried brick.

b. *Cambie según se indica, siguiendo el modelo.*

Les ruego a Uds. que estén de vuelta temprano. (a él)
Le ruego a él que esté de vuelta temprano.

1. Les ruego a Uds. que estén de vuelta temprano.
   a Ud. / a ellas / a Pepe / a ellos

2. Le permito a María que lo devuelva.
   a ellas / a ella / a Uds. / a la muchacha

3. Les dice a Uds. que lo hagan cuanto antes.
   a ellas / a Ud. / a los alumnos / a Dolores

4. Le propongo a él que lo termine mañana.
   a Uds. / al abogado / a los alumnos / a Marta

5. Les sugiero a ellos que vayan en avión.
   a Ud. / a mis amigos / a él / a mis hermanas

b. Verbs of *emotion* also require the subjunctive in a dependent noun clause. Note that the present subjunctive may express future as well as present time.

Espero que me acompañen. I hope they'll go with me.
Me alegro de que Uds. estén aquí. I'm glad (that) you're here.
Siento que no puedas ir al cine. I'm sorry you can't go to the movies.

Some common verbs of emotion are

sentir (ie)	to regret, be sorry	**alegrarse (de)**	to be glad
esperar	to hope	**es lástima**	it's too bad
temer	to fear	**extrañar**	to surprise

PRÁCTICA

Cambie según se indica.

Vendrán mañana. (Espero que . . .)
Espero que vengan mañana.

1. No están aquí.
   Siento que / Temo que / Es lástima que

2. Tú no la conoces.
   Me extraña que / Es lástima que / Siento que

3. Nos dan el dinero.
   Esperamos que / Nos extraña que / Nos alegramos de que

4. No irán a México.
   Temo que / Siento que / Es lástima que

5. Tienes tiempo para estudiar.
   Se alegra de que / Espera que / Le extraña que

2. AN INFINITIVE INSTEAD OF A NOUN CLAUSE

A few verbs of *causation* may be followed by an infinitive instead of a noun clause, even when the subject of the subordinate verb is different from the subject of the main verb. The following may take the infinitive:

mander	to order	**permitir**	to permit, allow
hacer	to make, have	**impedir**	to prevent
dejar	to let, allow		

Me permitió llevar a mis amigos. He allowed me to take my friends.
Déjele hacerlo. Let him do it. Allow him to do it.
Hicieron venir al médico. They had the doctor come.

PRÁCTICA

Diga en español.

1. I had the doctor come.
2. I had the boys work.
3. They permitted us to do it.
4. They permitted us to see it.
5. He ordered them to tell it.
6. He ordered them to answer.
7. You didn't let me speak.
8. You didn't let me listen.

Tareas

Diga en español.

1. Jaime Montero has just called her.
2. His father has told him to go to Cordova in his car.
3. He suggests that she and her friends accompany him.
4. He wants them to have the opportunity of seeing the south of Spain—Andalusia.
5. They would like to go, but they could not be ready at three o'clock.
6. Her friends are at El Escorial and will not be back until seven o'clock.
7. He advises her to take the ten o'clock train and go to look for them.
8. He suggests that she go out and take a taxi to the station.
9. Tell your friends to come, because we shall go to that marvellous Andalusian city, Seville.
10. Please telephone me from the station upon returning to Madrid.
11. He hopes they will be ready at three, because they ought to start as soon as possible.
12. He is glad they can go.

Composición oral o escrita

Tell how María's father has just telephoned from Texas. He wants her and her brother to come home at once, because their grandfather is ill. But Juan has gone off on a field trip, and María cannot reach him by phone. Advise her what to do in order to find him. Tell her you are sorry her grandfather is ill. You hope he will be better soon.

Diálogo

AL TELÉFONO

JAIME (*A la telefonista.*[1])—Una llamada interurbana,[2] si me hace el favor.[3] Madrid, 2327996. Cobro revertido,[4] por favor.[5]

EL SEÑOR MONTERO—Dígame.

JAIME—¡Papá! Estoy en Córdoba y necesito dinero urgentemente. ¿Puedes mandármelo[6] inmediatamente?

EL SR. M.—¡En absoluto![7] Te he dicho siempre que no me pidas tanto dinero.

JAIME—Pero, papá. Un camión[8] acaba de chocar con[9] mi coche y está casi totalmente destrozado.[10]

* * *

SECRETARIA—Diga.

JAIME—¿Está[11] el señor Pérez, el abogado?

SECRETARIA—¿De parte de quién, para decircle?[12]

JAIME—De Jaime Montero Álvarez. Mi padre es un cliente[13] suyo.

SECRETARIA—Ahorita[14] recuerdo que acaba de salir. Debe volver dentro de unos minutos. Desea Ud. que le dé un recado?[15]

JAIME—Sí, por favor. Le ruego que me llame tan pronto como posible. Es un asunto urgente. Estoy en el Hotel Fénix.

[1]telefonista *operator*

[2]la llamada interurbana *long distance call*

[3]si me hace el favor *please*

[4]cobro revertido *charges reversed*

[5]por favor *please*

[6]mandar *to send*

[7]en absoluto *absolutely not*

[8]el camión *truck*

[9]chocar con *to collide with*

[10]destrozado *wrecked*

[11]¿está? *is he in?*

[12]¿De parte de quién, para decirle? *Who may I say is calling?*

[13]el cliente *client*

[14]ahorita *this very minute*

[15]el recado *message*

PREGUNTAS PERSONALES

1. ¿Tienes teléfono en tu cuarto?
2. ¿Haces muchas llamadas interurbanas?
3. ¿Cuestan mucho?
4. Cuando llamas a tu familia y quieres que ellos paguen, ¿qué le dices a la telefonista?
5. Cuando llamas a tu familia, ¿siempre les pides dinero?
6. ¿Llamas a tu novia (a tu novio) todos los días?
7. ¿Cuánto tiempo hablas con tu novia (novio) las más de las veces?
8. ¿Te dice tu papá que no hables tanto tiempo?
9. ¿Has llamado alguna vez a un amigo en México?
10. ¿Cuál es tu número de teléfono?
11. ¿Quieres que te llame esta noche?

Notas culturales

1. We have noted how words for things of everyday life (like the terms for "bus") may differ from country to country in the Hispanic world. The way you answer the telephone differs, too. In Spain you say **"Dígame"** or **"Diga."** The person calling will say **"Oiga"** ("Listen") and may add **"¿Con quién hablo?"** ("Who is this," "With whom am I speaking?"). To the latter you may say **"Habla Fulano"** ("So-and-so speaking").

   In Mexico you answer the phone with a somewhat peremptory **"Bueno."** In Chile, you say **"Aló"**; in Argentina, **"Holá."** The most interesting of such expressions is the one used in Colombia, where you say **"A ver."** This means "Let's see." In Spanish it is an elliptical phrase, with the **Vamos** omitted. You can imagine the origin of this at the time when telephones were first installed in Bogotá. You can see someone answering a call, taking the receiver down from the new-fangled wall phone, and expressing his or her curiosity by saying "Let's see (who's on the other end of the line)."

2. Another such difference is the use of **voseo**, which means addressing a person as **vos**, instead of **tú**. This familiar usage is especially identified with Argentina, Uruguay, and Paraguay. It stems from an older use of the plural **vos** (modern **vosotros**) to address one person, much as English "you" came to have a singular as well as plural meaning. Verbs used with **vos** derive from the second person plural, but some have undergone a change in form:

   vos tenés = tú tienes
   vos estás = tú estás
   vos vivís = tú vives

Madrid. A busy street in the center of the city recently converted to a pedestrian mall.

4

A. *Conteste según el modelo.*

¿Puedes comprarlo?
Sí, y lo compraré.

1. ¿Puedes aprenderlo?
2. ¿Puedes hacerlo?
3. ¿Puedes decirlo?
4. ¿Puedes tenerlo?
5. ¿Puedes explicarlo?

B. *Conteste según el modelo.*

¿No va Rosita?
No, pero dijo que iría.

1. ¿No viene Luisito?
2. ¿No sale Dolores?
3. ¿No contesta Pancho?
4. ¿No puede hacerlo?
5. ¿No quiere hacerlo?

C. *Diga en español.*

1. They probably know it.
2. He must be in the library.
3. Can it be Pepe?
4. She probably was at home.
5. Where do you suppose they went?

D. *Use el adjetivo posesivo como se indica.*

1. ¿De quién es este coche? Es ____ (mine).
2. ¿De quién son estas flores? Son ____ (mine).
3. ¿De quién es esta finca? Es ____ (ours).
4. ¿De quién son estos zapatos? Son ____ (hers).
5. ¿De quién es este libro? Es ____ (theirs).
6. ¿De quién son estas corbatas? Son ____ (his).

E. *Conteste, usando el número siguiente, como el modelo.*

¿Es la primera vez?
No, es la segunda vez.

1. ¿Es el segundo día? No, es el _____ día.
2. ¿Es la cuarta semana? No, es la _____ semana.
3. ¿Es la lección sexta? No, es la lección _____.
4. ¿Es el libro octavo? No, es el libro _____.
5. ¿Era Alfonso IX? No, era Alfonso _____.

F. *Conteste según el modelo.*

¿Lo han escrito?
Lo están escribiendo ahora.

1. ¿Lo han hecho?
2. ¿Lo han dicho?
3. ¿Lo han pedido?
4. ¿Lo han comprado?

G. *Use **que** o **de**.*

1. Mi novia es más guapa ___ ella.
2. Es la más guapa ___ todas.
3. Esta película es mejor ___ la otra.
4. Tenía menos ___ cien pesos.
5. Había más ___ ochenta personas en el teatro.

H. *Continúe según el modelo.*

¿Quieres escribirlo?
Pues, escríbelo.

1. ¿Quieres decirlo?
2. ¿Quieres hacerlo?
3. ¿Quieres ir?
4. ¿Quieres salir?
5. ¿Quieres venir?

I. *Continúe según el modelo.*

¿No quieres comprarlo?
Pues, no lo compres.

1. ¿No quieres hacerlo?
2. ¿No quieres decirlo?
3. ¿No quieres aprenderlo?
4. ¿No quieres devolverlo?
5. ¿No quieres pedirlo?
6. ¿No quieres ir?

J. *Continúe según el modelo.*

¿No puedes proponerlo?
Pues entonces, que lo proponga Jorge.

1. ¿No puedes hacerlo?
2. ¿No puedes pagarlo?
3. ¿No puedes dármelo?
4. ¿No puedes venir?
5. ¿No puedes ir?

K. *Cambie según se indica.*

Desean vender la casa. (nosotros)
Desean que nosotros vendamos la casa.

1. Quieren ver la ciudad. (Uds.)
2. Desean volver temprano. (yo)
3. Quieren conocer a Inés. (Mario)
4. Desean ir a ese país. (sus hijos)
5. Quieren ponerlo sobre la mesa. (tú)

L. *Use el indicativo o el subjuntivo de los verbos entre paréntesis.*

1. Sé que Ramona _____ (estar) aquí esta mañana.
2. Les ruego a Uds. que _____ (estar) aquí esta noche.
3. Me dicen que _____ (ser) la una de la mañana.
4. Le dicen que _____ (sentarse) aquí.
5. ¿Insisten en que nosotros _____ (ir) con ellos?
6. Les aconsejo que lo _____ (hacer) ahora.
7. ¿Prefieres que yo te _____ (acompañar)?
8. ¿Me propones que _____ (pedir) el dinero?
9. Dígales que no _____ (ser) posible.
10. Dígales que tú no _____ (querer) que _____ (venir) hoy.

M. *Use el indicativo o el subjuntivo de los verbos entre paréntesis.*

1. Jaime espera que tú le _____ (dar) el reloj.
2. Sé que tú no _____ (ir) a dárselo.
3. Me alegro de que tú _____ (ir) conmigo.
4. Temen que yo no _____ (volver) a tiempo.
5. ¿Dices que tu padre _____ (ser) cubano?
6. Siento que Carmencita no _____ (estar) aquí.
7. ¿Es verdad que tu novia te _____ (escribir) todos los días?
8. Es lástima que mi novio no _____ (bailar) bien.
9. Me extraña que tu hermano no _____ (hablar) español.
10. Sentimos mucho que Ud. no _____ (poder) acompañarnos.

N. *Diga en español.*

1. Tell what you will do tomorrow: what time you will get up, what you will do when you get up, what classes you will attend, and what you will do in the afternoon and evening.

2. Tell what you would do this afternoon and evening if it were possible. You would go to the gym, you would play tennis or baseball, you would have dinner in a good restaurant, you would go to the movies. Begin by saying *"De ser posible"* ("If it were possible").

3. Describe your visit to a friend's family in Madrid.

4. Describe your visit to the Prado with Jaime. Tell who went with you, what you saw, and what happened.

5. Jaime telephones and says his father wants him to go to Cordova. He wants you and your friends to go with him. But your friends are at the Escorial. Tell what Jaime advises you to do.

19

El perro baila por dinero
y por pan, si se lo dan.
Money makes the world go round.

Present subjunctive of *ser* and *saber*

ser		saber	
sea	seamos	sepa	sepamos
seas	(seáis)	sepas	(sepáis)
sea	sean	sepa	sepan

PRÁCTICA

Cambie según se indica.

1. Prefieren que *Ud.* sea franco.
   tú / ellos / él / nosotros / yo

2. Insisten en que *yo* lo sepa.
   Uds. / tú / tú y yo / ellas / él

3. Deseo que *tú* seas honrado.
   él / nosotros / ella / ellos / Ud.

Present perfect subjunctive

The present perfect subjunctive of a verb is formed by combining the present subjunctive of **haber**, which is formed irregularly, with the past participle of the verb.

hablar		vivir	
haya hablado	hayamos hablado	haya vivido	hayamos vivido
hayas hablado	(hayáis hablado)	hayas vivido	(hayáis vivido)
haya hablado	hayan hablado	haya vivido	hayan vivido

PRÁCTICA

Cambie según se indica.

1. Esperan que *él* haya llegado temprano.
   ellas / yo / tú / nosotros / Paco

2. Me alegro de *Uds.* hayan vuelto a la universidad.
   nosotros / él / tú / ellos / Ana

3. Es lástima que *ella* lo haya dicho.
   nosotros / yo / tú / los alumnos / él

Escuchar y hablar

la Alhambra (*palace of the Moorish kings in Granada*)
el azulejo   colored tile
el camarero   waiter
el cante flamenco   flamenco (*Andalusian gypsy singing*)
la catedral   cathedral
la comedia   comedy
la copa   (wine) glass
creer   to believe, think
el dramaturgo   playwright
dudar   to doubt
entender (ie)   to understand
estrecho   narrow
el flan   custard
la función   performance, show
la Giralda (*cathedral tower in Seville*)
la mezquita   mosque
el monumento   monument
negar (ie)   to deny
la pared   wall
posible   possible
el postre   dessert
sabroso   delicious

la sopa   soup
temer   to fear
todo   every
el vino   wine

IDIOMS AND OTHER EXPRESSIONS

el arroz (rice) **con pollo** (chicken)   chicken with rice
comerse las eses   to eat up (swallow) the (letter) "*s*"
darse prisa   to hurry
estar bien de salud   to be in good health
estar para (+ *infin.*)   to be about to
(le extraña) que haya . . .   (she is surprised) that there is, that there are . . .
es lástima   it's too bad
para que lo sepas   let me tell you; for your information
por aquí   this way
por las paredes   along the walls
de postre   as (for) dessert
quedar agradecido   to be grateful

EN UN CAFÉ DE SEVILLA

—Por aquí—dijo Jaime Montero.

Pasamos por una de esas calles estrechas de Sevilla y entramos en un café muy interesante. Por las paredes había azulejos muy hermosos. Había un guitarrista y una chica que cantaba cante flamenco.

The people of Buenos Aires enjoy the many restaurants of the La Boca section, which is in the port area of the city.

Nos sentamos a una mesa y Jaime pidió una comida muy sabrosa: una buena sopa, arroz con pollo y, de postre, flan. En la mesa había copas para vino, pero no tomamos vino, porque no nos gusta. Nos sirvió un camarero andaluz, naturalmente, y por ser andaluz no pudimos entenderle.

—Cuando salimos para España—dijo Carlos—yo no entendía muy bien el español. Aquí he aprendido mucho, pero no puedo entender a este camarero.

—Para que lo sepas—contestó Jaime—hablas y entiendes muy bien. No entiendes al camarero porque, como todo andaluz, se come las eses.

—Me alegro de que nos hayas invitado a hacer este viaje—dijo Virginia.

—Has hecho mucho por nosotros y te quedamos muy agradecidos. Sólo siento que mi padre no haya venido con nosotros. Siempre ha querido ver esos monumentos que acabamos de visitar: la Mezquita de Córdoba, la Catedral de Sevilla con su Giralda y sobre todo la Alhambra, que veremos mañana.

—Es lástima que no te haya acompañado. Pero algún día vendrá a España, ¿verdad?

—No creo que sea posible. Es muy viejo y no está muy bien de salud. Por eso dudo que haga el viaje.

—Bueno, ¡vámonos!—dijo Jaime. —Es hora de ir al teatro. Quiero que vean una comedia de dos dramaturgos andaluces, los hermanos Álvarez Quintero. Espero que sea divertida. Pero temo que sea un poco tarde. Por eso tenemos que darnos prisa. Debemos estar en el teatro a las diez y media. La función está para empezar.

—Me extraña que haya funciones a esa hora—exclamó María.

—Para nosotros no es tarde—explicó Jaime. —En España las funciones siempre empiezan a esa hora.

PREGUNTAS

1. ¿Por dónde fuimos para llegar al café?
2. ¿Cómo era el café?
3. ¿Quién tocaba y quién cantaba?
4. ¿Qué cantaba?
5. ¿Qué comieron Uds.?
6. ¿Qué copas había en la mesa?
7. ¿Qué era el camarero?
8. ¿Qué dijo Carlos?
9. ¿Qué le responde Jaime?
10. ¿Cómo hablan muchos andaluces?
11. ¿De qué se alegra Virginia?
12. ¿Qué siente ella?
13. ¿Qué ha querido siempre su padre?
14. ¿Cómo está el padre de Virginia?
15. ¿Qué duda Virginia?
16. ¿Adónde propone Jaime que vayan?
17. ¿Qué van a ver?
18. ¿Qué espera Jaime?
19. ¿Qué teme?
20. ¿Qué le extraña a María?

Estructura

1. SUBJUNCTIVE IN THE NOUN CLAUSE—CONTINUED

Verbs of *doubt, denial,* and *uncertainty* require the subjunctive in a dependent noun clause. Included in this group are verbs of *belief used negatively.*

> **Dudo** que *haga* el viaje. *I doubt* that *he will make* the trip.
> **Carlos** *niega* que lo *hayan hecho.* Charles *denies* that *they have done* it.
> *No creo* que *sea* posible. I *don't think* *it's* possible.

But verbs of doubt and denial when used negatively are followed by the indicative.

> **No dudo que está en la ciudad.** I don't doubt that he's in the city.
> **No niega que lo han hecho.** He doesn't deny that they've done it.

And verbs of belief when used affirmatively are followed by the indicative.

> **Creo que estarán aquí mañana.** I think they'll be here tomorrow.

PRÁCTICA

Cambie según se indica.

> **Juan estudia mucho.**
> **Dudo que Juan estudie mucho.**
> **No dudo que Juan estudia mucho.**

1. Eso será necesario, ¿verdad?
   Sí, creo que _____.
   No, no creo que _____.

2. Dicen que vendrán mañana.
   Sus amigos dudan que _____.
   Yo no dudo que _____.

3. Dicen que es la verdad.
   Niegan que _____.
   No niegan que _____.

4. ¿Volverán pronto?
   Sí, creo que _____.
   No, no creo que _____.

5. Roberto lo tiene, ¿verdad?
   Roberto niega que _____.
   Roberto no niega que _____.

6. ¿Lo sabe Mercedes?
   Dudo que Mercedes _____.
   No dudo que Mercedes _____.

2. USE OF THE PRESENT PERFECT SUBJUNCTIVE

The present perfect subjunctive is used wherever we use a present perfect tense in English, but where a subjunctive is required in Spanish.

Siento que mi padre *no haya venido*. I am sorry that my father *has not come.*

No creemos que *hayan visto* la Alhambra. We don't think *they have seen* the Alhambra.

PRÁCTICA

Lea en español, cambiando según el modelo.

Han perdido los libros. (Siento que . . .)
Siento que hayan perdido los libros.

1. ¿Ha vuelto el médico?
   Dudo que . . . / No creo que . . .

2. Han estado enfermos.
   Es lástima que . . . / Temo que . . .

3. Juanito la ha visto hoy, ¿verdad?
   Juanito niega que . . . / No niega que . . .

4. Yo he prometido hacerlo.
   Ellos se alegran de que . . . / No creen que . . .

5. Hemos llegado temprano.
   Les extraña que . . . / Se alegran de que . . .

6. Ha sido imposible hacer eso.
   Creo que . . . / Dudan que . . .

3. USES OF PARA AND POR

Para has the following meanings:

1. *in order to*

   Estudiamos para aprender. We study to (in order to) learn.

2. *by,* when used with expressions of future time

   Estaremos de vuelta para las nueve. We'll be back by nine.

3. *about to* in the set phrase **estar para** (*to be about to*)

La función está para empezar.   The performance is about to begin.

Por has the following meanings:

1. *by*, expressing *agent* (with the passive voice) or *means* (by phone, etc.)

La novela fue escrita por Cervantes.   The novel was written by Cervantes.
Enviaron la carta por correo aéreo.   They sent the letter by air mail.

2. *around, along*

Por las paredes había azulejos.   Along the walls there were colored tiles.
Estará por aquí.   He must be around here.
Lo haremos por Navidad.   We'll do it around Christmas.

3. *out of, because of, from* (expressing cause)

Lo hizo por caridad.   He did it out of charity.
Lo hicieron por temor.   They did it from fear.
Lo hago por gusto.   I do it because I like to.
Por ser andaluz no podemos entenderlo.   Because he's Andalusian (because of his being an Andalusian) we can't understand him.

4. *in* or *at* in time expressions

Tenemos clases por la mañana.   We have classes in the morning.
Estudiamos por la noche.   We study at night.

Both **para** and **por** have several meanings that are equivalent to English *for*. Here the meanings of English *for* must be carefully distinguished, since **para** and **por** are not interchangeable.

Para is equivalent to *for* with the following meanings:

1. *destination* (places), *intended for* (persons or things)

Salimos para España.   We left for Spain.
Este regalo es para ti.   This gift is for you.
Esta es la lección para mañana.   This is the lesson for tomorrow.
Había vasos para vino.   There were glasses for wine (wineglasses).

2. *comparison*

Para nosotros no es tarde.   For us it's not late.
Para yanqui hablas muy bien.   For a Yankee you speak very well.

Por is equivalent to *for* with the following meanings:

1. *in exchange for*

Pagué ocho pesos por las flores.   I paid eight pesos for the flowers.

2. *on behalf of, for the sake of*

Ud. ha hecho mucho por nosotros.   You've done a lot for us.
Lo hizo por su madre.   He did it for his mother (for his mother's sake).

3. *because of*

Por eso.   For that reason; therefore.
No lo compró por falta de dinero.   He didn't buy it for lack of money.

4. *for*, expressing duration of present or future (not past) time

Estarán aquí por ocho días.   They'll be here for a week.

5. *to take for* (*consider*)

Lo tomaron por español.   They took him for a Spaniard.
Lo tomamos por hombre honrado.   We take him for (consider him) an honest man.

6. *to go for, come for*, etc.

Vino por el dinero.   He came for the money.

7. in exclamations

¡Por Dios!   For heaven's sake!

PRÁCTICA

Lea en español, usando **para** *o* **por** *(y a veces las dos palabras)*.

1. Comemos _____ vivir.
2. Esta carta es _____ mi novia.
3. Lo harán _____ mí.
4. Lo han hecho _____ necesidad.
5. ¿Hay tazas _____ café?
6. ¿Estarán de vuelta _____ Pascuas?
7. Haz el favor de llamarme _____ teléfono.
8. _____ eso no dijeron nada.
9. Es muy temprano _____ ti.
10. Mariano fue a la biblioteca _____ los libros.
11. Se quedarán en la Argentina _____ varias semanas.
12. ¿Cuándo van a salir _____ México?
13. Jugaron al tenis _____ la tarde.
14. ¿Me han tomado _____ mexicano?
15. Esta corbata es _____ tu hermano.
16. ¿Cuánto pagaste _____ el coche?

Spain is a land of castles. The Alcazar in Segovia, shown here, was built in the thirteenth century as a residence for the kings and queens of Castile.

17. ¿Qué han preparado Uds. _____ hoy?
18. Vamos a hacer un viaje _____ Hispanoamérica.
19. No dejes de volver _____ las siete.
20. Estoy _____ salir ahora.

Tareas

Diga en español.

1. "This way," Jaime said to us, and we went into a very interesting café.
2. In the café there was a guitarist, and a girl was singing flamenco.
3. We ordered a delicious dinner of soup, chicken with rice, and custard.
4. Because the waiter was Andalusian, Carlos could not understand him.
5. Like many Andalusians, he swallowed his *s*'s.
6. Virginia is glad that Jaime has invited us, but she is sorry that her father has not come with us.
7. She doesn't think that he will make the trip to Spain, because he is old and is not in good health.
8. Jaime wants us to see a comedy of two Andalusian dramatists.
9. He hopes that it will be amusing.
10. We have to hurry, because the performance is about to begin.
11. María is surprised that there are performances at ten-thirty.

Composición oral o escrita

One of your friends is about to leave for Spain. He (or she) will travel through the country for six months. He speaks Spanish well for an American, but they won't take him for a Spaniard. He paid a lot for the ticket. At least it's a lot for you, and you're afraid you can't go with him for lack of money. You don't think he'll be able to call you by phone from Seville, but he'll write to you by air mail. You hope to see him around Christmas; he'll be back by then. You don't doubt that he'll have some gifts for you. (Be original: use as many other cases of **para** and **por** as you can think of.)

Diálogo

UN RESTORÁN EN ANDALUCÍA

CONCHA—¡Eres un ángel! ¡Qué bueno[1] que hayas consentido en[2] acompañarme!

JORGE—Sirvo para algo, ¿eh? ¡Para llevar todos estos paquetes![3] Pero despúes de tanto tiempo yendo de tienda en tienda[4] tengo un hambre atroz.[5] ¿Por qué no comemos ahora mismo?[6]

CONCHA—Quiero ir a una tienda más. No creo que vayas a morir de hambre.

JORGE—Déjalo para más tarde. Conozco un buen restorán que hay por aquí.[7]

* * *

JORGE—(*Al camarero.*) Tráiganos[8] la lista[9] por favor. (*A Concha.*) ¡Qué vas a tomar, Concha? Recomiendo[10] el asado de cabrito.[11]

CONCHA—¿Hay pescado?[12]

JORGE—Dudo que esté muy fresco.[13]

CONCHA—Bueno, pues, voy a tomar bistec con papas fritas y una ensalada.[14]

JORGE—Y yo, el asado de cabrito. Es sabrosísimo.[15]

CONCHA—¿No quieres legumbres?[16] Hay guisantes, zanahorias, espinacas.[17]

JORGE—¡Quiá![18] Las detesto.[19]

CAMARERO—¿Qué van a tomar de postre?

JORGE—Para mí, flan.

CONCHA—Para mí, nada. No quiero engordar.

[1]qué bueno *how nice*

[2]consentir en *to consent to*

[3]el paquete *package*

[4]de . . . en *from . . . to*

[5]atroz *terrible*

[6]ahora mismo *right now*

[7]por aquí *around here*

[8]tráiganos *bring us*

[9]la lista *menu*

[10]recomendar *to recommend*

[11]el asado de cabrito *roast kid*

[12]el pescado *fish*

[13]fresco *fresh*

[14]la ensalada *salad*

[15]sabrosísimo *absolutely delicious*

[16]la legumbre *vegetable*

[17]guisantes, zanahorias, espinacas *peas, carrots, spinach*

[18]¡Quiá! *Not on your life!*

[19]detestar *to detest, loathe*

PREGUNTAS PERSONALES

1. ¿Acompañas a tu novia (novio) cuando va de compras?
2. ¿Llevas los paquetes?
3. ¿Invitas a tu novia (novio) a comer en un restorán?
4. ¿Te gusta comer en un restorán?
5. ¿Hay por aquí un buen restorán?
6. ¿Te gusta el pescado?
7. ¿Te gustaría el asado de cabrito?
8. ¿Te gustan las legumbres?
9. ¿Qué legumbres te gustan más? ¿Los guisantes? ¿Las zanahorias? ¿Las espinacas?
10. ¿Siempre pides un postre?
11. Muchas chicas no toman postre. ¿Por qué?
12. ¿Le das siempre una propina (*tip*) al camarero?

Notas culturales

The Moors in Spain

Andalusia is the old Moorish Spain. In 711 the Berbers from North Africa invaded and by 718 had pushed their conquest through the whole peninsula, except for a few mountain strongholds in the north.

Under Moorish domination the Christians were generally treated well and prospered. The Moors were more advanced, by far, than the peoples of Europe in the Middle Ages, and a flourishing civilization developed. Impressive Moorish cities grew up at Valencia, Toledo, and Córdoba. By the tenth century Córdoba was the most civilized city in Europe and a great center of learning. Its library contained 400,000 books. Its university attracted students from other European countries and boasted the leading scholars in medicine, mathematics, astronomy, geography and botany, and in history, philosophy, and juris-prudence. These erudite men transmitted to Europe not only Arabic learning and culture, but that of ancient Greece as well.

The Moors brought to Spain skillful methods of agriculture, including irrigation, which enabled the country to support a greater population. They introduced the Moorish arch and built magnificent buildings like the Alhambra at Granada and the great Mezquita at Córdoba.

In 718 the Spaniards defeated the Moors in the battle of Covadonga, in Asturias, which was a great moral victory, though not so important militarily. This began the period of the Reconquest, which lasted for eight centuries. In 1492 the last Moorish kingdom, Granada, fell to Ferdinand and Isabel and the Moors were finally overcome.

20

No se ganó Zamora en una hora.
Rome was not built in a day.

Present subjunctive of verbs ending in *-car*, *-gar*, and *-zar*

You have seen that verbs in **-car, -gar,** and **-zar** have a spelling change in the
first person singular of the preterit.

busqué   **pagué**   **empecé**

These same changes occur throughout the present subjunctive.

buscar to look for		pagar to pay		empezar to begin	
bus*qu*e	bus*qu*emos	pa*gu*e	pa*gu*emos	empie*c*e	empe*c*emos
bus*qu*es	(bus*qu*éis)	pa*gu*es	(pa*gu*éis)	empie*c*es	(empe*c*éis)
bus*qu*e	bus*qu*en	pa*gu*e	pa*gu*en	empie*c*e	empie*c*en

PRÁCTICA

Cambie según se indica.

1. Prefieren que *Ud.* llegue temprano.
   tú / ellos / él / yo / nosotros

2. Ruegan que lo *busquemos* hoy.
   yo / ella / Ud. / ellas / tú / tú y yo

3. Sugieren que *yo* lo comience ahora.
   Ud. / nosotros / tú / Uds. / ella

259

Present indicative and present subjunctive of verbs ending in -*guir*

Verbs ending in **-guir** change **gu** to **g** in the first person singular of the present indicative and throughout the present subjunctive.

---

seguir (i)   to follow; to continue

PRESENT INDICATIVE		PRESENT SUBJUNCTIVE	
si*g*o	seguimos	si*g*a	si*g*amos
sigues	(seguís)	sigas	(sigáis)
sigue	siguen	siga	si*g*an

PRÁCTICA

Cambie según se indica.

1. Los alumnos siguen conversando.
   Ud. / ellas / tú / nosotros / yo

2. Esperan que *tú* sigas bien.
   Uds. / él / yo / Ud. / tú y yo / ellas

Escuchar y hablar

almorzar (ue)   to lunch
la animación   bustle, movement
antiguo   old, ancient
el árbol   tree
la cantidad   quantity
cartaginés   Carthaginian
el catalán   Catalan
citarse con   to make an appointment with
conviene   it is advisable
la derecha   right (hand)
derecho   straight (ahead)
enseñar   to teach
la esquina   corner
fabricar   to manufacture
fundar   to found

el habitante   inhabitant
industrial   industrial
la izquierda   left (hand)
lejos   far
lo *neuter def. art.*   the
lo que *rel. pron.*   that which, what
necesario   necessary
ofrecerse a   to offer to
la palabra   word
la Plaza (Square) **de Cataluña** (Catalonia) (*central square in Barcelona*)
preciso   necessary
probable   probable
producir   to produce
publicar   to publish
puntual   punctual

la rambla   boulevard (*in Barcelona*)
saludar   to greet
tacaño   stingy
el tejido   textile
varios   several
el yanqui   Yankee

IDIOMS AND OTHER EXPRESSIONS

lo de siempre   the same old thing
me han dicho que   I have been told that
parece mentira   it seems incredible
a pie   on foot
unos cuantos   a few

EN BARCELONA

—Es preciso que estemos en la Plaza de Cataluña a las nueve y media—le dije a Carlos mientras tomábamos el desayuno en el hotel en Barcelona. —Nos hemos citado con don Tomás Milá.

—¿Dónde queda[1] la Plaza de Cataluña?—le pregunté al camarero que nos servía.

—Está bastante lejos, señor. Si Ud. va a pie, vaya a la izquierda al salir del hotel. Al llegar a la esquina hay que ir a la derecha hasta la Rambla. Luego vaya otra vez a la izquierda y siga derecho.

—¡Son las nueve y veinte!—exclamé al salir del hotel. —Conviene que busquemos un taxi. Es necesario llegar a tiempo, porque me han dicho que estos catalanes son muy puntuales. ¡Son los yanquis de España!

Don Tomás era un viejo amigo del profesor Martínez. —¿Cómo sigue[2] mi buen amigo allá en América?—fue lo primero que nos dijo don Tomás después de saludarnos.[3] —Veo que les ha enseñado muy bien el español. Pero es probable que no les haya enseñado nada de catalán. ¡Lástima! Como aquí se habla catalán, conviene saber unas cuantas palabras.

Don Tomás iba a mostrarnos algunos de los puntos de interés de Barcelona. —Empecemos con la Catedral—nos dijo. —No está muy lejos.

Fuimos a ver la Universidad también, pero estaba cerrada.

Barcelona es una ciudad muy interesante y muy antigua. Fue fundada por los cartagineses. Tiene más de dos millones de habitantes. Es una ciudad industrial. Aquí se fabrican tejidos en grandes cantidades y se publican muchos libros.

Después de visitar varios puntos de interés, Carlos exclamó de pronto: —Propongo que almorcemos. ¡Tengo mucha hambre!

Almorzamos en un buen restorán en una de las Ramblas. —Lo mejor de Barcelona—dijo Carlos—es esta Rambla con sus flores y sus árboles.

—Para mí—dije—lo más interesante es la animación que se ve en todas partes. Estos catalanes se dan mucha prisa, como los norteamericanos. Parece mentira que sean españoles.

Después de hablar un rato de lo que habíamos visto, don Tomás se despidió. Al quedarme solo con Carlos, no me ofrecí a pagar la cuenta. Carlos no había pagado nada hasta entonces. Es un poco tacaño.

—¡Caramba!—exclamó de pronto. —¿Es posible que haya dejado mi dinero en el hotel? No lo encuentro.

—¡Lo de siempre!—pensé. —¡Ahora es necesario que yo pague otra vez!

NOTAS

1. **Quedar** sometimes means *to be.*

   Quedamos muy agradecidos.   We are very grateful.
   ¿Dónde queda la Plaza?   Where is the Square?

2. **Seguir** sometimes means *to be now, to still be.*

   ¿Cómo sigue el señor Martínez?   How is Mr. Martínez now?
   Sigue muy bien.   He is still very well.

3. You have been using **al** plus an infinitive to mean *upon (doing something).*
   This is a pattern in Spanish. After a preposition the infinitive must be used
   to translate the English verbal noun in *-ing.*

   Al entrar en el café . . .   On entering the café . . .
   Después de hablar un rato . . .   After talking a while . . .
   Antes de comer . . .   Before eating . . .

PRÁCTICA

Diga en español, cambiando según se indica.

1. before leaving
   lunching / sitting down / reading

2. after returning
   answering / writing / studying

3. upon getting up
   going to bed / waking up / getting dressed

PREGUNTAS

1. ¿Dónde es preciso que estemos a las nueve y media?
2. ¿Con quién nos hemos citado?
3. ¿Qué le pregunta Ud. al camarero?
4. Al salir del hotel, ¿cómo se llega a la Plaza de Cataluña?
5. ¿Qué conviene que busquemos?
6. ¿Quién es don Tomás?
7. ¿Qué nos pregunta?
8. ¿Qué lengua se habla en Barcelona?
9. ¿Qué nos sugiere don Tomás?
10. ¿Cuántos habitantes tiene Barcelona?
11. ¿Qué propone Carlos?

12. Para Ud., ¿qué es lo más interesante de Barcelona?
13. ¿Cómo es Carlos?
14. ¿Qué exclama él?
15. ¿Qué es necesario que haga Ud.?
16. Uds. no pudieron ver el interior de la Universidad de Barcelona, ¿verdad?
   ¿Por qué no?

Estructura

1. SUBJUNCTIVE MOOD IN THE NOUN CLAUSE—CONTINUED

Impersonal expressions that *do not stress a fact*, such as those of *necessity, possibility, probability,* and *advisability*, require the subjunctive in a dependent noun clause.

Ahora es necesario que yo pague. Now it's necessary for me to pay (that I pay).

Es preciso que estemos allí. It's necessary that we be there.

Es probable que no les haya enseñado el catalán. It's probable that he has not taught you Catalan.

Conviene que busquemos un taxi. It's advisable that we look for a taxi.

Some common impersonal expressions of this type are

es necesario	it is necessary	**conviene**	it is advisable
es preciso	it is necessary	**basta**	it is sufficient
es posible	it is possible	**parece mentira**	it seems incredible
es probable	it is probable		

When the dependent verb has no subject, the infinitive is used.

Es necesario llegar a tiempo. It's necessary to arrive on time.

Conviene saber unas cuantas palabras. It's advisable to know a few words.

Impersonal expressions that *stress a fact* take the indicative in a dependent noun clause.

Es verdad que están aquí. It's true that they are here.

Es cierto que lo han hecho. It's certain that they have done it.

PRÁCTICA

a. *Cambie según se indica.*

1. Es posible que ellos no vengan.
   yo / Ud. / nosotros / ellas / tú

2. Es probable que él lo haga mañana.
tú / nosotros / ellos / yo / él

3. Conviene que yo lo pague.
Uds. / ella / tú / tú y yo / ellos

4. Basta que Ud. lo diga.
Ud. y yo / ellos / tú / yo / Uds.

5. Parece mentira que hayan vuelto.
nosotros / Ud. / yo / tú / ellas

6. Es verdad que lo han visto.
nosotros / tú / ella / yo / Ud. y yo

b. *Diga en español, cambiando según se indica.*

1. It is advisable that we see it.
that you see it / that they see it / that I see it

2. It is sufficient for him to know it.
for me to know it / for them to know it

3. It seems incredible that she has left.
that you have left / that they have left

4. It is necessary that we read a lot.
that I read / that you read / that she read

5. It is possible that they have seen it.
that you have seen it / that he has seen it

2. REFLEXIVE VERB FOR THE PASSIVE VOICE

The commonest Spanish equivalent of the English passive voice is the reflexive verb. This is used when a *thing* is the subject and no *agent* is expressed. Note that the subject normally follows the verb. When the subject is plural, the verb is plural.

Aquí se habla catalán.   Catalan is spoken here.
Se fabrican tejidos.   Textiles are manufactured.
Ahora se publican muchos libros.   Many books are published now.
Se ve mucha animación en todas partes.   A great deal of movement is seen everywhere.

PRÁCTICA

Conteste según el modelo.

¿Qué se habla aquí? (español)
Aquí se habla español.

1. ¿Qué se habla aquí?
   inglés / italiano / portugués / francés

2. ¿Qué se estudia aquí?
   historia / francés / español

3. ¿Qué se fabrica aquí?
   zapatos / sombreros / tejidos

4. ¿Qué se ve aquí?
   muchas fincas / edificios interesantes / ranchos enormes

5. ¿Qué se produce aquí?
   muchos caballos / muchos automóviles / muchos zapatos

6. ¿Qué se lee aquí?
   muchos libros / muchos periódicos

7. ¿Qué se escribe aquí?
   muchas composiciones / muchos ejercicios

3. THE TRUE PASSIVE

Spanish has a true passive voice. Just as the English passive is formed with the verb *to be* plus a past participle, the Spanish passive is formed with the verb **ser** plus a past participle. This is used when the *agent* ("by someone") is expressed or clearly understood. The past participle agrees in gender and number with the subject. Spanish speakers, however, use the passive less frequently than the active voice.

SUBJECT	Ser	PAST PARTICIPLE	AGENT
La ciudad	fue	fundada	por los cartaginses.
Esas ciudades	fueron	fundadas	por los españoles.
El libro	fue	escrito	por Cervantes.
Estos libros	fueron	publicados	por Espasa-Calpe.
El criminal	fue	detenido	(agent clearly understood).

PRÁCTICA

a. *Cambie a la voz pasiva, siguiendo el modelo.*

Velázquez pintó ese cuadro.
Ese cuadro fue pintado por Velázquez.

1. Pepe escribió esta carta.
2. El chico cerró la puerta.
3. Pizarro fundó aquellas ciudades.
4. El Greco pintó esos cuadros.
5. Mi mamá hizo este vestido.
6. Nuestro abuelo vendió la finca.

b. *Conteste con voz activa y pasiva, según el modelo.*

¿Quién escribió esta novela? (Cervantes)
Cervantes escribió esta novela.
Esta novela fue escrita por Cervantes.

1. ¿Quién compró el rancho? (un médico)
2. ¿Quién preparó la comida? (la criada)
3. ¿Quién prestó el dinero? (un rico)
4. ¿Quién cerró las ventanas? (el profesor)
5. ¿Quién examinó el documento? (un abogado)
6. ¿Quién pintó esos cuadros? (un español)

4. ACTIVE INSTEAD OF THE PASSIVE VOICE WITH A LIVING SUBJECT

In English, a living being is often the subject of a passive verb:

The lieutenant was promoted.

The Spanish equivalent, when no agent is expressed, is the third person plural of the active verb. The English subject becomes the Spanish object.

Ascendieron al teniente.   The lieutenant was promoted. (They promoted the lieutenant.)
La vieron en el teatro.   She was seen in the theater.
Le dijeron que no era posible.   He was told that it was not possible.

PRÁCTICA

Diga en español.

1. He was sent to Spain.
2. He was seen in the gymnasium.
3. I was told that it was the truth.
4. I was asked if it was the truth.
5. They were offered a lot of money.
6. They were promised a new car.

*Antonio Gaudí's
Church of the Sagrada
Familia with its
parabolic forms and
textured surfaces was
his greatest project.
Unfinished at his
death in 1926,
Barcelona's landmark
is still under
construction and is to
be completed
according to the
original plans.*

5. ESTAR *WITH PAST PARTICIPLES ("RESULTANT CONDITION")*

You have been using **estar** with adjectives and past participles to express an accidental or temporary state or condition.

Los alumnos están cansados.

Such expressions may resemble a passive voice, but they are not. When the past participle denotes a state or condition (as the result of *previous* action on the subject), **estar** (not **ser**) is used.

$$\boxed{\text{estar} + \text{past participle} = \text{state or condition}}$$

La puerta está cerrada.   The door is closed.
Las ventanas estaban abiertas.   The windows were open.
El libro está escrito en español.   The book is written in Spanish.

PRÁCTICA

Conteste según el modelo.

¿Cerraron el museo?
Sí, el museo está cerrado.

1. ¿Abrieron las puertas?
2. ¿Publicaron el libro?
3. ¿Han vendido las casas?
4. ¿Han ocupado la sala?
5. ¿Han escrito bien las composiciones?
6. ¿Escribieron el documento en español?

Las Ramblas is one of the most famous avenues of Europe. With its center boulevard it lends itself to the pleasures of the paseo—*defined as a short, leisurely stroll—a popular pastime of people in Spain and Latin America alike. In the foreground is the entrance to the Metropolitano, Barcelona's subway system.*

6. *NEUTER ARTICLE* LO

The neuter article **lo** is used with the masculine singular of an adjective as the equivalent of an abstract noun. **Lo** in such expressions is often the equivalent of English *that which is* or *what is*.

> **lo bueno**   the good, that which is good
> **lo malo**   the bad, what is bad
> **lo bello**   the beautiful, that which is beautiful

Sometimes these expressions are equivalent to the corresponding English expression plus the word *thing* or *part* (*of*).

> **lo primero que nos dijo**   the first *thing* (that) he said to us
> **lo mejor de Barcelona**   the best *thing about* Barcelona
> **lo más interesante de la lección**   the most interesting *part of* the lesson

PRÁCTICA

Diga en español.

1. that which is good
2. that which is easy
3. that which is best
4. the difficult thing
5. the interesting thing
6. the worst part

Tareas

Diga en español.

1. It is necessary for us to be in the Plaza de Cataluña at nine-thirty.
2. On leaving the hotel, we go to the left, and at the corner we go to the right.
3. It's advisable for us to look for a taxi.
4. We tell Don Tomás that Mr. Martínez is still well.
5. He says it's probable that Mr. Martínez hasn't taught us Catalan.
6. It's too bad, because Catalan is spoken here.
7. Let's begin with the Cathedral, which isn't far away and is open.
8. The University was closed.
9. Barcelona has more than two million inhabitants, but Seville has fewer than 600,000.
10. In Barcelona textiles are manufactured.
11. "Let's have lunch in a restaurant," says Carlos.
12. For him the best part of Barcelona is the Rambla.
13. It seems incredible that the Catalans are not Yankees.
14. It's probable that Carlos has left his money in the hotel.

Composición oral o escrita

1. Pretend you are on a bus in Spain. Tell the person beside you where you are from and tell him or her something about your home town (when it was founded, how many inhabitants it has, what is manufactured there, etc.).

2. Tell a new student how to get from your dormitory to

   a. the library
   b. a good restaurant
   c. the shopping center (*zona de tiendas*)

   Tell where you go to the left, at which corner you go to the right, and where you go straight ahead.

Diálogo

LA LONJA[1] DE BARCELONA

RAMÓN—Hay muchas cosas que ver en Barcelona y en sus alrededores[2] . . .

LUISITO—Me imagino[3] que hay muchas cosas de interés. Pero sigue.

RAMÓN—Subimos a las dos famosas montañas, Montjuich, con sus jardines y su teatro griego,[4] y Tibidabo, donde hay un parque de atracciones[5] y desde donde se ve toda la ciudad. Vimos la iglesia de la Sagrada Familia,[6] cuya arquitectura[7] es la más original del mundo.

LUISITO—Fue construida por Gaudí,* ¿verdad?

RAMÓN—Así es. Pero lo más curioso de mi visita fue que quería ver un edificio muy antiguo y no pude encontrarlo. Quería ver la Lonja, que fue fundada en 1383. Me dijeron que debía hallarse en el Barrio Gótico.[8]

LUISITO—Es allí donde se hallan todos los edificios medievales[9] de Barcelona, ¿verdad?

RAMÓN—¡Exacto![10] Bueno, busqué en todas partes. Hice muchas preguntas. Nadie sabía decirme nada. Después de buscar más de una hora, fue preciso abandonar la búsqueda.[11] Por fin me dirigí a la Lonja actual,[12] en que no había tenido ganas de entrar, y allí encontré lo que buscaba. Dentro de ese vasto edificio se ha preservado la antigua Sala de Contratos[13] de la Lonja original.

[1]La Lonja *Exchange*
[2]los alrededores *surroundings*
[3]imaginarse *to imagine*
[4]griego *Greek*
[5]parque de atracciones *amusement park*
[6]Sagrada Familia *Holy Family*
[7]cuya arquitectura *whose architecture*

[8]Barrio Gótico *Gothic Quarter*
[9]medieval *medieval*
[10]¡Exacto! *Exactly!*
[11]la búsqueda *search*
[12]actual *present*
[13]Sala de Contratos *Hall of Contracts*

* Antonio Gaudí (1852–1926), Spanish architect and designer.

PREGUNTAS PERSONALES

1. ¿Ha estado Ud. en Barcelona?
2. Si no, Ud. piensa ir allá algún día, ¿verdad?
3. Hay muchas cosas que ver en Barcelona, ¿verdad? ¿Cuáles son algunas?
4. Ud. querrá ir a Tibidabo. ¿Qué se ve desde allí?
5. Ud. podrá divertirse mucho en Tibidabo. ¿Por qué?
6. Ud. querrá ver la iglesia de la Sagrada Familia. ¿Qué sabe Ud. de su arquitectura?
7. Ud. irá también al Barrio Gótico. ¿Qué clase de edificios verá Ud. allí?
8. ¿Adónde irá Ud. para ver lo que queda de la antigua Lonja de Barcelona?
9. ¿Qué se ha preservado allí?
10. ¿Hay edificios muy antiguos en la ciudad donde Ud. vive?

Notas culturales

Spain in Early Times

You read earlier that Barcelona was founded by the Carthaginians. In ancient times a number of peoples invaded the Iberian Peninsula and left varying degrees of influence on the racial mixture and the culture. Spain was inhabited in paleolithic times by men who reflected their surroundings in the marvelously realistic and graceful paintings of animals on the cave walls of Altamira in the northern province of Santander. At the beginning of recorded history, the peninsula was inhabited by the race known as Iberians, who are believed to have come from Africa. Around 1000 B.C., and in greater numbers in the sixth century B.C., the Celts penetrated Spain from Europe and mixed with the Iberians along the northern coast and on the central plateau to produce the Celtiberian race.

The Phoenicians arrived eleven centuries before Christ and established Cádiz in 1101 B.C. Later came the Carthaginians and Greeks, who founded colonies along the Mediterranean coast. These three peoples were essentially colonists and traders and, while they influenced the art and culture of the Peninsula, they did not contribute as much to the racial mixture as did the Celts.

The overwhelmingly important invasion in ancient times was that of the Romans, during the period of the Punic Wars with Carthage. In 218 B.C. powerful Roman armies landed on the coast of what is now Catalonia and began the conquest and Romanization of the territory, a project that would take two hundred years. Roman influence in Spain was of vast extent. The Romans gave the country its language, which evolved from the popular Latin spoken by soldiers and colonists. In addition, they gave it institutions: Roman administrative procedures and social customs and, later, the Christian religion.

They implanted Greco-Roman culture and Etrusco-Roman architecture, building roads, temples, theaters, aqueducts, coliseums, and walled towns.

The Romans were followed by the Goths, who entered the Peninsula in 409. After four hundred years of relative peace, Spain was easy prey for the northern barbarians. The period of Visigothic domination, which lasted until 711, was one of civil wars and anarchy. While the Visigoths did not make cultural contributions on the scale of the Romans, they brought an infusion of vigorous new blood and gave the country lasting legal codes.

21

No firmes carta que no leas, ni bebas agua que no veas.
Don't sign what you don't read nor drink what you don't
know the source of.

Past subjunctive

The past subjunctive* in Spanish has two forms. Both forms, in all verbs, derive from the third person plural of the preterit. The **-ron** is removed and one of the following sets of endings is added:

1. **-ra** endings   2. **-se** endings

-ra	**-ramos**	**-se**	**-semos**
-ras	**(-rais)**	**-ses**	**(-seis)**
-ra	**-ran**	**-se**	**-sen**

	hablar		aprender, vivir	
THIRD PERSON PLURAL PRETERIT	hablaron		aprendieron, vivieron	
-ra ENDINGS	hablara	habláramos	aprendiera	aprendiéramos
	hablaras	(hablarais)	aprendieras	(aprendierais)
	hablara	hablaran	aprendiera	aprendieran
-se ENDINGS	hablase	hablásemos	viviese	viviésemos
	hablases	(hablaseis)	vivieses	(vivieseis)
	hablase	hablasen	viviese	viviesen

Note that the stress always falls on the syllable before the ending, making necessary an accent on the first person plural. The same two sets of endings are used for all three conjugations. In most cases these two forms may be used interchangeably. The **-ra** endings are preferred in Spanish America.

* Also called imperfect subjunctive.

273

PRÁCTICA

Cambie según se indica.

1. Convenía que *tú* contestaras.
   nosotros / ellos / él / yo / Ud.

2. Esperaban que *Ud.* aprendiese mucho.
   yo / nosotros / Uds. / tú / ellas

3. Querían que *yo* escribiera la carta.
   tú / nosotros / Ud. / Ud. y yo / ellas

Past subjunctive of stem-changing verbs

Since the past subjunctive of all verbs is formed on the third person plural of the preterit, only stem-changing verbs in **-ir** have a change in this tense: **e** changes to **i**, and **o** changes to **u**. Verbs in **-ar** and **-er** do not change.

INFINITIVE	THIRD PERSON PLURAL PRETERIT	PAST SUBJUNCTIVE	
sentir	s*i*ntieron	s*i*ntiera	s*i*ntiese
pedir	p*i*dieron	p*i*diera	p*i*diese
dormir	d*u*rmieron	d*u*rmiera	d*u*rmiese
pensar	pensaron	pensara	pensase
volver	volvieron	volviera	volviese

PRÁCTICA

Cambie según se indica.

1. Sentían que *Ud.* lo perdiera.
   yo / nosotros / ellos / tú / él

2. Permitieron que *él* lo devolviese.
   tú / yo / Uds. / ella / Ud. y yo

3. Era lástima que *Ud.* no se sintiera bien.
   Uds. / tú / él / yo / nosotros

4. Rogaron que *nos vistiéramos* pronto.
   él / yo / tú / Ud. y yo / Uds.

5. Esperaban que *yo* durmiera bien.
   nosotros / ella / ellas / Uds. / tú

Escuchar y hablar

el **Cabildo**   Town Hall (*in Buenos Aires*)
la **clase**   kind
colonial   colonial
la **comisión**   commission
la **compañía**   company
el **contrato**   contract
el **destierro**   exile
el **dictator**   dictator
el **que** *rel. pron.*   who, the one who
el **entusiasmo**   enthusiasm
el **estudiante**   student
el **estudio**   study
extraño   strange
fascinar   to fascinate
fuera *past subj. of* **ir**   that he go
fuésemos *past subj. of* **ir**   that we go
ganar   to earn
histórico   historical
huir   to flee
impresionar   to impress
interesar   to interest
lleno   full
la **maquinaria agrícola**   agricultural
  (farm) machinery

el **monumento**   monument
negociar   to negotiate
el **oeste**   west
la **oficina**   office
la **ópera**   opera
el **período**   period
precioso   pretty, beautiful
quien *rel. pron.*   who
recibir   to receive
rosado   pink
sorprender   to surprise
los **tíos**   uncle and aunt

IDIOMS AND OTHER EXPRESSIONS

de aquí en (cuatro días)   (four days) from
  now
como de costumbre   as usual
haber de + *infin.*   to be to; to be
  supposed to; must
sin más ni más   just like that; without
  more ado

BUENOS AIRES

Esta mañana hablábamos de la América del Sur. El señor Martínez
preguntó: —¿Hay alguien en la clase que haya estado en la Argentina?

Dos estudiantes levantaron la mano.[1] Uno de ellos era Juan. El profesor
le pidió que nos hablara un poco de su viaje.

—Bueno,—dijo Juan, —han de[2] saber Uds. que un tío mío vende
maquinaria agrícola. Esta clase de maquinaria se vende mucho en la Argentina.
Un día mi tío recibió una carta de la oficina de su compañía en Chicago. Le
pedían que fuera a Buenos Aires para negociar un contrato muy importante,
porque no había nadie en la compañía que hablara español tan bien como él.

—Le sorprendió a mi tío que le pidiesen eso sin más ni más. «¡Dios mío!»
exclamó. «De aquí en cuatro días he de estar en Buenos Aires!» Le propuso a
mi tía que lo acompañase. Mis padres les rogaron a mis tíos que me llevaran a
mí también.

—Hicimos el viaje en avión. Buenos Aires nos impresionó mucho. Es una
ciudad tan grande como Chicago y con casi tantos habitantes como Chicago:

Calle Florida in Buenos Aires—the city that has been called the Paris of South America. Since 1910 Argentina has been an urban rather than a rural nation, with much of the population concentrated in Greater Buenos Aires.

casi tres millones. Mi tía y yo vimos más de la ciudad que mi tío. Él no tenía tanto tiempo como nosotros para visitar museos y monumentos históricos. Fuimos a ver el Cabildo, un precioso edificio colonial, y la Casa Rosada, que se encuentra en la Plaza de Mayo y que es la Casa Blanca de la Argentina. Una noche mi tía quería que fuésemos al famoso Teatro Colón. Esa noche se dio la ópera *Carmen*.

—Lo que me gustó más fue la excursión que hicimos a Luján, una pequeña ciudad al oeste de Buenos Aires, para ver la catedral y el maravilloso museo histórico. Nunca he visto ningún museo que me haya interesado más. Me fascina la historia argentina. Hice un estudio especial del período de Rosas, quien fue dictador de 1829 a 1852. Como muchos dictadores, tuvo que huir, y no es extraño que muriera en el destierro.

—Mientras nosotros nos divertíamos, mi pobre tío trabajaba tanto como de costumbre. Pero al fin le dieron el contrato. Naturalmente estaba lleno de entusiasmo. «¡Qué ciudad ésta para los negocios!» exclamó. «¡He de ganar más de diez mil dólares en comisiones! ¿Conocen Uds. otra ciudad que sea tan interesante?»

NOTAS

1. Where English uses the plural, Spanish uses the singular for parts of the body and articles of clothing of which *only one per person* is referred to.

   Dos estudiantes levantaron la mano.   Two students raised their hands.
   Se pusieron el sombrero.   They put on their hats.

2. **Haber de** followed by the infinitive expresses future time, sometimes with a slight degree of obligation. It means *to be to* or *to be supposed to*. It may translate English *must*, but without the degree of compulsion expressed by **tener que**.

De aquí en cuatro días *he de estar* en Buenos Aires.   Four days from now
  I am to be (am supposed to be) in Buenos Aires.

Ha de ganar diez mil dólares.   *He is to earn* ten thousand dollars.
Han de saber Uds. . . .   *You must know . . .*

But:

Tengo que estudiar.   *I must (have to) study.*

PRÁCTICA

Diga en español.

a. 1. They washed their faces.
   2. They raised their hands.
   3. They put on their hats.
   4. They put on their shirts.

b. 1. They are to be here tomorrow.
   2. They are to sing tomorrow.
   3. They are to speak tomorrow.
   4. I am supposed to study now.
   5. I am supposed to work now.
   6. I am supposed to go now.

PREGUNTAS

1. ¿Qué preguntó el señor Martínez?
2. ¿Qué hicieron dos estudiantes?
3. ¿Qué le pidió a Juan el señor Martínez?
4. ¿Qué vende un tío de Juan?
5. ¿Dónde se venden muchas de las máquinas?
6. ¿Qué recibió su tío?
7. ¿Qué le pedían en la carta?
8. ¿Por qué?
9. ¿Qué propuso el tío de Juan?
10. ¿Qué le rogaron al tío los padres de Juan?
11. ¿Cómo hicieron el viaje?
12. ¿Es grande Buenos Aires?
13. ¿Cuántos habitantes tiene?
14. ¿Por qué no visitó el tío tantos museos como Juan?
15. ¿Qué puntos de interés vieron Juan y su tía?
16. ¿Qué le gustó más a Juan?
17. ¿Cuándo fue Rosas dictador de la Argentina?
18. ¿Qué exclamó el tío de Juan?
19. ¿Cuánto dinero había de ganar en comisiones?

Estructura

1. USE OF THE PAST SUBJUNCTIVE

Up to this point our subordinate noun clauses have depended upon a main verb in the present tense. When the subjunctive was required in the dependent clause, we used the present or the present perfect subjunctive.

> **Quiero que Ud. me pague.**   I want you to pay me.
> **Dudo que hayan llegado.**   I doubt that they have arrived.

When, however, the main verb is in the imperfect, preterit, or conditional tense and a subjunctive is required in the subordinate clause, the verb in the dependent clause is normally in the past subjunctive.

IMPERFECT, PRETERIT, CONDITIONAL		PAST SUBJUNCTIVE	
Quería	que	**fuésemos al teatro.**	She wanted us to go to the theater.
Le pidieron	que	**fuera a Buenos Aires.**	They asked him to go to Buenos Aires.
Preferiría	que	**Ud. hablara en español.**	I would prefer that you speak in Spanish.

But the past subjunctive may follow any verb which logically calls for a simple past tense in the dependent clause.

> **Dudo que llegaran.**   I doubt that they arrived.
> **No es extraño que Rosas muriera en el destierro.**   It is not strange that Rosas died in exile.

PRÁCTICA

a. *Cambie según el modelo.*

Carlos salió. (Querían)
Querían que Carlos saliera.

1. Ud. llegó temprano.
   esperaban / se alegraban

2. Yo no volvería.
   sentían / temían

3. Él durmió en un hotel.
   convendría / preferirían

4. Ellos lo pidieron.
   fue necesario / convenía

5. Ella me buscó.
   fue preciso / parecía mentira

b. *Diga en español, cambiando según se indica.*

1. I am glad they saw it.
   they wrote it / they prepared it

2. They asked me to sing.
   to dance / to speak

3. She told us to study.
   to eat / to work

4. You doubted that we would return.
   we would leave / we would enter

5. It was advisable for me to learn.
   for me to pay / for me to answer

2. SUBJUNCTIVE IN THE ADJECTIVE CLAUSE

An adjective clause is one that is used as an adjective—that is, it modifies a noun or pronoun. The noun or pronoun which it modifies is called its antecedent. When the antecedent is not a definite person or thing, or is negative or non-existent, the verb in the adjective clause must be in the subjunctive.

	INDEFINITE OR NEGATIVE ANTECEDENT		SUBJUNCTIVE IN ADJECTIVE CLAUSE
¿Conoce Ud.	**una ciudad**	que	**sea tan interesante?**
¿Hay	**alguien**	que	**haya estado en Buenos Aires?**
No había	**nadie**	que	**hablara español.**

But when the antecedent is a definite person or thing in the mind of the speaker, the adjective clause is in the indicative.

Conozco una ciudad que es tan interesante.   I know a city (a definite city) that is as interesting.

Tengo un amigo que ha estado en Buenos Aires.   I have a friend (a definite friend) who has been in Buenos Aires.

Ayer conocí a una chica que hablaba español.   Yesterday I met a girl (a definite girl) who spoke Spanish.

A family at home in Buenos Aires. The economic development of Argentina has created a large middle class. Housing conditions are generally better than in most Latin American countries. The Argentines also eat better than some of their neighbors because of the abundance of domestically produced meat.

PRÁCTICA

a. *Use la forma correcta del verbo indicado, siguiendo el modelo.*

Conozco a una chica que _____ (hablar) portugués.
Conozco a una chica que habla portugués.

No conozco a nadie que _____ (hablar) portugués.
No conozco a nadie que hable portugués.

1. Tengo un libro que _____ (ser) fácil.
   Me hace falta un libro que _____ (ser) fácil.

2. Es una cosa que me _____ (gustar) mucho.
   No hay nada que me _____ (gustar) más.

3. Tengo un amigo que _____ (trabajar) mucho.
   No hay nadie que _____ (trabajar) tanto.

4. Conozco a un hombre que _____ (poder) hacerlo.
   ¿Conoces un hombre que _____ (poder) hacerlo?

5. Es una persona que _____ (saber) mucho.
   No hay nadie que _____ (saber) más.

6. Tenemos una secretaria que _____ (estar) bien preparada.
   Buscamos una secretaria que _____ (estar) bien preparada.

b. *Conteste, usando las palabras sugeridas.*

1. ¿Buscas un hotel que sea económico?
   No, porque vivo en un hotel que _____.

2. Ésta es una tienda donde venden barato, ¿verdad?
   No, no hay tiendas donde _____.

3. ¿Tienes un amigo que haya estudiado en España?
   Sí, tengo varios amigos que _____.

4. ¿Hay por aquí un teatro donde den películas españolas?
   No, por aquí no hay ningún teatro donde _____.

5. ¿Conoces a alguien que haya viajado por México?
   Sí, conozco a muchos que _____.

c. *Cambie al pasado, según el modelo.*

Aquí no hay nadie que baile bien.
Allí no había nadie que bailara bien.

1. No hay nada que cueste menos.
   No había nada que _____.

2. Le hace falta una secretaria que hable español.
   Le hacía falta una secretaria que _____.

3. No hay nadie que lo pida.
   No había nadie que lo _____.

4. Busco un restorán donde sirvan arroz con pollo.
   Buscaba un restorán donde _____.

5. ¿Hay alguien que duerma más?
   No había nadie que _____.

6. ¿Conoces a alguien que trabaje menos?
   No conocía a nadie que _____.

3. COMPARISONS OF EQUALITY

tan	+ adjective or adverb	+ **como** = as . . . as
tanto, tanta **tantos, tantas**	+ noun	+ **como** = as much (many) . . . as
verb	+ **tanto**	+ **como** = as much as

With adjectives and adverbs:

Buenos Aires es tan grande como Chicago. Buenos Aires is as large as Chicago.

Este museo no es tan interesante como aquél. This museum is not as interesting as that one.

Tú bailas tan bien como ella. You dance as well as she.

With nouns:

No tenía tanto tiempo como nosotros. He didn't have as much time as we.

No tienen tanta suerte como Ud. They haven't as much luck as you.

Tiene tantos habitantes como Chicago. It has as many inhabitants as Chicago.

Marta lee tantas novelas como él. Martha reads as many novels as he.

With verbs:

No estudio tanto como tú. I don't study as much as you.

Trabajaba tanto como de costumbre. He worked as much as usual.

PRÁCTICA

Cambie según los modelos.

a. **Este periódico es muy interesante.**
   Sí, es tan interesante como el otro.

   1. Este coche es muy barato.
   2. Esta lección es muy fácil.
   3. Esta lección es muy difícil.
   4. Estas corbatas son muy bonitas.
   5. Esta comedia es muy divertida.

b. **Tus amigos trabajan mucho, ¿verdad?**
   Sí, trabajan tanto como yo.

   1. Tus amigos estudian mucho,
      ¿verdad?
   2. Tus amigos juegan mucho,
      ¿verdad?
   3. Tus amigos se divierten mucho,
      ¿verdad?
   4. Tus amigos bailan mucho,
      ¿verdad?
   5. Tus amigos comen mucho,
      ¿verdad?

c. **No tengo muchos libros.**
   No tengo tantos libros como tú.

   1. No tengo mucho tiempo.
   2. No tengo muchas amigas.
   3. No tengo muchos vestidos.
   4. No tengo muchas camisas.
   5. No tengo muchos zapatos.

d. **Jaime llegó muy temprano.**
   Sí, llegó tan temprano como yo.

   1. Enrique llegó muy tarde.
   2. Roberto llegó muy pronto.
   3. Humberto llegó muy puntualmente.
   4. Benito llegó muy cansado.
   5. Juanito llegó muy enojado.

4. DEFINITE ARTICLE WITH GEOGRAPHICAL NAMES

You have learned certain geographical names with which the definite article is used: **la Argentina**, **el Brasil**, **la América del Sur**, etc. The following are some of the most common names with which the definite article is used:

la Argentina Argentina	**el Paraguay** Paraguay
el Brasil Brazil	**El Salvador** El Salvador
el Ecuador Ecuador	**el Canadá** Canada
el Perú Peru	**el Japón** Japan
el Uruguay Uruguay	

Nowadays, however, many Spanish speakers tend to omit the definite article with names of countries, especially in series or after prepositions. The exception is **El Salvador**, always used with the definite article, which here does not contract with the preposition **a**. (In the *Práctica* below use the definite article as it has normally been used.)

Geographical names of which adjectives or phrases are a part, or which happen to be modified by adjectives or phrases, almost always take the definite article. For example:

los Estados Unidos   the United States
la Gran Bretaña   Great Britain
la América del Sur   South America
la España meridional   Southern Spain

But:

Sudamérica   **Costa Rica**

PRÁCTICA

Diga en español.

a. 1. Let's go to Peru.
   2. Let's go to Spain.
   3. Let's go to Brazil.
   4. Let's go to France.
   5. Let's go to Paraguay.
   6. Let's go to El Salvador.

b. 1. They like Uruguay.
   2. They like central Spain.
   3. They like Ecuador.
   4. They like Costa Rica.
   5. They like Great Britain.

Tareas

Diga en español.

1. Is there any student in this class who has been to Argentina?
2. Juan was one of the students who raised their hands.

3. Mr. Martínez asked him to speak about his trip.
4. You must know that his uncle sells agricultural machinery.
5. His uncle's company asked him to go to Argentina.
6. It surprised him that they should ask him to go just like that.
7. There was no one in the company who spoke Spanish as well as he.
8. His parents asked his uncle to take him too.
9. He made the trip by plane with his uncle and aunt.
10. Buenos Aires is as large as Chicago and has nearly as many inhabitants.
11. One night his aunt wanted him to accompany her to the Teatro Colón.
12. He has never seen a museum that interested him as much as the historical museum of Luján.
13. It is not strange that the dictator Rosas died in exile.
14. They don't know any other city that is as interesting as Buenos Aires.

Composición oral o escrita.

One of your friends is feeling blue **(tiene murria)** today. Tell her a number of flattering things to cheer her up and bolster her ego. Tell her she's a very lucky girl **(una chica muy afortunada),** and she's as pretty as any **(cualquiera)** of the other girls. She has as many dates as they. Her boyfriend is as good-looking as any of the other boys. She's very talented **(tiene mucho talento)**; she's as talented as anybody. She sings and dances as well as any of the girls around here and plays the guitar as well as they. She's as intelligent as anybody you know. Cheer her up with as many comparisons as you can think of.

Diálogo

HUMBERTO NO HA LLAMADO

ANITA—¿Tienes murria,[1] ¿verdad?
ROSA—No lo creas.[2] Estoy como unas pascuas.[3]
ANITA—No mientas.[4] Se deja ver en la cara.[5]
ROSA—Estás viendo visiones.[6]
ANITA—Tiene que ver con el nuevo compañero.[7] ¡Sí, por cierto![8]
ROSA—¿Humberto? ¡No lo puedo ver![9]
ANITA—¡Y él tan simpático! ¡Y tan guapo! Es tan guapo como el que más.[10]
ROSA—No me había fijado.[11]
ANITA—Es el más guapo de todos estos chicos.
ROSA—No lo había notado.
ANITA—Vi que estabas charlando con él anteayer. La conversación parecía muy animada. ¿Qué te dijo?
ROSA—Que quería ponerse en contacto[12] con alguien que pudiera[13] invitar al baile.
ANITA—¿Te invitó?

ROSA—No, pero preguntó el número de mi teléfono y dijo que me llamaría.

ANITA—Bueno, ¿y qué?[14]

ROSA—Pues, ¡no ha llamado!

[1]tener murria   *to feel blue*

[2]No lo creas.   *Don't you believe it.*

[3]Estoy . . . pascuas.   *I'm as happy as a lark.*

[4]mentir   *to lie*

[5]Se deja . . . cara.   *It shows on your face.*

[6]ver visiones   *to be seeing things*

[7]compañero   *classmate*

[8]¡Sí, por cierto!   *Yes, of course!*

[9]¡No lo puedo ver!   *I can't stand him.*

[10]el que más   *the next one*

[11]fijarse   *to notice*

[12]ponerse en contacto   *to get in touch*

[13]pudiera   *might (be able to)*

[14]¿y qué?   *so what?*

PREGUNTAS PERSONALES

1. ¿Tienes murria de vez en cuando?
2. ¿Tienes murria cuando tu novia (novio) no te llama por teléfono?
3. ¿Tienes murria cuando no recibes cartas?
4. Al contrario, ¿cómo te sientes cuando recibes una carta de tu novio (novia)?
5. ¿Estás como unas pascuas cuando tu novio (novia) te llama por teléfono?
6. ¿Quieres una amiga que te escriba todos los días?
7. ¿Tenías antes una amiga que te escribiera todos los días?
8. ¿Buscas a alguien con quien puedas ir al baile?
9. ¿Buscabas a alguien con quien pudieras ir al baile?
10. ¿Tienes una amiga que te haya escrito todos los días?
11. ¿Tienes un amigo que te haya llamado desde Europa?

Notas culturales

The **gaucho** was perhaps the most colorful and picturesque popular type of Latin America and gave rise to a fascinating literature. The museum in Luján in Argentina contains an interesting collection of things relating to him and to his life and times.

A mixture of White and Indian blood, the gaucho had developed, with his own special characteristics and way of life, in Argentina, Uruguay, and southern Brazil, by the eighteenth century. He was a free, proud, and independent spirit, at home in the limitless distances of the vast pampa. It has been said that "the horse created the gaucho," and without the horse his way of life would have been impossible. He loved his horses and was at home only on horseback on the open plains. The greatest misfortune he could imagine was "to be in Chile and on foot." For use in the cattle roundups and his other work as he wandered from **estancia** to **estancia**, he maintained a **tropilla** of half a dozen horses, as nearly identical in color and markings as possible. He lavished what little money he had on their trappings, adorning the bridles with silver, while he himself, if he could, wore silver spurs.

His dress was simple but picturesque: a small-brimmed hat, a neckerchief, a short jacket, fringed pants, a **chiripá** (a kind of apron) for protection on horse-back, leather boots that he made himself, and in cooler weather a poncho. And always a sharp dagger (**facón**).

If the horse created the gaucho, it was the wire fence with which, in the later nineteenth century, the ranchers began to close off the **estancias**, that destroyed him. His descendants are the present-day ranch hands.

22

Quítate tú para que me ponga yo.
Beware of advice when the giver can gain.

More past subjunctives

You learned that the past subjunctive is formed on the third person plural of the preterit. Here are the past subjunctives of some common irregular verbs.

INFINITIVE	THIRD PLURAL PRETERIT	PAST SUBJUNCTIVE	
		-ra	-se
dar	dieron	diera	diese
decir	dijeron	dijera	dijese
estar	estuvieron	estuviera	estuviese
hacer	hicieron	hiciera	hiciese
ir	fueron	fuera	fuese
ser	fueron	fuera	fuese
poder	pudieron	pudiera	pudiese
poner	pusieron	pusiera	puiese
querer	quisieron	quisiera	quisiese
saber	supieron	supiera	supiese
tener	tuvieron	tuviera	tuviese
venir	vinieron	viniera	viniese

Verbs like **leer** (whose stem ends in a strong vowel) change the unstressed **i** of the personal endings to **y**.

leer	leyeron	leyera	leyese
creer	creyeron	creyera	creyese

PRÁCTICA

Cambie según se indica.

1. Convenía que *yo* estuviera allí.
   tú / él / Ud. / ellos / nosotros

2. No querían que *Ud.* fuese al café.
   Ud. y yo / ella / ellas / tú / yo

3. Sentían que *él* no pudiera hacerlo.
   tú / yo / ella / Uds. / nosotros

4. Parecía mentira que *Ud.* no quisiera hacerlo.
   Uds. / nosotros / yo / tú / él

5. No creían que *él* fuera español.
   yo / tú / nosotros / ellos / ella

6. Rogaron que *yo* les diera el dinero.
   tú / ellas / nosotros / ella

7. Es probable que *ella* dijera la verdad.
   Uds. / Ud. y yo / tú / Paco

8. Le pedí *a él* que lo hiciera.
   a ti / a ellos / a Uds. / a ella

9. Les dijo *a ellos* que se pusieran el sombrero.
   a mí / a tí / a Ud. / a Uds. / a ella

10. Dudaban que *yo* lo supiera.
    Ud. / nosotros / tú / Uds.

11. Esperaban que *Ud.* no tuviera miedo.
    yo / Ud. y yo / ellas / tú

12. Es posible que *ellos* vinieran ayer.
    tú / nosotros / Ud. / yo

13. Era preciso que *yo* lo leyera.
    Ud. / Ud. y yo / ellas / tú

14. Bastaba que *él* lo creyera.
    yo / ellas / tú y yo / tú

Escuchar y hablar

anunciar to announce
cierto (a) certain
el cliente cliente
confidencial confidential
decidir to decide
dentro de within
discutir to discuss
el documento document
entregar to hand over

imposible impossible
la línea aérea airline
la llegada arrival
de manera que so that
a menos que unless
para que in order that
¿para qué? for what reason?
el parecer opinion
el pasaje passage

quisiera I should like to
reservar to reserve
sino but
sumamente extremely, exceedingly
con tal que provided that
telefonear to telephone

IDIOMS AND OTHER EXPRESSIONS

debieras you (really) ought to
hacer la maleta to pack one's suitcase
poner un telegrama to send a telegram
al principio at first
sin embargo nevertheless

OTRO ASUNTO URGENTE

—Como el tío de Juan,—dijo Carlos—mi padre tuvo que hacer un viaje urgente el año pasado, a México. ¿Saben Uds. que mi padre es abogado? Pues lo es. Un cliente suyo le telefoneó desde Guadalajara rogándole que fuera allá. Le pidió que hiciera el viaje para que hablara con él de un asunto urgente y confidencial. Quería que mi padre leyese ciertos documentos y que le dijese ciertas cosas que no podían discutir por teléfono. Esperaba también que mi padre le diera su parecer sobre ciertos asuntos. Era necesario que estuviera en Guadalajara dentro de veinticuatro horas. Al principio mi padre no creía que fuera posible. Le dijo al cliente que sería imposible.

—«Quisiera ir» nos dijo después. Pero se sentía un poco enfermo y además no creía tener tiempo. Sobre todo no quería ir a menos que mi madre lo acompañara.

—«Debieras ir» le dijo mi madre. «Ya sabes que es sumamente importante.»

—«Lo sé» contestó mi padre. «Pero sólo iré con tal que vayas tú.»

—Pero fue imposible que mamá lo acompañase. Iba a visitarnos una tía suya. Sin embargo mi padre decidió hacer el viaje.

—«¿Quieres hacerme la maleta?» le preguntó a mi madre. Y buscó unas camisas y unas corbatas que le entregó a mi madre de manera que ella le hiciera la maleta.

—Mi padre casi siempre viaja en tren. Pero esta vez, naturalmente, no tomó el tren, sino el avión. Yo llamé a la línea aérea para que le reservasen el pasaje. Fue preciso también que yo pusiese un telegrama anunciando su llegada.

—«¿No te lo dije?» me preguntó mi madre después. «Es lo de siempre. Tu padre nunca quiere hacer un viaje a menos que yo vaya también. Pero al fin se va.»

PREGUNTAS

1. ¿Qué tuvo que hacer el padre de Carlos?
2. ¿Quién le telefoneó?
3. ¿Qué le rogó?
4. ¿Para qué le pidió que hiciera el viaje?
5. ¿Qué quería que leyese?
6. ¿Qué quería que le dijera?
7. ¿Qué esperaba que su padre le diera?

In the highlands of the Central Andes, Indian descendants of the Incas compose most of the rural population. They still speak Quechua, the language of their Inca ancestors. Full skirts, shawls, and wool derbies are typical of the Andean region.

8. ¿Cuándo era necesario que su padre estuviera en Guadalajara?
9. ¿Creía su padre que sería posible ir a Guadalajara?
10. ¿Qué le dijo el cliente?
11. ¿Qué dijo después a la familia?
12. ¿Por qué no quería ir?
13. ¿Por qué fue imposible que la madre de Carlos lo acompañara?
14. ¿Qué buscó su padre?
15. ¿Para qué se las entregó a la madre de Carlos?
16. ¿Tomó el tren?
17. ¿Para qué telefoneó Carlos a la línea aérea?
18. ¿Qué fue preciso que hiciera Carlos?
19. ¿Qué dijo después la madre de Carlos?

Estructura

1. SUBJUNCTIVE OR INDICATIVE IN ADVERB CLAUSES

An adverb clause is one which modifies a verb. It tells why, for what purpose, when, or in what circumstances the action of the main verb takes place.

You have learned that use of the subjunctive or indicative in a noun clause depends on the meaning of the main verb. In the adjective clause it depends on the meaning of the antecedent noun or pronoun. Some adverb clauses are in the subjunctive and some are in the indicative.

Whether you use the subjunctive or indicative in an adverb clause depends on the meaning of the clause itself. Two types of adverb clauses are always in the subjunctive:

those expressing purpose (introduced by "in order that," "so that")
those expressing proviso ("provided that," "unless," "in case")

Conjunctions introducing clauses of purpose are

para que   in order that
de modo que   so, so that
de manera que   so, so that

Conjunctions introducing clauses of proviso are

a menos que   unless
con tal que   provided (that)
en caso de que   in case

MAIN VERB	SUBJUNCTIVE IN ADVERB CLAUSE EXPRESSING PURPOSE OR PROVISO
Iremos al museo We'll go to the museum **Se las entregó** He handed them to her	**para que veas los cuadros.** in order that you may see the pictures. **de modo que ella hiciera la maleta.** so (that) she might pack the suitcase.
Mi padre irá My father will go **No quería ir** He didn't want to go	**con tal que mi madre vaya también.** provided my mother goes too. **a menos que mi madre fuera también.** unless my mother went (would go) too.

PRÁCTICA

Cambie según los modelos.

a. **Les daré el dinero.**
   Comprarán el coche.
   Les daré el dinero para que compren el coche.

1. Les daré el dinero.
   Irán a España.

2. Les daré el dinero.
   Verán la película.

3. Les daré el dinero.
   Saldrán.

4. Les daré el dinero.
   Tomarán un taxi.

5. Les daré el dinero.
   Harán el viaje.

b. **Les di el dinero.**
   Compraron el coche.
   Les di el dinero de manera que compraran el coche.

1. Les di el dinero.
   Fueron a España.

2. Les di el dinero.
   Vieron la película.

3. Les di el dinero.
   Salieron.

4. Les di el dinero.
   Tomaron un taxi.

5. Les di el dinero.
   Hicieron el viaje.

c. **Ella no irá al teatro.**
   Tú insistes.
   Ella no irá al teatro a menos que tú insistas.

1. Ella no irá al teatro.
   Tú vas.

2. Ella no irá al teatro.
   Tú quieres.

3. Ella no irá al teatro.
   Tú vuelves.

4. Ella no irá al teatro.
   Tú pagas.

d. **Dijeron que irían.**
   Ud. insistiría.
   Dijeron que irían, con tal que Ud. insistiera.

1. Dijeron que irían.
   Ud. iría.

2. Dijeron que irían.
   Ud. querría.

3. Dijeron que irían.
   Ud. volvería.

4. Dijeron que irían.
   Ud. pagaría.

2. PAST SUBJUNCTIVE IN SOFTENED STATEMENTS

The **-ra** form of the past subjunctive of **querer, deber,** and **poder** is used to soften
a statement, that is, to make it less brusque and more courteous than the
present indicative.

Quisiera ir a Panamá.   I should like to go to Panama.
Ud. debiera estudiar más.   You (really) should (*or* ought to) study more.
¿No pudieran Uds. hacerlo ahora?   Couldn't you do it now?

PRÁCTICA

Diga en español.

1. I should like to know it.
2. I should like to see it.
3. You should work more.

4. You should play more.
5. Couldn't you tell me?
6. Couldn't you return now?

3. DATIVE OF INTEREST

The indirect object pronoun is often used to indicate the person in whose interest, or to whose advantage or disadvantage, an act is done.

¿Quieres hacer*me* la maleta?   Will you pack the suitcase *for me?*
***Le* reservaron el pasaje.**   They reserved the passage *for him.*
***Nos* resultó muy fácil.**   It turned out to be very easy *for us.*

Sometimes this indirect object is untranslatable except with English colloquial expressions.

Se *me* murió el caballo.   The horse died (*"on me"*).

PRÁCTICA

Conteste según se indica en los modelos.

a. **¿Quieres hacerme la maleta?**
   ¡Cómo no! Te la hago ahora mismo.

1. ¿Quieres buscarme un taxi?
2. ¿Quieres reservarme una mesa?
3. ¿Quieres pagarme el billete?
4. ¿Quieres comprarme un café?
5. ¿Quieres envolverme el paquete?

b. **¿Le pago el billete ahora?**
   Sí, páguemelo, por favor.

1. ¿Le busco un taxi?
2. ¿Le reservo un pasaje?
3. ¿Le compro un café?
4. ¿Le envuelvo el paquete?
5. ¿Le limpio los zapatos?

4. NEUTER PRONOUN LO

The neuter pronoun **lo** (*it* or *so*) is regularly used as the object or predicate of a verb, even where its English counterparts are omitted.

¿No *lo* sabes? Sí, *lo* sé.   Don't you know (it)? Yes, I know (it).
Se *lo* dije.   I told you (so).
¿Es abogado? *Lo* es.   Is he a lawyer? He is.
¿Es rica la muchacha?   *Lo* es.   Is the girl rich? She is.

Airport in Lima, Peru.

PRÁCTICA

Diga en español.

1. We know.
2. We told you.
3. We asked you.
4. Are they doctors? They are.
5. Are they students? They are.
6. Are they intelligent? They are.

5. SINO *AND* SINO QUE

Sino means *but* in the sense of *but on the contrary*. It replaces **pero** after a negative statement when the following statement contradicts the preceding negative one.

No tomó el tren, sino el avión.   He did not take the train but the plane.
No es español, sino catalán.   He is not a Spaniard but a Catalan.

When a conjugated verb follows, **sino** becomes **sino que.**

No fui al museo, sino que me quedé en el hotel.   I did not go to the museum, but (I) stayed in the hotel.

PRÁCTICA

Cambie según el modelo.

No es español. (francés)
No es español, sino francés.

1. No es norteamericano. (mexicano)
2. No es alta. (baja)
3. No es viejo. (joven)
4. No es rubia. (morena)
5. No es rico. (pobre)

Tareas

Diga en español.

1. Some clients of Carlos' father telephoned him from Guadalajara.
2. They wanted him to go (down) there.
3. They asked him to make the trip in order that they might discuss a certain urgent matter.
4. They wanted him to read some documents and to tell them his opinion.
5. They hoped he would give them some advice.
6. It was necessary for him to be in Guadalajara within twenty-four hours.
7. His father didn't think it was possible and told them so.
8. "I should like to go," he said later.
9. But he didn't want to go unless Carlos' mother would go too.
10. It was impossible for her to accompany him.
11. He looked for some ties, so that she could pack the suitcase for him.
12. He didn't go by train but by plane.
13. Carlos phoned the airline in order that they might reserve a passage for him.
14. It was also necessary for him to send a telegram.

Composición oral o escrita

Tell how your father suddenly **(inesperadamente)** has to take a trip to Mexico City. He won't be able to get there in time unless he can take the eight o'clock plane. He'll be able to take it, provided you call the airline and reserve passage for him. He wants you to help with the preparations **(los preparativos)**. He asks you to look for his shoes, socks, and shirts in order that you may pack his suitcase for him. He also tells you to send a telegram, so that in Mexico City they will know the time of his arrival.

Diálogo

UN BOLETO[1] A GUADALAJARA

RICARDO—¿Hay plazas[2] en el avión de Guadalajara?

AGENTE—Sí, señor. ¡Cómo no!

RICARDO—Bueno, pues, un boleto a Guadalajara.

AGENTE—¿Sencillo,[3] o de ida y vuelta?[4]

RICARDO—De ida y vuelta.

AGENTE—Aquí lo tiene Ud.[5]

RICARDO—¿A qué hora es la salida[6] del avión?

AGENTE—A las tres y veinte.

RICARDO—¿Cuál es el número del vuelo?[7]

AGENTE—Número treinta y cuatro. ¿Cuál es su maleta, para que la pesen?

RICARDO—Ésta es mi maleta. Creo que no pesa demasiado.

AGENTE—Tiene derecho a[8] veinticinco kilos de equipaje.[9] Esta maleta pesa menos. Aquí tiene Ud. el talón[10] y su tarjeta de embarque.[11]

RICARDO—¿Se pueden escoger[12] los asientos?[13]

AGENTE—Sí, señor.

RICARDO—Quiero un asiento junto a[14] la salida de urgencia.[15] Siempre que[16] viajo en avión me pongo[17] un tanto nervioso.[18]

[1]el boleto *ticket*	[10]el talón *baggage check*
[2]la plaza *seat, place*	[11]la tarjeta de embarque *boarding pass*
[3]sencillo *one way*	[12]escoger *to choose*
[4]de ida y vuelta *round trip*	[13]el asiento *seat*
[5]aquí lo tiene *here you are*	[14]junto a *next to*
[6]la salida *departure*	[15]la salida de urgencia *emergency exit*
[7]el vuelo *flight*	[16]siempre que *whenever*
[8]tener derecho a *to have a right to*	[17]ponerse *to become, get*
[9]el equipaje *baggage*	[18]un tanto nervioso *a bit nervous*

PREGUNTAS PERSONALES

1. ¿Le gusta a Ud. viajar en avión? ¿Por qué?
2. ¿Se pone Ud. un tanto nervioso cuando viaja en avión?
3. ¿Qué viajes ha hecho Ud. en avión?
4. ¿Ha ido Ud. alguna vez a México en avion?
5. La última vez que viajó en avión, ¿qué clase de billete sacó? ¿Sencillo?
6. Al sacar el billete, le entregó su maleta al agente, ¿verdad? ¿Para qué?
7. Al entregarle su maleta, ¿qué le dio a Ud.?
8. Generalmente, ¿se pueden escoger los asientos en los aviones?
9. ¿Prefiere Ud. un asiento junto a la salida de urgencia?
10. El verano que viene, ¿irá Ud. a Europa en avión, con tal que unos amigos vayan también?

Notas culturales

Overview of Latin American Society

In colonial times Latin American society was highly stratified on racial and economic lines. At the top were Spaniards who came to America for relatively brief periods to hold the best offices as viceroys, captains-general, bishops, or archbishops. Next were the **criollos,** those born in America of Spanish blood. Among them were wealthy owners of lands and mines, as well as professional people, but they could hold only lesser posts in government, Church, or army. The strong antagonism between these two groups would be an important factor in the movement for independence from Spain. Below these were the **mestizos**—of Spanish and Indian descent—and the large number of Indians.

As time went on a two-tiered society developed, headed by great land-owners and their powerful families. The **terratenientes** (*landholders*) or **hacendados** (*owners of vast estates*) were heirs to the system of latifundia implanted by the Spaniards. Under this system the conquistadores were granted **encomiendas**—not only land, but the right to the labor of the Indians who lived on it. Locally the **terratenientes** held enormous power, their peons traditionally being bound to the land by accumulated debts. Regionally and nationally they constituted an oligarchy with immense influence over government and its decisions.

Present-day Latin America is a three-tiered society. The former ruling class, the landed oligarchy, has now been joined by financial, industrial, and military leaders. The nineteenth century marked the emergence of an ever-growing middle class, which historically had been almost non-existent in the Hispanic world. This was made possible by the growth of cities, the development of commerce and industry, and a substantial amount of European immigration. The size of the middle class varies from country to country, reaching twenty-five percent in some countries and remaining as low as five percent in others. At the base of the pyramid are the working classes whose numbers, again, vary by countries, ranging from two-thirds of the people in some to ninety percent in others. This group includes the unskilled workers of the cities and the **campesinos** (*peasants*). Large numbers of the latter, seeking escape from a marginal existence in the country, have migrated to the large cities where they live in surrounding shantytowns.

An ancient noble house in the Calle del Cid, León, Spain.

5

A. *Use el subjuntivo o el indicativo de los verbos indicados.*

1. Es necesario que nosotros lo _____ (saber).
2. Es verdad que Carmen lo _____ (saber).
3. Conviene que tus amigos _____ (empezar) ahora.
4. Es cierto que mis padres _____ (ir) allá.
5. Parece mentira que las chicas _____ (ir) allá.

B. *Use el subjuntivo o el indicativo de los verbos indicados.*

1. Era necesario que nosotros lo _____ (saber).
2. Es verdad que Juan _____ (leer) el libro ayer.
3. Fue preciso que yo _____ (leer) todo el libro.
4. Convenía que el niño _____ (dormir) ocho horas.
5. Era cierto que el abogado les _____ (pedir) demasiado.
6. Era probable que el abogado les _____ (pedir) demasiado.

C. *Conteste según el modelo.*

¿Han llegado? (Dudo)
Dudo que hayan llegado.

1. ¿Han estado aquí? (Niego)
2. ¿Hemos aprendido mucho? (No creo)
3. ¿Han dicho la verdad? (Dudo)
4. ¿Ha pagado Pepe demasiado por el coche? (No creemos)

D. *Use el verbo indicado.*

1. ¿Hay alguien que lo _____ (saber)?
2. ¿Había alguien que lo _____ (saber)?
3. ¿Hay alguien que lo _____ (creer)?
4. ¿Había alguien que lo _____ (creer)?
5. No hay nadie que _____ (querer) hacerlo.
6. No había nadie que _____ (querer) hacerlo.
7. Aquí no hay nada que _____ (ser) barato.
8. Allí no había nada que _____ (ser) barato.

299

E. *Use la forma apropiada de los verbos indicados.*

1. Te daré el dinero para que _____ (poder) comprar el reloj.
2. Te di el dinero para que _____ (poder) comprar el reloj.
3. No iré, a menos que tú _____ (ir) también.
4. Dijeron que no irían, a menos que tú _____ (ir) también.
5. Lo hallarás, con tal que lo _____ (buscar).
6. Creían que lo hallarías, con tal que lo _____ (buscar).

F. *Use **para** o **por**.*

1. Estas flores son _____ ti.
2. Me llamaron _____ teléfono.
3. ¿No han salido _____ México?
4. Tus amigos estarán _____ aquí.
5. Lo hizo _____ temor.
6. _____ mí es un poco temprano.
7. ¿Cuánto pagó _____ el radio?
8. Creo que estarán en España _____ quince días.
9. Estarán de vuelta _____ las nueve.

G. *Conteste según el modelo, usando la voz pasiva.*

¿Fabrican tejidos aquí?
Sí, aquí se fabrican tejidos.

1. ¿Hablan español aquí?
2. ¿Publican muchos libros aquí?
3. ¿Venden muchos automóviles aquí?
4. ¿Hacen muchos zapatos aquí?

H. *Conteste con voz activa y voz pasiva, según el modelo.*

¿Quién escribió estas cartas? (mi novia)
Mi novia escribió estas cartas.
Estas cartas fueron escritas por mi novia.

1. ¿Quién pintó ese cuadro? (Goya)
2. ¿Quién preparó esta comida? (mi abuela)
3. ¿Quién cerró las ventanas? (un alumno)
4. ¿Quién fundó esta universidad? (un hombre muy rico)

I. *Diga en español.*

1. She was seen in the theater.
2. I was told that they had been here.
3. He was promised a new car.
4. They were asked if they knew it.

J. *Conteste con* **estar**, *según el modelo.*

¿Se ha cerrado el teatro?
Sí, el teatro está cerrado.

1. ¿Se abrieron las ventanas?
2. ¿Se ha escrito la carta?
3. ¿Se escribió el libro en español?
4. ¿Se publicó la novela?

K. *Conteste según el modelo.*

¿Tiene Ud. muchos libros?
Tengo tantos libros como Ud.

1. ¿Tiene Ud. muchos amigos?
2. ¿Tiene Ud. mucho dinero?
3. ¿Tiene Ud. mucha suerte?
4. ¿Tiene Ud. muchas corbatas?

L. *Conteste según el modelo.*

¿Estudias mucho?
Estudio tanto como tú.

1. ¿Trabajas mucho?
2. ¿Sabes mucho?
3. ¿Lees mucho?
4. ¿Juegas mucho?

M. *Conteste según el modelo.*

Eres muy inteligente ¿no?
Soy tan inteligente como el que más.

1. Eres muy listo, ¿no?
2. Eres muy perezoso, ¿no?
3. Estás muy cansado, ¿no?
4. Estás muy enojado, ¿no?

N. *Use* **pero** *o* **sino**.

1. Es muy bueno, _____ caro.
2. No es española, _____ mexicana.
3. No son altas, _____ bajas.
4. Vi la película, _____ no me gustó.

O. *Diga en español.*

1. the beautiful
2. what is most interesting
3. the easiest (thing) about the lesson
4. the best (part) of the book

P. *Diga en español.*

1. Tell about having dinner with Jaime Montero in a café in Seville. Describe the café. Tell what you ordered. Tell about the Andalusian waiter. Tell what Jaime wanted you to do afterward.

2. Tell about seeing Don Tomás Milá in Barcelona. Tell what you learned about Barcelona. Tell about your experience with Charles in the café.

3. Describe John's experiences in Argentina.

4. Explain why Charles's father had to go to Guadalajara. Tell about his preparations for the trip.

23

Antes que te cases, mira lo que haces.
Before you marry, consider what you're doing.

Past perfect subjunctive

The past perfect subjunctive (also called the pluperfect subjunctive) of any verb
(*had spoken, had learned,* etc.) is formed by combining the past subjunctive of
haber with the past participle of the verb.

hubiera		hubiese	
hubieras		hubieses	
hubiera	hablado	hubiese	hablado
	aprendido		aprendido
hubiéramos	vivido	hubiésemos	vivido
(hubierais)		(hubieseis)	
hubieran		hubiesen	

PRÁCTICA

Cambie según se indica.

1. Dudaban que lo *hubiéramos* visto.
   tú / él / Uds. / ellas / yo

2. Negaron que *Ud.* lo hubiera dicho.
   yo / ella / Uds. / tú / tú y yo

3. No creían que *él* hubiese vuelto.
   ellos / yo / Ud. / tú / Ud. y yo

303

Orthographic-changing verbs in *-uir*

Verbs whose infinitive ends in **-uir** (except **-guir** and **-quir**) insert **y** before the ending (except before **i**) in the present tenses.

construir   to build, construct

PRESENT INDICATIVE		PRESENT SUBJUNCTIVE	
construyo	construimos	construya	construyamos
construyes	(construís)	construyas	(construyáis)
construye	construyen	construya	construyan

As in verbs like **leer**, unstressed **i** of the personal endings changes to **y**. This change occurs in the third person, singular and plural, of the preterit; throughout the past subjunctive; and in the gerund.

PRETERIT: **construyó**   **construyeron**
PAST SUBJUNCTIVE: **construyera**, etc.   **construyese**, etc.
PRESENT PARTICIPLE: **construyendo**
PAST PARTICIPLE: **construido**

PRÁCTICA

Cambie según se indica.

1. Su cliente construye edificios.
   tú / nosotros / Uds. / él / yo

2. Él no construyó ese edificio.
   yo / Ud. / Uds. / tú / nosotros

3. Desean que Ud. concluya el trabajo.
   ellos / yo / nosotros / tú / Uds.

4. Convenía que, al escribirle, incluyeran el dinero.
   Ud. / tú / ella / nosotros / yo

Escuchar y hablar

amistosamente   in a friendly way
animado   lively
antes (de) que   before
arreglar   to arrange

aun cuando   even though
la cabeza   head
la clínica   hospital
concluir   to finish, conclude

construir to build, construct
el consultorio doctor's office
crecer to grow
después (de) que after
el doctor doctor
doler (ue) to ache, hurt, pain
encantador, encantadora charming,
  delightful
enfermar to become ill, get sick
la fiebre fever
la garganta throat
grave serious
hasta que until
interrumpir to interrupt
el jarabe tapatío Mexican hat dance
mejorarse to get better

mientras while
a pesar de que in spite of the fact that
la pulmonía pneumonia
recomendar (ie) to recommend
resultar to turn out; result
la suerte luck
varios several
la visita visit

IDIOMS AND OTHER EXPRESSIONS

guardar cama to stay in bed
¡qué lástima! what a pity!
(dijo) para sí (he said) to himself
¿Qué tengo? What's the matter with
  me?

EL PADRE DE CARLOS Y EL MÉDICO

—No hay nadie que tenga tan mala suerte como mi padre—dijo Carlos.—
Mamá y yo sentíamos mucho que hubiera hecho el viaje a Guadalajara.

—¿Qué pasó? No le gustó Guadalajara?—pregunté.

—Al contrario, le gustó mucho. Cuando volvió, nos dijo que es la segunda
ciudad de México y que está creciendo. Se están construyendo edificios nuevos
en todas partes. Además, es una ciudad animada y encantadora. Para que lo
sepas, es la ciudad del jarabe tapatío. Sus habitantes la llaman «la ciudad más
mexicana.» El cliente de papá lo recibió muy amistosamente. Después que
concluyeron su negocio le dijo «Antes que se vaya, quiero que vea los puntos
de interés.» Y en efecto se los mostró. Después de dos días no había nada de
interés que no hubiera visto.

—Bueno, pues, dime—interrumpí. —¿Por qué sentían Uds. tanto que
hubiera ido allá?

—Porque mientras estaba allí, enfermó. Había estado un poco enfermo
cuando fue a México. «No sé qué tengo,» dijo para sí. «Debo consultar un
médico.» En Guadalajara fue al consultorio de un médico que le había recomen-
dado su cliente. «Me duele la cabeza y me duele la garganta,» le explicó al
médico.

—«Ud. tiene fiebre,» le dijo el médico. «Tendrá que volver a casa y
guardar cama por varios días. Debe guardar cama mañana y pasado mañana,
aun cuando no tenga fiebre.»

—«No puedo, doctor,» dijo papá. «Soy de Nueva York y es preciso que
vuelva allá esta tarde.»

—«Imposible,» le dijo el médico. «Aunque Ud. no quiera, tendrá que
quedarse aquí hasta que se mejore. Le aconsejo que vaya a la clínica. Esto
puede ser grave. Vaya a la clínica antes que enferme gravemente.»

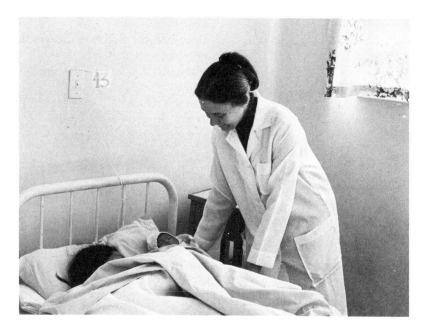

To counter historically high infant mortality and death rates, in recent decades many Latin American governments have expanded their efforts to provide health care to populations in remote areas, such as the Altiplano in Bolivia, the Sierra in Peru, and the Oriente in Ecuador.

—A pesar de que mi padre no quería hacerlo, fue a la clínica. Resultó que tenía pulmonía y tuvo que guardar cama quince días.

—¡Qué lástima que hubiera ido a México mientras estaba enfermo!

PREGUNTAS

1. ¿Qué sentían Carlos y su mamá?
2. ¿Qué dijo su padre de Guadalajara?
3. ¿Cómo la llaman sus habitantes?
4. ¿Qué le dijo el cliente al padre de Carlos?
5. Después de dos días, ¿qué resultó?
6. ¿Por qué sentía Carlos que su padre hubiera ido a México?
7. ¿Qué le dolía a su papá?
8. ¿Adónde fue?
9. ¿Qué le dijo el médico?
10. ¿Le dijo que guardara cama?
11. ¿Adónde le aconsejó que fuera?
12. ¿Qué tenía el padre de Carlos!
13. ¿Cuánto tiempo estuvo en la clínica?
14. ¿Qué exclamó Carlos?

Estructura

1. USE OF THE PAST PERFECT SUBJUNCTIVE

The past perfect subjunctive is used in Spanish wherever we use the past perfect in English, but where Spanish requires the subjunctive.

Sentía que mi padre hubiera hecho el viaje. I was sorry my father had made the trip.

No había nada que no hubiéramos visto. There wasn't anything that we hadn't seen.

¡Qué lástima que hubiera ido! What a pity he had gone!

PRÁCTICA

Cambie según los modelos.

a. **Ud. había llegado.**
Se alegraban.
Se alegraban de que Ud. hubiera llegado.

1. Ud. había vuelto.
2. Ud. había salido.
3. Ud. había ido.
4. Ud. había venido.
5. Ud. había terminado.

b. **Uds. lo habían comprado.**
Yo lo sentía.
Yo sentía que Uds. lo hubieran comprado.

1. Uds. lo habían hecho.
2. Uds. lo habían dicho.
3. Uds. lo habían vendido.
4. Uds. lo habían visto.
5. Uds. lo habían preguntado.

2. SUBJUNCTIVE OR INDICATIVE IN ADVERB CLAUSES—CONTINUED

Two types of adverb clauses may be in the subjunctive or the indicative: those expressing time ("when," "after," etc.) and those expressing concession ("although," "even though," etc.).

TIME CLAUSES

Time clauses are introduced by the following conjunctions:

cuando when		**tan pronto como** as soon as	
antes (de) que before		**hasta que** until	
después (de) que after		**mientras** while	

Such clauses are in the subjunctive when they refer to something that has not yet (or had not yet) happened.

MAIN CLAUSE	ACT NOT YET HAPPENED: SUBJUNCTIVE
Se lo diré I'll tell him	**cuando venga.** when he comes.
Quédese aquí Stay here	**hasta que se mejore.** until you get better.
Dijo que se quedaría aquí He said he'd stay here	**hasta que se mejorara.** until he got better.
Me prestará el libro He'll lend me the book	**tan pronto como lo haya leído.** as soon as he has read it.
Dijo que se marcharía He said he'd leave	**después que te hubiera visto.** after he had seen you.

Clauses introduced by **antes (de) que** are always in the subjunctive, because they always refer to something that has not yet, or had not yet, happened.

> **Antes que vuelvas a Nueva York, te mostraré la ciudad.**   Before you return to New York, I'll show you the city.
> **Le mostró la ciudad antes de que volviera a Nueva York.**   He showed him the city before he returned to New York.

Time clauses are in the indicative when they state what is already happening, what has already happened, or what regularly happens.

> **Cuando estudio, aprendo.**   When (whenever) I study, I learn.
> **Estaba enfermo cuando salió para México.**   He was sick when he left for Mexico.
> **Mientras él estudiaba, ella miraba la televisión.**   While he was studying, she was watching television.

PRÁCTICA

Cambie según los modelos.

a. **Los veo cuando vienen.**
   Los veré cuando vengan.

   1. Lo hago cuando puedo.
      Lo haré cuando _____.

   2. Los compro cuando tengo dinero.
      Los compraré cuando _____.

In some parts of Latin America, Catholicism is a blend of Christianity and pre-Christian practice. Indians in Guatemala will often light candles and burn incense on the steps of a church and then climb to a nearby mountain to pay homage to a black stone image of a Mayan diety.

3. Tomo el desayuno tan pronto como me visto.
   Tomaré el desayuno tan pronto como _____.

4. Estudio tan pronto como vuelvo a casa.
   Estudiaré tan pronto como _____.

5. Hablo con ellos mientras están en el café.
   Hablaré con ellos mientras _____.

6. Se lo expliqué después de que llegaron.
   Se lo explicaré después de que _____.

7. Yo salí después de que salieron.
   Yo saldré después de que _____.

8. Leo hasta que me duermo.
   Leeré hasta que _____.

b. **¿Saldrán tus amigos?**
   Sí, pero los veremos antes de que salgan.

   1. ¿Volverán tus amigos?
      Sí, pero los veremos antes de que _____.

   2. ¿Comerán tus amigos en un restorán?
      Sí, pero los veremos antes de que _____.

   3. ¿Irán al cine tus amigos?
      Sí, pero los veremos antes de que _____.

   4. ¿Se marchan hoy tus amigos?
      Sí, pero los veremos antes de que _____.

c. **¿Salieron tus amigos?**
   Sí, pero los vi antes que salieran.

   1. ¿Volvieron tus amigos?
      Sí, pero los vi antes que _____.

   2. ¿Comieron tus amigos en un restorán?
      Sí, pero los vi antes que _____.

   3. ¿Fueron al cine tus amigos?
      Sí, pero los vi antes que _____.

   4. ¿Se marcharon tus amigos?
      Sí, pero los vi antes que _____.

d. **Lo hará cuando sea posible.**
   Dijo que lo haría cuando fuera posible.

   1. Volverá tan pronto como pueda.
      Dijo que volvería tan pronto como _____.

   2. Iremos al café cuando ella llegue.
      Dijimos que iríamos al café cuando ella _____.

   3. Estarán aquí hasta que Ud. termine.
      Dijeron que estarían aquí hasta que Ud. _____.

   4. Estaré contigo tan pronto como escriba la composición.
      Dije que estaría contigo tan pronto como _____.

   5. Esperaremos hasta que vuelvan.
      Dijimos que esperaríamos hasta que _____.

CONCESSIVE CLAUSES

Adverb clauses of concession are introduced by the following conjunctions:

aunque although, even though
aun cuando even though
a pesar de que in spite of the fact that

Concessive clauses are in the subjunctive when they state something that is not a fact, but a mere possibility.

MAIN CLAUSE	ADVERB CLAUSE STATES POSSIBILITY, NOT FACT: SUBJUNCTIVE
No lo veré mañana I won't see him tomorrow	**aunque esté aquí.** although he may be here.
Tendrás que guardar cama You'll have to stay in bed	**aun cuando no tengas fiebre.** even though you may not have a fever.
Debes ir a la clínica You should go to the hospital	**a pesar de que no quieras.** in spite of the fact that you may not want to.

But when the clause states a fact, it is in the indicative.

No lo veo, aunque está aquí. I don't see him, even though he's here.
Tendrás que guardar cama, aunque no tienes fiebre. You'll have to stay in bed, although you don't have a fever.
Debes ir a la clínica, a pesar de que no quieres. You should go to the hospital, despite the fact that you don't want to.

PRÁCTICA

Diga en español.

a. **Harán el viaje:**

1. although they are ill
   although they may be ill

2. although I am not going
   although I may not go

3. even though they do not have the money
   even though they may not have the money

4. in spite of the fact that you do not recommend it
   in spite of the fact that you may not recommend it

b. **Dijeron que harían el viaje:**

1. although they might be ill
2. although I might not go
3. even though they might not have the money
4. in spite of the fact that you might not recommend it

---

3. PREPOSITIONAL FORMS OF THE REFLEXIVE PRONOUNS

All the forms of the reflexive pronouns used as objects of a preposition are the same as the other prepositional pronouns, except the third person, **sí.**

mí	myself	**nosotros (-as)**	ourselves
ti	yourself	**vosotros (-as)**	yourselves
sí	himself, herself, yourself, itself	**sí**	themselves, yourselves

You have already learned the forms **conmigo** and **contigo**, which are also reflexive. There is a corresponding reflexive form for the third person when the preposition is **con: consigo.**

> **Hablaba para mí.** I was talking to myself.
> **Me llevaron consigo.** They took me with them.

PRÁCTICA

Cambie según se indica.

1. Ellos hablaban para sí.
   Ud. / tú / ella / yo / él / Uds.

2. Ud. los llevó consigo.
   yo / ella / tú / ellos / Uds.

Tareas

Diga en español.

1. There is nobody who has such bad luck as my father.
2. We were sorry that he had gone to Mexico.
3. He liked Guadalajara: it's a lively city.
4. New buildings are being built everywhere.

5. "Before you leave, I want you to see the points of interest," said his client.
6. After two days there wasn't anything of interest that he had not seen.
7. But he became ill: his head ached and his throat hurt.
8. "You should stay in bed until the day after tomorrow, even though you may not have a fever," said the doctor.
9. "You'll have to stay here until you get better."
10. "Go to the hospital before you become seriously ill."
11. Despite the fact that he didn't want to, he went to the hospital.
12. What a pity he had gone to Mexico while he was sick!

Composición oral o escrita

Explain that you're feeling a bit ill. You don't know what's the matter with you. But even though you don't want to do it, you go to the doctor. You tell him your head aches and your throat hurts. He tells you to go to the hospital even though you may not want to. You should go before you become seriously ill. You'll have to stay there until you get well. It turns out that you have pneumonia, and it's necessary for you to stay in bed two weeks.

Diálogo

EN EL CONSULTORIO DEL MÉDICO

PRIMER ENFERMO[1]—Buenas tardes, señorita. ¿Está[2] el médico?

ENFERMERA[3]—No, señor. No estará hasta las seis. Ud. puede sentarse en la sala de espera.[4] Hay otro señor que lo espera también. (*Media hora después, dirigiéndose al otro enfermo.*) El doctor ha llegado. Ud. puede pasar a verlo.

EL MÉDICO—Bueno, ¿qué tiene Ud.? ¿Siempre usa Ud. muletas?[5]

SEGUNDO ENFERMO—No, tuve que comprarlas en una farmacia para poder venir acá.

EL MÉDICO—¿Qué le pasó?

SEGUNDO ENFERMO—Un accidente. O, mejor dicho,[6] dos accidentes. Estaba para cruzar[7] la calle, allí donde están construyendo ese nuevo edificio. Cayó un ladrillo[8] y me dio en[9] la cabeza. Al mismo tiempo me atropelló[10] un taxi. Me duele la cabeza. Me duele todo el cuerpo.[11] Creo que tengo contusiones[12] en todas partes. Y me parece que tengo rota[13] la pierna[14] izquierda.

EL MÉDICO—A ver[15] esa pierna. . . . No, no parece rota. Esto no es grave, aunque lo parezca. Vuelva Ud. a casa y tome dos aspirinas[16] cada cuatro horas.

(*Al Primer Enfermo*) Y Ud., ¿qué tiene?

PRIMER ENFERMO—Nada, doctor. Es sólo un arañazo.[17] Me arañó el gato.[18]

EL MÉDICO—A ver. . . . Esto parece grave. Le voy a poner unas inyecciones.[19] Luego vamos a llamar una ambulancia[20] para que lo lleven a la clínica.

[1]el enfermo *patient*	[12]la contusión *bruise*
[2]estar *to be in*	[13]roto *broken*
[3]la enfermera *nurse*	[14]la pierna *leg*
[4]la sala de espera *waiting room*	[15]a ver *let's see*
[5]las muletas *crutches*	[16]la aspirina *aspirin*
[6]mejor dicho *rather*	[17]el arañazo *scratch*
[7]cruzar *to cross*	[18]Me arañó el gato. *The cat scratched me.*
[8]el ladrillo *brick*	[19]la inyección *injection*
[9]dar en *to hit*	[20]la ambulancia *ambulance*
[10]atropellar *to run into*	
[11]el cuerpo *body*	

PREGUNTAS PERSONALES

1. ¿Ha ido Ud. recientemente al consultorio del médico?
2. La última vez que tenía la garganta mala, ¿le dolía mucho?
3. ¿Tuvo Ud. que guardar cama?
4. ¿Tomó Ud. aspirinas?
5. ¿Tuvo Ud. que ir a la clínica?
6. La última vez que Ud. tuvo que ir a la clínica, ¿cuánto tiempo estuvo allí?
7. ¿Qué tal las enfermeras cuando Ud. estuvo en la clínica?
8. ¿Se ha roto Ud. alguna vez una pierna?
9. ¿Ha usado Ud. muletas?
10. ¿Le ha arañado alguna vez el gato?
11. ¿Le duele ahora la cabeza?
12. ¿Se paga mucho en las clínicas por aquí?

24

Oye y calla, vivirás vida holgada.
Keep your ears open and your mouth shut
and you'll stay out of trouble.

Irregular verbs *oír*, *caer*, and *traer*

1. PRESENT INDICATIVE

oír to hear		**caer** to fall		**traer** to bring	
oigo	oímos	caigo	caemos	traigo	traemos
oyes	(oís)	caes	(caéis)	traes	(traéis)
oye	oyen	cae	caen	trae	traen

In **caer** and **traer** the only irregularity in the present indicative is the first person singular: **caigo, traigo.**

2. PRESENT SUBJUNCTIVE

As in most verbs, the present subjunctive is formed on the first person singular of the present indicative.

oiga, oigas, oiga, oigamos, oigáis, oigan
caiga, caigas, caiga, caigamos, caigáis, caigan
traiga, traigas, traiga, traigamos, traigáis, traigan

315

3. PRETERIT, PAST SUBJUNCTIVE, AND GERUND

The preterit of **oír** and **caer** is like that of **leer** (see Lesson 9). The unaccented **i** of the personal ending in the third person, singular and plural, changes to **y**. In the other forms the **i** bears a written accent. The preterit of **traer** is completely irregular.

PRETERIT	oí	caí	traje
	oíste	caíste	trajiste
	oyó	cayó	trajo
	oímos	caímos	trajimos
	(oísteis)	(caísteis)	(trajisteis)
	oyeron	cayeron	trajeron
PAST SUBJUNCTIVE	oyera oyese	cayera cayese	trajera trajese
GERUND	oyendo	cayendo	trayendo

PRÁCTICA

Cambie según se indica.

a. 1. Ud. lo oye.
   nosotros / tú / yo / ella / Uds.

   2. Ud. lo oyó.
   ellos / nosotros / yo / tú / Uds.

   3. Desean que Ud. lo oiga.
   tú / yo / tú y yo / él / Uds.

   4. Deseaban que Ud. lo oyera.
   Ud. / ellas / yo / tú / Ud. y yo

b. 1. No caen nunca.
   tú / nosotros / yo / ellos / Ud.

   2. No cayeron nunca.
   yo / tú / nosotros / él / ellas

   3. Parece mentira que no caigan.
   nosotros / ellas / yo / Ud. / tú

   4. Parecía mentira que no cayesen.
   ella / nosotros / yo / tú / Ud. y yo

c. 1. Él no lo trae.
   yo / tú / nosotros / ellos / Uds.

   2. Él no lo trajo.
   nosotros / tú / yo / ellos / Ud.

   3. Conviene que él lo traiga.
   yo / Uds. / tú / nosotros / Ud.

   4. Convenía que él lo trajera.
   Ud. / ellas / tú / yo / nosotros

One of the most popular tourist spots in Mexico is the coastal resort of Acapulco.

Escuchar y hablar

acercarse (a) to approach
el automóvil automobile
¡ay! oh!
caerse de to fall out of
la capital capital
cómodo comfortable
completamente completely
contar (ue) to tell
la cuna cradle
el chiste joke
hermosísimo most (very, exceedingly) beautiful
el individuo individual, person
limpio clean
llevar to wear
magnífico magnificent
muchísimo very much, a very great deal
nada *adv.* (not) at all
el Pacífico Pacific
el palacio palace
pintoresco picturesque
la pirámide pyramid

la playa beach
la prima cousin
progresista progressive
recobrar to recover
sin que without
el traje de baño bathing suit
el único the only one
viajar to travel
ya que since

IDIOMS AND OTHER EXPRESSIONS

al aire libre in the open air
ya caigo now I get it
concentrar la atención en to concentrate on
como lo oyes just as I'm telling you
¡ahora lo oigo! this is the first time I've heard about it!
oír decir to hear that, to hear it said that
a orillas de beside
yo sí I was (did, have, had, etc.)

VIRGINIA EN LA PLAYA DE ACAPULCO

Hace una hora que los estudiantes estudian en la biblioteca.

—Traigan sus libros y salgamos a la playa a[1] estudiar—dice Juan. —Hace una hora que trabajamos y aquí hace demasiado calor.

Pero nadie dice nada. El pobre Juan habla sin que nadie lo oiga. Los estudiantes concentran la atención en los libros.

—¿No me oyen? Les dije que trajeran los libros. Será más cómodo estudiar al aire libre.

Al salir de la biblioteca, Virginia empezó a contarles una cosa. —En la playa de Acapulco, cuando estuve en México hace dos años . . . —empezó.

—Tú has estado en México?—interrumpió Juan. —¡Ahora lo oigo!

—Como lo oyes—contestó ella. Fui a México con mi madre hace dos años. Ella quería ver ese país tan pintoresco. Como saben Uds., hace varios años que mi padre está enfermo. Cayó enfermo y no recobró completamente la salud. Pero ese verano se sentía mejor, de modo que fuimos a México. Hicimos el viaje en automóvil. De Nuevo Laredo fuimos a Monterrey . . .

—¿Por qué pasaron por Nuevo Laredo?—volvió a interrumpir Juan. —Ya que Uds. viven en California, debieron[2] ir a El Paso.

—Es que[3] tenemos una prima en San Antonio.

—Ya caigo—dijo Juan. —Uds. fueron a visitarla.

—Pues, como decía, pasamos por Monterrey, esa ciudad industrial, tan progresista y tan limpia. Luego fuimos a la capital. Es hermosísima la capital. Vimos los magníficos edificios de la nueva universidad. Fuimos a ver las pirámides de San Juan Teotihuacán. Visitamos el palacio de Cortés* en Cuernavaca y pasamos un par de días en Taxco. Habíamos oído decir que Acapulco tiene una playa muy buena. De manera que pasamos una semana en esa ciudad a orillas del Pacífico. Nos divertimos muchísimo.

—Una tarde estábamos en la playa. Mi madre no llevaba traje de baño, pero yo sí.[4] Se acercó un individuo a quien habíamos conocido en el hotel. «Señora,» dijo, dirigiéndose a mamá, «veo que no lleva Ud. traje de baño, ¿No nada nada?» «No, señor,» contestó ella. «Es que no traje traje.»

—¡Ay, Virginia! —exclamó Juan —Ese chiste es muy viejo. ¡La primera vez que lo oí me caí de la cuna!

NOTAS

1. You have learned that verbs of motion require **a** before a following infinitive. With such verbs **a** is used more frequently than **para** to express purpose. When **para** is used, it stresses the purpose (*in order to*).

*Hernán Cortés (1485–1547), conqueror of Mexico.

Salgamos a la playa a estudiar.   Let's go out to the beach to study.

But:

Fuimos a la biblioteca para estudiar.   We went to the library (in order) to study.

2. The preterit of **deber** plus an infinitive may be used in Spanish where English uses *ought* or *should* plus a perfect infinitive.

Uds. debieron ir a El Paso.   You ought to have gone to El Paso.
Debí hacerlo antes.   I should have done it before.

3. **Es que** . . . or **ello es que** . . . (*the fact is that*) may be used in beginning an explanation.

Es que no he estudiado hoy.   The fact is that I haven't studied today.

4. An emphatic **sí** or **no** may be used with a verb, or in place of a verb, where English uses an emphatic auxiliary verb. (We *did* go, but he *didn't*, etc.)

El niño no sabe escribir, pero *sí* sabe leer.   The child doesn't know how to write, but he *does* know how to read.
Ellos fueron, pero yo *no*.   They went, but I *didn't*.

PREGUNTAS

1. ¿Cuánto tiempo hace que los estudiantes están en la biblioteca?
2. ¿Qué les dice Juan?
3. ¿Qué dicen los amigos de Juan?
4. ¿Por qué no dicen nada?
5. ¿Qué quiere Juan que hagan los otros al salir de la biblioteca?
6. ¿Cuándo estuvo Virginia en México?
7. ¿Qué exclamó Juan?
8. ¿Cuándo fue Virginia a México con su madre?
9. ¿Qué quería su madre?
10. ¿Cuánto tiempo hace que el padre de Virginia está enfermo?
11. ¿Por qué pasaron por Nuevo Laredo Virginia y su madre?
12. ¿Cómo es Monterrey?
13. ¿Cómo es la capital de México?
14. ¿Qué habían oído decir de Acapulco Virginia y su madre?
15. ¿Quién se acercó a la madre de Virginia en la playa de Acapulco?
16. ¿Qué le dijo?
17. ¿Cómo contestó su madre?
18. ¿Qué le dijo Juan del chiste?

PRÁCTICA

Diga en español.

a. 1. He should have said so.
   2. I should have done it.
   3. They should have seen it.
   4. We should have read it.

b. 1. The fact is I didn't hear.
   2. The fact is he didn't fall.
   3. The fact is she didn't buy it.
   4. The fact is you didn't bring it.

c. 1. He doesn't hear, but I do.
   2. He doesn't know, but I do.
   3. She studied, but you didn't.
   4. She traveled, but you didn't.

Estructura

1. HACE QUE *WITH TIME EXPRESSIONS*

In English the following formula is used to express actions which began in the past and continue into the present:

have (has) been	+	present participle	+	for	+	period of time

I have been	studying	for	an hour.
He has been	living in Spain	for	ten years.

To express such ideas Spanish uses **hace que** and the *present tense.*

hace	+	period of time	+	**que**	+	present tense

Hace	una hora	que	estudio.
Hace	diez años	que	vive en España.

Hace que with the preterit tense is equivalent to "ago."

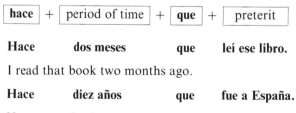

hace	+	period of time	+	**que**	+	preterit

Hace	**dos meses**	**que**	**leí ese libro.**

I read that book two months ago.

Hace	**diez años**	**que**	**fue a España.**

He went to Spain ten years ago.

The preterit may begin the sentence, in which case **que** is omitted.

    Leí ese libro hace dos meses.
    Fue a España hace diez años.

PRÁCTICA

Conteste según los modelos.

a. **¿Cuánto tiempo hace que lee Ud.? (media hora)**
   Hace media hora que leo.

   1. ¿Cuánto tiempo hace que estudia Ud.? (quince minutos)
   2. ¿Cuánto tiempo hace que trabaja Ud.? (dos horas)
   3. ¿Cuánto tiempo hace que escribe Ud.? (veinte minutos)
   4. ¿Cuánto tiempo hace que vive Ud. aquí? (diez años)

b. **¿Hace mucho tiempo que la conoces? (siete años)**
   Hace siete años que la conozco.

   1. ¿Hace mucho tiempo que estudian el español? (más de un año)
   2. ¿Hace mucho tiempo que viajan? (cuatro meses)
   3. ¿Hace mucho tiempo que esperas? (cuarenta minutos)
   4. ¿Hace mucho tiempo que se pasean Uds.? (más de una hora)

c. **¿Cuándo empezó la película? (cinco minutos)**
   Hace cinco minutos que empezó.
   Empezó hace cinco minutos.

   1. ¿Cuándo estuvo Ud. en México? (un año)
   2. ¿Cuándo fuiste a Panamá? (seis meses)
   3. ¿Cuándo trajeron la carta? (quince minutos)
   4. ¿Cuándo leyó Ud. ese libro? (unas semanas)
   5. ¿Cuándo llegaron a Puerto Rico? (varios días)
   6. ¿Cuándo salió ella de Cuba? (nueve semanas)

2. SUBJUNCTIVE OR INDICATIVE IN ADVERB CLAUSES— CONTINUED

De modo que and **de manera que** may express result as well as purpose. When they introduce an adverb clause expressing result, the verb of the clause is always in the indicative.

MAIN CLAUSE		ADVERB CLAUSE EXPRESSES RESULT: INDICATIVE
Se sentía mejor He felt better	**de modo que** so	**hizo el viaje.** he made the trip.
Me dio el dinero He gave me the money	**de manera que** so	**compré el reloj.** I bought the watch.

Sin que (*without*) expresses a negative result and always requires the subjunctive.

¿Podemos salir sin que nos vean?   Can we leave without their seeing us?
Juan hablaba sin que nadie lo oyera.   John was speaking without anyone
hearing him.

PRÁCTICA

Cambie según los modelos.

a. **Nos invitaron. Los acompañamos.**
   Nos invitaron, de modo que los acompañamos.

   1. Nos invitaron. Nos quedamos.
   2. Nos invitaron. Fuimos al cine.
   3. Nos invitaron. Tomamos un refresco.
   4. Nos invitaron. Bailamos.

b. **Insistieron mucho. Lo compré.**
   Insistieron mucho, de manera que lo compré.

   1. Insistieron mucho. Se lo dije.
   2. Insistieron mucho. Se lo expliqué.
   3. Insistieron mucho. Volví temprano.
   4. Insistieron mucho. Les prometí hacerlo.

c. **Siempre salen del hotel. No los oigo.**
   Siempre salen del hotel sin que los oiga.

   1. Siempre salen del hotel. No los oímos.
   2. Siempre salen del hotel. No los veo.
   3. Siempre salen del hotel. No los percibimos.
   4. Siempre salen del hotel. No lo sé.

3. ABSOLUTE SUPERLATIVE

To express a high degree of quality—for example, *exceedingly beautiful, very easy indeed*—Spanish frequently uses the "absolute superlative." This superlative contains no idea of comparison. It is formed by adding **-ísimo (-ísima)** to an adjective or adverb after dropping a final vowel.

hermoso	beautiful	**hermosísimo**	most (very, exceedingly) beautiful
fácil	easy	**facilísimo**	very easy
mucho	much	**muchísimo**	very much (indeed)

Occasionally a spelling change must also be made (as in orthographic-changing verbs) to preserve the original sound of the final consonant.

rico	rich	**riquísimo**	extremely rich
largo	long	**larguísimo**	exceedingly long

Adverbs in **-mente** add **-ísima** to the adjective stem before adding **-mente**.

correctamente   correctly
correctísimamente   most (extremely) correctly

PRÁCTICA

Conteste, siguiendo el modelo.

Ricardo está contento, ¿verdad?
Sí, está contentísimo.

1. El trabajo es difícil, ¿verdad?
2. Esta blusa es barata, ¿verdad?
3. Esa película es interesante, ¿verdad?
4. Inesita come mucho, ¿verdad?
5. Le pagan poco, ¿verdad?
6. Ese viaje es largo, ¿verdad?
7. La ciudad es grande, ¿verdad?
8. La vieja es rica, ¿verdad?
9. Viven pobremente, ¿verdad?

Tareas

Diga en español.

1. The students have been in the library for a long while.
2. "Bring your books," said Juan. "We've been working too long."
3. But he said it without anybody hearing him.
4. I told you to bring your books.
5. Virginia was in Mexico two years ago.
6. This is the first time I've heard it!
7. She went with her mother two years ago.
8. Her father has been ill for several years.
9. He was feeling better, so they took the trip.
10. They should not have gone to Nuevo Laredo, should they?
11. The fact is that they have cousins in San Antonio.
12. They had heard that Acapulco is a most interesting city.
13. So they spent a week there.
14. On the beach Virginia was wearing a bathing suit.
15. Don't you swim at all?
16. I didn't bring a suit.

Composición oral o escrita

1. Make up six statements about how long you have been doing certain things. Tell how long you have lived where you do now, how long you have been studying at the university, how long you have known some of your friends, etc.

2. Make up six sentences telling how long ago you did certain things. You had breakfast three hours ago; you went to the library half an hour ago; you took a trip a year ago, etc.

Diálogo

PACO LLEGA TARDE

RAÚL—¡Por fin! ¡Lo que has tardado![1] Creía que no venías.

PACO—¿Hace tiempo que me esperas?

RAUL—¡Claro! Hace más de una hora que te espero.

PACO—Lo siento muchísimo.

RAÚL—Dijiste que estarías aquí a las siete y ahora son las ocho y pico.[2] La película empezó hace cincuenta minutos.

PACO—Tuve unos disgustos.[3]

RAÚL—¿Qué pasó?

PACO—Fui a la peluquería para hacerme cortar el pelo.[4]

RAÚL—¡Ya era tiempo![5]

PACO—¡No, hombre! ¡Si[6] me lo hice cortar hace tres meses! Bueno, tuve que esperar. Y lo malo es[7] que hoy día[8] un corte de pelo[9] cuesta tanto que estoy sin blanca.[10]

RAÚL—¡Como siempre!

PACO—Tuve que buscar a Pepita para pedirle prestados[11] unos pesos.

RAÚL—¿Te los prestó?

PACO—No, no quiso prestármelos. Y luego mi coche no quiso arrancar.[12] Como estaba sin un céntimo,[13] no pude llamar al garaje[14] para que lo compusieran.[15] De manera que tuve que hacer autostop[16] para venir acá.

RAÚL—No debes hacer eso. Puede ser muy peligroso.[17]

PACO—Cerca de la universidad no es peligroso. Por aquí hay muchos autostopistas[18] y no corren peligro.[19]

[1]Lo que has tardado. *How late you are.*

[2]las ocho y pico *a little after eight*

[3]Tuve unos disgustos. *I had a little trouble.*

[4]hacerse cortar el pelo *to get a haircut*

[5]¡Ya era tiempo! *It was about time!*

[6]si *why*

[7]lo malo es *the trouble is*

[8]hoy día *nowadays*

[9]el corte de pelo *haircut*

[10]estar sin blanca *to be broke*

[11]pedir prestado *to borrow*

[12]arrancar *to start*

[13]estar sin un céntimo *to be broke*

[14]el garaje *garage*

[15]componer *to repair*

[16]hacer autostop *to hitch-hike*

[17]peligroso *dangerous*

[18]el autostopista *hitch-hiker*

[19]correr peligro *to be in danger*

PREGUNTAS PERSONALES

1. ¿Le molesta a Ud. cuando un amigo llega tarde a una cita?
2. Hay personas que siempre llegan tarde, ¿verdad?
3. ¿Qué les dice Ud. cuando llegan tarde?
4. ¿Siempre llega Ud. puntualmente?
5. ¿Llegó Ud. tarde a la última cita con su novia (novio)?
6. ¿Va Ud. con frecuencia a la peluquería?
7. ¿Cuándo se hizo Ud. cortar el pelo la última vez?
8. ¿Cuesta mucho hoy día un corte de pelo?
9. ¿Cuánto cuesta?
10. ¿Presta Ud. dinero a sus amigos.
11. ¿Le piden prestado dinero a Ud.?
12. ¿Está Ud. sin blanca (sin un céntimo) de vez en cuando?
13. ¿Hace Ud. autostop de vez en cuando?
14. ¿Es peligroso hacer autostop?
15. ¿Hay muchos autostopistas por aquí?

Metal wares on display in Mexico City's flea market.

25

Si quieres saber de aquí y de allá, el tiempo te lo dirá.
Time will tell.

Orthographic-changing verbs in *-ger* and *-gir*

In order to preserve the sound of the final consonant of the infinitive stem throughout the conjugation, verbs whose infinitive ends in **-ger** and **-gir** change **g** to **j** before the letters **o** or **a**. The forms affected are the first person singular of the present indicative and the entire present subjunctive. You will recall that the present subjunctive is derived from the first person singular of the present indicative.

PRESENT INDICATIVE		PRESENT SUBJUNCTIVE	
coger to pick up; to catch			
cojo	cogemos	coja	cojamos
coges	(cogéis)	cojas	(cojáis)
coge	cogen	coja	cojan
dirigir to direct			
dirijo	dirigimos	dirija	dirijamos
diriges	(dirigís)	dirijas	(dirijáis)
dirige	dirigen	dirija	dirijan

PRÁCTICA

Cambie según se indica.

1. Siempre cogen al criminal.
   él / tú / ellas / yo / Ud. y yo

2. Esperan que Ud. no coja una pulmonía.
   Uds. / nosotros / tú / yo / ella

3. Ahora se dirigen a la plaza.
ella / nosotros / yo / Ud. y yo / tú

4. Conviene que se dirijan a la plaza.
tú / nosotros / ellas / yo / él

Conditional perfect

The conditional perfect is formed by combining the conditional of **haber** with a past participle.

habría hablado   I should have spoken
habrías hablado   you would have spoken
habría hablado   he (she) would have spoken

habríamos hablado   we should have spoken
(habríais hablado)   you would have spoken
habrían hablado   they would have spoken

PRÁCTICA

Cambie según se indica.

1. Ud. lo habría dicho.
yo / nosotros / tú / ellos / Uds.

2. Tú lo habrías hecho.
ellos / nosotros / yo / Ud. y yo / él

3. Ellos lo habrían devuelto antes.
tú / nosotros / yo / ellas / Uds.

Escuchar y hablar

bello   beautiful
el bridge   bridge (*card game*)
el cielo   sky
como si   as if
el ejemplo   example
ello   it
la estrella   star

la filosofía   philosophy
lo que *rel. pron.*   that which, what
la lluvia   rain
el millonario   millionaire
el mundo   world
la necesidad   necessity
nublado   cloudy

Panamanian dancers in local costume. The folklore of Latin America has been influenced by three currents—Indian, European, and that of the Blacks brought over from Africa as slaves. Each country has its own distinctive songs and dances.

el ocio idleness
¡ojalá (que) . . . ! oh, that; if only
  I wish!
el producto product
el resfriado cold (*illness*)
rico rich
soñar (ue) to dream
el sueño dream

IDIOMS AND OTHER EXPRESSIONS

llegar a ser to become
pensar en to think of
poner por ejemplo to take for example
soñar (ue) con to dream of

LA VIDA ES SUEÑO

Todos soñamos en este mundo. Si somos pobres, soñamos con ser ricos. Si estamos enfermos, soñamos con estar bien de salud. Casi siempre deseamos lo que no tenemos y soñamos con ello.[1]

Conviene que haya en el mundo los que sueñan. La filosofía y el arte son productos de los sueños. El hombre no podría vivir sin soñar.

Pongamos por ejemplo un día típico. Es una tarde de primavera, pero el cielo está nublado y está lloviendo. Juan y las dos muchachas están hablando de lo que harían si pudieran.

—¡Ojalá[2] pudiéramos ir al partido de béisbol!—dice Juan. —Si no hubiera llovido, yo habría ido.

—Si Carlos estuviera aquí,—dice María—podríamos jugar al bridge. Ojalá que no hubiera cogido ese resfriado.

—Con esta lluvia—dice Virginia—no hay nada que hacer. ¡Tendremos que estudiar!

—Pensemos en lo que haremos mañana—propone Juan. —Si no llueve mañana, chiquita, ¿quieres jugar un partido de tenis conmigo?—pregunta, dirigiéndose a Virginia.

—Con mucho gusto. Pero si lloviese otra vez, no sería posible jugar.

—¡Cuántas cosas no son posibles!—exclama María. —Si fuera posible, me gustaría ser actriz. ¡Ojalá fuera tan bella como las estrellas de Hollywood!

—¡Ojalá fuera millonario!—dice Juan. —Si fuera rico, no haría nada más que viajar y divertirme.

—Pero Juan,—le dice María—si algún día llegases a ser rico, no te gustaría pasar la vida sin trabajar. Los sueños y el ocio son agradables, pero el trabajo es una necesidad. Los hombres necesitan trabajar.

—¡Ay, María,—responde Juan—tú hablas como si fueras mi abuela! ¡Con tus buenos consejos hablas como si tuvieras ochenta años!

NOTAS

1. **Ello** (*it*) is a neuter personal pronoun. It is used chiefly as object of a preposition, less commonly as subject of a verb. When used as object of a preposition it refers to a previously expressed idea, never to a specific object of determined gender. Its use as subject of a verb is practically limited to the expression **ello es que** (*the fact is that*).

   Deseamos lo que no tenemos y soñamos con ello.   We want what we do not have, and we dream of it.

   No tengo tiempo para ello.   I have no time for it.

   Ello es que no puedo ir.   The fact is that I can't go.

2. **¡Ojalá (que) . . . !** (*oh, that; if only; I wish*) is used with the past subjunctive when referring to present time and with the past perfect subjunctive when referring to past time. **Que** may be used or omitted.

   ¡Ojalá fuera rico!   Oh, that (if only) I were rich!

   ¡Ojalá que hubieran venido!   If only (I wish that) they had come!

PREGUNTAS

1. ¿Qué hacemos todos en este mundo?
2. ¿Con qué soñamos?
3. ¿Qué son la filosofía y el arte?
4. ¿Qué tiempo hace esta tarde de primavera?
5. ¿De qué hablan Juan y las dos muchachas?
6. ¿Qué exclama Juan?
7. ¿Qué harían los estudiantes si Carlos estuviera con ellos?
8. ¿Qué le pregunta Juan a Virginia?

9. ¿Es cierto que jugarán al tenis mañana?
10. ¿Qué quisiera ser María?
11. ¿Qué exclama ella?
12. ¿Qué haría Juan si fuera rico?
13. ¿Qué le dice María?
14. ¿Cómo habla María?
15. ¿Habla como una señorita de dieciocho años?

PRÁCTICA

Diga en español.

a.
1. Oh, that I were tall!
2. Oh, that I were intelligent!
3. If only she were here!
4. If only she were in Spain!
5. I wish they had come!
6. I wish they had left!
7. If only I had seen it!
8. If only I had done it!

b.
1. I dream of it.
2. I am glad of it.
3. We haven't the time for it.
4. We haven't the money for it.

Estructura

1. CONDITIONAL ("IF") CLAUSES

a. Most conditional clauses, introduced by **si** ("*if*"), are in the indicative. Spanish normally uses the same tenses as English in both the "if" clause and the main clause.

PRESENT	PRESENT OR FUTURE	
Si estudio,	**aprendo.**	If I study, I learn.
Si estudias,	**aprenderás.**	If you study, you will learn.

PAST	PAST	
Si tenía frío,	**se ponía el abrigo.**	If he was cold, he put on his coat.
Si recibió la carta,	**la contestó.**	If he received the letter, he answered it.
Si ha vuelto,	**lo han visto.**	If he has returned, they have seen him.

However, neither the future, the conditional, nor the present subjunctive may be used in an "if" clause.

>   **Si *estás* aquí mañana, lo discutiré contigo.**   If you *will be* here tomorrow, I'll discuss it with you.
>   **Si esto *es* traición . . .**   If this be treason . . .

b. "If" clauses may state something contrary to fact or something not likely to occur. Clauses stating what is contrary to fact are in the past subjunctive or the past perfect subjunctive. The main clause is in the conditional or the conditional perfect. Clauses stating something not likely to happen are in the past subjunctive. Their main clauses are in the conditional.

Contrary to fact:

PAST OR PAST PERFECT SUBJUNCTIVE	CONDITIONAL OR CONDITIONAL PERFECT
Si fuera rico, If I were rich (I'm not), **Si hubiera sido rico,** If I had been rich (I wasn't),	**iría a Sudamérica.** I would go to South America. **habría ido a Sudamérica.** I would have gone to South America.

Clause states something not likely to occur:

PAST SUBJUNCTIVE	CONDITIONAL
Si lloviese mañana, If it should rain tomorrow,	**no iría.** I wouldn't go.

PRÁCTICA

Cambie según los modelos.

a. **Tienen hambre.**
   Comerán.
   Si tienen hambre, comerán.

   1. Llueve mucho.
      No saldremos.

   2. Hace frío.
      Nos quedaremos en casa.

3. Tenemos tiempo.
Jugaremos al bridge.

4. Ella llega temprano.
La veremos.

5. Ud. estudia mucho.
Aprenderá mucho.

b. **Si tienen hambre, comerán.**
Si tuvieran hambre, comerían.

1. Si llueve mucho, no saldremos.
2. Si hace frío, nos quedaremos en casa.
3. Si tenemos tiempo, jugaremos al bridge.
4. Si ella llega a tiempo, la veremos.
5. Si Ud. estudia mucho, aprenderá mucho.

c. **Si ha cogido un resfriado, irá a la clínica.**
Si hubiera cogido un resfriado, habría ido a la clínica.

1. Si ha llamado, me lo dirán.
2. Si ha estado aquí, lo sabremos.
3. Si ha comprado el coche, lo pagará.
4. Si llegamos temprano, asistimos a la clase.
5. Si vendió la casa, ganó mucho dinero.
6. Si se levantaron tarde, no tomaron el desayuno.

2. CLAUSES INTRODUCED BY COMO SI

Como si (*as if*) introduces a clause which is essentially a contrary-to-fact condition. It is followed by the past subjunctive to express present time and by the past perfect subjunctive to express past time.

Hablas como si fueras mi abuela.   You talk as if you were my grandmother.
Hablaba como si lo hubiera visto.   He spoke as if he had seen it.

PRÁCTICA

Cambie según el modelo.

No tiene el dinero.
Habla como si lo tuviera.
Hablaba como si lo hubiera tenido.

1. No lo comprende.
Lo explica como si lo _____.
Lo explicó como si lo _____.

2. No está allí.
   Lo describe como si _____.
   Lo describió como si _____.

3. No lo sabe.
   Habla como si lo _____.
   Habló como si lo _____.

3. *SI MEANING "WHETHER"*

When **si** means "whether," it is followed by the future, the conditional, or any indicative tense.

No sé si lo hará.   I don't know whether (if) he'll do it.
No sabía si vendría.   I didn't know whether (if) he would come.
No sé si lo hicieron.   I don't know whether they did it.

PRÁCTICA

Cambie según se indica.

a. **¿Volverán pronto?**
   No sé si volverán pronto.

   1. ¿Vendrán mañana?
   2. ¿Irán allá?
   3. ¿Saldrán temprano?
   4. ¿Devolverán el dinero?

b. **¿Sabes si Juan volverá pronto?**
   No, no dijo si volvería pronto.

   1. ¿Sabes si vendrá mañana?
   2. ¿Sabes si irá allá?
   3. ¿Sabes si saldrá temprano?
   4. ¿Sabes si devolverá el dinero?

4. *DEFINITE ARTICLE WITH GENERAL AND ABSTRACT NOUNS*

The definite article is required before general nouns—that is, nouns that stand for *all* of whatever they name.

Los hombres necesitan trabajar.   Men (all men) need to work.
Me gusta la música.   I like music (all music in general).

It is also required before abstract nouns.

La vida es sueño.   Life is a dream.
El trabajo es una necesidad.   Work is a necessity.

PRÁCTICA

Diga en español.

1. I like horses.
2. I like soup.
3. I like flowers.
4. Life is interesting.
5. Philosophy is interesting.
6. Art is interesting.

5. DIMINUTIVES

Spanish attains a great variety of effect by the use of diminutive suffixes, which are added to nouns, adjectives, or adverbs after a final unstressed vowel has been dropped. Diminutives imply small size and may also express affection.

a. **-ito (-ita)** and **-illo (-illa)** are the commonest diminutive suffixes. To many words they are added directly. To others they are added after a final vowel has been dropped.

animal	animal	**animalito**	little animal
niña	girl	**niñita**	little girl
perro	dog	**perillo**	little dog

b. **-cito (-cita)** and **-cillo (-cilla)** are added to words of two or more syllables ending in **-n** or **-r** and to words ending in **-e**.

canción	song	**cancioncita**	little song
mujer	woman	**mujercita**	(dear) little woman
pobre	poor man	**pobrecillo**	poor little fellow

c. **-ecito (-ecita)** and **-ecillo (-ecilla)** are added to words of one syllable ending in a consonant.

pan	bread	**panecillo**	roll
flor	flower	**florecilla**	little flower

Spelling changes are sometimes necessary to preserve the sound of the final consonant of the original word.

amigo	friend	**amiguito**	little friend
poco	little	**poquito**	tiny bit
pez	fish	**pececito**	little fish

PRÁCTICA

Cambie al diminutivo.

¿Dónde está ese animal?
¿Dónde está ese animalito?

a. 1. ¿Dónde está el gato?
   2. ¿Dónde está el pájaro?
   3. ¿Dónde está el niño?
   4. ¿Dónde está la pequeña?

b. 1. El pobre está muy triste.
   2. La mujer está muy triste.
   3. ¿Me echas un café?
   4. ¿Me das una ración?

c. 1. Es muy chica.
   2. Hay un poco.
   3. ¿Qué tal, Paca?
   4. ¿Qué tal, amigo?

Tareas

Diga en español.

1. We all dream.
2. If we are poor, we dream of being rich.
3. They always want what they don't have and they dream of it.
4. Philosophy and art are the products of dreams.
5. This spring afternoon the sky is cloudy, and it is raining.
6. The students are talking of what they would do, if they could.
7. I wish I could go to the baseball game!
8. If it had not rained, I would have been able to go.
9. If our friend were here, we would play bridge.
10. If only he had not caught a cold!
11. There was nothing to do that afternoon.
12. Will you play a game of tennis tomorrow, if it doesn't rain?
13. If it should rain tomorrow, we would not be able to play.
14. If it were possible, María would like to be an actress.
15. If Juan were rich, he would do nothing but have a good time.
16. If he should become rich, he would want to work.
17. María talks as if she were eighty years old and as if she were Juan's grandmother.

Composición oral o escrita

Tell what you would do today, if you could, and what you would have done yesterday, if you had been able to. (You would go to the movies this evening, if you didn't have to study. You would have played tennis yesterday, if it hadn't rained, and so forth.)

Diálogo

ENRIQUE NO VA AL BAILE

INESITA—¿Vas al baile del sábado?

ENRIQUE—Todavía[1] no sé si iré.[2] No me he decidido.[3]

INESITA—Si te decides a ir, ¿a quién vas a invitar?

ENRIQUE—No lo sé. Ni siquiera he pensado en ello.

INESITA—¿Por qué no invitas a Carmencita?

ENRIQUE—No baila bien. Además si la invitara, no aceptaría.

INESITA—¿Estás seguro?

ENRIQUE—Iría con Carlitos. Está loca por él.

INESITA—¿Y Anita?[4] Si la invitas, seguro[5] que aceptará.

ENRIQUE—No está aquí. Ha ido a casa con motivo del[6] cumpleaños de su papá. Pero si estuviera aquí no la invitaría.

INESITA—¿Por qué no?

ENRIQUE—No congeniamos.[7]

INESITA—Lolita, entonces.

ENRIQUE—Tampoco. Es tan presumida.[8]

INESITA—Bueno, pues, ¿y Paquita?

ENRIQUE—¡Ni por pienso![9] Es todavía más presumida.

INESITA—¿Has pensado en Rita?

ENRIQUE—No puedo con ella.[10]

INESITA—¡Eres imposible! ¡Todas estas chicas te resultan antipáticas![11] ¿Por qué no invitas a Blancanieves?[12]

[1]todavía *yet, still*

[2]si iré *whether I'll go*

[3]decidirse *to decide*

[4]¿Y Anita? *And what about Anita?*

[5]seguro *surely*

[6]con motivo de *because of*

[7]congeniar *to get along (well)*

[8]presumido *snooty*

[9]¡Ni por pienso! *Never! The very idea!*

[10]No puedo con ella. *I can't stand her!*

[11]Todas . . . antipáticas. *You don't like any of these girls.*

[12]Blancanieves *Snow White*

PREGUNTAS PERSONALES

1. Si vas al baile, ¿con quién irás?
2. Si invitas a Dorotea, ¿aceptará?
3. Si tienes tiempo, ¿irás conmigo al centro?
4. Si tienes el dinero, ¿me lo prestarás?
5. Si llueve, ¿te quedarás en casa?
6. Si no estuviera lloviendo, ¿jugarías al béisbol?

7. Si pudieras, ¿harías un viaje?
8. Si tuvieras el tiempo, ¿irías conmigo al centro?
9. Si hubieras tenido el dinero, ¿habrías comprado el coche?
10. Si hubieras visto a Inesita, ¿la habrías invitado a tomar un refresco?

26

El que no se aventura no pasa la mar.
Nothing ventured, nothing gained.

Verbs in -eír

Verbs like **reír** (*to laugh*), whose infinitive ends in **-eír,** follow the pattern of the **pedir** type of stem-changing verb, with the following exceptions:

1. Wherever the **i** is stressed, it bears a written accent.

PRESENT INDICATIVE		PRESENT SUBJUNCTIVE	
río	**reímos**	**ría**	**riamos**
ríes	**(reís)**	**rías**	**(riáis)**
ríe	**ríen**	**ría**	**rían**

PAST PARTICIPLE **reído**

2. Two contiguous **i**'s are reduced to one. Among the forms affected are the third person singular and plural of the preterit, the entire past subjunctive, and the present participle.

PRETERIT		PAST SUBJUNCTIVE
reí	**reímos**	**riera, rieras,** etc.
reíste	**(reísteis)**	
rió	**rieron**	**riese, rieses,** etc.

PRESENT PARTICIPLE **riendo**

Notice that the first and second persons, singular and plural, of the preterit follow the rule stated in 1 above. Another common **-eír** verb is **sonreír** (*to smile*).

PRÁCTICA

Cambie según se indica.

1. Ellos ríen siempre.
   Ud. / tú / nosotros / yo / ella

2. Ud. no se rió de eso.
   yo / Ud. y yo / él / ellas / tú

3. Conviene que no se rían tanto.
   nosotros / tú / yo / ellas / él

4. Convenía que no se rieran tanto.
   Uds. / ella / yo / tú / Ud. y yo

Verbs in *–iar* and *–uar*

Some verbs whose infinitive ends in **-iar** accent the **i** throughout the singular and in the third person plural of both the present indicative and the present subjunctive.

enviar   to send

PRESENT INDICATIVE		PRESENT SUBJUNCTIVE	
envío	**enviamos**	**envíe**	**enviemos**
envías	**(enviáis)**	**envíes**	**(enviéis)**
envía	**envían**	**envíe**	**envíen**

But compare **estudiar: estudio, estudias, estudia,** etc.

PRÁCTICA

Cambie según se indica.

1. *Él* les envía el dinero.
   yo / nosotros / vosotros / tú / Uds.

2. Quieren que *Ud.* se lo envíe.
   tú / yo / nosotros / él / Uds.

*Spain has many
different kinds of
lotteries, most of
them sponsored by
some charity. The
most popular is the
Christmas lottery
which offers prizes as
high as 40,000,000
pesetas.*

Some verbs whose infinitive ends in **-uar** (except **-guar**) accent the **u** throughout
the singular and in the third person plural of both the present indicative and
the present subjunctive.

continuar   to continue

PRESENT INDICATIVE		PRESENT SUBJUNCTIVE	
continúo	continuamos	continúe	continuemos
continúas	(continuáis)	continúes	(continuéis)
continúa	continúan	continúe	continúen

PRÁCTICA

Cambie según se indica.

1. Carlos continúa hablando.
   nosotros / yo / la chica / tú / ellas
2. Conviene que continuemos buscando.
   tú / Ud. / Uds. / yo / tus amigos

Escuchar y hablar

añadir to add
artístico artistic
asegurar to assure, affirm
bilingüe bilingual
la compañía company
conseguir (i) to get, obtain
la contribución contribution
el cual, la cual who, whom, that, which
lo cual which (fact)
cualquiera *pron.* anybody
cualquier(a) *adj.* whichever, whatever
cursar to take, study (*a course*)
cuyo whose
la disminución diminution, decrease
dondequiera wherever
la ecología ecology
egoísta selfish
el empleo job
extravagante extravagant, odd
la felicidad happiness
hacerse to become
la herencia heritage
la humanidad humanity
el idioma language
interesarse por (*or* **en**) to be interested in, take an interest in

literario literary
el maestro teacher
materialista materialistic
la minoría minority
la polución de la atmósfera air pollution
práctico practical
el presidente president
la profesión profession
el que, la que he who, the one who, the one which
los que, las que those who, those which
reírse (de) to laugh (at)
el representante representative
la satisfacción satisfaction
sonreír to smile
el valor value

IDIOMS AND OTHER EXPRESSIONS

con todo empeño with great determination
lo que no me explico what I can't explain
al menos at least
de todos modos at any rate
valer por to be worth

¿QUÉ VAS A HACER DE TU VIDA?

Carlos, cuyas ideas son algo extravagantes, ha dicho que va a ser millonario.

—¡No se rían Uds!—continúa Carlos. —He dicho que voy a ser millonario y lo seré. Hay muchas compañías que envían representantes a Hispanoamérica. Voy a cursar al menos otros dos años de español. Estaré bien preparado para ir allá. Luego, después de terminar mis estudios, voy a conseguir un empleo en una compañía que tenga intereses en los países hispanoamericanos. Me enseñarán lo que hay que saber. Iré allá y dondequiera que me envíen trabajaré con todo empeño. Tal vez[1] llegue a ser presidente de la compañía. De todos modos voy a ser muy rico.

—Hombre,—responde Juan—no me río de eso. Es muy posible que resulte así. Si eso es lo que quieres, te deseo buena suerte. Lo que no me explico es esto: eres tan materialista. Cualquiera diría que eres egoísta. El dinero no trae la felicidad. Hay otras muchas cosas en la vida que dan mayor satisfacción.

Si te hicieras médico, por ejemplo, podrías ayudar a los enfermos y a los pobres, lo cual te daría gran satisfacción. O podrías interesarte por la ecología y trabajar por la disminución de la polución de la atmósfera. Los que trabajan por la humanidad son los que hacen una verdadera contribución al mundo.

—Dices que vas a aprender bien el español—añade María, sonriendo.

—Como has oído decir, el que sabe dos idiomas vale por dos personas. Aprendiendo bien el español, podrías hacerte maestro bilingüe. Es la profesión para la cual me preparo yo. Hacen mucha falta los maestros bilingües para enseñar a los niños de las minorías en este país.

—Y no pienses sólo en el valor práctico del español—dice Virginia.

—Como asegura el señor Martínez, vale la pena de continuar estudiándolo para comprender la rica herencia artística y literaria de España e Hispanoamérica.

NOTA

1. **Tal vez, quizá(s),** and **acaso** (*perhaps*) may take the subjunctive when followed by the verb and uncertainty is stressed.

   Tal vez llegue a ser presidente de la compañía. Perhaps he may become president of the company.

   But:

   Llegará a ser presidente, tal vez. He will become president, perhaps.

PREGUNTAS

1. ¿Cómo son las ideas de Carlos?
2. ¿Qué quiere ser Carlos?
3. Después de terminar sus estudios, ¿qué quiere conseguir Carlos?
4. ¿Cómo dice Carlos que trabajará?
5. ¿Qué llegará a ser, tal vez, en la compañía?
6. ¿Se ríe Ud. de las ideas de Carlos?
7. ¿Cómo es Carlos?
8. ¿Qué diría de él cualquier persona?
9. ¿Cree Ud. que el dinero trae la felicidad?
10. ¿Qué satisfacción tienen los que se hacen médicos?
11. ¿Se interesa Ud. por la ecología?
12. ¿Quiénes son los que hacen una verdadera contribución al mundo?
13. ¿Quisiera Ud. ser maestro (maestra) bilingüe?
14. ¿Qué hacen los maestros bilingües?
15. ¿Qué asegura el señor Martínez?

PRÁCTICA

Conteste según el modelo.

¿Crees que llegarán tarde?
Tal vez lleguen tarde.
Quizás lleguen tarde.

1. ¿Crees que saldrán temprano?
2. ¿Crees que volverán pronto?
3. ¿Crees que lo harán bien?
4. ¿Crees que enviarán el dinero?
5. ¿Crees que continuarán viajando?

Estructura

1. RELATIVE PRONOUNS AFTER PREPOSITIONS

a. *Whom*, as the object of a preposition, is **quien (quienes).**

   el tío *con quien* fui a Sudamérica   the uncle *with whom* I went to South America
   las personas *a quienes* me dirijo   the people *to whom* I speak

b. *Which* is **que** after the prepositions **a, de, en,** and **con.**

   la compañía *con que* trabaja   the company *with which* he works
   la ciudad *a que* vamos   the city *to which* we are going

c. *Which* is **el cual (la cual, los cuales, las cuales)** after other prepositions.

   la mesa *sobre la cual* puso los libros   the table *on which* he put the books
   los países *por los cuales* viajamos   the countries *through which* we traveled
   la iglesia *detrás de la cual* vivimos   the church *behind which* we live

RELATIVE PRONOUNS AFTER PREPOSITIONS

whom (*person*)	**quien, quienes**
which (*after* **a, de, en, con**) which (*after other prepositions*)	**que** **el cual, la cual,** **los cuales, las cuales**

PRÁCTICA

Diga en español.

a. **la amiga:**

1. for whom he bought it
2. to whom I sent it
3. with whom I went out

b. **los alumnos:**

1. for whom you bought it
2. to whom you sent it
3. with whom you went out

c. **el país:**

1. to which he is going
2. from which he has come
3. through which he traveled
4. about (*acerca de*) which he spoke to us

d. **la casa:**

1. in which they live
2. to which they are going
3. near which they live
4. in front of which they parked the car

---

2. RELATIVE PRONOUNS AS SUBJECT OR OBJECT OF A VERB

a. As subject or object of a verb, *who, whom, that,* or *which* is usually **que,** the commonest relative pronoun.

Hay muchas compañías *que* envían representantes a Sudamérica.   There are many companies *that* send representatives to South America.
las personas *que* vemos en la calle   the people *whom* we see in the street

b. *Who* or *whom* introducing a nonrestrictive or nonessential clause—that is, one set off by commas—may be **quien (quienes)** as well as **que.**

Mi padre, *quien* vive en Nueva York, está aquí ahora.   My father, *who* lives in New York, is here now.
Su hermana, *a quien* acabo de conocer, es muy linda.   His sister, *whom* I have just met, is very pretty. (Note the personal **a** when **quien** is the object, *whom.*)

c. *Which* introducing a nonrestrictive clause and referring to a previously expressed idea or statement (not to a concrete object) is the neuter **lo cual.**

Nuestras inversiones en México son alrededor de seiscientos millones de dólares, *lo cual* me sorprende.   Our investments in Mexico are around six hundred million dollars, *which* surprises me.

Se levantó temprano esta mañana, *lo cual* es extraordinario.   He got up early this morning, *which* is unusual.

RELATIVE PRONOUNS AS SUBJECT OR OBJECT OF VERB

who, whom, that, which	usually **que**
who, whom (*in clause set off by commas*)	**que** or **quien**
which (*neuter, in clause set off by commas*)	**lo cual**

PRÁCTICA

Cambie según los modelos.

a. **Ésta es la señora.**
   Vive aquí.
   Ésta es la señora que vive aquí.

   1. Ésta es la muchacha.
      Habla español.

   2. Éste es el muchacho.
      La conoce.

   3. Éstos son los hombres.
      Lo trajeron.

   4. Éstos son los individuos.
      Me lo enviaron.

b. **Ésta es la cinta.**
   La escuchamos.
   Esta es la cinta que escuchamos.

   1. Éste es el libro.
      Lo leemos.

   2. Éstas son las lecciones.
      Las estudiamos.

   3. Éste es el ejercicio.
      Lo escribimos.

   4. Éstas son las canciones.
      Las cantamos.

c. **Su padre vive en Chile.**
   Está aquí.
   Su padre, quien vive en Chile, está aquí.

   1. Su madre es española.
      Está aquí.

   2. Su tía es muy joven.
      Está aquí.

   3. Sus primas son muy ricas.
      Están aquí.

   4. Sus amigas son venezolanas.
      Están aquí.

d. **Conozco a sus padres.**
   No han llegado.
   Sus padres, a quienes conozco, no han llegado.

   1. Conozco a su hermano.
      No ha llegado.

   2. Busco a su hermana.
      No ha llegado.

   3. He conocido a sus abuelos.
      No han llegado.

   4. No veo a sus primos.
      No habrán llegado.

e. **Dicen que tiene cinco automóviles.**
   Me sorprende.
   Dicen que tiene cinco automóviles,
       lo cual me sorprende.

   1. Dicen que ha comprado el edificio.
       Es muy posible.

   2. Dicen que ganaremos el campeonato.
       Es imposible.

   3. Dicen que será presidente.
       No es probable.

   4. Dicen que tiene noventa años.
       Parece mentira.

3. COMPOUND RELATIVE PRONOUNS

A compound relative pronoun is one which contains its own antecedent, for example, *he who, those who, that which.*

a. *He who* (*the one who, those who, the one which, those which,* etc.) is **el que (la que, los que, las que).**

   El que se prepara hallará grandes oportunidades.   *He who* prepares himself will find great opportunities.
   De estas corbatas prefiero *las que* son de seda.   Of these ties I prefer *the ones which* are of silk.

b. *That which* (often contracted to *what*) is the neuter **lo que.**

   Me enseñarán *lo que* hay que saber.   They will teach me *what* it is necessary to know.
   Haré *lo que* Ud. quiera.   I shall do *what(ever)* you wish.

Note that the neuter **lo cual** (*which*) is a simple relative pronoun and never has this function.

PRÁCTICA

Diga en español.

a. 1. Juan is the one who is laughing.
    2. Teresa is the one who is laugning.
    3. The students are the ones who are laughing.
    4. The girls are the ones who are laughing.

El Paseo de la Reforma connects the center of Mexico City with the great iron gates at the entrance to Chapultepec Park. The wide, tree-shaded boulevard is interrupted with numerous glorietas— *small squares— adorned with monuments and attractive landscaping. Inexpensive one-peso cabs called* peseros *cruise up and down the Reforma, picking up and dropping off passengers anywhere along their fixed routes.*

b. 1. He who studies learns.
   2. Those who study learn.
   3. He who speaks Spanish will have opportunities.
   4. Those who speak Spanish will have opportunities.

c. 1. What you are doing is easy.
   2. What you are saying is interesting.
   3. What they see is amusing.
   4. What they sell is expensive.

4. CUALQUIERA *AND* DONDEQUIERA

Clauses following the indefinite pronoun or adjective **cualquiera** and the indefinite adverb **dondequiera** require the subjunctive.

> **cualquier ciudad que visitáramos**   whatever city we visited
> **dondequiera que me envíen**   wherever they (may) send me

Cualquiera may drop the final **a** before any noun. The plural of **cualquier(a)** is **cualesquier(a).** Notice that **que** introduces the clause following both **cualquier(a)** and **dondequiera.**

PRÁCTICA

Diga en español.

a. 1. whatever book you read
    2. whatever country you visit
    3. whatever suit you buy
    4. whatever movie you see

b. 1. wherever they go
    2. wherever they are
    3. wherever they live
    4. wherever they eat

5. *RELATIVE ADJECTIVE* CUYO

Cuyo (cuya, cuyos, cuyas) is a relative adjective. It never has the interrogative meaning "whose?" Interrogative "whose?" is **¿de quién?** or **¿de quiénes?**

Este es el autor cuyas obras leí.   This is the author whose works I read.

But:

¿De quién es este libro?   Whose book is this?

PRÁCTICA

Cambie según los modelos.

a. **El muchacho.**
    Vi su sombrero en la mesa.
    El muchacho cuyo sombrero vi en la mesa.

    1. El individuo.
       Compré su coche ayer.

    2. El alumno.
       Hallé sus libros en la biblioteca.

    3. Las personas.
       Visité sus casas en México.

    4. El pintor.
       Vendí sus cuadros la semana pasada.

b. **He hallado este sombrero.**
    ¿De quién es este sombrero?

    1. He hallado este reloj.

    2. He hallado esta guitarra.

    3. He hallado estas raquetas.

    4. He hallado estos zapatos.

Tareas

Diga en español.

1. Carlos, whose ideas are a bit odd, says he wants to be a millionaire.
2. There are many companies that send representatives to Hispanic America.
3. Carlos wants to get a job with one of them.
4. Wherever they send him, he will work with great determination.
5. Perhaps he may become president of the company.
6. Carlos is very materialistic. This is what Juan can't understand.
7. Anybody would say he is selfish.
8. Money isn't very important; many other things bring more satisfaction.
9. He who becomes a doctor can help the poor and the sick, which is a great satisfaction.
10. Those who work for humanity are the ones who make a real contribution.
11. If you learn Spanish well, you can become a bilingual teacher.
12. You could teach the children of the minorities, which would also bring great satisfaction.
13. This is the profession for which María is preparing herself.
14. Mr. Martinez, with whom we were talking, assured us that it is worth while to study the rich literary and artistic heritage of Hispanic America and Spain.

Composición oral o escrita

Tell about your plans for the future. What are you going to be—a doctor, a lawyer, a teacher, an engineer, or what? How will you prepare yourself for your chosen profession? Tell about the satisfactions you expect your life work to bring.

Diálogo

¿UNA OPORTUNIDAD PARA CONCHA?

CONCHA—¿Qué carrera[1] estudias? ¿Estudias para médico o abogado, o qué?

RAMON—No estudio para ninguna de esas profesiones que requieren[2] tanto trabajo. Son muy nobles, eso sí.[3] Pero los que se preparan para las profesiones tienen trabajo hasta por encima de las cejas.[4] Y yo soy un tanto perezoso.

CONCHA—Ya me fijé en tu pereza.[5] ¡Cuántas veces has faltado a la clase por no prepararla! Pero volviendo a lo de la carrera, si no vas a ser hombre profesional, lo cual no me explico, ¿qué vas a hacer de tu vida?

RAMÓN—Voy a ser millonario. ¡No te rías! Tengo mis planes. Voy a meterme en[6] un negocio[7] fantástico con mi tío. Los que tienen oportunidades así[8] pueden hacerse ricos de la noche a la mañana.[9] Yo sé lo que me digo.[10]

CONCHA—Y tienes razón. ¿Sabes por qué? En vez de dedicar largos años[11] a estudios profesionales, podrás casarte mucho más pronto.

[1]carrera   *course of study*

[2]requerir   *to require*

[3]eso sí   *certainly*

[4]tienen . . . cejas   *have their work cut out for them*

[5]la pereza   *laziness*

[6]meterse en   *to get into*

[7]el negocio   *business*

[8]así   *like this*

[9]de la noche a la mañana   *overnight*

[10]sé lo que me digo   *I know what I'm talking about*

[11]largos años   *long (many) years*

PREGUNTAS PERSONALES

1. ¿Estudia Ud. para médico (médica) o para abogado (abogada)?
2. En ese caso, ¿tendrá Ud. que dedicar largos años a sus estudios?
3. Para la carrera médica, ¿cuántos años se requieren?
4. Muchos políticos son abogados. Si Ud. estudia para abogado (abogada), ¿piensa dedicarse a la política también?
5. ¿Tienen que trabajar mucho los que se dedican a las profesiones?
6. ¿Prefiere Ud. dedicarse a los negocios?
7. ¿Hay individuos que puedan hacerse ricos de la noche a la mañana?
8. ¿Tiene Ud. planes para hacerse rico (rica)?
9. Ramón ha dicho que es perezoso. ¿Cree Ud. que puede hacerse rico?
10. ¿Cree Ud. que Concha ve una oportunidad para sí?

San Juan, Puerto Rico. Modern structures in the Condado section.

6

A. *Use el subjuntivo o el indicativo de los verbos indicados.*

1. Siempre jugamos al tenis cuando mis amigos _____ (estar) aquí.
2. Cuando _____ (venir) mis tíos, se lo preguntaré.
3. Saldremos tan pronto como _____ (llegar) José.
4. Siempre miro la televisión mientras _____ (estudiar).
5. Mientras tú _____ (estudiar) esta noche, no mires la televisión.
6. Iremos a comer después que tú _____ (terminar) tu trabajo.
7. No comeremos hasta que _____ (volver) los otros.
8. Quiero hablar contigo antes de que te _____ (ir).
9. Cuando le _____ (pedir) el dinero, me lo dará.
10. Dijo que me daría el dinero tan pronto como lo _____ (recibir).
11. Quieren hacerlo antes que yo _____ (salir).
12. Quierían hacerlo antes de que yo _____ (salir).

B. *Use el subjuntivo o el indicativo de los verbos indicados.*

1. Aunque mi novia _____ (estar) aquí anoche, no fuimos al baile.
2. Aunque mi novio _____ (estar) aquí mañana, no iremos al baile.
3. A pesar de que me _____ (sentir) enfermo ahora, asistiré a la clase.
4. No ganaremos el partido, a pesar de que el equipo _____ (jugar) bien mañana.
5. Aun cuando _____ (llover) mañana, iré al centro.

C. *Lea, usando los verbos que van entre paréntesis.*

1. Siempre entran sin que yo los _____ (oír).
2. Anoche entraron sin que yo los _____ (oír).
3. No vamos al restorán sin que tú _____ (ir) también.
4. Nunca iban al restorán sin que yo _____ (ir) también.

D. *Conteste según el modelo.*

¿Cuánto tiempo hace que vives aquí? (diez años)
Hace diez años que vivo aquí.

1. ¿Cuánto tiempo hace que estás aquí? (quince minutos)
2. ¿Cuánto tiempo hace que esperas aquí? (media hora)
3. ¿Cuánto tiempo hace que escuchas la cinta? (más de veinte minutos)
4. ¿Cuánto tiempo hace que conoces a Isabel? (más de un año)

E. *Conteste según el modelo.*

¿Cuándo llegó Ud? (tres días)
Hace tres días que llegué.
Llegué hace tres días.

1. ¿Cuándo volvió Ud.? (un mes)
2. ¿Cuándo fue Ud. a Costa Rica? (seis meses)
3. ¿Cuándo puso Ud. el telegrama? (cinco minutos)
4. ¿Cuándo construyeron la casa? (varios años)
5. ¿Cuándo trajeron los regalos? (una hora)

F. *Conteste según el modelo.*

¿Es larga la calle?
Sí, es larguísima.

1. ¿Es interesante el libro?
2. ¿Es pobre ese hombre?
3. ¿Son ricos tus amigos?
4. ¿Tienen mucho dinero?
5. ¿Tienen poca suerte?

G. *Lea, usando la forma necesaria de los verbos indicados.*

1. Si Paquita _____ (venir) mañana, la veremos.
2. Si _____ (hacer) calor mañana, iremos a la playa.
3. Si _____ (llover) mañana, no haremos la excursión.
4. Si tus amigos _____ (volver) pronto, podremos ir al cine.

H. *Cambie según el modelo.*

Si tenemos tiempo, jugaremos al bridge.
Si tuviéramos tiempo, jugaríamos al bridge.

1. Si está aquí, la veremos.
2. Si son ricos, harán el viaje.
3. Si lo saben, nos lo dirán.
4. Si llueve, nos quedaremos en casa.
5. Si estás cansada, no podrás ir al teatro.

I. *Cambie según el modelo.*

Si vienen mañana, lo harán.
Si vinieran mañana, lo harían.

1. Si llegan mañana, estarán aquí temprano.
2. Si llueve mañana, no iremos a la playa.
3. Si están aquí mañana, nos lo explicarán.
4. Si vuelven mañana, nos traerán el dinero.

J. *Use* **que, quien, quienes** *o una forma de* **el cual.**

1. el amigo a _____ conocí en Caracas
2. las chicas para _____ lo compré
3. la ciudad a _____ fueron
4. el país por _____ viajaron
5. los países por _____ viajaron
6. la ciudad en _____ vivían
7. la casa delante de _____ estacionaron el coche.

K. *Use* **que, quien** *o* **quienes.**

1. Su padre, _____ vive en España, acaba de llegar.
2. Sus padres, a _____ conozco, acaban de llegar.
3. Su hermana, _____ es muy guapa es actriz.
4. Su hermana, a _____ acabo de conocer, es muy guapa.
5. Sus hermanos, _____ trabajan aquí, son amigos míos.

L. *Use* **lo que** *o* **lo cual.** (*En algunas frases se puede usar cualquiera de las dos expresiones.*)

1. _____ han dicho es muy interesante.
2. Ha dicho que lo hará mañana, _____ no creo.
3. Eso no fue _____ dijo.
4. No quieren hacerlo, _____ me extraña.
5. ¿Es eso _____ preguntó?

M. *Use la forma apropiada de* **el que.**

1. Tomás es _____ está riendo.
2. Dolores es _____ acaba de llegar.
3. _____ estudia aprende.
4. Esas chicas son _____ conozco.
5. Carmencita es _____ me lo dijo.
6. _____ llegaron tarde no pudieron entrar.

N. *Diga en español.*

1. Explain how Charles's father went to the doctor in Guadalajara, what the doctor told him to do, and what happened then.
2. Describe Virginia's trip to Mexico and what happened on the beach at Acapulco.
3. Tell some of the things you would do today, if you could. Tell what you would have done yesterday, if it had been possible.
4. Explain how Charles wants to get a job with an American company in Latin America, how he will prepare himself for it, and what he will do, if he gets it. Tell some of the things it would be better for him to do, if he were not so materialistic.

APPENDIX

Verb forms not studied in the text

1. THE PRETERIT PERFECT TENSE

In addition to the past perfect (pluperfect) indicative (for example, **había hablado, había aprendido, había vivido**) Spanish has another form which is equivalent to the English pluperfect. This is the preterit perfect tense, formed by combining the preterit of **haber** with a past participle.

hube hablado I had spoken	**hubimos hablado** we had spoken
hubiste hablado you had spoken	**hubisteis hablado** you had spoken
Ud. hubo hablado you had spoken	**Uds. hubieron hablado** you had spoken
hubo hablado he had spoken	**hubieron hablado** they had spoken

The use of this tense is restricted to dependent clauses introduced by expressions meaning essentially "as soon as."

> **En cuanto hube comido, fui al cine.**   As soon as I had eaten, I went to the movies.
> **Apenas hubieron llegado, nos dieron los regalos.**   They had scarcely arrived when they gave us the gifts.

2. THE FUTURE PERFECT TENSE

Spanish, like English, sometimes uses the future perfect tense, which is formed by combining the future of **haber** with a past participle.

> **Habré estudiado la lección.**   I shall have studied the lesson.

The future perfect, like the simple future, sometimes expresses conjecture or probability.

> **¿Adónde habrán ido?**   Where can they have gone?
> **Habrá llegado.**   He probably has arrived.

357

3. THE FUTURE SUBJUNCTIVE

Spanish has a future subjunctive which is used rarely now except in proverbs and in legal terminology. It is the same in form as the **-ra** past subjunctive except that **-re** is substituted throughout for **-ra**.

hablare, hablares, etc.
aprendiere, aprendieres, etc.

Adonde fueres, haz lo que vieres.   When in Rome, do as the Romans do.
(*Literally,* Wherever you go, do what you see.)

Regular verbs

THE SIMPLE TENSES

INFINITIVE

| **hablar**   to speak | **aprender**   to learn | **vivir**   to live |

PRESENT PARTICIPLE

| **hablando**   speaking | **aprendiendo**   learning | **viviendo**   living |

INDICATIVE MOOD

PRESENT

I speak (do speak, am speaking), etc.	I learn (do learn, am learning), etc.	I live (do live, am living), etc.
hablo	aprendo	vivo
hablas	aprendes	vives
habla	aprende	vive
hablamos	aprendemos	vivimos
habláis	aprendéis	vivís
hablan	aprenden	viven

IMPERFECT

I was speaking (used to [would] speak, spoke), etc.	I was learning (used to [would] learn, learned), etc.	I was living (used to [would] live, lived), etc.
hablaba	aprendía	vivía
hablabas	aprendías	vivías
hablaba	aprendía	vivía
hablábamos	aprendíamos	vivíamos
hablabais	aprendíais	vivíais
hablaban	aprendían	vivían

PRETERIT

I spoke (did speak), etc.	I learned (did learn), etc.	I lived (did live), etc.
hablé	aprendí	viví
hablaste	aprendiste	viviste
habló	aprendió	vivió
hablamos	aprendimos	vivimos
hablasteis	aprendisteis	vivisteis
hablaron	aprendieron	vivieron

FUTURE

I shall (will) speak, etc.	I shall (will) learn, etc.	I shall (will) live, etc.
hablaré	aprenderé	viviré
hablarás	aprenderás	vivirás
hablará	aprenderá	vivirá
hablaremos	aprenderemos	viviremos
hablaréis	aprenderéis	viviréis
hablarán	aprenderán	vivirán

CONDITIONAL

I should (would) speak, etc.	I should (would) learn, etc.	I should (would) live, etc.
hablaría	aprendería	viviría
hablarías	aprenderías	vivirías
hablaría	aprendería	viviría
hablaríamos	aprenderíamos	viviríamos
hablaríais	aprenderíais	viviríais
hablarían	aprenderían	vivirían

SUBJUNCTIVE MOOD

PRESENT

(that) I may speak, etc.	(that) I may learn, etc.	(that) I may live, etc.
hable	aprenda	viva
hables	aprendas	vivas
hable	aprenda	viva
hablemos	aprendamos	vivamos
habléis	aprendáis	viváis
hablen	aprendan	vivan

-ra PAST

(that) I might speak, etc.	(that) I might learn, etc.	(that) I might live, etc.
hablara	aprendiera	viviera
hablaras	aprendieras	vivieras
hablara	aprendiera	viviera
habláramos	aprendiéramos	viviéramos
hablarais	aprendierais	vivierais
hablaran	aprendieran	vivieran

-se PAST

(that) I might speak, etc.	(that) I might learn, etc.	(that) I might live, etc.
hablase	aprendiese	viviese
hablases	aprendieses	vivieses
hablase	aprendiese	viviese
hablásemos	aprendiésemos	viviésemos
hablaseis	aprendieseis	vivieseis
hablasen	aprendiesen	viviesen

(There is also a future subjunctive, rarely used in modern Spanish except in proverbs and in legal terminology. The forms for **hablar** are **hablare, hablares, hablare, habláremos, hablareis, hablaren**; for **aprender, aprendiere,** etc.; for **vivir, viviere,** etc.)

IMPERATIVE MOOD

speak	learn	live
habla (tú)	aprende (tú)	vive (tú)
hablad (vosotros)	aprended (vosotros)	vivid (vosotros)

THE PERFECT TENSES

PERFECT INFINITIVE	PERFECT PARTICIPLE
haber hablado to have spoken	**habiendo hablado** having spoken
haber aprendido to have learned	**habiendo aprendido** having learned
haber vivido to have lived	**habiendo vivido** having lived

INDICATIVE MOOD

PRESENT PERFECT	PAST PERFECT	PRETERIT PERFECT
I have spoken, etc.	I had spoken, etc.	I had spoken, etc.
he hablado	había hablado	hube hablado
has hablado	habías hablado	hubiste hablado
ha hablado	había hablado	hubo hablado

hemos hablado	habíamos hablado	hubimos hablado
habéis hablado	habíais hablado	hubisteis hablado
han hablado	habían hablado	hubieron hablado

FUTURE PERFECT	CONDITIONAL PERFECT
I shall have spoken, etc.	I should have spoken, etc.
habré hablado	habría hablado
habrás hablado	habrías hablado
habrá hablado	habría hablado
habremos hablado	habríamos hablado
habréis hablado	habríais hablado
habrán hablado	habrían hablado

SUBJUNCTIVE MOOD

PRESENT PERFECT	-RA PLUPERFECT	-SE PLUPERFECT
(that) I may have spoken, etc.	(that) I might have spoken, etc.	(that) I might have spoken, etc.
haya hablado	hubiera hablado	hubiese hablado
hayas hablado	hubieras hablado	hubieses hablado
haya hablado	hubiera hablado	hubiese hablado
hayamos hablado	hubiéramos hablado	hubiésemos hablado
hayáis hablado	hubierais hablado	hubieseis hablado
hayan hablado	hubieran hablado	hubiesen hablado

Stem-changing verbs

1. CLASS I: VERBS IN -AR AND -ER

Stem vowel **e** becomes **ie** and stem vowel **o** becomes **ue** when stressed, that is, throughout the singular, in the third person plural of both the present indicative and the present subjunctive, and in the singular of the familiar imperative.

1. pensar   to think

Pres. Ind.   **pienso, piensas, piensa,** pensamos, pensáis, **piensan**
Pres. Subj.   **piense, pienses, piense,** pensemos, penséis, **piensen**
Imperative   **piensa** (tú), pensad (vosotros)

Like **pensar: cerrar** to close, **despertar** to awaken, **empezar** to begin, **negar** to deny, **sentar** to seat

2. contar   to count

Pres. Ind.	**cuento, cuentas, cuenta,** contamos, contáis, **cuentan**
Pres. Subj.	**cuente, cuentes, cuente,** contemos, contéis, **cuenten**
Imperative	**cuenta** (tú), contad (vosotros)

Like **contar: acordarse** to remember, **acostar** to put to bed, **costar** to cost, **encontrar** to find, **mostrar** to show, **recordar** to recall, **rogar** to beg, **sonar** to sound, **soñar** to dream

Jugar (to play) has this same change, despite the **u.**

Pres. Ind.	**juego, juegas, juega,** jugamos, jugáis, **juegan**
Pres. Subj.	**juegue, juegues, juegue,** juguemos, juguéis, **jueguen**
Imperative	**juega** (tú), jugad (vosotros)

3. perder   to lose

Pres. Ind.	**pierdo, pierdes, pierde,** perdemos, perdéis, **pierden**
Pres. Subj.	**pierda, pierdas, pierda,** perdamos, perdáis, **pierdan**
Imperative	**pierde** (tú), perded (vosotros)

Like **perder: atender** to attend, **entender** to understand

4. volver   to return

Pres. Ind.	**vuelvo, vuelves, vuelve,** volvemos, volvéis, **vuelven**
Pres. Subj.	**vuelva, vuelvas, vuelva,** volvamos, volváis, **vuelvan**
Imperative	**vuelve** (tú), volved (vosotros)

Like **volver: devolver** to return (give back), **mover** to move, **oler** to smell,* **resolver** to solve, **torcer** to turn

2. CLASS II: VERBS IN -IR

Stem vowel **e** becomes **ie** and stem vowel **o** becomes **ue** when stressed, that is, wherever the same changes occur in **-ar** and **-ir** verbs.

In addition **e** becomes **i** and **o** becomes **u** (1) in the present subjunctive, first and second persons plural; (2) in the preterit, third person singular and plural; (3) throughout the past subjunctive (both forms); and (4) in the present participle.

* Wherever stem vowel **o** of **oler** is stressed, **o** becomes **hue,** because the diphthong **ue** does not occur at the beginning of a word.

Pres. Ind.	**huelo, hueles, huele,** olemos, oléis, **huelen**
Pres Subj.	**huela, huelas, huela,** olamos, oláis, **huelan**
Imperative	**huele** (tú), oled (vosotros)

1. sentir   to feel, regret

Pres. Part	**sintiendo**
Past Part.	sentido
Pres. Ind.	**siento, sientes, siente,** sentimos, sentís, **sienten**
Pres. Subj.	**sienta, sientas, sienta,** sintamos, sintáis, sientan
Preterit	sentí, sentiste, **sintió,** sentimos, sentisteis, **sintieron**
Past Subj.	**sintiera (sintiese), sintieras (sintieses),** etc.
Imperative	**siente** (tú), sentid (vosotros)

Like **sentir: advertir** to warn, advise, **consentir** to consent, **divertir** to amuse, **preferir** to prefer, **referir** to relate, refer

2. dormir   to sleep

Pres. Part.	**durmiendo**
Past Part.	dormido
Pres. Ind.	**duermo, duermes, duerme,** dormimos, dormís, **duermen**
Pres. Subj.	**duerma, duermas, duerma,** durmamos, durmáis, duerman
Preterit	dormí, dormiste, **durmió,** dormimos, dormisteis, **durmieron**
Past Subj.	**durmiera (durmiese), durmieras (durmieses),** etc.
Imperative	**duerme** (tú). dormid (vosotros)

Like **dormir: morir** to die (*except in the past participle,* **muerto**)

3. *CLASS III: VERBS IN* -IR

Stem vowel **e** becomes **i** when stressed and wherever the **e** of **sentir** becomes **i**.

Pres. Part.	**pidiendo**
Past Part.	pedido
Pres. Ind.	**pido, pides, pide,** pedimos, pedís, **piden**
Pres. Subj.	**pida, pidas, pida,** pidamos, pidáis, **pidan**
Preterit	pedí, pediste, **pidió,** pedimos, pedisteis, **pidieron**
Past Subj.	**pidiera (pidiese), pidieras (pidieses),** etc.
Imperative	**pide** (tú), pedid (vosotros)

Like **pedir: conseguir** to get, obtain, **despedirse** to say good-by, **impedir** to prevent, **reír** to laugh, **reñir** to scold, quarrel, **repetir** to repeat, **seguir** to follow, continue, **servir** to serve, **sonreír** to smile, **vestir** to dress

Verbs with orthographic changes

1. Verbs whose infinitive ends in **-car** change **c** to **qu** before **e**.

buscar   to look for

Preterit   **busqué,** buscaste, buscó, buscamos, buscasteis, buscaron
Pres. Subj.   **busque, busques, busque, busquemos, busquéis, busquen**

Like **buscar: acercarse** to approach, **equivocarse** to be mistaken, **explicar** to explain, **indicar** to indicate, **sacar** to take out, **tocar** to touch, play

2. Verbs whose infinitive ends in **-gar** change **g** to **gu** before **e**.

pagar   to pay

Preterit   **pagué**, pagaste, pagó, pagamos, pagasteis, pagaron
Pres. Subj.   **pague, pagues, pague, paguemos, paguéis, paguen**

Like **pagar: llegar** to arrive, **obligar** to oblige, **negar (ie)** to deny, **jugar (ue)** to play

3. Verbs whose infinitive ends in **-zar** change **z** to **c** before **e**.

cruzar   to cross

Preterit   **crucé,** cruzaste, cruzó, cruzamos, cruzasteis, cruzaron
Pres. Subj.   **cruce, cruces, cruce, crucemos, crucéis, crucen**

Like **cruzar: alcanzar** to overtake, **almorzar (ue)** to lunch, **comenzar (ie)** to commence, **gozar** to enjoy, **empezar (ie)** to begin

4. Verbs whose infinitive ends in **-guar** change **gu** to **gü** before **e**.

averiguar   to find out

Preterit   **averigüé**, averiguaste, averiguó, averiguamos, averiguasteis, averiguaron
Pres. Subj.   **averigüe, averigües, averigüe, averigüemos, averigüéis, averigüen**

5. Verbs whose infinitive ends in **-ger** or **-gir** change **g** to **j** before **a** and **o**.

coger   to catch

Pres. Ind.   **cojo,** coges, coge, cogemos, cogéis, cogen
Pres. Subj.   **coja, cojas, coja, cojamos, cojáis, cojan**

Like **coger: dirigir** to direct, **elegir (i)** to elect, **escoger** to select, **recoger** to pick up

6. Verbs whose infinitive ends in **-guir** change **gu** to **g** before **a** and **o**.

distinguir   to distinguish
Pres. Ind.   **distingo,** distingues, distingue, distinguimos, distinguís, distinguen
Pres. Subj. **distinga, distingas, distinga, distingamos, distingáis, distingan**

Like **distinguir: conseguir (i)** to get, **seguir (i)** to follow, continue

7. Verbs whose infinitive ends in consonant + **-cer** or consonant + **-cir** change **c** to **z** before **o** and **a**.

convencer   to convince

Pres. Ind.   **convenzo,** convences, convence, convencemos, convencéis, convencen
Pres. Subj. **convenza, convenzas, convenza, convenzamos, convenzáis, convenzan**

Like **convencer: vencer** to conquer

8. Verbs whose infinitive ends in vowel + **-cer** or vowel + **-cir** insert **z** before **co** and **ca**.

conocer   to know
Pres. Ind.   **conozco,** conoces, conoce, conocemos, conocéis, conocen
Pres. Subj. **conozca, conozcas, conozca, conozcamos, conozcáis, conozcan**

Like **conocer: agradecer** to thank, be grateful for, **conducir** to conduct, **nacer** to be born, **merecer** to deserve, **ofrecer** to offer, **parecer** to seem, appear, **producir** to produce, **traducir** to translate, **conducir** to conduct, drive

Verbs ending in **-ducir** have a further irregularity in the preterit and in the past subjunctive:

Preterit   **conduje, condujiste, condujo, condujimos, condujisteis, condujeron**
Imperf. Subj.   **condujera (condujese), condujeras (condujeses),** etc.

9. Verbs whose infinite ends in **-uir** (except **-guir** and **-quir**) insert **y** before the ending (except before **i**) and change unstressed **i** to **y** between vowels.

huir   to flee

Pres. Part.   **huyendo**
Past Part.   huido
Pres. Ind.   **huyo, huyes, huye,** huimos, huís, **huyen**
Preterit   huí, huiste, **huyó,** huimos, huisteis, **huyeron**
Pres. Subj.   **huya, huyas, huya, huyamos, huyáis, huyan**
Past Subj.   **huyera, (huyese), huyeras (huyeses),** etc.
Imperative   **huye** (tú), huid (vosotros)

Like **huir: concluir** to conclude, **construir** to construct, **incluir** to include

10. Verbs whose infinite ends in vowel + **-er** or vowel + **-ir** (except **-eír**) change unstressed **i** to **y** between vowels. An accent on the stressed **i** of the ending is necessary to prevent a diphthong.

leer   to read

Pres. Part.	**leyendo**
Past Part.	**leído**
Preterit	**leí, leíste, leyó, leímos, leísteis, leyeron**
Past Subj.	**leyera (leyese), leyeras (leyeses),** etc.

Like **leer: caer** to fall, **creer** to believe, **oír** to hear. But **caer** and **oír** have other irregularities: see Irregular Verbs, pp. 368 and 370.

11. Verbs whose infinitve ends in **-eír** are stem-changing verbs (see Class III Verbs in **-ir**). They bear a written accent over the stressed **i**. Two contiguous **i**'s are reduced to one.

reír (i)   to laugh

Pres. Part.	**riendo**
Past Part.	**reído**
Pres. Ind.	**río, ríes, ríe, reímos, reís, ríen**
Pres. Subj.	**ría, rías, ría, riamos, riáis, rían**
Preterit	**reí, reíste, rio, reímos, reísteis, rieron**
Past Subj.	**riera (riese), rieras (rieses),** etc.
Imperative	**ríe** (tú), **reíd** (vosotros)

Like **reír: sonreír** to smile, **freír** to fry (*past part.*: **frito**)

12. Some verbs whose infinitive ends in **-iar** bear a written accent on the **i** throughout the singular, in the third person plural of both the present indicative and the present subjunctive, and in the imperative singular.

enviar   to send

Pres. Ind.	**envío, envías, envía**, enviamos, enviáis, **envían**
Pres. Subj.	**envíe, envíes, envíe**, enviemos, enviéis, **envíen**
Imperative	**envía** (tú), enviad (vosotros)

Like **enviar: confiar** to confide, **fiarse** to confide, trust

But other **-iar** verbs used in this book are regular: **estudiar** to study, **cambiar** to change.

13. Verbs whose infinitive ends in **-uar** (except **-guar**) bear a written accent on the **u** throughout the singular, in the third person plural of both the present indicative and the present subjunctive, and in the imperative singular.

continuar   to continue

Pres. Ind.   **continúo, continúas, continúa,** continuamos, continuáis, **continúan**
Pres. Subj.   **continúe, continúes, continúe,** continuemos, continuéis, **continúen**
Imperative   **continúa** (tú), continuad (vosotros)

Like **continuar: actuar** to act, **conceptuar** to judge, think

Irregular verbs

INFINITIVE	PARTICIPLES IMPERATIVE	PRESENT INDICATIVE	IMPERFECT INDICATIVE	PRETERIT
andar to go	andando andado anda andad	ando	andaba	anduve anduviste anduvo anduvimos anduvisteis anduvieron
caer to fall	cayendo caído cae caed	caigo caes cae caemos caéis caen	caía	caí caíste cayó caímos caísteis cayeron
dar to give	dando dado da dad	doy das da damos dais dan	daba	di diste dio dimos disteis dieron
decir to say	diciendo dicho di decid	digo dices dice decimos decís dicen	decía	dije dijiste dijo dijimos dijisteis dijeron
estar to be	estando estado está estad	estoy estás está estamos estáis están	estaba	estuve estuviste estuvo estuvimos estuvisteis estuvieron

FUTURE	CONDITIONAL	PRESENT SUBJUNCTIVE	PAST SUBJUNCTIVE	
andaré	andaría	ande	anduviera	anduviese
			anduvieras	anduvieses
			anduviera	anduviese
			anduviéramos	anduviésemos
			anduvierais	anduvieseis
			anduvieran	anduviesen
caeré	caería	caiga	cayera	cayese
		caigas	cayeras	cayeses
		caiga	cayera	cayese
		caigamos	cayéramos	cayésemos
		caigáis	cayerais	cayeseis
		caigan	cayeran	cayesen
daré	daría	dé	diera	diese
		des	dieras	dieses
		dé	diera	diese
		demos	diéramos	diésemos
		deis	dierais	dieseis
		den	dieran	diesen
diré	diría	diga	dijera	dijese
dirás	dirías	digas	dijeras	dijeses
dirá	diría	diga	dijera	dijese
diremos	diríamos	digamos	dijéramos	dijésemos
diréis	diríais	digáis	dijerais	dijeseis
dirán	dirían	digan	dijeran	dijesen
estaré	estaría	esté	estuviera	estuviese
		estés	estuvieras	estuvieses
		esté	estuviera	estuviese
		estemos	estuviéramos	estuviésemos
		estéis	estuvierais	estuvieseis
		estén	estuvieran	estuviesen

INFINITIVE	PARTICIPLES IMPERATIVE	PRESENT INDICATIVE	IMPERFECT INDICATIVE	PRETERIT
haber to have	habiendo habido	he has ha hemos habéis han	había	hube hubiste hubo hubimos hubisteis hubieron
hacer to do, make	haciendo hecho haz haced	hago haces hace hacemos hacéis hacen	hacía	hice hiciste hizo hicimos hicisteis hicieron
ir to go	yendo ido ve id	voy vas va vamos vais van	iba ibas iba íbamos ibais iban	fui fuiste fue fuimos fuisteis fueron
oír to hear	oyendo oído oye oíd	oigo oyes oye oímos oís oyen	oía	oí oíste oyó oímos oísteis oyeron
poder to be able	pudiendo podido	puedo puedes puede podemos podéis pueden	podía	pude pudiste pudo pudimos pudisteis pudieron

FUTURE	CONDITIONAL	PRESENT SUBJUNCTIVE	PAST SUBJUNCTIVE	
habré	habría	haya	hubiera	hubiese
habrás	habrías	hayas	hubieras	hubieses
habrá	habría	haya	hubiera	hubiese
habremos	habríamos	hayamos	hubiéramos	hubiésemos
habréis	habríais	hayáis	hubierais	hubieseis
habrán	habrían	hayan	hubieran	hubiesen
haré	haría	haga	hiciera	hiciese
harás	harías	hagas	hicieras	hiciese
hará	haría	haga	hiciera	hiciese
haremos	haríamos	hagamos	hiciéramos	hiciésemos
haréis	haríais	hagáis	hicierais	hicieseis
harán	harían	hagan	hicieran	hiciesen
iré	iría	vaya	fuera	fuese
		vayas	fueras	fueses
		vaya	fuera	fuese
		vayamos	fuéramos	fuésemos
		vayáis	fuerais	fueseis
		vayan	fueran	fuesen
oiré	oiría	oiga	oyera	oyese
		oigas	oyeras	oyeses
		oiga	oyera	oyese
		oigamos	oyéramos	oyésemos
		oigáis	oyerais	oyeseis
		oigan	oyeran	oyesen
podré	podría	pueda	pudiera	pudiese
podrás	podrías	puedas	pudieras	pudieses
podrá	podría	pueda	pudiera	pudiese
podremos	podríamos	podamos	pudiéramos	pudiésemos
podréis	podríais	podáis	pudierais	pudieseis
podrán	podrían	puedan	pudieran	pudiesen

Irregular verbs

INFINITIVE	PARTICIPLES IMPERATIVE	PRESENT INDICATIVE	IMPERFECT INDICATIVE	PRETERIT
poner to put	poniendo puesto pon poned	pongo pones pone ponemos ponéis ponen	ponía	puse pusiste puso pusimos pusisteis pusieron
querer to wish	queriendo querido quiere quered	quiero quieres quiere queremos queréis quieren	quería	quise quisiste quiso quisimos quisisteis quisieron
saber to know	sabiendo sabido sabe sabed	sé sabes sabe sabemos sabéis saben	sabía	supe supiste supo supimos supisteis supieron
salir to go out	saliendo salido sal salid	salgo sales sale salimos salís salen	salía	salí
ser to be	siendo sido sé sed	soy eres es somos sois son	era eras era éramos erais eran	fui fuiste fue fuimos fuisteis fueron

FUTURE	CONDITIONAL	PRESENT SUBJUNCTIVE	PAST SUBJUNCTIVE	
pondré	pondría	ponga	pusiera	pusiese
pondrás	pondrías	pongas	pusieras	pusieses
pondrá	pondría	ponga	pusiera	pusiese
pondremos	pondríamos	pongamos	pusiéramos	pusiésemos
pondréis	pondríais	pongáis	pusierais	pusieseis
pondrán	pondrían	pongan	pusieran	pusiesen
querré	querría	quiera	quisiera	quisiese
querrás	querrías	quieras	quisieras	quisieses
querrá	querría	quiera	quisiera	quisiese
querremos	querríamos	queramos	quisiéramos	quisiésemos
querréis	querríais	queráis	quisierais	quisieseis
querrán	querrían	quieran	quisieran	quisiesen
sabré	sabría	sepa	supiera	supiese
sabrás	sabrías	sepas	supieras	supieses
sabrá	sabría	sepa	supiera	supiese
sabremos	sabríamos	sepamos	supiéramos	supiésemos
sabréis	sabríais	sepáis	supierais	supieseis
sabrán	sabrían	sepan	supieran	supiesen
saldré	saldría	salga	saliera	saliese
saldrás	saldrías	salgas		
saldrá	saldría	salga		
saldremos	saldríamos	salgamos		
saldréis	saldríais	salgáis		
saldrán	saldrían	salgan		
seré	sería	sea	fuera	fuese
		seas	fueras	fueses
		sea	fuera	fuese
		seamos	fuéramos	fuésemos
		seáis	fuerais	fueseis
		sean	fueran	fuesen

Irregular verbs

INFINITIVE	PARTICIPLES IMPERATIVE	PRESENT INDICATIVE	IMPERFECT INDICATIVE	PRETERIT
tener to have	teniendo tenido ten tened	tengo tienes tiene tenemos tenéis tienen	tenía	tuve tuviste tuvo tuvimos tuvisteis tuvieron
traer to bring	trayendo traído trae traed	traigo traes trae traemos traéis traen	traía	traje trajiste trajo trajimos trajisteis trajeron
valer to be worth	valiendo valido val valed	valgo vales vale valemos valéis valen	valía	valí
venir to come	viniendo venido ven venid	vengo vienes viene venimos venís vienen	venía	vine viniste vino vinimos vinisteis vinieron
ver to see	viendo visto ve ved	veo ves ve vemos veis ven	veía veías veía veíamos veíais veían	vi viste vio vimos visteis vieron

FUTURE	CONDITIONAL	PRESENT SUBJUNCTIVE	PAST SUBJUNCTIVE	
tendré	tendría	tenga	tuviera	tuviese
tendrás	tendrías	tengas	tuvieras	tuvieses
tendrá	tendría	tenga	tuviera	tuviese
tendremos	tendríamos	tengamos	tuviéramos	tuviésemos
tendréis	tendríais	tengáis	tuvierais	tuvieseis
tendrán	tendrían	tengan	tuvieran	tuviesen
traeré	traería	traiga	trajera	trajese
		traigas	trajeras	trajeses
		traiga	trajera	trajese
		traigamos	trajéramos	trajésemos
		traigáis	trajerais	trajeseis
		traigan	trajeran	trajesen
valdré	valdría	valga	valiera	valiese
valdrás	valdrías	valgas		
valdrá	valdría	valga		
valdremos	valdríamos	valgamos		
valdréis	valdríais	valgáis		
valdrán	valdrían	valgan		
vendré	vendría	venga	víniera	viniese
vendrás	vendrías	vengas	vínieras	vinieses
vendrá	vendría	venga	viniera	viniese
vendremos	vendríamos	vengamos	viniéramos	viniésemos
vendréis	vendríais	vengáis	vinierais	vinieseis
vendrán	vendrían	vengan	vinieran	viniesen
veré	vería	vea	viera	viese
		veas		
		vea		
		veamos		
		veáis		
		vean		

The following abbreviations are used in the vocabularies:

abbr. = abbreviation   *indef.* = indefinite   *plu.* = plural
adj. = adjective   *indir. obj.* = indirect object *poss.* = possessive
adv. = adverb   *inf.* = infinitive   *prep.* = preposition
conj. = conjunction   *int.* = interrogative   *pres. part.* = present participle
def. = definite   *invar.* = invariable   *pron.* = pronoun
demonstr. = demonstrative   *m* = masculine   *reflex.* = reflexive
dir. obj. = direct object   *n* = neuter   *rel.* = relative
f = feminine   *past part.* = past participle *subj.* = subject

The sign — means a repetition of the word printed in boldface type at the beginning of the entry; thus, — **mismo** under **ahora** means **ahora mismo**. When the word is a noun preceded by its article, the sign — stands for the noun alone.

a   to; at
abierto   open
el abogado   lawyer
el abrigo   overcoat
abril *m*   April
abrir   to open
absolutamente   absolutely
absoluto: en —   absolutely not
la abuela   grandmother
el abuelo   grandfather
acá   here
acabar   to finish; **— de** + *inf.*   to have
    just + *past part.*
el aceite   oil
aceptar   to accept
acerca de   about, concerning
acercarse (a)   to draw near (to),
    approach
el acero   steel
acompañar   to accompany, go with
aconsejar   to advise
acordarse (ue) (de)   to remember
acostarse (ue)   to go to bed
acostumbrado   accustomed
el actor   actor
la actriz   actress
actual   present
además *adv.*   besides; **— de** *prep.*
    besides

adiós   good-by
¿adónde?   where?
la aduana   customs
aéreo *adj.*   air; **la línea aérea**   airline
el aeropuerto   airport
agosto *m*   August
agradable   agreeable
agradecido   grateful
agrícola   agricultural
el agua   water
ahí   there; **— mismo**   right over there
ahora   now; **— mismo**   right now;
    ¡ — lo iogo!   this is the first time I've
    heard about it
el aire   air; **al — libre**   in the open air;
    — acondicionado   air conditioning
al (a + el)   to the; **— +** *inf.*   upon
    + *pres. part.*
alegrarse (de)   to be glad
la alergia   allergy
algo   something, anything; somewhat
alguien   someone, somebody, anybody
alguno, algún   some, any; someone,
    anyone
almorzar (ue)   to lunch
alrededor de   about, around
los alrededores   outskirts
alto   tall
la alumna   student *f*

el alumno student *m*

allá there, back there

allí there

amable kind

amar to love

la ambulancia ambulance

América *f* America; **la — del Norte**
North America; **la — del Sur** South
America

la amiga friend *f*

el amigo friend *m*

amistosamente in a friendly way

el amor love

Andalucía Andalusia

andaluz, -a Andalusian

andar to walk, go; **¡anda!** come on!

el animal animal

la animación animation; bustle,
movement

anoche last night

anteayer day before yesterday

antes *adv.* before; **— de** *prep.* before;
— (de) que *conj.* before; **cuanto —**
as soon as possible

antiguo old

anunciar to announce

añadir to add

el año year; **el — pasado** last year;
tener (veinte) años to be (twenty)
years old; **¿cuántos —s tiene Ud.?**
how old are you?

el apartamento apartment

aprender to learn

aprobado: salir — to pass (*a course*)

aprovechar to· take advantage of

el apuro difficulty

aquel, aquella, aquellos, aquellas
demonstr. adj. that, those; the former

aquél, aquélla, aquéllos, aquéllas
demonstr. pron. that, those; the
former

aquí here; **— lo tiene Ud.** here it is;
de — en (cuatro días) (four days)
from now; **por —** this way, around
here

arañar to scratch

el arañazo scratch

el árbol tree

el arete earring

la Argentina Argentina

argentino Argentine

la arquitectura architecture

arreglar to arrange

arriba above; **río —** up the river

el arroz rice

el arte art

artístico artistic

el artículo article

el ascensor elevator

asegurar to assure, affirm

así thus, so; **— soy yo** that's the way
I am

la asignatura course

asistir (a) to attend

asombroso astonishing, amazing

la aspirina aspirin

el asunto matter

la atención attention; **prestar —** to pay
attention

la atmósfera atmosphere

atropellar to run into (*or* over)

atroz terrible

aun, aún even, yet, still

aun cuando even though

aunque although

la ausencia absence

el automóvil automobile

autostop: hacer — to hitchhike

el autostopista hitch-hiker

averiguar to find out

el avión plane, airplane; **en —** by
plane, by air

avisar to inform, let know

ay oh

ayer yesterday

ayudar to help

azul blue

el azulejo colored tile

bailar to dance

el baile dance

bajar to go down; — **de** to get out of, off (*a vehicle*)

bajo short

bañarse to bathe

barato cheap

bastante enough, sufficient; rather, quite; a good deal

bastar to be enough, be sufficient

el béisbol baseball

bello beautiful

la biblioteca library

bien well; very; **está** — all right

bilingüe bilingual

la bisabuela great-grandmother

el bistec steak, beefsteak

blanco white

la blusa blouse

la boca mouth

el boleto ticket; — **de ida y vuelta** round-trip ticket

bonito pretty

bordo: a — on board

el Brasil Brazil

el bridge bridge (*card game*)

brillante brilliant

la broma joke; **en** — jokingly

bueno, buen good; **¡bueno!** all right, O.K.; — **pues** all right then, well then; —**s días** good morning; **¡qué** —**!** how nice!

la busca search

buscar to look for

la búsqueda search

el caballero gentleman

el caballo horse; **(montado) a** — on horseback

la cabeza head

el Cabildo Town Hall

cada *invar. adj.* each, every

caer to fall; **ya caigo** now I get it; —**se de** to fall out of

el café coffee; coffeehouse, café

los calcetines socks

el calentador heater

caliente hot

California California

el calor heat; **hace** — it is warm, hot; **tener** — to be warm (*of living beings*)

la calle street

la cama bed

el camarero waiter

cambiar to change, exchange

caminar to walk

el camino road, way

el camión truck

la camisa shirt

el campeón champion

el campeonato championship

el campo country

la canción song

la cancha court (*tennis, etc.*)

cansado tired

cantar to sing

el cante flamenco flamenco (*Andalusian gypsy singing*)

la cantidad quantity

la capital capital

la cara face

¡caramba! confound it! gracious!

el Caribe Caribbean

Carlos Charles

caro dear, expensive

la carrera career; course of study

la carta letter

el cartaginés Carthaginian

la casa house, home; **a** — (to) home; **en** — at home

casarse con to marry

casi nearly, almost

el caso case; **en** — **de que** in case

el catalán Catalan

Cataluña Catalonia

la catedral cathedral

catorce fourteen

célebre famous, celebrated

el cenicero ashtray

el centavo cent (*Spanish America*)

el céntimo   cent (*Spain*)
central   central
el centro   center, downtown
cerca de   near
cerquita de *diminutive of* **cerca de**   close to
cerrar (ie)   to close
certificar   to register
ciento, cien   a (one) hundred
cierto   (a) certain
cinco   five
cincuenta   fifty
el cine   movies
la cinta   tape
la cita   date (*engagement*)
citarse con   to make an appointment with
la ciudad   city
¡claro!   of course!
la clase   class; kind
clásico   classic
el cliente   client
el clima   climate
la clínica   hospital
cobro revertido   charges reversed
el coche   car
coger   to catch, pick up
la colección   collection
Colombia   Colombia
colonial   colonial
colorado   red
la comedia   comedy
el comedor   dining room, dining salon
comenzar (ie)   to begin
comer   to eat; **—se**   to eat up; **—se las eses**   to swallow the letter *s*
la comida   dinner, meal
la comisión   commission
como   like, as; **— si**   as if
¿cómo?   how? **¿a — se vende?**   how is it sold? what is the price? **¿— te va?**   how goes it? **¡— no!**   of course!
cómodo   comfortable
el compañero   companion; **— de cuarto**   roommate

la compañía   company
completamente   completely
componer   to repair
la composición   composition
la compra   purchase; **ir de —s**   to go shopping
comprar   to buy
comprender   to understand
el compromiso   engagement, appointment
con   with; **— tal que**   provided that
concentrar   to concentrate; **— la atención en**   to concentrate on
el concierto   concerto
conducir   to lead, conduct
confesar   to confess, admit
confidencial   confidential
¡conforme!   agreed!
congeniar (con)   to get along (with)
conmigo   with me
conocer   to know; to meet, make the acquaintance of
conocido   well-known
conseguir (i)   to get, obtain
el consejero   adviser
el consejo   (piece of) advice
consentir en   to consent to
consigo   with himself, with herself, with yourself, etc.
construir   to build, construct
el consultorio   doctor's office
el contacto   contact
contar (ue)   to count, tell
contener   to contain
contento   happy
contestar (a)   to answer
continuar   to continue
contra   against
contrario: al —   on the contrary
el contrato   contract
la contribución   contribution
la contusión   bruise
convencer   to convince
conversar   to converse, talk
el convidado   guest

conviene   it is advisable
la copa   wine glass
el coral   coral
el corazón   heart
la corbata   tie, necktie
el cordero   lamb
la cordillera   mountain range
Córdoba   Cordova
el correo   mail; **— aéreo**   air mail
correr   to run; **— peligro**   to be in danger
el corte   cut; **— de pelo**   haircut
cortés   polite
la cosa   thing; matter
costar (ue)   to cost
la costumbre   custom
crecer   to grow
creer   to believe, think; **ya lo creo**   I should say so
la criada   servant, maid
cruzar   to cross
el cuadro   picture, painting
el cual, la cual, los cuales, las cuales *rel. pron.*   that, which, who, whom; **lo —** *n*   which
¿cuál?   which (one)? what?
la cualidad   quality
cualquier(a)   any(one); whichever, whatever
cuando   when; **aun —**   even though
¿cuándo?   when?
cuanto   all that; **— antes**   as soon as possible; **en —** *conj.*   as soon as; **unos —s**   a few
¿cuánto?   how much? **¿a —?**   at how much? at what price? **¿—s?**   how many?
cuarenta   forty
cuarto   fourth
el cuarto   room; quarter; **las diez menos —**   a quarter to ten
cuatro   four
cuatrocientos   four hundred
cubano   Cuban
la cubierta   deck

cubierto *past part. of* **cubrir**   covered
cubrir   to cover
la cuenta   bill, check; **darse — (de)**   to realize
el cuerpo   body
el cuidado   care; **tener —**   to be careful; **pierda Ud. —**   don't worry
la cultura   culture
cultural   cultural
el cumpleaños   birthday
la cuna   cradle
cursar   to take, study (*a course*)
cuyo   whose, of which
la chaqueta   jacket; **— sport**   sport jacket
charlar   to chat
la chica   girl
chico   small; **el —**   boy
chiflado   daft; **estar — por**   to be crazy about
Chile *m*   Chile
chileno   Chilean
la chiquita   little girl
el chiste   joke
chistoso   witty
chocar con   to collide with
el chocolate   chocolate
la chuleta   chop

dar   to give; to show (*a movie*); **— con**   to meet, run into; **— en**   to hit; **—se cuenta de**   to realize; **—se prisa**   to hurry
de   of, from; **más — dos**   more than two; **el alumno más intelegente — la clase**   the most intelligent student in the class; **el —**   the one of, the one with; **— ...en**   from ... to
deber   to owe; ought, should, must
decidir, decidirse a   to decide
décimo   tenth
decir   to say, tell; **— que si (no)**   to say yes (no); **oír — que**   to hear that; **querer —**   to mean; **¡diga! ¡dígame!**   hello! (*on the telephone*)

dejar   to leave; to let, allow

del (de + el)   of the, from the

delante de   in front of

delgado   thin

demasiado   too, too much

dentro de   within

el deporte   sport

la derecha   right hand; **a la —**   to (at, on) the right

derecho   right; straight; **tener — a**   to have a right to

el desayuno   breakfast

descansar   to rest

describir   to describe

descubierto *past part. of* **descubrir** discovered

el descubrimiento   discovery

descubrir   to discover

desde   from, since

desear   to desire

el deseo   desire; **tengo vivo — de**   I'm eager to

desgraciado   unfortunate

desocupado   unoccupied

despacio   slowly

el despacho de billetes   ticket office

despedirse (i)   to take leave; to say good-bye

despertarse (ie)   to wake up, awaken

después *adv.*   afterwards; **— de** *prep.* after; **— (de) que** *conj.*   after

el destierro   exile

destrozar   to wreck

el detalle   detail

detrás de   behind

devolver (ue)   to return, give back

el día   day; **¡buenos días!**   good morning! **todos los —s**   every day

diciembre *m*   December

el dictador   dictator

dicho *past part. of* **decir**   said; **mejor —** rather

diecinueve   nineteen

dieciocho   eighteen

dieciséis   sixteen

diecisiete   seventeen

el diente   tooth

diez   ten

difícil   difficult

el dineral   large amount of money

el dinero   money

Dios   God; **¡— mío!**   my goodness! **¡por —!**   for heaven's sake! **quiera —** God grant; **¡vaya Ud. con —!**   off with you! good-by!

dirigir   to direct; **—se a**   to address, speak to; to go toward

el disco   (phonograph) record

la discoteca   record shop

discutir   to discuss

discusión   discussion

el disgusto   trouble

la disminución   diminution, decrease

divertido   amusing

divertirse (ie)   to amuse oneself, have a good time

doce   twelve

la docena   dozen

el doctor   doctor

el doctorado   doctorate

el documento   document

el dólar   dollar

doler (ue)   to ache, pain, hurt

el domingo   (on) Sunday

don (*abbr.* **D.**)   Mr., Don (*title used with first names only*)

donde   where

¿dónde?   where? **¿a —?**   where?

dondequiera   wherever

doña (*abbr.* **Da.**)   Mrs., Miss, Doña (*title used with first names only*)

dormir (ue)   to sleep; **—se**   to go to sleep

dos   two

doscientos   two hundred

el dramaturgo   playwright

dudar   to doubt

el dueño   owner

durante   during

la ecología ecology

la economía economy

ecuatorial equatorial; **la línea —** equator

la edad age **¿qué — tiene?** how old is he?

el edificio building

efecto: en — in fact

egoísta selfish

el ejemplo example; **poner por —** to take for example

el ejercicio exercise

el *m* the; **— de** that of, the one of, the one with; **— que** he who, the one who (which), that which; **tan listo como — que más** as clever as the next one

él he; *after prep.* him, it (*m*)

ella she; *after prep.* her, it (*f*)

ellas they; *after prep.* them (*f*)

ello it (*n*); **— es que** the fact is that

ellos they (*m*); *after prep.* them (*m*)

embargo: sin — nevertheless, however

empezar (ie) to begin

el empleado employee, clerk

el empleo job

en in, into; on

enamorado in love; **el —** sweetheart

encantado delighted (to meet you)

encantador, -a charming, delightful

encantar to charm, enchant

encima de on top of

encontrar (ue) to find

enero *m* January

enfermar to become ill, get sick

la enfermera nurse

enfermo ill; **el —** patient

engordar to get fat, put on weight

engrasar to grease

enojado angry

enorme enormous

la ensalada salad

enseñar to teach; to show

entender (ie) to understand

entonces then

entrar (en) to enter, go in(to)

entre between, among

entregar to hand over

entretanto meanwhile

entretener to entertain

el entusiasmo enthusiasm

enviar to send

envolver to wrap

el equipaje baggage

el equipo team

escoger to choose

escribir to write

escrito *past part. of* **escribir** written

escuchar to listen (to)

ese, esa, esos, esas *demonstr. adj.* that, those

ése, ésa, ésos, ésas *demonstr. pron.* that (one), those

la ese (letter) s; **comerse las — s** to swallow the (letter) s

eso *n demonstr. pron.* that; **— de** that matter of; **por —** therefore, for that reason, that's why; **— sí** certainly

España *f* Spain

español, -ola Spanish; **el —** Spanish, Spaniard

especial special

especialmente especially

esperar to wait; to hope

la esposa wife

el esposo husband

esquiar to ski

la esquina corner

la estación station; season

estacionar to park

el estadio stadium

el estado state

los Estados Unidos United States

estar to be; **— para** to be about to; **está bien** all right

este, esta, estos, estas *demonstr. adj.* this, these

éste, ésta, éstos, éstas *demonstr. pron.* this (one), these; the latter

el este east

esto *n demonstr. pron.* this
estrecho narrow
la estrella star
el estudiante student
estudiar to study
el estudio study
¡estupendo! great!
Europa *f* Europe
evidentemente obviously
el examen examination
examinar to examine
exclamar to exclaim
la excursión excursion, trip; **— de estudio** field trip; **hacer una —** to take *or* go on a trip, excursion
explicar to explain; **no me explico** I can't explain
la exportación export
exportar to export
el extranjero foreigner
extrañar to surprise
extraño strange

la fábrica factory
fabricar to manufacture
fácil easy
facturar to check
la falda skirt
la falta lack; **me hace —** I need
faltar to be lacking, missing; **— a la clase** to miss class
la familia family
famoso famous
fascinar to fascinate
fastidiado annoyed
el fastidio boredom
el favor favor; **por —** please; **haga Ud. el — de** please
favorito favorite
febrero *m* February
la fecha date
la felicidad happiness
feliz happy
feroz ferocious
el ferrocarril railroad

la fiebre fever
la fiesta holiday; celebration
fijarse (en) to notice
la filosofía philosophy
el fin end; **al —** finally; **por —** finally, at last; **a — de que** in order that
la finca farm
el flan custard
la flor flower
flotante floating
formal serious
la fortuna fortune
francés, francesa *adj.* French; **el —** French, Frenchman
Francia *f* France
franco frank
fresco fresh; cool; **hace —** it is cool
el frío cold; **hace —** it is cold; **tener —** to be cold (*of living beings*)
frito fried
la fruta fruit
fuerte strong
la función performance
funcionar to work, run
fundar to found
el fútbol football

la gana inclination, desire; **no me da la —** I don't feel like it
ganar to win; to earn
la ganga bargain
el garaje garage
el garajista garage attendant
la gardenia gardenia
la garganta throat
el gasto expense
el gato cat
generoso generous
genial brilliant
la gente people
la geografía geography
geográfico geographical
la geología geology
el gimnasio gymnasium

gordo fat

¡gracias! thank you! thanks!
  muchas —! thank you very much!

grande, gran large, big; great

grave serious

el guante glove

guapa pretty

guapo good-looking, handsome

guardar to keep; **— cama** to stay in bed

el guisante pea

el guitarrista guitarist

gustar (a) to be pleasing (to); **me gusta** I like it; **me gustan** I like them; **me gusta más** I like it better

el gusto pleasure; **con mucho —** with pleasure, gladly; **¡cuánto — de verlo!** how pleased (I am) to see you! **mucho — de verlo** (I am) very pleased to see you; **tanto — de conocerlo** so pleased to meet you; how do you do

haber to have (*auxiliary*); **— de** + *inf.* to be to, be supposed to, must; **hay** there is, there are; **había** there was, there were; **habrá** there will be; **hay que** it is necessary, one must; **no hay de qué** you're welcome, don't mention it

la habichuela string bean

el habitante inhabitant

hablar to speak; **— para sí** to talk to oneself; **¡ni —!** not on your life!

hacer to do, make; **— la maleta** to pack one's suitcase; **— una excursión** to go on an excursion; **— una pregunta** to ask a question; **— un viaje** to take a trip; **hace calor, frio, etc.** it is warm, cold, etc.; **hace buen tiempo** the weather is good; **hace una semana** a week ago; **hace tres meses que estudio** I have been studying for three months; **hacía mucho tiempo que esperaban** they had been waiting for a long time; **se hace tarde** it is becoming late

hacerse to become

la hacienda landed estate, ranch

hallar to find; **—se** to be

el hambre *f* hunger; **tener —** to be hungry

hasta until; even; **— luego** until later, see you later; **— que** *conf.* until

hay *see* **haber**

hecho *past part. of* **hacer** done, made

el helado ice cream

la herencia heritage

la hermana sister

el hermano brother

hermosísimo most (very, exceedingly) beautiful

hermoso beautiful

la hija daughter

el hijo son

hispánico Hispanic

Hispanoamérica *f* Hispanic America

hispanoamericano Hispanic American

la historia history

histórico historical

el hockey hockey

hola hello, hi

el hombre man

el honor honor

honrado honest

la hora hour; **la — de comer** dinner time; **a estas —s** at this time

el horno furnace

el hotel hotel

hoy today; **— día** nowadays

el huaso cowboy (*Chilean*)

el huevo egg

huir to flee

la humanidad humanity

la idea idea

la identidad identity

el idioma language

imaginarse to imagine

impaciente impatient

impedir (i) to prevent

importante important

importar to matter; **no importa** it doesn't matter

imposible impossible

la impresión impression

impresionante impressive

impresionar to impress

el inconveniente objection

la independencia independence

el individuo individual, person

la industria industry

industrial industrial

el ingeniero engineer

Inglaterra *f* England

inglés, -esa English; **el —** English, Englishman

inmediatamente immediately

insistir to insist

inteligente intelligent

la intención intention; **tener la — de** to intend to

el interés interest

interesante interesting

interesar to interest; **—se por (en)** to be interested in

interrumpir to interrupt

el invierno winter

la invitación invitation

invitar to invite

la inyección injection

ir to go; **— de compras** to go shopping; **—se** to go off, go away; **¿cómo te va?** how goes it? **¡vaya un viaje!** what a trip! **¡qué va!** nonsense!

la isla island

Italia *f* Italy

el italiano Italian

la izquierda left hand; **a la —** to (at, on) the left

jamás never, not . . . ever, ever

el jardín garden

la jaula cage

joven young; **el —** young man

Juan John

Juanito Johnny

el jueves (on) Thursday

la jugada play (*in a game*)

jugar (ue) to play

el jugo juice

julio *m* July

junio *m* June

junto a next to, beside

la *f* the; *pron.* her, you, it; **— de** that of, the one of, the one with; **— que** she who, the one who (which), that which

el laboratorio laboratory

el lado side; **al — de** beside; **(la cancha) de al —** the next (court)

el ladrillo brick

la lana wool

largo long

la lástima pity; **es —** it's a pity; **¡qué —!** what a pity!

lavar to wash; **—se** to wash, get washed

le him, you; to him, to her, to it, to you

leal loyal, faithful

la lección lesson

la leche milk

leer to read

la legumbre vegetable

lejos far. distant

la lengua language

lentamente slowly

la lenteja lentil

el león lion

levantarse to get up, rise

libre free; **al aire —** in the open air

la librería bookstore

el libro book

ligero light

limpiar to clean

limpio clean

lindo pretty

la línea line; **— aérea** airline

la lista (de platos) menu

listo ready

literario literary

la literatura literature

el litro liter

lo *n def. article* the; *pron.* it, so; **— de** that of; **— que** that which, what

el lobo wolf

loco crazy

la Lonja Exchange

luego then; **hasta —** until later, see you later

la luna moon; **a la luz de la —** by moonlight

el lunes (on) Monday

la luz light

la llamada call; **— interurbana** long distance call

llamar to call; **—se** to be called; **me llamo** my name is; **¿cómo se llama?** what is his name?

la llegada arrival

llegar to arrive; **— a** to arrive at, reach; **— a ser** to become

llenar to fill

lleno full

llevar to take; to wear

llover (ue) to rain

la lluvia rain

la madre mother

el maestro teacher

magnífico magnificent, superb

mal badly; **salir —** to flunk, fail

la maleta suitcase; **hacer la —** to pack one's suitcase

malo bad; ill, sick; **lo — es que** the trouble is that

la mamá mother, mama

la manera manner, way; **de — que** so (that)

la mano hand

manso gentle

mañana *adv.* tomorrow; **— por la mañana** tomorrow morning; **pasado —** day after tomorrow

la mañana morning; **por la —** in the morning; **a las diez de la —** at ten o'clock in the morning

la maquinaria machinery

maravilloso marvellous

María Mary

el martes (on) Tuesday

marzo *m* March

más more, most; **— que** more than; **no . . . — que** only; **¡qué vestido — bonito!** what a pretty dress! **sin — ni —** just like that, without more ado

las matemáticas mathematics

materialista materialistic

mayo *m* May

mayor older, oldest; greater

me me; to me, myself

la medianoche midnight

las medias stockings

el médico doctor

medieval medieval

medio *adj.* half; **media docena (de)** half a dozen; **a las dos y media** at half past two, at two-thirty

el mediodía noon

mejor better, best

mejorarse to get better, recover

menor younger, youngest

menos less, least; fewer, fewest; **a — que** unless; **al —** at least; **las diez — cuarto** a quarter to ten

la mentira lie; **parece —** it seems incredible

el mercado market

la merienda light lunch, picnic lunch

el mes month

la mesa table

mexicano Mexican

México *m* Mexico

la mezquita mosque

mi, mis *poss. adj.* my

mí *after prep.* me, myself

el miedo fear; **tener —** to be afraid

mientras (que) while

el miércoles (on) Wednesday

mil a (one) thousand

el millón million

el millonario   millionaire

la minoría   minority

mío *poss. adj.* my; of mine; **el —** *poss. pron.* mine

mirar   to look (at), watch

mis, mis   here, kitty (*calling cat*)

mismo   same; self; **el — que** the same (one) as; **ahí —** right over there

la mitad   half

moderno   modern

el modo   way, manner; **de — que** so (that); **de todos — s** at any rate

molestar   to bother

el momento   moment

mono   cute

la montaña   mountain

montar a caballo   to ride horseback, go (horseback) riding; **montados a caballo**   on horseback

el monumento   monument

moreno   dark-haired, dark

morir (ue)   to die

mostrar (ue)   to show

motivo: con — de   because of

el movimiento   movement

el mozo   young man; **buen —** good-looking

la muchacha   girl

el muchacho   boy

muchísimo   very much, a very great deal

mucho *adj.* much, a great deal of; *plu.* many; *adv.* much, a great deal, a lot, hard, very

la mujer   woman

las muletas   crutches

el mundo   world; **todo el —** everybody

la murria   blues, depression

el museo   museum

la música   music

muy   very

nacer   to be born

nada   nothing; *adv.* not at all; **de —** you're welcome, don't mention it

nadar   to swim

nadie   nobody, no one, not anybody

la naranja   orange

natural   natural

necesario   necessary

la necesidad   necessity

necesitar   to need

negar (ie)   to deny

negociar   to negotiate

el negocio   business

negro   black

nervioso   nervous

nevar (ie)   to snow

ni   nor, (not) . . . or; **ni . . . ni** neither . . . nor

la nieve   snow

el nilón (*usually pronounced as if spelled* **nailon**) nylon

ninguno, ningún   none, no one, no, not any

la niña   girl

el niño   child, boy

no   not, no

la noche   night; **esta —** tonight; **a las once de la —** at eleven o'clock at night; **¡buenas — s!** good night! good evening!

el norte   north

Norte América *f* North America

norteamericano   (North) American; **el —** American

nos   us, to us, ourselves

nosotros   we; *after prep.* us, ourselves

notar   to notice

novecientos   nine hundred

noveno   ninth

noventa   ninety

la novia   sweetheart

noviembre *m* November

el novio   sweetheart

la nube   cloud; **por las — s** sky high

nublado   cloudy

nuestro *poss. adj.* our, of ours; **el —** *poss. pron.* ours

Nueva York   New York

nueve   nine

nuevo new
el número number
nunca never, not . . . ever

o or
la obra work (*of art*)
observar to observe
el ocio idleness
octavo eighth
octubre *m* October
ocupado busy
ocurrir to occur; happen
ochenta eighty
ocho eight
ochocientos eight hundred
el oeste west
la oficina office
ofrecerse a to offer
oír to hear; — **decir que** to hear that,
  hear it said that; **¡ahora lo oigo!** this
  is the first time I've heard it! **¡oiga Ud.!**
  listen! **¡oye!** listen, hey! **como lo oyes**
  just as I'm telling you
¡ojalá! oh that! I wish that . . . !
el ojo eye
once eleven
la onda wave
la ópera opera
la oportunidad opportunity
la orilla bank, shore; **a —s de** beside
la orquesta orchestra
os *dir. and indir. obj. pron.* you, to you,
  yourselves
el otoño autumn
otro other, another

el Pacífico Pacific (*Ocean*)
el padre father; **los —s** father and
  mother, parents
pagar to pay
el país country
el paisaje landscape
el pájaro bird
la palabra word
el palacio palace
la pampa pampa(s)

el pan bread; — **tostado** toast
el panecillo roll
el papá father, dad
las papas potatoes; — **fritas** french
  fries
el papel paper; **hacer un —** to play a
  role
el paquete package
para to, in order to; for; — **que** in
  order that; **¿— qué?** for what reason?
  — **con** towards; **estar —** to be
  about to; **dijo — sí** he said to
  himself
parecer to seem, appear; **¿qué le
  parece . . . ?** how do you like . . . ?
el parecer opinion
la pared wall
el parque park; — **zoológico** zoo
la parrillada mixed grill
la parte part; **la mayor — de** most of;
  en todas —s everywhere; **¿de — de
  quién, para decirle?** who may I say is
  calling?
el partido game (*match*)
partir to start, leave
pasado past; last; — **mañana** day after
  tomorrow; **el verano —** last summer
el pasaje passage
el pasaporte passport
pasar to pass, spend (*time*); happen;
  — **por** to stop by; **pase Ud.** come in
pasearse to stroll, ride
el paseo walk, stroll, promenade;
  dar un — to take a walk
patinar to skate
pedir (i) to ask (for), request; to order
  (*in a restaurant*); — **prestado** to
  borrow
peinarse to comb one's hair
la película movie, film
el peligro danger; **correr —** to be in
  danger
peligroso dangerous
el pelo hair; **hacerse cortar el —** to get
  a haircut; **el corte de —** haircut;

tomar el — a uno   to kid someone
pensar (ie)   to think; **— en**   to think of;
  — + *inf.*   to intend; **no — más en**   to
  forget; **ni por pienso**   never! not on
  your life!
peor   worse, worst
pequeño   small
perder (ie)   to lose; **pierda Ud. cuidado**
  don't worry
la pereza   laziness
perezoso   lazy
el periódico   newspaper
el período   period
permanecer   to remain
permitir   to permit, allow
pero   but
el perro   dog
la persona   person
el Perú   Peru
pesar: a — de   in spite of; **a — de que**   in
  spite of the fact that
el pescado   fish
pescar   to fish
la peseta   peseta (*monetary unit of
  Spain*)
el peso   weight; peso
pico: las ocho y —   a little after eight
el pie   foot; **a —**   on foot
la pierna   leg
pintar   to paint
el pintor   painter
pintoresco   picturesque
la pintura   paint
la pirámide   pyramid
el piso   floor; **— bajo**   ground floor;
  — principal   main floor
el placer   pleasure
la plata   silver
el plato   plate, dish; **— del día**   day's
  speciality; **lista de —s**   menu
la playa   beach
la plaza   square; place, seat (*in a plane,
  etc.*)
pobre   poor
poco *adj. and pron.*   little; *adv.*   little,
  a bit; **—s**   few

poder   to be able; **no puedo con ella**
  I can't stand her
el político   politician
la polución   pollution
el pollo   chicken; **arroz con —**   chicken
  with rice
poner   to put, place; **— por ejemplo**   to
  take for example; **— un telegrama**   to
  send a telegram; **—se**   to put on; to
  become
popular   popular
poquito   very little, a tiny bit
por   for; by, through; along, around;
  on behalf of; in exchange for; for
  the sake of, on account of; **—   eso**
  therefore, for that reason, that's why;
  — favor   please; **— fin** ¡ finally;
  — supuesto   of course; **¡ — Dios!**   for
  heaven's sake! **— la tarde**   in the
  afternoon; **— ser**   because he (it) is
¿por qué?   why?
porque   because
el portugués   Portuguese
el porvenir   future
poseer   to possess
la posesión   possession
posible   possible
el postre   dessert
práctico   practical
el precio   price
precioso   pretty, beautiful; precious
precisamente   just at this moment
preciso   necessary
preferir (ie)   to prefer
la pregunta   question
preguntar   to ask
preocuparse (por)   to worry (about)
preparar   to prepare
la presentación   introduction
presentar   to introduce
el presidente   president
prestar   to lend; **— atención**   to pay
  attention
la prima   cousin *f*
la primavera   spring
primero, primer   first

el primo cousin *m*
principal principal
el principio beginning; **al —** at first
la prisa haste; **darse —** to hurry
probable probable
probablemente probably
producir to produce
el producto product
la profesión profession
el profesor professor, teacher
el programa program
progresista progressive
el progreso progress
prometer to promise
pronto soon; **de —** suddenly; **tan — como** as soon as
propio own
proponer to propose, suggest
propósito: a — by the way
próximo next
la psicología psychology
público public
el pueblo town
la puerta door
el puerto port
puertorriqueño Porto Rican
pues as, for, since; well, then; **bueno, —** well then, all right then
la pulmonía pneumonia
el punto point; **las tres en —** three o'clock sharp
puntual punctual
el puré: — de papas mashed potatoes

que *rel. pron.* who, whom, that, which; *conj.* that; than; **el —** *rel. pron.* who, whom, that, which, he who, the one who, the one which; **lo —** *rel. pron. n* that which, what
¿qué? *int. pron. and adj.* what? which? **¿y qué?** so what?
¡qué! what a . . . ! how . . . ! **¡— va!** nonsense
quedar to remain; **— agradecido** to be grateful; **—se** to remain, stay; **—se con** to take

querer to wish, want; **— a** to like, love; **— decir** to mean; **quiera Dios** God grant
¡quiá! not on your life!
quien who, whom, he who
¿quién? who? **¿de —?** whose?
quince fifteen; **— días** two weeks
quinientos five hundred
quinto fifth
quizá, quizás perhaps

la ración portion, helping
la radio radio
la rambla boulevard
el rancho ranch
la raqueta racket
el rato while; **largo —** a long while
el ratón mouse
la razón right; **tener —** to be right
la realidad reality
realizar to realize, carry out, fulfill
rebajar to lower
el recado message
recibir to receive
recientemente recently
recobrar to recover
recoger to pick up
recomendar (ie) to recommend
recordar (ue) to remember
los recuerdos regards
el refresco refreshment; **tomar un —** to have (get) something to drink
refrescarse to cool off
regalar to give (*as a gift*)
el regalo gift
la regla rule; **estar en —** to be in order
reír to laugh; **—se de** to laugh at
el reloj clock; watch
repetir (i) to repeat
el representante representative
la república republic
requerir (ie) to require
reservar to reserve
el resfriado cold (*illness*)
la residencia de estudiantes dormitory

resistir   to resist; to stand
responder (a)   to answer
el restorán   restaurant
resultar   to result, turn out to be
revisar   to inspect
rico   rich
el río   river; **— arriba**   up the river
el rodeo   roundup
rogar (ue)   to beg
rojo   red
la ropa   clothing
rosado   pink
roto *past part. of* **romper**   broken
rubio   blond

el sábado   (on) Saturday
saber   to know; to learn, find out;
   **— + *inf.*   to know how to
sabroso   delicious
sacar   to take out
la sala   room; **— de clase**   classroom;
   — de espera   waiting room
la salida   departure; **— de emergencia**
   emergency exit
salir (de)   to leave, go out (of);
   — aprobado   to pass (*a course*);
   — mal   to fail, flunk (*a course*)
la salud   health; **estar bien de —**   to be
   in good health
saludar   to greet
el salvaje   savage
el santo   saint
San, Santo   Saint
santo *adj.*   saintly
la satisfacción   satisfaction
se   himself, herself, yourself, etc; each
   other
la secretaría de policía   police
   headquarters
la sed   thirst; **tener —**   to be thirsty
la seda   silk
seguida: en —   at once
seguir (i)   to follow; to continue
segundo   second
seguro   sure; surely

seis   six
seiscientos   six hundred
la selva   forest
el sello   stamp
la semana   week; **la — que viene**   next
   week
sencillo   one-way (*ticket*)
sentado   seated, sitting
sentarse (ie)   to sit down
sentir (ie)   to regret, be sorry; **lo siento
   mucho**   I am very sorry; **—se**   to feel
señalar   to indicate, point out
señor (*abbr.* **Sr.**)   Mr., sir; **el —**
   gentleman; **el Señor**   the Lord
señora (*abbr.* **Sra.**)   Mrs., madam;
   la —   lady
señorita (*abbr.* **Srta.**)   Miss; **la —**
   young lady, miss
septiembre *m*   September
ser   to be; **es que**   the fact is that;
   llegar a —   become
serio   serious
el servicio   service
servir (i)   to serve; **no — para nada**   to be
   of no use, to be good for nothing
sesenta   sixty
setecientos   seven hundred
Sevilla   Seville
sexto   sixth
si   if, whether; why (*in exclamations*)
sí   yes; **yo —**   I am (did, was, etc.)
sí *after prep.*   himself, herself, yourself,
   etc.; **dijo para —**   he said to
   himself
la sicología   psychology
siempre   always; **lo de —**   the same old
   thing; **— que**   whenever
siete   seven
simpático   nice, congenial
simple   simple
sin   without; **— que** *conj.*   without;
   — embargo   however
sino   but
siquiera: ni —   not even
la situación   situation

sobre   on, upon; **— todo**   especially
el sol   sun; **hace —**   it is sunny
solicitar   to apply for
solo   alone
sólo   only; **— que**   only
el sombrero   hat
sonar (ue)   to sound; to ring
sonreír (i)   to smile
soñar (ue)   to dream; **— con**   to dream of
la sopa   soup
sorprender   to surprise
su, sus *poss. adj.*   his, her, its, your, their
subir (a)   to go up; to get in, get on
Sudamérica   South America
el suelo   ground
el sueño   dream; sleep; **tener —**   to be sleepy; **me quita el —**   it keeps me awake
la suerte   luck
sugerir (ie)   to suggest
sumamente   extremely, exceedingly
supuesto: por —   of course
el sur   south
suyo *poss. adj.*   his, her, your, their; of his (hers, yours, theirs); **el —** *poss. pron.*   his, hers, yours, theirs

tacaño   stingy
tal   such, such a; **— vez**   perhaps; **con — que**   provided (that
el talón   baggage check
el tamaño   size
también   also, too
tampoco   neither, not . . . either
tan *adv.*   as, so; such; **— . . . como** as . . . as; **— pronto como**   as soon as; **¡qué flores — lindas!**   what pretty flowers!
el tanque   tank
tanto   as much, so much
el tanto   point (*in a game*)
tardar en   to be long in, take (time) to

tarde   late; **se hace —**   it is becoming late
la tarde   afternoon, evening; **¡buenas —s!** good afternoon!
la tarjeta   card; **— de identidad** identification card
el taxi   taxi
la taza   cup
te   you, to you; yourself
el teatro   theater
le técnica   technique
Tejas *m*   Texas
el tejido   textile
telefonear   to telephone
la telefonista   (telephone) operator
el teléfono   telephone
el telegrama   telegram; **poner un —**   to send a telegram
la televisión   television
el tema   theme
temer   to fear
temprano   early
tener   to have; **— que**   to have to; **— calor, etc.**   to be warm, etc; **¿qué tengo?**   what is the matter with me? **aquí lo tiene Ud.**   here it is; **¿cuántos años tiene Juan?**   how old is John?
el tenis   tennis
tercero, tercer   third
terminar   to finish
ti *after prep.*   you, yourself
la tía   aunt
el tiempo   time; weather; **a —**   in, on time; **¿cuánto —?**   how long? **más —** longer; **¡ya era —!**   it was about time! **hace buen —**   the weather is good; **¿qué — hace?**   what kind of weather is it, how is the weather?
la tienda   shop, store
la tierra   land
el timbre   bell
el tío   uncle
típico   typical
el título   title
tocar   to play (*an instrument, song*)

todavía   still, yet

todo   all; every; **— el mundo**
everybody; **sobre —**   especially; **—s
los días**   every day; **toda la lección**
all the lesson, the whole lesson

tomar   to take; to have (*with liquids*);
— un refresco   to have something to
drink; **— el sol**   to sit in the sun

Tomás   Thomas

el total   total

trabajar   to work

el trabajo   work

traer   to bring

el traje   suit; **— de baño**   bathing suit

tranquilo   calm

trece   thirteen

treinta   thirty

el tren   train

tres   three

trescientos   three hundred

triste   sad

tropical   tropical

tú   you

tu, tus *poss. adj.*   your

tus, tus   here, boy (*calling dog*); **no
decir — ni mus**   to say nothing

tuyo *poss. adj.*   your, of yours; **el —**
poss. pron.   yours

¡uf!   phew!

último   last

un, una   a (an); one

único   only

la universidad   university

uno, un, una   one

unos   some

urgente   urgent

urgir   to be urgent

usar   to use

usted   you

la vaca   cow; **asado de —**   roast beef

las vacaciones   vacation

valer   to be worth; **vale la pena**   it is
worth while

el valor   value

vamos   let's go; **— a estudiar**   let's study

el vapor   steamer, boat

el vaquero   cowboy

varios   several

el vaso   glass

vasto   vast

vecino   neighboring

veinte   twenty

vender   to sell

venir   to come; **la semana que viene**
next week

la ventanilla   window (*of a bank, etc.*)

ver   to see; **a —**   let's see

el verano   summer

la verdad   truth; **es —**   it is true;
¿—? ¿no es —?   isn't he? doesn't it?
don't you? etc.

verdadero   true

verde   green

la vergüenza   shame; **me da —**   it makes
me ashamed

el vestido   dress

vestirse (i)   to dress, get dressed

la vez   time; **en — de**   instead of;
otra —   again; **por primera —**   for
the first time; **tal —**   perhaps;
alguna —   ever

la vía   way; **por — aérea**   by air

viajar   to travel

el viaje   trip; **— de vuelta**   return trip;
hacer un —   to take a trip

la vida   life

viejo   old

el viento   wind; **hace —**   it is windy

el viernes   (on) Friday

el vino   wine

la virgen   virgin

Virginia   Virginia

la visita   visit

visitar   to visit

visto *past part. of* **ver**   seen

la viuda   widow

vivaracho   lively, sprightly

vivir   to live

volver (ue) to return, go back; **— a** + *inf.* to (do) again

vosotros you, yourselves

la voz voice

el vuelo flight

la vuelta return; **el viaje de —** return trip; **estar de —** to be back; **de ida y —** round trip

vuelto *past part. of* **volver** returned

vuestro *poss. adj.* your, of yours; **el —** *poss. pron.* yours

y and

ya already, now; **— caigo** now I get it; **— no** no longer; **— que** since

el yanqui Yankee

yendo *pres. part. of* **ir** going

yo I

el zapato shoe

a, an un, una
able: to be — poder
about acerca de, sobre, de; alrededor de; **to be — to** estar para
absolutely absolutamente; **— not** en absoluto
accept aceptar
accompany acompañar
ache doler (ue)
acquaintance: to make the — of conocer
actor el actor
actress la actriz
add añadir
address dirigirse a
admit confesar
advice el consejo
advisable: it is— conviene
advise aconsejar
afraid: to be — tener miedo
after después de *prep.*; después (de) que *conj.*
afternoon la tarde; **in the —** por la tarde; **good —** ¡buenas tardes!
afterwards después
again otra vez; **to do —** volver (ue) a hacer
agreeable agradable
agreed! ¡conforme!
agricultural machinery la maquinaria agrícola
air el aire; **by —** en avión, por vía aérea; **in the open —** al aire libre
air conditioning el aire acondicionado
air pollution la polución de la atmósfera
airline la línea aérea
airplane el avión
airport el aeropuerto
all todo; **— right then** bueno pues; **— that** todo lo que, cuanto; **not at —** nada
all right está bien; ¡bueno!
allergy la alergia
allow dejar, permitir
almost casi

alone solo
already ya
also también
alternative: there's no — no hay remedio
although aunque
always siempre
amazing asombroso
ambulance la ambulancia
America América
American americano; norteamericano
among entre
amuse oneself divertirse (ie)
amusing divertido
and y
Andalusia Andalucía
Andalusian andaluz
angry enojado
animal el animal
animation la animación
announce anunciar
annoyed fastidiado
another otro
answer contestar (a), responder (a)
any alguno; cualquier(a); **if there are —** si los hay
anybody alguien
anyone alguien
anything algo
apartment el apartamento
appear parecer; presentarse
appetite el apetito
apply for solicitar
appointment el compromiso; **to make an — with** citarse con
approach acercarse a
April abril *m*
architecture la arquitectura
Argentina la Argentina
Argentine argentino
around por; alrededor de; **— here** por aquí
arrange arreglar
arrival la llegada
arrive llegar (a)

397

art   el arte

artistic   artístico

as   como; tan; — **good** —   tan bueno como; — **for**   en cuanto a; — **if**   como si; — **much** —   tanto como; — **soon** —   en cuanto, tan pronto como

ashamed: to be —   tener vergüenza; **it makes me** —   me da vergüenza

ashtray   el cenicero

ask   preguntar; — **a question**   hacer una pregunta; — **for**   pedir (i)

aspirin   la aspirina

assure   asegurar

astonishing   asombroso

at   en, a

attend   asistir (a)

attention: to pay — **to**   prestar atención a

August   agosto *m*

aunt   la tía

auto   el coche, el automóvil

automobile   el automóvil

autumn   el otoño

awaken   despertarse (ie)

back: to be —   estar de vuelta

bad   malo; **it's too** —   es lástima

badly   mal

baggage   el equipaje; — **check**   el talón

bank   el banco

baseball   el béisbol

bath: take a —   bañarse

be   ser; estar; hallarse; **to** — **about to**   estar para; **to** — **to,** — **supposed to**   haber + *inf.*; **there is, there are**   hay; **there was, there were**   había

beach   la playa

beautiful   bello, hermoso; precioso

because   porque; — **of**   a causa de

become   llegar a ser; ponerse; hacerse

bed   la cama; **to go to** —   acostarse (ue), **to stay in** —   guardar cama

beefsteak   el bistec

before   antes de *prep.*; antes (de) que *conj.*

beg   rogar (ue)

begin   empezar (ie), comenzar (ie), echar(se) a + *inf.*

behind   detrás de

believe   creer

bell   el timbre

beside   al lado de; a orillas de

besides   además

best   mejor

better   mejor; **to get** —   mejorarse

between   entre

big   grande

bilingual   bilingüe

bill   la cuenta

bird   el pájaro

birthday   el cumpleaños

bit: a —   algo; **not a** —   nada

black   negro

blond   rubio

blouse   la blusa

blue   azul

board: on —   a bordo (de)

boat   el vapor

body   el cuerpo

book   el libro

bookstore   la librería

boredom   el fastidio

borrow   pedir (i) prestado

boulevard   la rambla (*in Barcelona*)

boy   el muchacho, el chico

Brazil   el Brasil

bread   el pan

break   romper (*past part.* roto)

breakfast   el desayuno

brick   el ladrillo

bridge (*card game*)   el bridge

brillant   brillante

bring   traer

brother   el hermano

bruise   la contusión

brunet   moreno

build   construir

building   el edificio

business   el negocio
bustle   la animación
busy   ocupado
but   pero; sino
buy   comprar
by   por; — **ten o'clock**   para las diez
café   el café
cage   la jaula
California   California
call   la llamada; **long distance** —   la
   llamada interurbana
call   llamar; **to be called**   llamarse;
   who may I say is calling?   ¿de parte
   de quién, para decirle?
calm   tranquilo
can   poder (ue)
capital   la capital
car   el coche, el auto
careful: to be —   tener cuidado
Caribbean   el Caribe
carry   llevar
Carthaginian   cartaginés
case: in —   en caso de que
cat   el gato
Catalan   el catalán
Catalonia   Cataluña
catch   coger
cathedral   la catedral
celebrated   célebre
celebration   la fiesta
cent   el centavo   (*Spanish America*);
   el céntimo (*Spain*)
center   el centro
central   central
certain   cierto
certainly   eso sí
champion   el campeón
championship   el campeonato
charges: — **reversed**   cobro revertido
Charles   Carlos
charming   encantador, -a
cheap   barato
check   la cuenta; el cheque
chicken   el pollo; — **with rice**   el arroz
   con pollo

child   niño, niña
Chile   Chile
choose   escoger
church   la iglesia
city   la ciudad
class   la clase; **in** —   en la clase
classic   clásico
classroom   la sala de clase
clean   limpio; **to** —   limpiar
client   el cliente
climate   el clima
clock   el reloj
close   cerrar (ie)
cloudy   nublado
coffee   el café
coffeehouse   el café
cold   el frío; (*illness*)   el resfriado; *adj.*
   frío; **to be** — (*living beings*)   tener frío;
   it is cold (*weather*)   hace frío
collection   la colección
collide with   chocar con
Colombia   Colombia
colonial   colonial
comb   peinar; **to** — **one's hair**   peinarse
come   venir; — **in!**   ¡pase Ud.!; — **on!**
   ¡anda!; **to** — **by here**   pasar por aquí
comedy   la comedia
comfortable   cómodo
commerical   comercial
commission   la comisión
company   la compañía
composition   la composición
concentrate   concentrar; **to** — **on**
   concentrar la atención en
concert   el concierto
confidential   confidencial
confound it!   ¡caramba!
congenial   simpático
construct   construir
contact   el contacto
contain   contener
continue   continuar, seguir (i)
contract   el contrato
contrary   el contrario; **on the** —   al
   contrario

contribution la contribución
conversation la conversación
converse conversar
convince convencer
cool fresco; **to — off** refrescarse
Cordova Córdoba
corner la esquina
cost costar (ue)
count contar (ue)
country el país; el campo
couple el par
course la asignatura; **— of study** la carrera; **of —** claro (que), ¡cómo no! por supuesto, desde luego
court (*tennis*) la cancha
cousin el primo, la prima
cow la vaca
cowboy el vaquero
cradle la cuna
crazy loco, chiflado
cross cruzar
crutches las muletas
Cuban cubano
cultural cultural
culture la cultura
cup la taza
custard el flan
custom la costumbre
cute mono

dad el papá
dance el baile; bailar
danger el peligro
dangerous peligroso
dark, dark-haired moreno
date la fecha; (*engagement*) la cita; **to make a — with** citarse con
daughter la hija
day el día; **— after tomorrow** pasado mañana; **— before yesterday** anteayer; **all —** todo el día; **every —** todos los días
deal: a good — bastante; **a great —** mucho; **a very great —** muchísimo
December diciembre *m*

decide decidir, decidirse a
deck la cubierta
decrease la disminución
delicious sabroso
deny negar (ie)
departure la salida
describe describir
desire desear; el deseo
dessert el postre
detail el detalle
devil el diablo
dictator el dictador
die morir (ue)
different diferente, distinto
difficult difícil
dining room el comedor
dinner la comida; **— time** la hora de comer
direct dirigir
discover descubrir
discovered descubierto
discuss discutir
dish el plato
distant lejos
do hacer
doctor el médico, el doctor
doctorate el doctorado
dollar el dólar
done hecho (*past part. of* hacer)
door la puerta
dormitory la residencia de estudiantes
doubt dudar
down: to go — bajar
downtown el centro
dream soñar; **to — of** soñar con
dress el vestido; **to —** vestirse
drink beber; **to have (get) something to —** tomar un refresco
during durante

each cada; **— one** cada uno; **to speak to — other** hablarse
eager impaciente; **I'm — to** tengo vivo deseo de
early temprano

earn ganar
earring el arete
east el este
easy fácil
eat comer
ecology la ecología
Ecuador el Ecuador
egg el huevo
eight ocho
eight hundred ochocientos
eighteen diez y ocho, dieciocho
eighth octavo
eighty ochenta
elevator el ascensor
eleven once
emergency exit la salida de emergencia
end el fin
engagement el compromiso
engineer el ingeniero
England Inglaterra
English inglés; el inglés
Englishman el inglés
enormous enorme
enough bastante
enter entrar (en)
entertain entretener
enthusiasm el entusiasmo
entire entero
especially especialmente
Europe Europa
even aun, aún; hasta; **— though** aun cuando; **not —** ni siquiera
evening la tarde; **good —** ¡buenas noches! **in the —** por la noche; **this —** esta noche
ever jamás; alguna vez
every cada; todo; **— day** todos los dias
everybody todo el mundo
everything todo
everywhere en (a) todas partes
examination el examen
examine examinar
example el ejemplo; **for —** por ejemplo; **to take for —** poner por ejemplo

exceedingly sumamente
exchange cambiar
exclaim exclamar
excursion la excursión
excuse dispensar
exercise el ejercicio
exile el destierro
expense el gasto
expensive caro
explain explicar
export la exportación; exportar
extremely sumamente

face la cara
fact: in — en efecto; **the — is that** (ello) es que
factory la fábrica
fail (*a course*) salir mal
faithful leal
fall (*season*) el otoño; **to —** caer; **— out of** caerse de
family la familia
famous famoso, célebre
far lejos
farm la finca
fascinate fascinar
fat gordo; **to get —** engordar
father el padre, el papá
favor el favor
favorite favorito
fear el miedo; temer
February febrero *m*
feel sentir (ie), sentirse (ie); **I don't — like it** no me de la gana
ferocious feroz
fever la fiebre
few pocos; **a —** unos, unos cuantos
fewer, fewest menos
field trip la excursión de estudio
fill llenar
fifteen quince
fifth quinto
fifty cincuenta
film la película
finally al fin, por fin

find hallar, encontrar (ue); — **out** averiguar, saber

finish terminar, acabar

first primero, primer; **at —** al principio

fish el pescado; pescar

five cinco

five hundred quinientos

flamenco el cante flamenco

flee huir

flight el vuelo

floating flotante

floor el piso; **ground —** el piso bajo; **main —** el piso principal

flower la flor

flunk (*a course*) salir mal

follow seguir (i)

foot el pie; **on —** a pie

football el fútbol

for por, para *prep.*; pues *conj.*; **as —** en cuanto a

foreigner el extranjero

forest la selva

forget olvidar

forty cuarenta

found fundar

four cuatro

four hundred cuatrocientos

fourteen catorce

fourth cuarto

France Francia

frank franco

free libre; desocupado

French francés; el francés

Frenchman el francés

frequently con frecuencia

fresh fresco

Friday viernes *m*

fried frito

friend el amigo, la amiga

from de; desde; **— . . . to** de . . . en

front: in — of delante de

fruit la fruta

full lleno

furnace el horno

future el porvenir

game el partido

garage el garaje

garage attendant el garajista

garden el jardín

gardenia la gardenia

gay alegre

generous generoso

gentle manso

gentleman el caballero

geographical geográfico

geography geografía

geology la geología

get conseguir (i); **— in, on** subir (a); **— off** bajar (de); **— up** levantarse; **— along (with)** congeniar (con); **now I — it!** ¡ya caigo!

gift el regalo

girl la muchacha, la chica; **little —** la chiquita

give dar; (*as a gift*) regalar; **— back** devolver (ue)

glad: to be — alegrarse (de); **I am very — to meet you** tengo mucho gusto en conocerlo

glass el vaso; **wine —** la copa

glove el guante

go ir; **— away, — off** irse; **— back** volver (ue); **— down** bajar; **— horseback riding** montar a caballo; **— in** entrar; **— out** salir; **— shopping** ir de compras; **— to bed** acostarse (ue); **— toward** dirigirse a; **— up** subir; **— with** acompañar; **let's —** vamos; **how goes it?** ¿cómo te va?

God Dios

good bueno, buen; **good-looking** guapo, buen mozo; **to be — for nothing** no servir para nada

good-by adiós; **to say — to** despedirse (i) de

good-looking guapo

goodness: my —! ¡Dios mío!

grandfather   el abuelo

grateful   agradecido; **to be —**   quedar agradecido

grease   engrasar

great   grande, gran; **a — idea**   una idea genial

great-grandmother   la bisabuela

greet   saludar

ground   el suelo

green   verde

grill: mixed —   la parrillada

grow   crecer

guest   el convidado

guitarist   el guitarrista

gymnasium   el gimnasio

hair   el pelo, el cabello

haircut   el corte de pelo; **get a —**   hacerse cortar el pelo

half   medio; la mitad; **— past one**   la una y media

hand   la mano; **to — over**   entregar

handsome   guapo

happen   occurrir

happiness   la felicidad

happy   contento

hat   el sombrero

have   tener; haber (*with past part.*); **to — to**   tener que; **— a good time**   divertirse (ie); **to — just**   acabar de + *inf.*; **— something to drink**   tomar algo, tomar un refresco

he   él; **— who**   el que

head   la cabeza

health   la salud; **to be in good —**   estar bien de salud

hear   oír; **to — that**   oír decir que; **this is the first time I've heard about it**   ahora lo oigo

heat   el calor

heater   el calentador

heaven   el cielo; **for —'s sake!**   ¡por Dios!

hello   hola

help   ayudar

her   su, sus *poss. adj.*; la *dir. obj.*; le *indir. obj.*; ella *after prep.*

here   aquí; acá; **— is**   he aquí, aquí (lo) tiene Ud.; **around —**   por aquí; **—, boy** (*calling dog*)   tus, tus

heritage   la herencia

hers   el suyo, etc., *poss. pron.*; el (la, los, las) de ella; **of —**   suyo *poss. adj.*

herself   se; sí *after prep.*

hey!   ¡oye!

hi   hola

him   le *dir. and indir. obj.*; él *after prep.*; **with —**   consigo *reflex.*

himself   se; sí *after prep.*; **he says to —**   dice para sí

his   su, sus *poss. adj.*; el suyo *poss. pron.*; el (la, los, las) de él; el suyo *poss. adj.*

Hispanic   hispánico

Hispanic America   Hispanoamérica

Hispanic American   hispanoamericano

historical   histórico

history   la historia

hit   dar en

hitchhike   hacer autostop

hitch-hiker   el autostopista

hockey   el hockey

home   la casa; **at —**   en casa; **to go —**   ir a casa

honest   honrado

hope   esperar

horse   el caballo

horseback: to ride —   montar a caballo

hospital   la clínica

hot: to be — (*living beings*)   tener calor, **it is —** (*weather*)   hace calor; caliente *adj.*

hotel   el hotel

hour   la hora

house   la casa

how?   ¿cómo? **— long?**   ¿cuánto tiempo? **— much?**   ¿cuánto? **— many?**   ¿cuántos?

how . . . !   ¡qué . . . !

humanity   la humanidad

hundred   ciento, cien

hunger el hambre *f*
hungry: to be— tener hambre
hurry darse prisa
hurt doler (ue)
husband el esposo

I yo
idea la idea; **the very —!** ¡ni por
  pienso!
idleness el ocio
if si; **as —** como si
ill enfermo; **to become —** enfermar
imagine imaginarse
immediately inmediatamente
impatient impaciente
important importante
impossible imposible
impress impresionar
impression la impresión
impressive impresionante
in en; **— the morning** por la mañana;
  at ten o'clock — the morning a las
  diez de la mañana
incredible: it seems — parece mentira
independence la independencia
indicate señalar
individual el individuo
industrial industrial
industry la industria
inform avisar
inhabitant el habitante
injection la inyección
insist (on) insistir (en)
instead of en vez de
intelligent inteligente
intend pensar en + *inf.*; tener la
  intención de + *inf.*
interest el interés; interesar
interested: to be — in interesarse por (en)
interesting interesante
interrupt interrumpir
introduce presentar
investment la inversión
invitation la invitación
invite invitar

island la isla
it lo, la *dir. obj.*; le *indir. obj.*; él, ella,
  ello *after prep.*
Italian el italiano
Italy Italia

jacket la chaqueta; **sport —** la
  chaqueta sport
January enero *m*
job el empleo
John Juan
Johnny Juanito
joke el chiste
jokingly en broma
juice el jugo
July julio *m*
June junio *m*
just: to have — acabar de + *inf.*; **— at**
  this moment precisamente

kid (*someone*) tomar el pelo (*a uno*)
kind amable *adj.*; la clase
kindness la bondad; **have the — to**
  tenga Ud. la bondad de
know saber; conocer; **to let —** avisar

laboratory el laboratorio
lack la falta; faltar
lady la señora; **young —** la señorita
land la tierra
landscape el paisaje
language la lengua, el idioma
large grande
last último; **— summer** el verano
  pasado; **— night** anoche
late tarde; **it is becoming —** se hace
  tarde
later: till —, see you — hasta luego
laugh reír; **to — at** reírse de
lawyer el abogado
laziness la pereza
lazy perezoso
lead conducir
learn aprender; saber
least menos; **at —** al menos

leave salir (de); dejar; partir; **to take one's —** despedirse (i)

left la izquierda

leg la pierna

lend prestar

less menos

lesson la lección

let dejar, permitir; **to — know** avisar; **let's go** vamos; **let's study** vamos a estudiar

letter la carta

library la biblioteca

life la vida; **not on your —!** ¡ni hablar! ¡quiá!

light la luz; ligero *adj.*

like como *prep.*; gustar a; **— that** así; **just — that** sin más ni más; **how do you —?** ¿qué le parece? **I — it better** me gusta más; **I should —** quisiera; **I don't feel — it** no me da la gana

likely: it is — es fácil

lion el león

list la lista

listen escuchar; ¡oiga! ¡oye!

liter el litro

literary literario

literature la literatura

little pequeño; poco; **a —** un poco; **a very —** un poquito

live vivir

lively vivaracho

located situado

long largo; (*time*) mucho tiempo; **how —?** ¿cuánto tiempo?

longer más tiempo; **any —** más; **no —** ya no

look: — for buscar; **— at** mirar

lose perder (ie)

lot: a — mucho

love querer a; **to be in —** estar enamorado

lower (*a price*) rebajar

luck la suerte

lunch almorzar (ue); **light —, picnic —** la merienda

machinery la maquinaria

made hecho (*past part. of* hacer)

Madrid Madrid

magnificent magnífico

maid la criada

mamma mamá

man el hombre

manner la manera

manufacture fabricar

many muchos

March marzo *m*

market el mercado

marry casarse con

marvelous maravilloso

Mary María

materialistic materialista

mathematics las matemáticas

matter el asunto; importar; **it doesn't —** no importa; **that — of** eso de; **what's the — with you?** ¿qué tiene Ud.?

May mayo *m*

me me *dir. and indir. obj.*; mí *after prep.*; **with —** conmigo

meal la comida

mean querer decir

meanwhile entretanto

medieval medieval

meet encontrar (ue); conocer; dar con

menu la lista

message el recado

Mexican mexicano

Mexico México

midnight la medianoche

milk la leche

million el millón

millionaire el millonario

mine mío; el mío; **of —** mío

minority la minoría

minute el minuto

miss faltar; **to — class** faltar a la clase

Miss señorita

modern moderno

moment el momento; **just at this —** precisamente

Monday lunes *m*

money el dinero; **large amount of —** el dineral

month el mes

monument el monumento

moon la luna

moonlight: by — a la luz de la luna

more más; **— than** más que, más de

morning la mañana; **good —** buenos días; **in the —** por la mañana

mosque la mezquita

most más; **— of** la mayor parte de

mother la madre; la mamá

motion picture la película

mountain la montaña; **— range** la cordillera

movie(s) el cine

Mr. señor

Mrs. señora

much mucho; **as (so) —** tanto; **how —?** ¿cuánto? **very —** muchísimo

museum el museo

music la música

must deber; tener que; **one —** hay que

my mi; mío

name el nombre; **his — is** se llama; **what is his —?** ¿cómo se llama?

narrow angosto, estrecho

natural natural

near cerca de

nearly casi

necessary necesario, preciso; **it is —** es necesario, es preciso, hay que + *inf.*

necessity la necesidad

necktie la corbata

need necesitar

neighboring vecino

negotiate negociar

neither tampoco; ni; **— ... nor** ni ... ni

nervous nervioso

never nunca, jamás

nevertheless sin embargo

new nuevo

newspaper el periódico

New York Nueva York

next próximo; **— week** la semana que viene; **— court** la cancha de al lado; **— to** junto a

nice simpático; **how —!** ¡qué bueno!

night la noche; **good —** buenas noches; **last —** anoche

nine nueve

nine hundred novecientos

nineteen diez y nueve, diecinueve

ninety noventa

ninth noveno

no no *adv.*; ninguno, ningún *adj.*; **— longer** ya no; **— one** nadie; **to say —** decir que no

nobody nadie

none ninguno

nonsense! ¡qué va!

noon el mediodía

nor ni

north el norte

North America la América del Norte

North American norteamericano

nothing nada; **to be good for —** no servir (i) para nada

notice notar; fijarse (en)

November noviembre *m*

now ahora; ya; **from — on** de aquí en adelante; **(four days) from —** de aquí en (cuatro días); **right —** ahora mismo

nowadays hoy día

nurse la enfermera

objection el inconveniente

observe observar

obtain conseguir (i)

obviously evidentemente

occur ocurrir

o'clock: one — la una; **two —** las dos

October octubre *m*

of de

offer ofrecerse a

office   la oficina; **doctor's —** el consultorio

often   a menudo, muchas veces

oh   oh, ay

oil   el aceite

old   viejo; antiguo; **to be twenty years —** tener veinte años; **how — is he?** ¿cuántos años tiene?

older, oldest   mayor

on   en, sobre; **— entering** al entrar; **— Saturday** el sábado; **— time** a tiempo

once   una vez; **at —** en seguida

one   uno, un, una; se *indef. subj. pron.*; **the — of (with)** el (la) de; **the — (s) who (which)** el (la, los, las) que; **it is — o'clock** es la una; **no —** nadie; **some —** alguien

oneself   se *dir. and indire. obj.*; sí *after prep.*; **to talk to —** hablar para sí

one-way (ticket)   sencillo

only   único *adj.*; sólo, no . . . más que; **the — thing** lo único

open   abrir

opera   la ópera

operator (*telephone*)   telefonista

opinion   la opinión, el parecer

opportunity   la oportunidad

or   o

orange   la naranja

orchestra   la orquesta

order   mandar; (*in a restaurant*) pedir; **in — to** para; **in — that** para que, a fin de que; **to be in —** estar en regla

other   otro

ought   deber

our   nuestro

ours   el nuestro; **of —** nuestro

out: get — of (*a vehicle*) bajar de; **go — (of)** salir (de)

overcoat   el abrigo

owe   deber

own   propio

Pacific (*Ocean*)   el Pacífico

pack (*a suitcase*)   hacer (*una maleta*)

package   el paquete

paint   la pintura; pintar

painter   el pintor

painting   el cuadro

pair   el par

palace   el palacio

pampas   la pampa

parents   los padres

pardon   dispensar, perdonar

park (*a car*)   estacionar (*un coche*)

part   la parte; **the greater —** la mayor parte

pass   pasar; (*a course*) salir aprobado

passage   el pasaje

passport   el pasaporte

patient   el enfermo

pay   pagar; **— attention to** prestar atención a

people   la gente

performance   la función

perhaps   quizá(s), tal vez

period   el periodo

permit   permitir

person   la persona, el individuo

Peru   el Perú

phew!   ¡uf!

philosophy   la filosofía

pick up   coger; recoger

picnic lunch   la merienda

picture   el cuadro; **motion —** la película

picturesque   pintoresco

pink   rosado

pity: it's a —   es lástima

plane   el avión; **by —** en avión

play   jugar (ue); (*an instrument*) tocar; (*in a game*) la jugada

player   el jugador

playwright   el dramaturgo

please   gustar a; por favor; haga Ud. el favor de . . . ; tenga Ud. la bondad de . . .

pleased: how — (I am) to see you! ¡cuánto gusto de verlo! **so — to meet you!** ¡tanto gusto de conocerlo!

pleasure el gusto; **with —** con mucho gusto; **the — is mine** el gusto es mío

pneumonia la pulmonía

point el punto; (*in a game*) el tanto; **— at** señalar

polite cortés

politician el político

pollution la polución; **air —** la polución de la atmósfera

poor pobre

popular popular

port el puerto

Porto Rican puertorriqueño

Portuguese el portugués

possess poseer

possible posible; **as soon as —** cuanto antes

potatoes las papas

practical práctico

prefer preferir (ie)

prepare preparar

present (day) actual

president el presidente

pretty bonito, lindo, precioso; guapa

prevent impedir (i)

price el precio; **what is the — of?** ¿a cómo se vende? ¿cuál es el precio de . . . ? **at what —?** ¿a cuánto?

principal principal

private particular

probable probable

probably probablemente

produce producir

product el producto

professor el profesor

program el programa

progressive progresista

progress el progreso

promise prometer

propose proponer

provided (that) con tal que

psychology la sicología

public público

punctual puntual

purchase la compra

put poner; **— on** ponerse

pyramid la pirámide

quarter el cuarto; **it is a — to five** son las cinco menos cuarto

question la pregunta; **ask a —** hacer una pregunta

quickly pronto

quite bastante

racket la raqueta

radio la radio; **—** (*set*) el radio

railroad el ferrocarril

rain la lluvia; llover (ue)

raise levantar

ranch el rancho, la hacienda

rate: at any — de todos modos

rather bastante; mejor dicho

reach llegar (a)

read leer

ready listo

reality la realidad

realize darse cuenta de

reason la razón; **for that —** por eso; **for what —?** ¿para qué?

receive recibir

recommend recomendar (ie)

record (*phonograph*) el disco

record shop la discoteca

recover mejorarse; recobrar

red rojo, colorado

refreshment el refresco

regret sentir (ie)

relative el pariente

remain quedarse

remember recordar (ue), acordarse (ue) (de)

repair componer

repeat repetir (i)

representative el representante

republic la república

request pedir (i)

require requerir (ie)

reserve reservar

resist resistir

rest descansar

restaurant el restorán

result resultar

return la vuelta; volver (ue); (*give back*) devolver (ue); — **trip** el viaje de vuelta

rice el arroz

rich rico

ride pasearse; — **horseback** montar a caballo; **take a —** dar un paseo

right la razón; (*hand*) la derecha; — **now** ahora mismo; **all —** está bien; **all —, then** bueno, pues; **to be —** tener razón

ring sonar (ue)

rise levantarse

river el río; **up the —** río arriba

role el papel; **to play a —** hacer un papel

room la sala, el cuarto

roommate el compañero de cuarto

roundup el rodeo

run correr; funcionar; — **into** dar con; — **over (into)** atropellar

s la ese

sad triste

said dicho (*past part. of* decir)

saint Santo, San; el santo

salad la ensalada

salesgirl la vendedora

same mismo; **the — (one) as** el mismo que

satisfaction la satisfacción

Saturday sábado *m*

say decir

scratch arañar; el arañazo

season la estación

seat asiento; plaza (*in a plane, etc.*)

second segundo

see ver

seem parecer

seen visto (*past part. of* ver)

selfish egoísta

sell vender

send enviar; — **a telegram** poner un telegrama

September septiembre *m*

serious grave; serio, formal

servant la criada

serve servir (i)

service station la estación de servicio

seven siete

seven hundred setecientos

seventeen diez y siete, diecisiete

seventh séptimo

seventy setenta

several varios

Seville Sevilla

shame la vergüenza

sharp: three o'clock — las tres en punto

she ella

shirt la camisa

shoe el zapato

shop la tienda

shopping: to go — ir de compras

short bajo

show mostrar (ue); enseñar; (*a movie*) dar

sick enfermo; **to become —** enfermar

side el lado

silk la seda

simple simple

since desde; como; pues; ya que

sing cantar

sister la hermana

sit down sentarse (ie)

sitting sentado

six seis

six hundred seiscientos

sixteen diez y seis, dieciséis

sixth sexto

sixty sesenta

size el tamaño

skate patinar

ski esquiar

skirt la falda

sky el cielo; — **high** por las nubes

sleep dormir (ue); **to go to —** dormirse (ue)

slowly lentamente

small pequeño, chico

smile sonreír

snow la nieve; nevar (ie)

so así; tan (*with adj. or adv.*); **— much** tanto; **— that** de modo que, de manera que

socks los calcetines

some alguno, algún; unos

somebody, someone alguien

something algo

sometimes a veces, algunas veces

somewhat algo

son el hijo

song la canción

soon pronto; **as — as** en cuanto, tan pronto como; **as — as possible** cuanto antes

sorry: to be — sentir (ie); **I am very —** lo siento mucho

sound sonar (ue)

soup la sopa

south el sur

South America Sudamérica, la América del Sur

Spain España

Spaniard el español

Spanish español; el español

speak hablar

spend gastar; (*time*) pasar

spite: in — of a pesar de; **in — of the fact that** a pesar de que

sport el deporte

spring la primavera

square la plaza

stadium el estadio

stand (*resist*) resistir; **I can't — her** no puedo con ella, no la puedo ver

star la estrella

start partir

state el estado

station la estación

stay quedarse

steak el bistec

steamer el vapor

steel el acero

still todavía, aun, aún

stingy tacaño

stockings las medias

stop: to — by pasar por

store la tienda

straight derecho

strange extraño

street la calle

stroll pasearse

strong fuerte

student el alumno, la alumna, el estudiante

study estudiar; el estudio

such tan *adv.*; **— a** tal *adj.*

suddenly de pronto

suffer sufrir

sufficient bastante, suficiente; **to be —** bastar

suggest proponer, sugerir (ie)

suit el traje; **bathing —** el traje de baño

suitcase la maleta

summer el verano

sun el sol; **to sit in the —** tomar el sol

Sunday domingo *m*

sunny: it is — hace sol

sure seguro

surprise sorprender, extrañar

swallow: to — the (letter) *s* comerse las eses

sweetheart el novio, la novia, el enamorado

swim nadar

table la mesa

take tomar; llevar; llevarse; (*a course*) cursar; **— a trip (an excursion)** hacer un viaje (una excursión); **— for example** poner por ejemplo

talk conversar

tall alto

tank el tanque

tape   la cinta

taxi   el taxi

tea   el té

teacher   el profesor, la profesora; el maestro, la maestra; **Spanish —**   el profesor de español

team   el equipo

technique   la técnica

teeth   los dientes

telegram   el telegrama

telephone   el teléfono; telefonear

television   la televisión

tell   decir; contar (ue)

ten   diez

tennis   el tenis; **— court**   la cancha de tenis

tenth   décimo

Texas   Tejas

textile   el tejido

than   que; **more — ten**   más de diez

thank   dar las gracias a; **—s!** ¡gracias! **— you very much**   ¡muchas gracias!

that   que *conj. and rel. pron.*; el cual, el que *rel. pron.*; ese, esa, aquel, aquella *demonstr. adj.*; ése, ésa, eso, aquél, aquélla, aquello *demonstr. pron.*; **— of**   el (la, lo) de; **— which**   lo que; **all — which**   todo lo que, cuanto; **oh, —**; **would —**   ojalá

the   el, la, los, las

theater   el teatro

their   su, sus, de ellos

theirs   el suyo, el de ellos; **of —**   suyo, de ellos

them   los, las *dir. obj.*; les *indir. obj.*; ellos, ellas *after prep.*; **with them**   consigo *reflex.*

themselves   se; sí *after prep.*

then   entonces; luego, después; pues; **all right —, well —**   bueno pues

there   allí; allá; **back —**   allá; **right over —**   ahí mismo; **— is, — are**   hay; **— was, — were**   había; **if — are any**   si los hay

therefore   por eso; por consiguiente

these   estos, estas *demonstr. adj.*; éstos, éstas *demonstr.-pron.*

they   ellos, ellas

thin   delgado

thing   la cosa; **the same old —**   lo de siempre

think   pensar (ie); creer; **to — of**   pensar en

third   tercero, tercer

thirst   la sed

thirsty: to be —   tener sed

thirteen   trece

thirty   treinta

this   este, esta *demonstr. adj.*; **— (one)**   éste, ésta, esto *demonstr. pron.*

Thomas   Tomás

those   esos, esas, aquellos, aquellas *demonstr. adj.*; ésos, ésas, aquéllos, aquéllas *demonstr. pron.*; **— who (which)**   los (las) que; **— of**   los (las) de

though: even —   aun cuando

thousand: a (one) —   mil

three   tres

three hundred   trescientos

throat   la garganta

through   por

Thursday   jueves *m*

thus   así

ticket   el boleto, el billete

tile: colored —   el azulejo

tie   la corbata

time   el tiempo; la vez; la hora; **at this —**   a estas horas; **at the same —**   a la vez; **dinner —**   la hora de comer; **in (on) —**   a tiempo; **for the first —**   por primera vez; **this is the first — I've heard about it**   ahora lo oigo; **to have a good —**   divertirse (ie); **at what —?**   ¿a qué hora? **what — is it?**   ¿qué hora es? **it was about —?**   ¡ya era tiempo!

tired   cansado

title   el título

to   a, para; **in order —**   para; **a quarter — nine**   las nueve menos cuarto

toast   el pan tostado

today   hoy

tomorrow   mañana; **— morning** mañana por la mañana; **day after —** pasado mañana

too   también; demasiado; **— much** demasiado

tooth   el diente

total   el total

tourist   el turista

towards   hacia; para con

town   el pueblo

train   el tren

travel   viajar

tree   el árbol

trip   el viaje; la excursión; **return —** el viaje de vuelta; **to take a —** hacer un viaje

tropical   tropical

truck   el camión

true   verdadero; **it is —** es verdad

truth   la verdad

try   pretender, tratar de

Tuesday   martes *m*

turn: — out to be   resultar

twelve   doce

twenty   veinte

two   dos

two hundred   doscientos

typical   típico

uncle   el tío

understand   comprender, entender (ie)

United States   los Estados Unidos

university   la universidad

unless   a menos que

unoccupied   desocupado

until   hasta *prep.*; hasta que *conj.*

up   arriba; **— the river**   río arriba

upon: — leaving   al salir

Uruguay   el Uruguay

urgent   urgente; **to be —**   urgir

us   nos *dir. and indir. obj.*; nosotros *after prep.*

use   usar; **to be of no —**   no servir (i) para nada

vacation   las vacaciones

value   el valor

various   varios

very   muy; bien

view   la vista

Virginia   Virginia

visit   la visita; visitar

wait   esperar

waiter   el camarero

waiting room   sala de espera

walk   caminar; **take a —**   dar un paseo

wall   la pared

want   querer

warm: to be —   tener calor (*living beings*): **it is —**   hace calor (*weather*)

wash   lavar(se)

washed: to get —   lavarse

watch   el reloj; **to —**   mirar

water   el agua *f*

way   la manera; el camino; **this —**   por aquí; **that's the — I am**   así soy yo; **by the —**   a propósito

we   nosotros, nosotras

wear   llevar

weather   el tiempo; **the — is good**   hace buen tiempo

Wednesday   miércoles *m*

week   la semana; **two —s**   quince días

weigh   pesar

welcome: you're —   no hay de qué; de nada

well   bien; pues; **— then**   bueno pues; **to get —**   mejorarse

well-known   conocido

west   el oeste

what   lo que *rel. pron.*; **—?**   ¿qué? ¿cuál? **— a . . . !**   ¡qué . . . ! **what a beautiful dress!**   ¡qué vestido más hermoso! **— a trip!**   ¡vaya un viaje!

whatever   cualquier(a)

when   cuando; **—?**   ¿cuándo?

whenever siempre que

where donde; *int.* ¿dónde? ¿adónde?

wherever dondequiera

whether si

which que, el cual, el que, lo cual *rel. pron.*; **—?** ¿qué? ¿cuál?
 those — los (las) que

while el rato; **a long —** largo rato; mientras (que) *conj.*

white blanco

who que, quien, el cual, el que *rel. pron.*; **—?** ¿quién? **the one —, he (she) —** el (la) que

whole entero; **the — lesson** toda la lección

whom que, a quien, al cual, al que *rel. pron.*; **—?** ¿a quién?

whose cuyo *rel. adj.*; **—?** ¿de quién?

why? ¿por qué?

widow la viuda

wife la esposa

win ganar

window la ventana

wind el viento

windy: it is — hace viento

wine el vino

winter el invierno

wish querer

with con

within dentro de

without sin *prep.*; sin que *conj.*

witty chistoso

wolf el lobo

woman la mujer

wool la lana

woolen de lana

word la palabra

work el trabajo; (*of art*) la obra; trabajar; funcionar

world el mundo

worry (*about*) preocuparse (por); **don't —** pierda Ud. cuidado

worse peor

worst peor

worth: to be — valer; **it's — while** vale la pena (de)

wrap envolver

wreck destrozar

write escribir

written escrito (*past part. of* escribir)

Yankee el yanqui

year el año; **last —** el año pasado

yes sí; **— I am (was, did,** *etc.***)** yo sí; **to say —** decir que sí

yesterday ayer; **— afternoon** ayer por la tarde; **day before —** anteayer

yet todavía, aun, aún; **not —** todavía no

you usted (Ud.), ustedes (Uds.) *subj. and after prep.*; le, la, lo, los, las *dir. obj.*; le, les *indir. obj.*; *familiar forms:* tú, vosotros *subj. pron.*; te, os *dir. and indir. obj.*; ti, vosotros *after prep.*

young joven; **— man** el joven; **— lady** la joven, la señorita; **— people** los jóvenes

younger menor

youngest menor

your su, sus, de Ud., de Uds.; tu, tus (*familiar*); vuestro (*familiar plu.*)

yours el suyo, el de Ud. (Uds.); el tuyo, el vuestro (*familiar*); **of —** suyo, de Ud. (Uds.); tuyo, vuestro (*familiar*)

zoo el parque zoológico

PHOTOGRAPH ACKNOWLEDGMENTS

Photography International: Robert Rapelye, pages 44, 51, 73, 119, 133, 155, 190, 212, 223, 235, 268, 341

Ginger Chih from Peter Arnold: pages 33, 40

Yoram Lehmann from Peter Arnold: pages 203, 306

E.P. Jones: page 329

Courtesy of Spanish National Tourist Office: pages 100, 112, 124, 220, 232, 239, 256, 267

Courtesy of Mexican National Tourist Council: pages 172, 227

Editorial Photocolor Archives: pages 54, 290; Steve Dunwell, page 166; Alain Keller, pages 16, 24, 28, 36, 65, 78, 89, 145, 148, 161, 218, 249, 276, 280, 294, 309, 317, 348

Courtesy of World Bank: Ray Witlin, pages 86, 137; Mary Hill, page 96; Paul Sanche, page 102

Courtesy of American Airlines: pages 74, 183, 192, 201, 326; Bob Takis, page 106

Ernst Schrader: pages 176, 244, 298, 352

INDEX

417

LOS ESTADOS UNIDOS

Océano Atlántico

70°   30°

Nogales   Ciudad Juárez

Chihuahua

BAJA CALIFORNIA

Golfo de México

ISLAS BAHAMAS

Durango   Monterrey

Mazatlán

Guadalajara

TRÓPICO DE CÁNCER   La Habana

Tampico

Mérida

CUBA

HISPANIOLA   San Juan

Ciudad Trujillo

PUERTO RICO

ANTILLAS

20°

Veracruz

YUCATÁN

Oaxaca

JAMAICA

Kingston   Port-au-Prince

Océano Pacífico

Acapulco

Bélice

HONDURAS BRITÁNICA

HONDURAS

MAJORES

Mar de las Antillas

MÉXICO Y AMÉRICA CENTRAL

Guatemala

EL SALVADOR   Tegucigalpa

Managua

NICARAGUA

COSTA RICA

10°

San José

Panamá

AMÉRICA DEL SUR

ESCALA   600 Millas

0   965 Kilómetros

110°   100°   80°

45°   5°

ESPAÑA

La Coruña

FRANCIA

Golfo de Viscaya

Santander

Vigo

Océano Atlántico

Oporto

Burgos

Valladolid

Río Ebro

Duero

Zaragoza

Barcelona

Tarragona

40°

Coimbra

Río

Salamanca

Madrid

Río

Lisboa

Toledo

Setúbal

Valencia

ISLAS BALEARES

MENORCA

Océano

Río

Guadiana

MALLORCA

IBIZA

FORMENTERA

MORENA

Sevilla

Guadalquivir

Alicante

Huelva

Cádiz

Granada

Mar Mediterráneo

Cartagena

ESCALA   100 Millas

0   160 Kilómetros

Málaga   Almería

Gibraltar

Tánger   Estrecho de Gibraltar

0°

ÁFRICA

10°